5. 6. '01
K 200

COURT AND CULTURE

Holland-Bavarian cavalcade on the (Zeeland?) shore. The central figure must be William VI (with the Order of Saint Anthony around his neck) praying for God's protection. Fifteenth-century miniature. School of Van Eyck. (Turin Breviary, Durrieu facsimile ed., Leiden University Library, MS. Dousa 88-3842, pl. XXXVII)

COURT AND CULTURE

DUTCH LITERATURE,

1350–1450

FRITS PIETER VAN OOSTROM

TRANSLATED BY ARNOLD J. POMERANS

FOREWORD BY JAMES H. MARROW

University of California Press
Berkeley · Los Angeles · Oxford

Originally published as *Het woord van eer: Literatuur aan het Hollandse hof omstreeks 1400*, © 1987 by F. P. van Oostrom and Meulenhoff Nederland bv, Amsterdam.
English-language translation © 1992 by Arnold J. Pomerans. The preparation of this work was made possible in part by a grant from the National Endowment for the Humanities, an independent federal agency.
The publisher also gratefully acknowledges a generous grant given this book by the Netherlands Organization for Scientific Research (NWO).

University of California Press
Berkeley and Los Angeles, California

University of California Press, Ltd.
Oxford, England

Library of Congress Cataloging-in-Publication Data

Oostrom, F. P. van.
  [Woord van eer. English]
  Court and culture : Dutch literature, 1350–1450 / Frits Pieter van Oostrom ; translated by Arnold J. Pomerans ; foreword by James H. Marrow.
      p.   cm.
  Translation of: Het woord van eer.
  Includes bibliographical references and index.
  ISBN 0-520-06777-0 (cloth : alk. paper)
  1. Dutch literature—To 1500—History and criticism.
  I. Title.
PT5420.O5713   1992
839.3'109001—dc20   91-36301
                                                                        CIP

Printed in the United States of America
9 8 7 6 5 4 3 2 1

The paper used in this publication meets the minimum requirements of American National Standard for Information Sciences—Permanence of Paper for Printed Library Materials, ANSI Z39.48-1984. ⊗

Contents

Illustrations

Foreword

Court and Culture is an exemplary work of cultural history, one that demonstrates new possibilities for this genre of historical inquiry. The disarmingly simple aim of Van Oostrom's study is to consider the Dutch court in relation to its literature, and its literature in relation to the court. The real achievement of the book is that in addition to expanding and redefining our knowledge of the Dutch court and its literature at this time, it openly and imaginatively addresses the fundamental questions of what constitutes "cultural history" and how we can effectively reconstruct and interpret essential aspects of the past. Such concerns come to the fore especially in the final chapter, but in fact underlie the entire study.

I learned of Van Oostrom's study of Dutch court literature shortly after its publication in the Netherlands. Within a span of about a month, a host of colleagues with whom I correspond regularly about medieval Dutch culture wrote to alert me to the existence of what they termed an extraordinary, and an extraordinarily well written, book. Inasmuch as this kind of report had never reached me about *any* book published in the Netherlands, and came, moreover, from scholars working in widely diverse fields (history, theology, literature, art history, and manuscript studies), I made it a point to acquire and read the book forthwith. On first reading, I was impressed enough to write the author a letter of admiration and five pages of detailed comments and to arrange to meet with him on my next visit to the Netherlands. I was also impressed enough to ask him if he had considered the possibility of publishing an English translation of the book, and to suggest that I would be willing to recommend such a publication to various presses in the United States. My resolve was fortified by the reception of the book in Europe: after selling out its first printing in a mere six months, it earned one of the most distinguished awards presented in the Netherlands for books of its class, the Wijnaendts Francken Prize, given by the Society of Dutch Literature (Maatschappij der Nederlandse Letterkunde) once every six years for a distinguished book of cultural history.

Van Oostrom's book is distinguished in many respects, a few of which I shall try to summarize. On one level, it is a ground-breaking study of the Dutch court in the late fourteenth and early fifteenth centuries. It defines more fully and insightfully than any previous study the forms, attitudes, and character of this court, succeeding in this aim because of the breadth of vision Van Oostrom brings to bear on these issues. Dynastic and personal history, documentary evidence (including some provocative new material unearthed in the archives by the author and his colleagues and students), the testimony of art, architecture, and literature, are brought together to produce a vivid picture of Dutch courtly life at one of its important formative moments.

Van Oostrom's book is also a seminal study of Dutch literature in the years around 1400. One of its most important achievements is to have taken types of literature usually studied independently of one another (typically, in relation only to works of the same genre) and to have considered them as complementary facets of contemporary Dutch court life. Chapters II through VI treat, respectively: the works of William of Hildegaersberch, an orator who delivered set pieces in verse on quasi-public occasions; works found in collections of contemporary songs, especially those in the Hague Song Manuscript; the historical chronicles written by the official herald of the Dutch court, who is known by the name "Bavaria"; the religious tract known as the "Table of the Christian Faith" (*Tafel vanden kersten ghelove*), written by the Dominican monk Dirk of Delft, who served as chaplain to the Dutch court in the years around 1400—a work that is, as Van Oostrom brings out, probably the most learned and extensive catechetical treatise produced anywhere in Europe at this time; and the writings of Dirk Potter, a functionary at the court whose oeuvre includes the most important treatise on love written in Dutch in this period, "The Course of Love" (*Der minnen loep*), as well as works of overtly moralizing character, such as "Flower of Virtue" (*Blome der doechden*). Precisely because he views them as complementary facets of realities and values of the Dutch court at this time—because, that is, he has the confidence, the ability, and the sensitivity to interpret them as more than mere representatives of different literary genres—Van Oostrom produces original readings of each of these authors and works.

Van Oostrom's book is also an important piece of revisionist history, counterbalancing the predominantly negative view of Dutch culture at this time, not to mention of late-medieval culture in Northern Europe as a whole. I refer especially to the pessimistic viewpoints given wide currency in such well-known works as Johan Huizinga's *Waning of the Middle Ages* and Barbara Tuchman's *A Distant Mirror*, in relation to which this book provides a welcome corrective. Drafted from a different perspective and focused on different questions and evidence, it casts light on the structures and workings of quintessentially constructive elements and forces in the historical fabric of the period.

What is really at issue here are such questions as how cultures shape themselves, how they define their forms and values, how they situate themselves in relation to essential traditions (historical, ethical, religious, and moral), and how they constitute their "history." Masterfully negotiating history *and* historiography, Van Oostrom shows that cultural history can be powerfully and insightfully written through a synthetic approach focused on the reciprocal and symbiotic relationships between its guiding figures and fictions.

James H. Marrow
Professor of Art History
Princeton University

Preface

"The literature that emerged in the county of Holland between about 1350 and 1450 deserves much more attention than literary historians have given it"—so we are told in A.M.J. van Buuren's 1979 dissertation. One major reason for writing this book has been my wish to give these Dutch texts the greater attention they deserve. Another reason was more strictly academic. These writings are most relevant to a study of Middle Dutch court literature; the store of available texts is considerable, as is our historical knowledge of the Holland-Bavarian court. Such a combination made it possible to try an approach based on the fusion of literature and history—an approach that has proved fruitful in foreign studies of medieval (court) literature but had still to be applied to Middle Dutch texts. Nor would I wish to conceal a third reason, one quite different, namely the wish to write a book on my own subject in the hope that it might stimulate further research, encourage students, and also appeal to a wider public.

While I was writing this book, the concern and help of many people greatly assisted me. In many (but by no means all) instances, I have acknowledged my debt. Here I shall merely record my general thanks to the many students at Leiden who have shared my thoughts in lectures, papers, and conversations over the past few years and who have persuaded me that it is both possible and desirable to combine university teaching and research. The fact that some of them have meanwhile graduated and are working on theses concerning various topics raised here holds out a hopeful prospect.

Most of the essential studies were done in 1982–86 at the University of Leiden. During the academic year 1986–87 I was fortunate in being able to continue research at the Netherlands Institute for Advanced Studies, Wassenaar. Thanks to the excellent working environment of the institute, I was able to round off my work in book form within just one year. But during that year I was also reminded more than once that Paul Valéry's famous dictum applies not only to poetry but also to such aca-

demic studies as mine: they are never finished—you merely let go of
them.

Wassenaar/Leiden
31 July 1987

NOTE TO THE SECOND EDITION

In this, the second edition, a number of errors have been corrected. I
am indebted to all those who have drawn my attention to them.

May 1988

NOTE TO THE ENGLISH-LANGUAGE EDITION

My involvement in the publication of *Court and Culture* has been both
a pleasure and a privilege. I wish to thank James H. Marrow for his
enthusiasm and initiative, Arnold J. Pomerans for his sense and sensibility, Anne Geissman Canright for her meticulous editing, Roberta
Engleman for her thorough preparation of the index, and, at the Press,
Deborah Kirshman and Rose Vekony for their effective and professional coordination from start to finish. Thanks to all their devoted expertise, working on this book will remain a memorable experience.

Fritz van Oostrom
Leiden, May 1992

A Note on Editions

The following Dutch-Bavarian works constitute the primary focus of this book and are referred to throughout, in some cases in an abbreviated form. Excerpts from these medieval texts have been translated so as to facilitate the lay reader's grasp of the original rather than to follow the text with strict philological accuracy.

Bavaria Herald. *Wereldkroniek* (Chronicle of the world). (Abbreviated in text and notes as *WK*.) Quotations are from the manuscript (128 E 10) in the Royal Library, The Hague, with the relevant folio numbers (e.g., 79r) indicated. Modern punctuation has been added; some minor changes have been made.

———. *Hollandse kroniek* (Chronicle of Holland). (Abbreviated in text and notes as *HK*.) Quotations are from the manuscript (17914) in the Royal Library, Brussels, with the relevant folio numbers indicated. Modern punctuation has been added; some minor changes have been made.

Dirk of Delft. *Tafel vanden kersten ghelove* (Table of the Christian faith). 4 vols. Edited by Father L. M. Daniëls, O.P., Ons Geestelijk Erf Publications 4–7. Antwerp, 1937–39. (Abbreviated in text and notes as *TKG*.) The references are to "Winterstuc" (Winter piece: "W") or "Somerstuc" (Summer piece: "S") followed by chapter numbers and, if necessary, line numbers (e.g., "S" XXIV/45–160). Diacritical signs have been omitted.

Dirk Potter. *Der minnen loep* (The course of love). 2 vols. Edited by P. Leendertz Wz., Leiden, 1845–46. (Abbreviated in text and notes as *ML*.) The references are to the (roman) book numbers followed by the line numbers in that edition (e.g., II, 270–86).

———. [*Blome der doechden*] *Dat Bouck der Bloemen* ([Flower of virtue] The book of flowers). Edited by Fr. S. Schoutens, Hoogstraten, 1904. (Abbreviated in text and notes as *BD*.) The references are to the page numbers in that edition, followed by the line number (e.g., 72/24–29); modern punctuation has been added to the quotations.

Since the editor has sometimes censored the original text (see Chapter VI, sec. 1), I have also referred to (a microfilm of) the manuscript in the Franciscan Monastery, Vaalbeek. In those instances the folio number of the manuscript is given.

————. *Mellibeus*. Edited by B.G.L. Overmaat, Arnhem, 1950. (Abbreviated in text and notes as *Mell.*) The references are to the page numbers in that edition; diacritical signs have been omitted from the quotations.

Haags Liederenhandschrift. *Die Haager Liederenhandschrift. Faksimile des Originals mit Einleitung und Transkription* (The Hague song manuscript. Facsimile of the original with introduction and transcription). 2 vols. Edited by E. F. Kossmann, The Hague, 1940. (Abbreviated in text and notes as *HLH.*) The references are to the arabic numerals used to identify the poems in that edition, if necessary followed by line numbers (e.g., no. 62; 31/10–15). Small changes have been made to some of the quotations in accord with Kossmann's annotations.

Martinus Fabri and Hugo Boy. *Two Chansonniers from the Low Countries. French and Dutch Polyphonic Songs from the Leiden and Amsterdam Fragments (Early Fifteenth Century)*. Monumenta musica neerlandica XV. Edited by J. van Biezen and J. P. Gumbert, Amsterdam, 1985. The references are to the identifications of the songs in that edition (e.g., L6); diacritical marks have been omitted from the quotations.

William of Hildegaersberch. *Gedichten* (Poems). Edited by W. Bisschop and E. Verwijs, The Hague, 1870 (reprint Utrecht, 1981). The references are to the (roman) numerals used to identify the poems in that edition, sometimes followed by line numbers (e.g., CV/15–27). The punctuation of the quotations may differ slightly from that of the Bisschop/Verwijs edition.

I

Court and Literature

1. A NEW COUNT

In the matter-of-fact language of reference books it sounds almost commonplace: "Count William V of Holland became of unsound mind in 1357 and was forced to hand government over to his brother, Albert, duke of Bavaria, in 1358."[1] But then, what misfortunes do not befall a country whose prince goes mad? In the Middle Ages, such incidents occurred more often than people think; indeed, during the second half of the fourteenth century mental illness seemed almost epidemic in European dynasties, striking down Philip IV and Charles VI of France, Joan and Louis of Bourbon, John II of Forez—and William V of Holland. It seems unlikely that William's full case history can ever be wholly reconstructed; when it comes to such forbidden subjects as the disgraceful fact of a ruler's insanity, historical sources prefer to keep silent. The anonymous fifteenth-century continuator of Van Boendale's *Brabantsche Yeesten* hints that he knew more:[2]

> Niet al te wel en der ic sagen
> Welc die sake was deser plagen:
> Ic beveelt der verborghenheit
> Des Vader inder eeuwicheit.

I dare not speak the cause of this illness too plainly: I commend that secret to our Eternal Father.

It was no accident that such hints should have been dropped by a Brabanter. His contemporaries in Holland, after all, kept their own counsel. Yet the deeper we enter into this murky affair, the more we are persuaded that our researches will have to accommodate not only a psychiatrist, but also a master detective. What were the true circumstances surrounding Count William's insanity, and what—and who—was behind it?[3]

We certainly know that William V bore a hereditary taint: as the grandson of the crazed Jeanne of Valois he carried mental illness in his blood. It is partly against this background that historians of psychiatry have identified William's mental condition as a form of chronic psychosis that steadily worsened after 1357. If we probe further, we shall discover in William's behavior symptoms of mental instability, ones extending beyond his hereditary predisposition, even before 1357. We need only recall his brutality in burning alive one of his clerks or in killing the nobleman Gerard of Wateringen with his own hands, in which case we will share the psychological conclusion of Jean le Bel, the Hainaut chronicler who described William V as being *de desguisé manière* and *estrange*: stealthy and strange.

But even though the historian-psychologist may be satisfied with that description, the historian-detective's suspicions continue to play on the mysterious circumstances surrounding William's downfall. He will soberly note that Count William V continued to reign with a firm hand until 1357, the year he traveled to England on family business, only to return home one month later (at the age of twenty-five) "of unsound mind." Could he have been poisoned? Had he perhaps been the victim of a plot? Whatever the answer, during January and February 1358 William was clearly being edged out. Although he was apparently still trying to cling to office, preparations to put his brother, Duke Albert, into power were by then well advanced. That must have been a time full of covert diplomatic activity. In early January, when Albert was still in Prague, his quartermaster arrived in Holland from Bavaria. On the twenty-sixth of that month, Albert was appointed *ruwaard* (regent; literally, keeper of the peace) under a settlement. A few weeks later he arrived in The Hague where, on 23 and 26 February, he agreed (as confirmed by covenant on 6 March) to serve as *ruwaard* of Holland, "an evident necessity imposed by the illness of our dear brother [. . .] whom it may please God to succor." Simultaneously, the pitiable, beloved brother was giving orders to have the court in The Hague guarded by fifty soldiers. Self-defense or paranoia?

The spring of 1358 saw *ruwaard* Duke Albert's inauguration as count of Holland and the removal of William V. The latter was packed off to Delft, a town well disposed toward him of old and where, on 11 March, he was still being tended by "four masters of medicine." Yet his departure from Holland was imminent: in May, he and his wife, the Countess Matilda, repaired to Dordrecht, whence—this time accompanied by Duke Albert—they journeyed on to estates in remote Hainaut. And while his brother was busy removing the last obstacles in the way of his own *ruwaard*ship, poor William, nominally still officiating as count, was put in irons and locked up in Quesnoy Castle, where he was to spend the next thirty years "in safe keeping"—like a bird in a cage, as the continuator of the *Brabantsche Yeesten* put it. William's condition seems to have worsened steadily in prison (cause or effect?), and when he died in 1389, the event was recorded in The Hague without the least semblance of mourning or regret. Late into the fifteenth century, however, certain sections of the main prison building continued to be referred to as the "mad count's chamber."

Count William V vanished, supplanted by Duke Albert of Bavaria. Although he had been designated heir as early as 1346, at age ten, and although he had several times gone to The Hague in the years that followed, the Bavarian duke must have been surprised by his actual investiture as count of Holland. In the middle of January, he was still in Prague; three weeks later he was received as *ruwaard* in The Hague.

The twenty-one-year-old Albert, incidentally, was becoming *ruwaard* over a wasps' nest. Under William V, the counties of Holland, Zeeland, and Hainaut had never fully recovered from the crisis following the accession of the Bavarian dynasty to the House of Hainaut. In this struggle, the young regent was given little support and much trouble by his family. His reign opened on a clash with his brother Louis the Roman, and within three years he was involved in a bitter quarrel with the Countess Matilda, who had originally supported her brother-in-law. Albert, though, was able to handle both conflicts; indeed, according to H. A. van Foreest, it was then that he donned "the mantle of the wise statesman he would wear so honorably for so long."[4]

The conflicts with his brother and sister-in-law, however, were no more than minor pinpricks when compared with the permanent struggle in which the county of Holland was involved from the mid–fourteenth century: the fight between the Hooks (*Hoekse*) and the Cods (*Kabeljauwse*). In Dutch elementary schoolbooks, these quarrels are blithely reduced to petty and picturesque provincial squabbles; yet in fact, they constituted a most perilous web of feuds that kept the county almost permanently on the verge of civil war. Many times during his reign Albert had to confront this volcano of tensions, which plagued Holland for almost another century.

The most violent eruption occurred during the early years and came to a head in Albert's quarrel with Delft.[5] In October 1358, the new ruler seemed to be in absolute control, so much so that he judged the time ripe for the first official display of festivities: an ambitious tournament at his new manor of Edingen in Hainaut. Invitations went out to the

1.   William V and Albert of Bavaria. (Sixteenth-century woodcut by J. C. van Oostzanen; reproduced from Jansen 1971, 424)

Brabant ducal couple, to the duchess of Guelders, and to other prominent dynastic connections. At the end of the month, Albert himself set out for Hainaut, having just appointed a commission (wisely composed of two Hooks and two Cods) to "keep the country safe" during his absence. In mid-November, however, the duke was still at his residence in Middelburg making the final arrangements for the festival, and he was forced to change his entire design. He let it be known that "the festivities at Adighem had to be called off" and that a general mobilization had been declared, all because of unrest in North Holland.

At Kennemer Sands near Haarlem, Reynold of Brederode, one of the two Hook bailiffs appointed by Albert, had been ambushed by a party of Cods and barely escaped with his life. Understandably, Albert considered the attack a flagrant challenge to his sovereignty, one requiring harsh reprisals. The Cod culprits entrenched themselves in Delft, the town most bitterly opposed to Albert; indeed, it had at first refused to pay homage to him as *ruwaard*. The upshot was a bitter struggle between the duke and one of his most important towns, beginning in December 1358 and leading to the siege of Delft, from April to June 1359. The conditions that Albert imposed on the fallen town were harsh: a fine of 50,000 Bruges écus, the razing of all fortifications, and a large-scale display of public penance in which one thousand Delft citizens, bareheaded and barefoot, would beg the duke's mercy outside the city walls, while five hundred Delft women, arrayed in their best garments and with their hair let down, did likewise before the Countess Matilda. In the Middle Ages, wise statesmanship often called for iron severity.

Acting thus—that is, keeping as aloof as possible from the rival factions but striking hard when necessary—Albert was able to consolidate his position in the county of Holland. From about 1365, Holland even enjoyed relative peace, a peace that endured until 1390 and was accompanied, moreover, by economic progress. Throughout this period, Albert greatly expanded his power. The very titles that he often paraded in early documents show clearly that he enjoyed conceiving himself as much more than a mere substitute for his afflicted brother: "We, Albert, by the grace of God, Count Palatine of the Rhineland, Duke of Bavaria, *Ruwaard* of the duchies of Hainaut, Holland, and Zeeland and of the seigneury of Friesland." It was also in keeping with his ambitions that Albert seized a prominent role on the European political stage—as a prince whose support or enmity such great powers as England, France, and Burgundy did well to respect. Within his county, too, the duke succeeded in establishing a reasonable balance of power, with himself at the center.

The geographical fragmentation of Albert's possessions raised a special problem, however. His dominion included, in the northern coastal region, the counties of Holland and Zeeland, which were separated from the remote county of Hainaut by stretches of Brabant and Flanders; finally, twice that distance again separated him from his original patrimony, the duchy of Bavaria-Straubing. Governing these scattered lands required constant travel, even more than medieval princes were already accustomed to. Throughout the period of Bavarian rule in Holland, messengers hurried from one possession to another, and quite often the duke himself would make the journey. Eventually, however, Albert chose a capital where he remained as long as possible and from which he tried to maintain centralized authority. That capital was not in his native Bavaria, nor was it in the county of Hainaut chosen by his predecessors William III and William IV. Instead, Albert decided on the Binnenhof (Inner Court) in The Hague, a town that would become the "count's hedge"—*'s graven hage*—in the true sense of the word only under Albert's own reign.

2. INFRASTRUCTURE

During the first half of the fourteenth century, the Hainaut line governed Holland as much as possible from its birthplace in the southern Netherlands. Matters of state regularly brought the rulers north, of course, but the court was summoned to The Hague—as to other smaller capitals in Holland, such as Middelburg and Dordrecht—only on special occasions. During the Hainaut period, Holland was thus controlled largely from the south, and The Hague was just one of the palaces where the counts of Holland regularly stayed, without really residing there. Upon the death of Count William IV, when authority over Holland passed to the Bavarians, all this was to change. Under Duke Albert and his Bavarian successors, as we have seen, The Hague became the seat of government. Although the counts' residence there had been used thus earlier—before the Hainaut rulers, such counts of Holland as William II and Floris V had held court in The Hague—only under Albert did the hunting castle in The Hague begin to look like a real palace: an establishment from which the sovereign governed his territory almost without interruption from 1365 onward.

To transform The Hague into a capital city with a certain splendor, many alterations were required. And here, Albert was self-indulgent. As a son of Emperor Louis of Bavaria he had grown up in a court far more resplendent than that in Holland. To be sure, the hall completed under Floris V (today called the Knights' Hall) was easily comparable to the best of its rivals; even the staunch Burgundian Chastellain, who was certainly a connoisseur, praised this hall as "une des plus belles du

2.   The Hague court. (From C. H. Peters 1909, accompanying 134–35)

monde et des plus propres à tenir grant feste."[6] Otherwise, however, until about 1360 the court in The Hague decidedly lacked grandeur.

Accordingly, as soon as Duke Albert was firmly installed he moved to add luster to his court. The most visible change was physical: architectural extension.[7] Not a year passed but carpenters and masons erected major works on the several hectares of the court complex. In 1366, the duke added apartments for his wife, their children, and retainers. In 1378, Albert's then thirteen-year-old son, William of Oostervant (his successor as William VI), was given his own quarters on the southern side of the palace; these were then extended further after William's marriage in 1385. Room was also made for more lowly followers: with the count's approval, certain nobles, such as members of the council, acquired temporary quarters in the inner and outer courts, and many permanent officials, too, settled in the count's keep. Along the northern side of the palace stood a mass of small thatched cottages for lower personnel; thus the court merged into what, by 1356, had become an independent craftsmen's village—the *Haagambacht*—peopled with artisans and peasants and studded with *stoven*, bathhouses of dubious repute where the counts liked to be pampered. And so, on the Binnenhof, the

Buitenhof (Outer Court), the Plaats (Courtyard), the Tournooiveld (Tiltyard), and the Spui (Sluice) there grew up a large community revolving about the duke and his family. Here it was, and especially at the center, that the literary life—this book's theme—began to evolve.

Very closely connected with Albert's transformation of the court into a royal residence was the growth of the administration.[8] If the court was effectively to manage its increasingly complex holdings, it needed an efficient bureaucracy. That, too, had already been brought to The Hague by the Hainaut line, under whom the first signs of a regular government were to be seen in the extension of the staff quarters. Under Duke Albert, however, such changes grew steadily more apparent. Here again, Albert's background served as a spur: after all, he had grown up in the immediate vicinity of the imperial chancellery.

Thus, accompanied by the elite of the Bavarian administration, who surely benefited his first years in The Hague, the new count of Holland reorganized government along more modern patterns. The residence became a professional center of authority, where he conferred regularly with bailiffs and stewards "from the province" and where legal, financial, and other official services could be performed. A novelty was the introduction, in 1363, of the office of *tresorier*. The treasurer was put in charge of all the staff concerned with financial affairs; at the same time, he was made head of the ducal chancellery and, in the absence of the duke, president of the council. He was, in short, a powerful man surrounded by an ever-growing number of officials. These administrators were recruited from the necessarily literate clergy, but also increasingly from the nobility and the middle classes. Even these circles had begun to recognize the opportunities to be found in basing life on the pen.

There would be no need to emphasize such residential and bureaucratizing features had they not had a special influence on the infrastructure of *literary* life, not only in The Hague, but at many other medieval courts as well. Indeed, J. Bumke has argued that these conditions were necessary if courts were to develop into centers of literature.[9] Only through the establishment of large royal and ducal households could a stable court culture flourish, with a sophisticated audience permanently present and a much larger public at hand for regular celebrations and performances. No wonder, then, that itinerant poets preferred to journey to these glittering palaces, large and small, where they were almost certain to find the rulers in person—in contrast to ambulatory courts, where the princes were most often absent on official travels. A royal residence thus exerted centripetal forces—not least those found in literature and song.

The emergence of texts ampler and more important than the evanescent creations of itinerant reciters was further encouraged by the growing significance of the chancellery. The court's administrative nerve center, this office was equipped with a staff of lettered clerks, allowing for production of not only functional, but also literary texts. This fact explains why medieval court literature so often emerged in the shadow of a chancellor.

How these administrative developments stimulated literary life in The Hague is something I shall now try to demonstrate. It was not by chance, for instance, that before Albert established himself in Holland, the court of John of Blois in Schoonhoven (to be examined later), and not the prince's court, had been the site of the chief literary circle in Holland. For unlike his Hainaut relatives, John of Blois remained almost permanently in the north. Similarly, the differences in the development of the court of Holland under Duke Albert and the contemporary Guelders court can probably be explained, at least in part, by the fact that the Guelders remained ambulatory much longer.[10] An itinerant writer such as William of Hildegaersberch could usually expect a hearing in The Hague with its settled court; in Guelders, the chance of finding an audience was considerably smaller.

The existence of direct links between the literature produced at Albert's court and the work of his chancellery is confirmed by several documents. For instance, jotted in the margins of dry account books we occasionally find such pleasures as a short verse (in Middle Dutch, or even in Latin) by Philip Persoenresone or a drinking song by Peter Potter.[11] Dirk Potter, Peter's more famous brother, and also the most inspired man of letters in that family, worked all his life in the count's chancellery and was the very embodiment of the union of administrative and literary penmanship. While this distinction was less marked in the literary output of Bavaria Herald, the handwriting on his autographs nevertheless bears typical chancellery flourishes.[12] And even the writing in that purely literary work the *Haags liederenhandschrift* (Hague song manuscript), with its elongated *h*'s and *n*'s, is reminiscent of chancellery script.

Thus two political-administrative developments having critical links provided the Hague court with the infrastructure to foster (Middle Dutch) literature. Yet a third factor was equally important: in the ducal

House of Bavaria, Holland had acquired a dynasty that, unlike the Hainaut line, from birth had spoken German rather than French. For a century, then, until the coming of the Burgundians in 1433, the mother tongue of prince and subjects derived from the same stem.

Under the Hainaut princes, French had been the first language of the court of Holland. Indeed, for the aristocracy of the day, French functioned as Latin did for the clergy; medieval court culture was international and polyglot, and French served well as the lingua franca. It therefore follows that under the Bavarian dukes, too, the language remained in prominent use among the nobility, particularly where contacts with "foreign" relations were concerned.[13] Certainly, the Bavarian princes maintained French for their dealings with Hainaut, as their excellent relations with Froissart, the celebrated chronicler of the grander courts of Burgundy France and England, vividly reflect.[14]

Even so, the ability to understand one another's mother tongues must have greatly helped communication between these princes and their Dutch subjects. The dialects of Holland and Bavaria were actually much closer than the territories themselves were physically. People from Straubing could make themselves understood in The Hague, if they were prepared to take some trouble. Where there was a will there certainly was a way.[15] And the will was spurred by political trends, which culture once again followed.

Remarkably, from the second half of the fourteenth century—that is, precisely upon the arrival of the Bavarian house—many Middle Dutch texts took on a clear German sound. And of these texts, those from the court at The Hague assume a central place. This phenomenon has often been attributed to the political links between Holland and the empire, an explanation that continues to sound plausible.[16] Yet the question still demands study, because it raises many different problems. The German influence is much clearer in some of the writers at the court of Holland than in others: of those whom we shall be discussing at some length, for example, William of Hildegaersberch and Bavaria Herald used eastern dialectal elements (the second despite his Guelders past) much less than Dirk Potter and the authors of most of the lyrics in the *Haags liederenhandschrift*, with Dirk of Delft apparently holding an intermediate position. How is this difference in tone to be described and explained? The relationship between literature and popular speech, too, needs further study, with the language of court accounts—frequently of German appearance thanks to the presence of numerous *ts*-forms—probably representing an interesting halfway house. In any case, corroborative evidence indicates that, in the late-fourteenth-century Hague court, the Dutch and Bavarian languages were fused into a practicable linguistic compromise. This development, too, was surely a great advance over the Hainaut period, when the sharp linguistic barrier between the Romance and Germanic tongues must often have been quite an obstacle. In 1344, for example, Ysebout of Asperen, an accounts clerk, was forced to enlist the help of Walloon colleagues to translate his accounts into French, while four accounts written in French had to be rendered into Dutch with the help of two other clerks.[17] Clearly, in those days the language boundary was crossed only with great difficulty.

This gap between the mother tongue of the Hainaut rulers and that of their subjects in Holland is reflected at least as strongly in their respective literatures. In the final analysis, Middle Dutch writing has little in common with the literary culture of Hainaut. The counts of Hainaut, in fact, held themselves aloof from the literary life of Holland, which, not surprisingly—for lack of encouragement from on high?—remained underdeveloped. The very fact that the Hainaut rulers spent as much time as possible in their southern domains would hardly have encouraged an interest in Middle Dutch culture. Rather, in their opulent court in Hainaut they surrounded themselves with French texts, including those of the minstrel Colin, not to mention such crusader epics as *Baudouin de Sebourc*.[18] The list of books owned by John II of Avesnes, too, which descends to us as an unusually early example of such records, shows clearly how little interest this count of Holland took in the literature of the Low Lands: all his books were in French.[19] And when the Hainaut rulers did occasionally venture north, they took along only French artists. The trumpeters who served Count William IV in the Hague, for example, were immigrants from the south,[20] and the accounts of Middelburg record an appearance in 1326–27 of the Hainaut poet Jean de Condé, traveling in the wake of William III.[21] When that poet later wrote an elegy to William III, extolling his generosity and referring to him as "li pères de menestrés," he must have been thinking of William's patronage of *French* minstrels.

Were, then, the Hainaut counts of Holland totally biased in literary matters? The case of two Middle Dutch authors indicates that matters were not quite so simple. The first of these men, Melis Stoke, may still be called a cultural heir to the previous noble house, for in 1305 he completed for Count William III the Middle Dutch rhymed chronicle he had started for Floris V. The generous treatment of the second author, however, was more than the settlement of an old Hainaut debt of honor: in 1337, William IV granted "Willem van Delft den dichter" (William of Delft, the poet—who we may assume used Middle Dutch as his first language) an annuity of five Holland pounds, as well as an annual issue of "a set of clothes with lining befitting his estate."[22] Still, one poetic swallow does not a literary summer make, and we have reason to doubt that Count William often listened to this poet. Perhaps the count looked on court poetry as a sort of cultural front for the entertainment of visiting local nobles from Holland—among whom interest in Middle Dutch literature naturally continued into the first half of the fourteenth century.[23]

In fact, Middle Dutch authors could not expect any real help except from one Hainaut noble, Count John of Blois, who was related to the ruling dynasty through his mother and was also of French origin on his father's side. Unlike the rest of the Hainaut line, he seems to have been deeply rooted in the Low Countries. He chose Schoonhoven Castle (near Gouda) as his primary residence and, moreover, was fluent in the *Dietse*, or Old Dutch, language, an accomplishment that Froissart considered unusual. Thanks to John of Blois, a flourishing court life emerged at Schoonhoven, patronizing not only French but also Middle Dutch poets (for instance, Augustijnken).[24] In the years before Duke Albert of Bavaria arrived, the Schoonhoven court was the most important focus of literary life in the county of Holland; thereafter, although Albert seized cultural leadership, John of Blois nevertheless continued to live in high style and remained one of Albert's most loyal allies (even acting as his deputy in the duke's absence).

John of Blois thus represented political as well as cultural continuity between the Hainaut and Bavarian traditions in Holland. With this sole exception, however, the (early) Hainaut rulers of Holland were devotees of French culture and of French culture alone. A signal proof is the gigantic Arthurian *Perceforest*, a rudimentary and fitfully powerful romance that was probably presented to Count William III in about 1335.[25] Although written in Old French (as far as is known, it was never translated into Middle Dutch), it by no means ignored Holland. Its references to that country, however, were not very flattering. One day, a hero lands in Zeeland and looks around in amazement. First he remarks how flat and bare the landscape is; a moment later he sees a flock of sheep speeding toward a hill and hears the shepherd call out to him to follow. But too late: a spring tide overwhelms the Hainaut nobleman, and it is only thanks to the panic-stricken paddling of his horse (the rider himself, of course, is quite unable to swim, like most nobles in fourteenth-century Holland) that he survives the ordeal. With its literary exaggeration, this scene characterizes how the counts of Hainaut saw their domains in Holland: as flat, wet, and rather eerie.

With the new Bavarian dynasty, the ties between the ruling house and the county were strengthened, a process helped by the blurring of the linguistic boundary. Where once there had been a barrier, now cultural currents could flow freely. That a German wave washed over the Low Countries is clearly reflected in the accounts of the county of Holland—as I shall show in greater detail below. The number of poets from German-speaking lands who presented themselves at Albert's court was considerable:[26] the records mention guest appearances of poets and reciters not only from his native Bavaria, but also from Mainz, Bohemia, Guliche, Meissen, Westphalia, Heidelberg, Nuremberg, Holstein, Cleves, Cologne, and Austria. In addition, there were many other *Duutsche segghers* (German declaimers), whose precise place of origin is not mentioned. Undoubtedly, these artists recited in their mother tongue, or perhaps in an "intermediate" language specially adapted for the benefit of the listening Hollanders.

With so large an influx of writers and performers, the German influence must have grown swiftly, though we still know very little about it. The courtier Dirk Potter, for instance, in his (heavily German-flavored) work displays a familiarity with such German literature as the writings of (pseudo-)Neidhard and the *Titurel*, a long epic poem—and he apparently expected no less from his own readers.[27] Perhaps even more arresting was the library of Count John IV of Nassau, born at Dillenburg, but resident in Breda from the early fifteenth century on. In addition to Middle Dutch translations of Old French and Latin works (possibly including the celebrated *Lancelot* compilation), his collection contained chivalric romances by Rudolf von Ems.[28] Whereas court literature in Holland had previously been dominated by the great French and Latin medieval writers, a marked German influence became prominent during the Bavarian period and, in the absence of a genuine language barrier, gave added impetus to the rise of Middle Dutch court literature.[29] In light of other propitious elements—particularly the residential and administrative trends mentioned earlier—these developments paved the way for a new heyday of Middle Dutch literature at the royal court in Holland. What had been smouldering in the first half of the fourteenth century now burst into flame.

3. COURT AND COURTLY LIFE

The word *court* is easier to use than to define. Walter Map, the Welsh writer and archdeacon of Oxford under Henry II, puzzled about its meaning as early as the twelfth century: "In the court I exist and of the court I speak," he wrote, "and what the court is, God knows, I know not."[30] Map's confession shows that any attempt to make a sharp distinction between what a court comprised and what it did not is bound to be futile: the concept was simply not well defined in the Middle Ages. At best, medieval courts can be called centers of worldly authority, organized around a lord and his retinue. As administrative bases, they were the primary seats of political power. Hardly less important, however, was their social function of allowing the attending nobles to mingle with those of the governing classes who, though less illustrious than themselves, were no less essential. At court, officials made staff appointments, governed, legislated, and consulted—but also lived, married, mourned, celebrated, feasted, or merely dined. Here a jostling throng of visitors gravitated toward a core of more or less constant inhabitants and those more intimate courtiers who accompanied the prince on his travels. For a clearer picture of these two groups at the court of Holland-Bavaria, we can do no better than study the register of court personnel for May 1354 (still under William V), which has fortunately survived.[31]

The permanent staff attached to the Bavarian house was composed mainly of clerks and their lordly supervisors who administrated the Inner and Outer Courts. Beneath them were more menial figures: gatekeepers and prison wardens; a "swans' count" who tended the swans on the *hofvijver*, the court's picturesque inner lake; nightwatchmen; those in charge of the kitchen gardens on the east side and the stables (*bouverie*) on the west; a professional staff of building workers; and a hunting staff, including a forester, various huntsmen, and a falconer or hawker. Higher in rank were the courtiers directly attached to the count's person, constituting what Philip of Leiden called the "societas familiaris ac domestica." Of these, the person most intimately linked to the count was the knight "of my lord's life," the personal bodyguard who never left his side. Equally exalted—an honorary post, in fact— was the master chamberlain, an official who, attended by several valets, organized and maintained his lord's private accommodation. At table, the count was under the daily care of three young noblemen, one of whom guarded his eating utensils, while the other two ensured that his

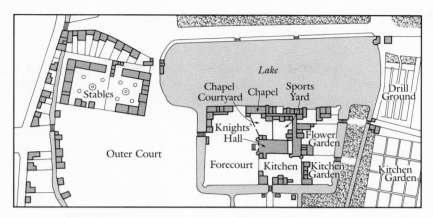

3. Ground plan of the court complex. (Based on C. H. Peters 1909, accompanying 160–61)

plate and cup were never empty. An usher, finally, was always firmly ensconced at the entrance of any chamber in which the count happened to be.

In addition to the count's personal retainers were officials in charge of supplies. At their head were two masters of the household, a knight and a shield bearer, both with personal assistants. Then there was the staff of the five central divisions of the court: the pantry (for grain and bread storage), the buttery (for the storage of liquors), the kitchen, the (count's) chamber, and the marshalcy, which oversaw hundreds of horses. Each of these offices—to which the *taelgerie*, or court tailor, should be added—was presided over by a master with one or more *garsoenen* (pages) or servants. As remuneration these men usually received wages according to rank, together with board and clothing (particularly the count's cherished pale blue livery), and often, according to their function, special emoluments. Thus the masters of the stable had a share in the proceeds from the sale of skins and fat, and valets were allowed to keep the wax of spent candles from the count's apartments. (Apparently the new candles made from that wax provided a brisk trade.) The court also employed a small army of mounted *messagiers* and runners, a following further swollen by such more exalted dignitaries as the personal physician and the chaplain.

The complete court officialdom thus amounted to some seventy persons—to which must be added the more modest, yet far from undermanned, personal establishments of the count's heir and successor, as well as of the countess, whose personal staff was, of course, composed of ladies and maids. The total roll would thus have exceeded one hundred.

Still, even this figure does not include what was, in essence, the most important group of all: the clerks employed in the chancellery and the treasury. In 1354, they, like the household, were divided into five categories, each probably managed by at least one master clerk assisted by several lesser clerks. The archives were staffed by clerks of the register, whose particular task it was to deal with the administrative correspondence. The clerks of the blood (of whom Dirk Potter [see Chapter VI] was one) were concerned with court jurisprudence, while the clerks of affairs dealt with general business. The final two categories—the clerks of the money and the clerks of the kitchen or board—are of special interest, for they superintended the household finances. The board invoices at Albert's court were listed, generally speaking, under three main headings: *cost*, *provanchen*, and *foreynen*. *Cost* covered all the personal expenditures of Albert and his wife in their domains; *provanchen* comprised expenditures, trade by trade, on provisions in the widest sense, that is, on acquisitions by and for the pantry, the buttery, the kitchen, the count's quarters, and the marshalcy. *Foreynen*, finally, included all expenses beyond the court's normal routine, again with subdivisions: unusually large expenses, as well as expenditures on gold and silver work, on fabrics, furriery, horses, and saddlery, on pipers and heralds, on messengers, on various small items, and on carpentry. Related to the extent of the count's domains and the large number of his retainers, the precision with which these accounts record the most trifling disbursements can seem almost comical. Nevertheless, their pedantic character has proved a blessing for us: it is thanks to the devotion of these clerks that we can form so clear a picture of life at the Holland-Bavarian court.

Since we shall be examining these accounts at some length in our reconstruction of court literary life, it is worth considering briefly the scope and limitations of this source. One limitation is obvious: by their very nature, the accounts are confined to transactions involving the exchange of money. Common though such transactions clearly were, we must not forget that many court dealings involved no financial considerations or cash payments—and in those cases our sources are silent. Moreover, the accounts sometimes appear to be much more precise than they actually are; for example, some disbursements, though described as annual expenses, are in fact booked on only one occasion. Clearly, and for whatever reason, honest or otherwise, not every payment found its way into the accounts, and some clerks were more punctilious than others. Moreover, not all accounts have come down to us for every year, so our sources have gaps—even though the available material is much more ample than a single person can digest. Lastly, the administration was not equally lavish in furnishing details for every sphere; we have, for instance, no inventory that lists what books or objects of art were found at the court in any one year.

What accounts have survived, however, are far too numerous to be listed in full, even in our age of large-scale academic projects. In any event, it is doubtful whether such a vast inventory would render comparable findings. Nevertheless, it should be stressed that our knowledge of these invaluable sources can never be comprehensive, and that from every fresh study new facts emerge. What a boon it is for anyone trying to reconstruct life at a baronial court to have access to accounts covering so many decades. They tell us more about *daily* life at court than any other historical source can hope to do; literary sources at that period, namely, tended to concentrate on less humdrum events. In addition, the sober exactitude of the accounts underpins their historical authenticity. Hence it is not surprising that so many students have already delved to good advantage into the Holland-Bavarian account books. Still, much remains to be done; thus we still await an integral study of daily routine at the court of Holland, a study that, thanks to these accounts, ought to be far more concrete than researches devoted to other European courts. Here, in contrast, we must make do with a brief sketch of that life, based on previously published sources and with only the occasional mention of a new discovery, especially with relevance to literature.[32] Such references may, at least, make the reader crave further information.

Court life in The Hague under Duke Albert of Bavaria and, later, his son William VI had undeniable allure. If we place the Burgundians—then already at spectacularly lofty heights—beside the kings of England and France, and the German emperors themselves at the top of the dynastic scale, then the Bavarian court in Holland must be recognized as among the most distinguished of the second rank. To attain and preserve that ranking, the court had to maintain a grand life-style—indeed, it would be quite an error to underestimate the political importance of such pomp and flamboyance. The medieval value system demanded a lavish show of power from its lords: at home, to leave no doubt about their greatness; abroad, lest they be outshone by others.[33] It was a case of *magnificence oblige*. But besides political considerations, aesthetics fulfilled other vital needs in the sumptuous court round as well. The

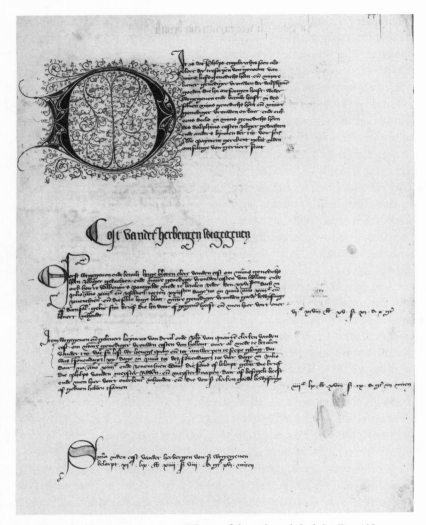

4. Household account entry ("Cost of board and lodging"). (Algemeen Rijksarchief, The Hague, MS. AGH 1269, fol. 22r)

men at the top were the leaders of fourteenth-century society and had enough leisure and means to indulge freely in what Huizinga has called "the ideal of the sublime life."

The accounts are thus quite explicit about the Holland-Bavarian table. Meals, let alone banquets, were impressive in quality no less than in quantity. The vast larders bulged with provisions from the count's own manors and holdings, as well as from such sources as his small personal fishing fleet. He would also add lavish purchases from elsewhere, including wines from French and Rhenish vineyards and beer from Hamburg. In addition, delicatessen goods were favorite presents, for example the oysters with which the bailiff of Den Briel regaled the court in June 1393, or the gift of sturgeon from the city of Kampen and for which the Kampen messenger, Jan Peterszoon, received a handsome gratuity of six new guilders—three times as much as the entire Hague stage company had been paid a few days earlier. Especially at such ritual ceremonies as christenings, the dubbing of knights, weddings, and Shrove Tuesdays or other great Christian festivals, the count's table would be overloaded. During the three dinners Albert held for the countess of Guelders in 1369, the rich silver-bedecked boards—the forks, as good medieval custom decreed, being used exclusively for taking meat from the platters before eating it with one's fingers—were filled with roast swan, wild gosling, rabbit, ham, poultry, suckling pig, and wild boar, together with lamprey, pike, salmon, and crayfish, and not excluding meat pies, mutton, and, for dessert, fruit, preserves, pastries, and fish in warm jelly.

We cannot tell if the celebrants were aware of the health hazards of such unbridled eating (Count Guy of Blois was so stout in later days that he was unable to ride a horse and had to be conveyed in a special cart). In any event, Albert and his friends and relations regularly and conscientiously exercised. Thus, on 3 April 1394, as soon as Albert's second wife, Margaret of Cleves, arrived in The Hague, she diverted herself by repairing to the seaside town of Scheveningen in the company of Albert's son and his wife—probably the first time the future countess of Holland had seen the sea.[34] The accounts also record frequent outings to Rijnsburg Abbey to visit friends or relatives among the (mostly noble) nuns, and also for dancing; the visits were usually concluded with a lordly gift—duly entered in the accounts—to the distinguished convent. Within the court itself, moreover, dancing, sports, and games abounded. There were tournaments large and small, in earnest or for sport, some in boats on the *hofvijver*. Courtiers also enjoyed shooting, tilting at quintains or each other, handball, rounders, skittles, and various other ball games. Gambling and guessing games were other favorites (both being played for money): the accounts mention dicing, cards, trictrac, and chess, for which the local champion, Janne *den scaker*, was often invited. What happened on Monday after St. Nicholas's Day in 1395 was typical of Holland: "My lord and my lady, being desirous of repairing to Delft over the ice, [went] equipped with clubs, balls, hired sledges. . . ." In 1398, the court purchased "for my lord twelve pikestaffs for flitting with irons under his feet"—perhaps a medieval cross between skates and skis?

Albert's favorite sport, though, was of course hunting. Situated on the edge of dunes, the Hague court was ideally suited to this pursuit. Boars, foxes, and (scarce) wolves were hunted down with weapons and with hounds; small game and wildfowl were also pursued. For the smaller prey, the use of hawks, sparrowhawks, and falcons was customary, though these occasionally flew off for good, even despite their training by professional experts. This fact is shown by the fairly frequent mention in the accounts of fees for errand boys who followed "my lord's falcon," sometimes as far as Amsterdam, or repaired to Brabant and Flanders to buy replacements. All sorts of larger hunting beasts were kept in the court stables as well.

In general, interest in animals was a notable aspect of medieval European court culture. There, zoological gardens were still private menageries, and in this regard Holland was no exception.[35] The stork's nest kept in permanent readiness on the roof of the Great Hall was probably the most "Haguish" example of courtly care for wildlife—"Haguish" inasmuch as the city's coat of arms boasts a stork to this day. But lions, too, were kept in The Hague, with special provision being made for straw and the slaughter of sheep; there were also bear pits, which, together with the lion cages, were managed by a keeper nicknamed Vos van der Lewen—Fox of the Lions. Jacqueline of Bavaria maintained a number of monkeys during her youth, and these accompanied her from The Hague to Hainaut; Albert's mistress, Adelaide of Poelgeest, owned a female monkey (evidently given to her by the Duke for reasons of gallantry), together with a hutch of rabbits and an ambling horse, the price of which his lordship had managed to get reduced.[36] The accounts contain many other entries about presents of animals, such as the beautiful dog Albert brought from Montpellier to The Hague in July 1362 for his wife;[37] the two greyhounds given him by Dirk of Polanen, which were allowed to sleep in the duke's bedroom; and the dromedary William V received from the Lady Egmont in 1408, and which he presented, in his turn, to the duchess of Brabant.[38]

This dromedary, a rarely seen and romantic beast, is a reminder of the many unusual luxuries with which the Hague court was so richly endowed.[39] Nor was it the only exotic rarity to reach Holland from oriental pavilions and pleasure domes. In 1416, at Hainaut, Jacqueline of Bavaria and John of Touraine received a visitor from Rhodes. A knight in the service of the King of Cyprus, he delighted the noble couple with a luxuriant variety of eastern presents: a leopard (accompanied by a page and a little Negress), a special bow, and a set of tambourines for John; and an assortment of cosmetics for Jacqueline.[40]

Not all luxuries came from afar, however. The accounts abound with payments for clothes bedecked with pearls or noble metals of less exotic provenance, the acme of *haute couture* being a robe owned by the Duchess Margaret and decorated in 1373 by the court purveyor Jan de Lauwe of Delft with more than two thousand letters in gilded silver. Gentlemen's attire, too, was often trimmed, not only with fur (for instance, the red-white-and-blue robe of state of William VI),[41] but also with motifs taken from nature and embroidered in silver thread. One entry from 1358 mentions a hundred silver buttons, supplied by a Dordrecht silversmith for "my lord's coat." Silver and gold clasps, too, were part of the ducal family's glittering wardrobe, as were expensive belts. Among the jewels, the crown was literally weighed down with an extravagantly precious diadem, bought in Hainaut in 1369 for the duchess. Gold rings figure in the accounts almost by the gross; of these, Her Grace in 1374 bought no less than three ounces for New Year presents. In 1417, Jacqueline and John of Touraine bought gold, pearls, diamonds, and rubies from a Parisian jeweller, all said to be "pour le fait du premier jour de l'an," as the Hainaut accounts put it.[42] At Christmas, too, the duke would try to express his friendship for courtiers with small presents; thus, in 1358, the Dordrecht gold and silversmith Jacob of Oudewater supplied the court with "small gold brooches set with pearls, which my lord presented on Christmas Eve to the ladies and damsels."

Crafted luxuries also included large quantities of silver tableware, bonbon dishes, and ornamental chests and cases, the latter often of precious leather but also made of silver or even of gold. Unfortunately, all these articles of undisputed Holland-Bavarian provenance are now lost. The same is true of the court's many religious *objets d'art*. Thus we can only imagine the golden crown of thorns, set with fourteen pearls, two emeralds, ten rubies, and eight sapphires, or the expensive tapestries that must have adorned many walls in the castle.[43] (Floors, incidentally, were usually covered with sand, grass, or sweet-smelling herbs.) The treasury (how helpful it would be if we had an inventory of that department!) apparently boasted a wall hanging embroidered with stars and clouds as well as a (symbolic?) tree. No less astonishing must have been the hundreds of shields (of nobles from Holland, Zeeland, and Bavaria) embroidered in Brussels on red velvet in 1371–72.

Then there were the paintings that graced many a wall and ceiling at court. Entries of payments for such paintings are, alas, all too scanty in the accounts. Only occasionally is there a mention of *tableaux*, and when they are mentioned they are usually those with religious motifs bought for court ladies. Much the same is true of the statues, for here, too, religious motifs were the most common, and the majority were ordered on behalf of female relatives of the noble lord.[44] (In the next section [4. Literary Life] we shall return to the leading cultural role of women, in particular to their interest in literature.)

The plastic arts may have been rather neglected by the rulers of Holland, but they seem to have rejoiced in music all the more.[45] To begin with there were the musicians attached to the court chapel, which was not only kept in good architectural repair by Duke Albert but also provided with a choir and organist. Even so, most of the music at the Hague court had a more worldly tenor. Under the board accounts we encounter a whole parade of players gracing the duke's table with their music: fiddlers, trumpeters, harpists, singers, and above all, countless pipers. Not a day seems to have gone by without music. Indeed, not only Duke Albert, but the separate establishments of his wife and of William of Oostervant, too, employed a host of musicians. On special occasions, moreover, countless guest performers appeared, adding even greater luster to the festivities in The Hague in the name of their own (absent) masters. The accounts covering the christening of Albert's daughter in 1372, for instance, mention payments (in addition to those for anonymous "speakers," waffle bakers, and two fools) to drummers and a viol player from Dordrecht; to a fiddler from the lord of Brederode; to pipers from the Lords of Arkel, Egmont, and Putten and from the duke of Brabant; to pipers from Guelders; and to wind players from 's Gravensande, Rotterdam, and Leiden.[46]

The nobles seem to have delighted in playing music themselves, and especially in accompanying their own singing on strings—though, of course, only as a hobby. Jacqueline of Bavaria bought a lute, a clavichord, and a harp in 1423, and two years later her second husband was presented with a beautiful harp. Yet the most remarkable entry in this area concerned Albert personally. On 3 May 1400, "my dear lord's pipers" received two Dordrecht guilders to "toast the new air to May that my lord hath made"[47]—a tune that the duke himself apparently composed (both text and music?) and may well have sung previously to the court. In this, of course, he was merely following an old tradition of medieval aristocrats; after all, troubadour lyrics were in large measure written by noblemen, Duke John I of Brabant being the most famous adept in the Low Countries. Clearly Albert of Bavaria, too, was occasionally inspired to produce new airs, for instance to celebrate spring, and to sing them himself or have them presented by others. And songs need words, which introduces what for us is the most important aspect of the leisure activities at the court of Holland: the literary life.

4. LITERARY LIFE

There were many books at the court of Holland,[48] not least among them the account books, which, most fortunately, are preserved in large number in the Netherlands State Archives. Most of the expenditures made on parchment, paper, pens, and ink, mentioned so often in these volumes, were probably requisitioned for the official texts and books issued by the treasury and the chancellery. Similarly, the "books and letters" transferred so hurriedly from The Hague to Vianen during the siege of Hagestein in 1405 most likely concerned administration; the same is true of the jurisprudential "plaints . . . concerning the disabilities of the Hollanders under the French," handed over in the form of "a booklet" to Andries Pesselssoen in 1407 for translation into French.

Yet the court also owned books of a nonadministrative nature. The most important will be discussed in detail in later chapters, namely Duke Albert's (extant) presentation copy of the *Tafel van den kersten ghelove* (Table of the Christian faith) by Dirk of Delft (Chapter V) and an autograph of the *Hollandse kroniek* (Chronicle of Holland) dedicated to Count William VI by Bavaria Herald (Chapter IV, sec. 3). Nevertheless, the invaluable accounts provide us with glimpses of other books— most of which, sadly, have disappeared, making it all the more fortunate that their existence has been thus recorded. For example, Dirk of Delft appears to have written a second book—even earlier than the *Tafel*, this time for Albert's wife, to whom a finished copy was handed on 10 January 1401: "Master Dirk the monk paid on my lady's behalf [. . .] for a book he hath made for my lady and brought to her all finished."[49] While we are left wondering about the (undoubtedly pious) contents of this work, we are puzzled even more by the mysterious *boeck van de orloghe* (book of the war), which required three "great quires of paper and 1 large white sheet" to make; do such materials suggest an illustrated

5.   Breviary of Margaret of Cleves: opening miniature. (Fundação Calouste Gulbenkian Museu, Lisbon, MS. L.A. 148, fol. 19v)

book, or was the work rather a distant offshoot of Vegetius's *Epitome rei militaris*? We may never know.

There is less uncertainty about the prayer books and breviaries that figure repeatedly in the accounts. All of them were probably in Latin, though the entries do not specify. The only extant breviary from the court of Holland-Bavaria is, however, in that language; it was made for Margaret of Cleves, the second wife of Duke Albert, and dates back to her life in The Hague as countess of Holland (ca. 1395–1400).[50] The opening miniature (see fig. 5) depicts her kneeling before Mary and Jesus, saying, by means of a banderole, "Pater adveniat regnum tuum" (Father, thy kingdom come), with Christ adding, "Fiat" (So be it). The execution of the breviary is sublime; specialists consider it one of the earliest examples of the French style, soon afterward to be used by the brothers Limburg in the famous breviaries they made for the duke of Berry, late medieval masterpieces for that time and all time. The craftsmen who created Margaret's breviary also produced the first, no less lavishly illustrated, copies of Dirk of Delft's *Tafel* for Duke Albert and his entourage; thus they provided the court with many splendid books. Other breviaries and prayer books at the court of Holland-Bavaria must have been equally exquisite. In 1358, the court acquired a small breviary written on exclusive *aportyf*, velvet-soft parchment obtained from lambs aborted for that purpose. And thirty years later, in 1388, an accounts entry mentions two such breviaries, "very costly and well gilded," brought to the court by a "young woman from Haarlem" (a Beguine?) and intended for "my lady of Oestervant and my lady of Hainaut." The one from 1358 was made for a third great lady at court, presumably Albert's daughter Margaret; whereas in 1389 another daughter, Joanna, was the probable recipient of a breviary bought for six guilders "on my lady of Holland's" behalf.

Usually, breviaries and prayer books were made for the court ladies, whose association with books was remarkable. Indeed, the earliest recorded mention of a manuscript at the court of Holland-Bavaria concerns a lady: in 1361, Voghelaer, a messenger from the countess of Voorne, handed the (then) Countess Matilda a chessboard as well as a "German book."[51] Then, too, the "new poetry books" that "a man from France" brought to the court in 1408 were meant for "my dear lady," that is, the wife of William VI, who, as the daughter of Philip the Bold, duke of Burgundy, must have longed to keep up with the latest French literary fashions. Other examples of acquisitions of books by women abound. Moreover, as in the fine arts, the number of literary purchases made for ladies was much higher than for men.

Various indications thus confirm the predominance of women in the culture of medieval courts.[52] Perhaps it was equally symptomatic that, at the court of Holland, the countess not only had a separate household but, whenever she and her husband were in residence simultaneously, was in charge of both establishments.[53] Thus, although ladies at court rarely exerted direct political influence, their cultural sway was comparatively powerful.[54] The stereotype of the well-read woman with a husband too busy with matters of state to bother about refined manners and culture seems to have had some basis as early as the fourteenth century in The Hague.

The schooling of ladies at court seems to have been in no way inferior to their husbands'. The accounts of 14 October 1404, for example, mention "my lady's first schoolmaster," yet no reference is made anywhere to a private instructor for Duke Albert or William IV.[55] Neither cost nor pain was spared in the education of Jacqueline of Bavaria, either.[56] When she was about ten, *maistre* Aubert Loison gave her and John of Touraine, the same age and her fiancé, a solid French education in Hainaut, including lessons in Latin, history, geometry, and elementary moral philosophy. The books purchased for this training were not only handsome but also, according to the Hainaut accounts, *très bien glosés*, that is, accompanied by many instructive examples. If all this was done in the hope that Jacqueline might one day become queen of France (John of Touraine was the dauphin), that prospect collapsed with John's sudden death in 1417. Nevertheless, Jacqueline benefited well from that early education; we find her, toward the end of her life in Castle Teylingen, surrounded by a multitude of books, including works on medicine and history.[57] In addition, Jacqueline (who did marry, among others, Humphrey of Gloucester, for a time protector of England for the infant Henry VI and whose generous gift of books to Oxford University places him as the virtual founder of the world-famous Bodleian Library) seems to have been the only person in her circle to have read English books—which, on her death, "no one hereabouts having any liking for them, . . . were sold to a foreign English merchant."

Still, the male scions of the House of Holland-Bavaria were anything but illiterate: quite possibly they could read Latin fluently—a possibility that would become a certainty if only we knew that they actually read the Latin texts dedicated to them. These works included Philip of Leiden's guide for princes, dedicated to William V before his mental illness.[58] Much less well known is the fact that, in about 1395 in a monastery at Valenciennes, the Franciscan friar Jacques de Guise wrote a chronicle of Hainaut (*Annales Hannoniae*), which he dedicated to the lords of that county, who were then also (Bavarian) counts of Holland.[59] A dedication-miniature of that chronicle included in the Brussels manuscript shows the author presenting the book to Duke Albert; but whether the duke did more than look pleased at the dedication is uncertain. Much the same is true of a third, perhaps even more remarkable book: an account of the travels to the Holy Land by the wealthy Venetian patrician Marino Sanudo, published in book form upon his return from Jerusalem and presented, in about 1335, in a large and luxurious edition, to the foremost European nobles and the pope (fig. 6).[60] The

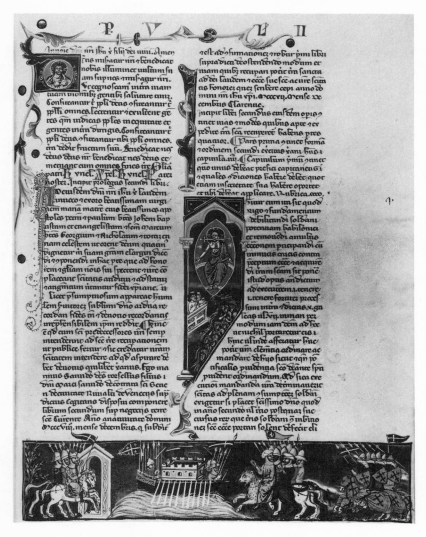

6. Book from the Dutch court's collection(?): Sanudo's description of the Holy Land. (Bibliothèque royale Albert Ier, Brussels, MS. 9404–05, fol. 18r)

author did not forget the House of Holland-Hainaut; two fine specimens of Sanudo's text, which must have passed into Burgundian hands through the Bavarian dynasty in the fifteenth century, are today owned by the Royal Library in Brussels. But could Sanudo be certain that all these princes were at ease with Latin? Perhaps not; nevertheless, we should be quite wrong to dismiss these princes' learning and to consider them less educated than they were clearly expected to be in their age. At the very least, Albert of Bavaria and his son had mastered the arts of reading and writing; this fact appears unequivocally in account entries indicating that both, for reasons of confidentiality, themselves read and wrote various diplomatic letters.[61] Indeed, to another of Duke Albert's sons, John of Bavaria, count of Holland in succession to his brother William VI, reading even proved fatal. In 1424, a Hook enemy (perhaps an accomplice of Jacqueline, who may have allied with the count's enemies to pursue her own private goals) smeared "poison over my lord's book, which was about as large as a walnut"; the description suggests that the book was a miniature prayer book—used, in the event, for what resulted in the deadliest of private devotions.[62] Albert and William VI, too, owned prayer books. For Albert, a profusely illustrated copy was ordered from Utrecht, then the center of book illumination in the northern Netherlands.[63] No less beautiful was a (Latin) breviary that was probably made for William VI and was later included among the treasures of the Turin Library, which burned down in 1904.[64] The private accounts of Duke Albert and of his son William further mention a small "chest in which my lord's books" were stored.[65]

Still, a bookcase, let alone a small chest, does not make a library. And unfortunately, we have no way of telling whether The Hague boasted a court library in the fullest sense. What it probably did have was a small library in the court chapel, as accounts and an inventory from the early Burgundian period imply.[66] In 1460, for example, twenty-five tin-plated chains were bought, "that the books might be secured therewith in the said library"—which suggests the presence of as many (chained) items. According to the inventory, these books were liturgical, and almost certainly in Latin. This mention does not, of course, reflect the existence of a proper court library, and perhaps the very fact that no references to one can be found entitles us to think that the stock of books possessed by the ruling family indeed was confined to one chest or shelf in their private chambers. Then again, this collection may well have been larger and more accessible than the accounts indicate: for where else would Bavaria Herald, for instance, have obtained the copious writings of Jacob van Maerlant, which, according to his chronicles, he had constantly within reach? In addition, extant lists of books owned by nobles close to the Bavarian court—including the recently discovered catalogue of books owned by the counts of Egmont, the partly reconstructible library of Count John IV of Nassau, and the fairly impressive collection of some forty books owned by one of Albert's vassals in the duchy of

Straubing—suggest that these men, too, were collectors, however amateurish.[67]

But perhaps even more important than the number of books to be found at court is the quality of its literary life, for that quality seems to have been considerably greater than the total cost of the volumes entered in the accounts would suggest. Students of medieval culture often project the apparently clear-cut conditions of the early Middle Ages onto the later Middle Ages; in terms of educational achievement, this projection can easily give an oversimplified picture of a clergy with a monopoly on knowledge, a studious middle class, and an ignorant nobility. In fact, it would be a mistake to underestimate the learning and education at the court of Holland during the Bavarian period, even if we omitted such exceptionally cultivated courtiers as Dirk of Delft. According to historians of medieval education, Albert of Bavaria was one of the first princes to advocate the extension of education to the laity.[68] In particular, he helped to set up schools in Haarlem (1389), Alkmaar (1390), Oudewater (1394), and other towns; nearer home, he presented his own court chapter with a village school in The Hague in 1393 and at the same time introduced something very much like compulsory education: "[We] enjoin and command all our inhabitants in The Hague to send [. . .] their children to school under them [i.e., the schoolmasters of the chapter]."[69]

Yet the existence of these "public" schools should not cause us to ignore the importance of private education in these privileged circles. The accounts for 1408–9, for instance, mention that two of the countess's pages went to school in the house of "Walter the Scribe in The Hague to learn writing and reading"[70]—which suggests that village scribes may have served as private tutors to young nobles as well. This entry, then, shows that the court of Holland-Bavaria prized at least an elementary education for young noblemen and future courtiers. More literary sources at court convey a similar message: although they do not say that nobles should attend universities, they nevertheless present a decent education as a worthy end. Dirk of Delft, better educated than any other Holland courtier, even articulated this sentiment in a saying famous in the Middle Ages: "An uneducated king is like unto a crowned ass" (*TKG*/"S" XLI/26). Just how educated the counts of Holland-Bavaria themselves were is hard to say, because so often servants did their writing for them; in any case, the days when aristocrats could remain self-satisfied illiterates were certainly past by about 1400. At court, one was no longer expected to cultivate muscles and manners alone; one had to attend to the intellect as well.[71] And that entailed acquiring not only some useful French, but at least some elementary Latin as well and, certainly, the ability to read and write. Most courtiers were, so to speak, functionally literate.

An example was Dirk Potter. Just where he stood in terms of general education is debatable; as a declared admirer of classical letters, however, he must have had more than an average interest in general intellectual matters. To be sure, his intellectual profile is not nearly as unusual as Dirk of Delft's. It therefore seems safest to rank Potter among the better educated laymen at court, but not to consider him a marked exception in terms of cultural attainment. He, too, associated books primarily with the clerical cloth, and the nobility primarily with arms, but he also considered reading and writing a normal attribute of young people of good family.[72] He himself tried to set them a good example, modestly though he appraised his own skills, especially in his prologues (*ML* I, 36–40):

> Mijn konst en prisic niet een ey:
> Doch donct my prisens weerdich wesen,
> Datmen kan scriven ende lesen
> Ende te maten Latijn verstaen;
> Daer om heb ic ter scole ghegaen.

My skills I do not greatly praise; yet praiseworthy I deem the ability to read and write and a fair grasp of Latin; for these I went to school.

Apart from school learning, which must have given him the thorough grounding in Latin that his writings reflect, Potter also acquired considerable knowledge of subjects outside the academic curriculum.[73] Thus his French was proficient enough to translate the *Livre de Mellibee*, and his Italian enabled him not only to travel to Rome on diplomatic business but also to use the *Fiore di Virtú* as a sourcebook for his *Blome der doechden* (Flower of virtue).[74] The educated man of the world can be seen in those parts of his work where—not without chauvinism—he muses on the character of various European peoples; in *Der minnen loep* (The course of love), for example, he states that "good courtly love" can be found in full measure throughout the German Empire—and hence in Holland—while the Mediterranean inhabitants of France and Italy, no less than those of England, "rarely understand its language" (II, 724).

Potter's travels and life went hand in hand with a broad familiarity with books, which explains why students today wrestle so persistently with his literary and personal sources. We shall return to this subject in Chapter VI; here, however, let us consider what literary knowledge Potter assumed in his *public*, for that will help us assess the literary luggage that courtiers carried in Holland in around 1400. Judging by Potter's output, we can say that that luggage was far from light. True, that he expected little knowledge of Latin is revealed by the pedantry with which he explains the Latin names of the sins and virtues in his *Blome*.[75] Otherwise, though, his writings presuppose a wide familiarity with the great medieval popular texts. In *Der minnen loep*, he refers to the Tristan saga, Perceval and the quest for the Grail, the story of Troy, and the Reynard cycle, as well as (less obviously, but understandably given the Bavarian influence) to the *Titurel* epic and Neidhard von Reuental.[76] In addition, he parades lists of characters from various romances.[77] And when he retells the tragic love story of the *Chatelaine of Vergi*, he openly relies on his readers' thorough knowledge of it: "As you will likely have read" (II, 560) and "Now, you will doubtless know how these matters ended" (II, 543–44).

This last quotation raises a crucial question. Familiarity with the major works of popular medieval writing did not necessarily entail ownership of books, or even direct contact with books. Certainly in 1400, literary life still largely bypassed written texts, for anyone interested in literature was free to listen to reciters. The student of literary life at the court of Holland, then, does well to concentrate on the spoken rather than the written word; indeed, there are many signs that literary life hinged not so much on "books read in private nooks" as on small groups of listeners.

Here again, the accounts yield our chief evidence. Most of the books named in them are of a devotional, even sacred, character: breviaries and prayer books predominate.[78] The French manuscript with secular poems mentioned earlier was an exception. Commonly in medieval Europe, poets and storytellers presented their work by reciting or singing, at the hour when the lord and his family gathered at table. In this the Hague court was no exception, for meals were regularly accompanied by music and often by other entertainment, including storytelling. Storytellers are usually listed as "speakers" in the accounts, with numerous entries for persons who, as the standard formula put it, "spoke at my lord's table." All were itinerant performers paid from a special account. Indeed, their large numbers almost make one forget that the count also had table performers in his permanent employ, whose appearances, being part of their regular duties, did not have to be booked separately. Their names crop up in the accounts only if they performed some extraordinary feat deserving special recompense or made a guest appearance elsewhere, in which case the expenses were debited to the court in question. The Blois accounts for 1359 in fact show that, within a year of his taking office, Albert had at least five minstrels in his regular service.[79] The countess of Holland, too, seems to have employed personal minstrels in 1362, and the accounts for the separate establishment of William of Oostervant mention two "little singers" and the appearance of "minstrels."[80]

In addition to the regular court entertainers, many passing reciters enlivened the duke's meals in The Hague. Occasionally these were professional poets, but as often as not they were servants of the master's kinsmen, who, while frequently conveying messages, also helped to maintain literary links between their own masters and the ruler of Holland. In this role, a host of guest speakers from within and without the county performed before the court. The largest group of speakers came from the German Empire: emissaries of cities such as Nuremberg, Heidelberg, Meissen, Cleves, and Cologne and of their lordly residents, and of nobles from such regions as Austria, Westphalia, and Bavaria. But the court also received guest speakers from England (did they address the court in French?), France, and even Poland (the last were servants of Albert's father-in-law and received rewards unusually lavish).

The poetry recited during dinners must have been as artistically variable as it was multilingual. No particular occasion or excuse for entertainment was needed; on many an ordinary weekday one or another "speaker at my lord's table" received his testimonial gift. True, the number increased on special occasions, and we may assume that distinguished visitors were treated not only to culinary but also to literary delights. The "pipers and heralds" rubric of the accounts for 1388, for example, lists, in connection with a visit the lord of Heusden paid Albert in Dordrecht,

alrehande lude, die vor minen here op die tijt aldaer ghesonghen, ghepepen ende ghespeelt hadden; eerst der stede pipers van Dordrecht, 2 gulden. Item Ydekijn mit 2 ghesellen die songhen, 2 gl. Item 2 andere sanghers 1 gl. Item Alijt van Bult, van licht broet ende van clareyt, 1 gl. Item noch 2 lude mit 1 lute ende mit gheterne, 1 gl. Item meester Jan mitter santorie, 1 gl. Item een man mit 1 kinde, die pijpten, 1 gl.

various persons who on that occasion did sing and pipe and play for my Lord; first the town pipers of Dordrecht, 2 guilders. Item Ydekijn with two companions who sang, 2 gl. Item 2 other singers 1 gl. Item Alijt van Bult [= Hump], light bread and claret [to the value of] 1 gl. Item another two persons with 1 lute and guitars, 1 gl. Item Master Jan with cither, 1 gl. Item one man with 1 child who did piping, 1 gl.[81]

As this one entry shows, poets were lumped together with many other performers—in this case even a (hunchbacked?) dealer in comestibles; they were treated like anything but princes of Parnassus. Sometimes it is quite impossible to determine whether a particular entertainer accompanied himself on an instrument while he sang or recited. On one occasion our ignorance is particularly glaring, for we have no inkling how the artist performed—whatever could the *catridder* (cat's knight?) mentioned in the accounts for 1378 have offered? Was his act perhaps similar to that of the "wild knights" who so often erupt in the Blois accounts, one of whom Duke Albert seems to have had in his permanent employ?[82]

Overall, the accounts present us with a motley crew of entertainers.[83] The largest group was of musicians; we read of "Master Geraerd the fiddler, Crayenbliec my lord's trumpeter, a poor priest from Ireland who played for my lord on the lute," anonymous viol, organ, guitar, lyre, and harp players, and a legion of pipers. Conjurers and jugglers were a small group apart; their ranks included Master Christian, an anonymous "damsel who could juggle," and another performer who gave of his best in 1387, "just as my Lord was preparing to ride to Haarlem," and who "pleased my Lord greatly" (reward: 1 guilder). The accounts also, and repeatedly, mention "fools" from the retinues of the lord of Culemborg, the bishop of Utrecht, and others. Animal acts were popular: one man appeared with a dog and two netfuls of warbling finches. The court furthermore welcomed masters of physiognomy, who presumably read, from their features, the character of the distinguished diners. In 1345, a "Brabanter" was paid a fee for "letting himself be beaten about the head as much as anyone liked." More subtle, no doubt, were the skills of "Noyden the dancer," the occasional tumbler, and the many child artists. Sometimes acrobatics were combined with other forms of table entertainment, as in the case of the "two players who performed with glasses on their noses" and the artist "who played on the lute and balanced a sword on his forehead even while he was playing." Even the distinction between the recital of poetry or stories and acrobatics was not always clear; the popularity of the oft-mentioned blind poets, for example, must have been due, at least in part, to their success in overcoming their handicap. And the name "Snelryem de spreker" (Quickrhyme the speaker) must have designated a juggler of rhymes. Indeed, stage names are quite common in the accounts. Sometimes they indicate the professional competence of their owners: thus Jonkheer vander Minnen (Squire of Love) and Jan Vrouwentroost (John Ladies' Solace) must have been minnesingers, and Ruutentuut a virtuoso piper or flautist. Another artist turned his favorite season into a trademark: Hopezomer (Hopesummer), the best time for anyone trying to earn his bread as an itinerant performer.

Although the total number of "word artists" figuring in the Hague accounts is difficult to compute because of the large proportion of anonymous performers, several hundred poets, speakers, declaimers, singers, and heralds can be definitely identified. Nevertheless, even when they are listed by name—a distinction probably reserved for the most renowned—they still mean nothing to us, because no single poem or song is attributable to them. Master Jan of Raemsdonc, the poetess Trude of Nymaghen, Jan of Bot, Mees of Dordrecht, Bertelmees of Delft—unique though all these entries may be as sources of literary history, the disappearance of their associated works only makes them enigmatic. How wonderful it would be to know something about the repertoire of, say, the noble singer Damsel Adelaide of Hochusen, who, in 1394, traveled about with her *cokerelle* (probably a kind of serenade) and so moved the count that he presented her with twelve silver bowls.[84]

Most regrettable of all is the loss of a whole genre, namely the stage play. The accounts mention payments for several theatrical performances, but we are unable to imagine what was being performed, for none of the plays have survived. To be sure, sometimes the question of survival is moot: the *dockenspiel* "opened up for my lord in his chamber" in 1396, for example, must have been a kind of puppet or marionette act in which few words were spoken, making transcription virtually impossible.[85] For the majority of the stage performances recorded in the accounts, however, texts undoubtedly did exist. Such plays must have varied considerably, from a modest one-man show by a reciter who "said a little play for my lord," through "two players who treated my lord and my lords of Oestervant to a play about Saint George and King Charles," to performances by large companies.[86] Prominent among the latter were the scholars from The Hague, who on one occasion arrived, accompanied by their "bishop," near the end of the year to treat the court to a (burlesque) performance. Under the same heading we must probably place the carnival play given in 1415 by "diverse persons, women and men, who came to masquerade monks in the Great Hall."[87] The most important actors to entertain the court of Holland, though, were undoubtedly the fourteenth-century forerunners of the Hague Comedy, the "companions of the play from The Hague." Their repertoire seems to have had a mainly religious flavor: the accounts mention plays with such pious titles as "Of Holy Cross Day," "Of Our Lord's Resurrection," and "Of Our Sweet Lady's Attendance at Church."[88] Furthermore, in 1413–14, four young men treated the count's council to a performance of "the contumacy of the magpie and the crossbill"—a comical disputation of birds, and pointedly appropriate for the select audience.

The stage on which these performances were enacted was as variable as the repertoire. The "companions of the play" performed in the Plaats (Courtyard), on the Vijverberg (Lake Hill), in the chapel, and even in the resplendent Knights' Hall. The links that these entertainers enjoyed with the nascent town of The Hague, moreover, were apparently quite close, reflecting the association between urban background and the medieval stage that students of the period usually assume existed. In Holland, however, that association did not preclude court patronage. Yet what kind of text would have been suitable for both town and court? The *abele spelen*—the oldest known dramatic works in the Dutch language—make attractive candidates, but we cannot be certain: no text used for court performances at The Hague has been discovered.[89] Hence, what might have been a cornerstone of Dutch literary history remains little more than soft clay, at least for the moment. In what follows we shall thus have to ignore the court stage.

Clearly, the survival of a text presented at court by a poet or storyteller and recorded in the accounts depended on special circumstances. Much of these performers' work was never written or printed, but was communicated and perpetuated orally. If an author did wish to commit his repertoire to paper (and hence was more literate than many of his colleagues), then, for practical and economic reasons, he recorded it in such small volumes as would be easily mislaid or destroyed; for example, only one fragment of what can be considered a work by Augustijnken's own (or a colleague's) hand has come down to us.[90] A fortiori, natural wear and tear has taken a drastic toll on those rare manuscripts presented by reciters to the count after particularly successful performances: passing centuries had little respect for loose sheets.[91] Where short literary gems were nevertheless preserved, it was usually through incorporation into a larger (and hence more solid) manuscript. This is certainly true of the only extant *bispel* (short poem) by Jan Visier, which owes its existence to Bavaria Herald copying it into his *Kladboek* (Jotter). For the public generally, this petty art form was not worth taking home in a book; poems, in essence, were disposable. Hence it was quite exceptional when, in 1409, Count William VI of Holland chose to purchase a book containing "many fine stories." Not surprisingly, they were by the undisputed master of this genre, the only one from whom a substantial oeuvre has come down to us. His name was William of Hildegaersberch.

II

William of Hildegaersberch

1. MARRIAGE AND POETRY

In April 1394, a wedding was celebrated at the Hague court. It was Duke Albert's second marriage. He had lost his first wife, Margaret of Brieg, in 1386, after she had borne him seven children. Though now in his fifties, the widower was still virile: from 1387 onward, the noble Adelaide of Poelgeest figured in the accounts as the duke's *amye*, or sweetheart. Morally, the affair was no problem; politically, however, it seems to have been a disaster.[1] Thus, on Sunday, 22 September 1392, while strolling in the Outer Court with the courtier William Cuser, Adelaide was stabbed to death by hired assassins. The motives for the murder were much less clear than many romanticized historical accounts have suggested; but whatever the reasons, the effect was that Holland was shaken by a grave crisis. Worst of all, perhaps, the duke quarreled with his son and heir, William of Oostervant, suspecting him of complicity in the murder. His retaliation was harsh: scores of nobles—including William—were banished, their goods and chattels declared forfeit and their castles razed. (The 700,000 bricks that had once been Castle Hodenpijl Duke Albert used in restoring his Inner Court.)[2]

In the aftermath of all this turmoil, the duke decided to contract a fresh marriage. A causal relation seems likely: Albert may well have been trying to consolidate his position through wedlock. If that was indeed his purpose, it would explain why, in his fraught state, he chose a bride of so inferior a rank—after all, a prince for whose favors the great European powers had begun to vie could have done much better than Margaret of Cleves. Yet the situation was in fact more complex than that. Indeed, his foreign standing may well have benefited from a liaison with Cleves—which explains the suggestion that Philip the Bold, duke of Burgundy and powerful father-in-law of Albert's daughter Margaret, had acted as matchmaker behind the scenes. And—a final guess—perhaps Albert wanted a second son to thwart the pretensions of the rebellious William of Oostervant. But even if that consideration was serious—and to be sure, the marriage plans of medieval aristocrats, in those times of high mortality, often did include hopes for more male births—it finally came to nothing: when Albert died in 1404, Margaret of Cleves had still not presented him with a child.

One is almost tempted to say that the laborious logistics of the wedding were an omen of a sterile union. Originally, the nuptials were to have been held in Heusden in late March 1394; to make all the necessary contractual and ceremonial preparations, Albert's "steward" and various trusted nobles traveled frequently between North Holland and Cleves.[3] Then, at the last moment, Albert sent this steward to Margaret's mother with the urgent request (as a clerk has faithfully recorded in the messenger-service accounts) "that she convey my dear lady of Hollant [the bride] to The Hague and let him [Albert] sleep with her there, as he is unable to repair to Heusden and sleep with my dear lady there." This request was probably at once obeyed. To receive the wedding guests from Cleves in due ceremony and splendor, Albert had the Rijswijk road improved and on it rode out to meet his bride in ducal style on 3 April. Two days later, the marriage was consecrated in the court chapel, with the sexton and priest receiving a joint fee of three guilders.

Necessarily, the wedding night saw a mighty banquet and lively entertainments. The treasury accounts for 5 April mention a small army of musicians and reciters (see fig. 7):[4]

Item V dagen in aprille: 35 piperen van der heren wapen gegeven die tot mijns heren brulofte gecomen waren 60 gulden. Item alrehande stede pipers tsamen gegeven 56 gulden. Item 6 herauden tsamen 30 gulden. Item 3 parsevanten elcx 4 gulden. Item enen speelre uptie quintaerne, toebehorende den coninc van Beem 8 gulden. Item enen vedelair, toebehorende den hertoge van Oistenrijc 20 gulden. Item heren drie toebehorende den hertoge van Sassen spelende upten quintaerne 15 gulden. Item enen orgelaer ende enen vedelair toebehorende den bisscop van Wyertsberch 8 gulden. Item meester Willem van Hildegaertsberge, meester Jan van Raemsdonc ende enen spreker toebehorende den grave van Hoensten elc 4 gulden. Item enen vreemden spreker sonder wapen 2 gulden. Item jonchere Otten spelende uptie quintaernen 40 groot. Item Bom, dez heren knecht van Zevenbergen 80 groot. Item Wijs Neve, die mit minre vrouwen van Hollant quam gegeven 6 gulden. Item Heynken mitter stelt enen gulden. Item 4 sanghers elcx enen gulden.

Item V days into April: 35 pipers in the lords' arms [i.e., in the service of various nobles] who were come to my lord's wedding 60 guilders. Item various local pipers 56 guilders in all. Item 6 heralds 30 guilders in all. Item 3 pursuivants 4 guilders each. Item one player on the quintern [guitar] appurtenant to the king of Bohemia 8 guilders. Item one fiddler appurtenant to the duke of Austria 20 guilders. Item three gentlemen appurtenant to the duke of Saxony playing upon

7. Artists' charges for the wedding of Duke Albert and Margaret of Cleves, 1394. (Algemeen Rijksarchief, The Hague, MS. AGH 1248, fol. 26r)

the quinterns 15 guilders. Item one organist and one fiddler appurtenant to the bishop of Wyertsberch [Würzburg] 8 guilders. Item master William of Hildegaertsberge, master John of Raemsdonc and an orator appurtenant to the count of Hoensten 4 guilders each. Item a foreign orator without arms [i.e., armorial bearings] 2 guilders. Item *jonkheer* Otto playing on the quintern 40 groats. Item Bom, the lord's servant from Zevenbergen 80 groats. Item Wise Neve who came with my lady from Hollant 6 guilders. Item Heynken with his wooden leg one guilder. Item 4 singers one guilder each.

This list seems to have been quite systematically compiled. First come musicians in the permanent employ of nobles or towns, next artists from the guild of heralds, then musicians in the livery of exalted foreign lords (and rewarded accordingly), then poets from Holland, and finally a motley group comprising the noble guitarist Jonkheer Otto, a man-servant from Zevenbergen, a member of the Cleves wedding party, a man (who may well have been a juggler) with a wooden leg, and four anonymous singers. Of the more than sixty artists noted here, we can make an informed guess about the precise role of only one, and that was "master William of Hildegaertsberge"—for of the more than 120 poems that survive under his name, one was eminently suited to recitation at the showy wedding feast of 5 April 1394, namely the occasional poem entitled "Van feeste van hylic" (On the wedding feast; LVI).

The work contains fewer than two hundred lines, but it covers a considerable variety of topical matters. William starts with a conventionally pious reference to the festive mood (1–14).

> Menighe feeste wort opheven
> Opdat die tijt van onsen leven

Mit ghenoechten overgae.
Elck bedenck hem ende versta,
Waermen feeste mach bedriven
Ende buten sonden mach off bliven;
Want blyde te sijn sonder zonde
Dat quam uut reynre herten gronde;
Oeck ist Gode wel bequame.
Doe hy Yeve gaff Adame,
Hi maecte daer feest van hoghen prise,
Ende setse inden paradise,
Ende hadden si buten sonden ghebleven,
Wy mochten sonder sterven leven.

Many a feast is given so that we may pass the time of our life agreeably. Let each of us reflect how he may feast without sinning; for gladness without sin ever springs from a pure heart and pleases God withal. When he gave Eve to Adam, he held a magnificent feast and placed them in Paradise; and had they continued without sin, we should now be living without death.

This was plain speaking: our poet is certainly not objecting to a merry feast—provided sin is kept at bay. And if, by introducing this qualification, William is more reserved than befits an epithalamium, his recital grows even more somber as it unfolds. With his reference to the spoiled feast held for Adam and Eve in Paradise, he introduces the theme of death, and also the question of free will, which ensures (31–33)

Dat elcman is sijns selfs vry
Te comen daer ghenoechte sy,
In feeste die niet en mach vergaen . . .

That every man is free to come where there is pleasure, to a feast that does not fade away . . .

Thus, anyone wishing to partake of an everlasting feast holds the key in his own hands: his free will enables him to reach out for heaven. Compared with such eternal bliss, the delights of a wedding feast are evanescent and full of pitfalls (34–44):

Hoe hoghe feeste wy hier begaen
Om vreuchde te driven mit jolijt,
Tis al verganc in corter tijt.
Hierom selmen feesten maken
Buten sondeliken zaken,
Gode te loven, der werlt te vromen.
Soe wye in brulofts feeste comen,
Die moghen sonder zonde hoven,
Gode te dancken ende te loven,

Laten sijt hoff in sijnre waerde
Sonder nijt of hoveerde.

No matter how splendid a feast we hold to rejoice down here, it is over all too soon. Hence we should feast without sin, to God's glory and the good of the world. Any who come to a wedding may feast without sin, thanks be to God, provided they do not detract from the honor of the court, and act without envy or pride.

In the last two lines, William is stepping on dangerous ground. Of course, we can read these verses as so many banal rhymes, as verbose and platitudinous poetics. But if this poem was indeed recited at the 1394 wedding, then the reference to honoring the court surely had a specific meaning. Those present must have been startled and perhaps embarrassed by the absence from the festivities of the bridegroom's son and heir. Hildegaersberch knew better than to be overexplicit—but perhaps his remarks about the desirable absence of envy and pride were aimed at William of Oostervant and his supporters. The lines immediately following could have referred to them even more specifically (45–56):

Hoveerde, nijt ende ghierichede
Daer wort een hoff onzuver mede;
Daer by machmense mit goeden reden
Te hove laten onghebeden.
Want hoghe bruloften off edel feeste,
Wat soude daer nijt of tempeeste?
Vruechde, blyschap, melody,
Die wil God selve datter sy,
Want in sijn lof ist al ghesticht,
Man ende wijff, dese edel gycht,
Die si malcander moeten gheven,
Trouwe te houwen al hoer leven.

Pride, envy, and avarice sully a court; hence they are best left uninvited. For what business have envy and anger at a noble wedding or at a nobleman's feast? Joy, gladness, music, these God himself desires, for in his praise was conceived the gift husband and wife have to give each other: lifelong faithfulness.

With that William arrives at the actual reason for feast and poem: the duke's wedding. He continues with a rhymed eulogy to a hallowed institution sanctified by God that, by virtue of the sacrament of marriage, unites man and wife in harmony and affection unto death (v. 67). Characteristically, William says nothing about true love. Aristocratic circles did not then consider marriage a seal upon love; for emotional love, and sometimes for mere affection, a nobleman kept mistresses. Thus, even after marriage, Albert continued to maintain his accustomed suite of ladies, his lavish gifts meticulously entered as "expenses" in the court accounts. In short, a noble marriage was a contract, more political than amorous, less between two individuals than between their countries or estates (80–88):

> Hoghe heren ende edel vrouwen,
> Die mogher by in rusten bliven.
> By hilijc letmen menich kiven,
> Want als twee landen te gader minghen
> By hilic, dat si te samen bringhen,
> Hoer vyande worder mede versaecht.
> Hoe groeten hoemoet datmen draecht,
> Groet ontsich van felre wrake
> Dat doet verhoeden menighe zake.

Noble lords and ladies may live in peace thanks to marriage. Marriage helps to avert many quarrels, for when two countries join together by marriage, they fill their enemies with fear. No matter how haughty they may be, dire fear of fierce revenge prevents many things.

Marriage, therefore, is a powerful weapon to deter an enemy. Generally speaking, of course, this seems no very moral or domestic justification of matrimony; in the troubled and uncertain context of 1394, however, marriage was certainly an important aid to social and political survival. The county of Holland was in desperate need of peace and security, and Hildegaersberch warmly welcomed the fact that a marriage could serve these goals well. Foreign enemies had been warned off; moreover, the marriage would assure peace at home as well: a mighty lord inspires awe, which dissuades his subjects from expectations too ambitious, too greedy, too unrealistic. Differences in rank at least induce obedience: "Inequality is good, for it fosters submission" (Daer by is onghelike goet, wantet wel verdraghen doet; 95–96).

In addition to immediate peace and order, though, William of Hildegaersberch had another important reason for considering marriage, and particularly the wedding he was attending that day, a gift from God: to wit, long-term continuity. As long as a strong ruler is alive, everyone seems to know his place, but upon on his death quarrels frequently erupt—unless, of course, a legitimate and powerful heir to the throne stands ready to take over. Thus, it is even more important for noblemen to marry than it is for commoners—or, as William puts it (121–23):

> Want als sy kinder afterlaten,
> Tcomt den lande te meerre baten
> Dan off die mate kinder winnen.

For if they have children, the country benefits more than when the common people have children.

In short (126–28):

> By hylic quam die werlt voert,
> By hilic machse staende bliven,
> Doet ons God sijn hulp beclyven.

Through marriage came mankind about, through marriage can it continue, so long as God proffers his help.

True, William felt he must add the warning that lasting concord between the partners (and their countries) is essential; after all, a harmonious marriage is not to be found in the jumble of wedding presents (144–48):

> Te hilic hoort wel grote hoede;
> Al is die coop al thants ghedaen,
> Die dach die moet al langher staen,
> Ende wye misraect op sinen dach,
> Ic waent hem langhe dencken mach.

Marriage calls for great care; for no matter how quickly the bargain is struck, the day is not yet over, and whoever slips up later will, I believe, rue it at his leisure.

Having uttered that warning, William apparently became impatient. Had some fresh delicacy been served up, or did another performer stand waiting in the wings? In any case, it seems it was time to conclude (149–52):

> Van hilic mochtmen dichten vele;
> Soud ic tende vanden spele
> Dichten, tworde ons te lanc,
> Soe waert een arbeit sonder danck.

Of marriage many verses can be written; were I inclined to draw the game of poetry out too long, it would be a labor without thanks.

Was William hinting at his fee? After all, he had entertained the august company in the hope of reaping their thanks, preferably in a form more substantial than high-flown compliments and stately nods. And so he concludes with another morsel of self-advertisement (156–68):

Ghi heren, peynst om Goods ghebot,
Ende laet U niet verlanghen zeer,
Als ghi wat hoert van goeder leer.
Want goede leer ende wel besloten
Is dickent wijsheit uutghevloten.
Doch hoert tot allen dinghen maet:
Een dichter die hem wel verstaet
Ende overdenct wat hem mach deren,
Dien dicht niet al sijns selfs begheren.
Want goet ghedicht ende niet te langhe,
Een schoen vertreck van nyewen sanghe,
Dat heeftmen gaern ter heren hove;
Tis best dat icket mede love.

My lords, think of God's command and do not tire of hearing what is instructive. For from good instruction, well framed, wisdom has often sprung. Yet all things have their measure: a poet who knows his trade and reflects on what may cause it harm will not write whatever poetry pleases him. A good poem, but not too long, a fine presentation in a new tone, is gladly heard at the court of noblemen; that is why I prefer it to all others.

In short, finish the performance and put out your hand! If the entry in the accounts does indeed refer to this particular poem, then we know the reward William received for it: four guilders, or twice his normal remuneration—and half the monthly wage of a master craftsman. But then, he had journeyed far and had had to compose a new poem (though one suitable for other marriages as well, doubtless with a slight change here or there).[5] Indeed, however closely these verses may be linked to the festivities of 5 April 1394, three standard themes of William's court poetry come across strongly in this epithalamium: the state of the country, God's will, and—most remarkably—the poet's role in all this.

2. THE ART OF TRUTH

William of Hildegaersberch had to survive by his art; poetry was not only his vocation, but also his livelihood, his literary bread and wine. That association was less self-evident then than it is today. To all the other authors discussed in this book—the court chaplain Dirk of Delft, Bavaria Herald, or the secretary Dirk Potter, for example—writing was at most a sideline. William of Hildegaersberch, as far as we know, was exclusively a professional poet-reciter, and he was also the only one of this group to be listed as *literator* in the Holland accounts. William ap-

8. Account mentioning "William of Hildegaersberch, the speaker." (Algemeen Rijksarchief, The Hague, MS. AGH 1243, p. 160)

peared before the court purely by virtue of his poetry. The first mention of Hildegaersberch in the accounts is quite specific on that point: on 5 February 1383 the obviously still obscure "Willem van Hilgaertsberghe, enen spreker" (a "speaker") was paid one guilder for his performance in The Hague. By the end of that same year, the accounts already refer to him as "Master William the speaker," and in 1385 he is named as "Master William the poet." Subsequently he is referred to variously as "poet" and (more often) "speaker" (see fig. 8). From about 1392 on his name needed less and less qualification: "Master William of Hildegaersberch" was usually thought sufficient.

Master William's craft was thus that of poet, or more precisely, itinerant poet. We know nothing of any permanent commitment to the court or town of The Hague, though William does seem to have maintained close ties with them. But we also have records of his reciting in Egmont Abbey, before the duke of Guelders (then staying in Leiden), and before the magistrates of the towns of Middelburg and Utrecht. Yet other connections outside The Hague may be inferred from the very character of William's work.[6] If we rely on what little data we possess, William seems to have traveled mainly in the western parts of the Netherlands (in its modern configuration), reciting his verse before various local notables—at courts, but also occasionally at monasteries and municipalities, and with The Hague as his base. As compensation he received at least board and lodging and perhaps also the infrequent payment in kind—of stable value and hence, in times of almost constant devaluation, no less attractive than solid, ringing coin. Still, most commonly the accounts record cash payments, which were essential in helping him endure until his next engagement (LXXXIII/83–93):

> Waer vrou Eren vrienden hoven,
> Daer sietmen dichters conste loven
> Ende ander constenaers daer by;
> Dat doet—het is een melodi
> Die den goeden toebehoert.
> Ende als die dichters willen voert,
> Soe selmen hem een luttic gheven,
> Daer si voort op moghen leven,
> Twisschen tyden al daer si wanderen
> Vanden enen totten anderen,
> Want si sel worden wel ontfaen.

Where the friends of Lady Honour abide, praises are sung to the art of poets and of other artists; that is as it should be, it is only what persons of rank deserve. And when the poets depart, they must be given something on which to live until their next sojourn; this gift will be extremely welcome.

Still, we must be cautious when drawing conclusions about William's life from his work. That he was indeed a native of Hillegersberg we may assume from his toponymic name and also from several passages in his poems. Much of the rest of his life, however, remains obscure. On the evidence of such a poem as "Ic bin al moede, ic wil ga rusten" (I have grown tired, I shall seek rest) (no. CXI), for instance, it has been suggested that William, though disappointed at the poor reception of his work, continued to write verse until a fairly advanced age. Yet that assumption ignores the fact that the *sproken* genre—short medieval Dutch tales in verse form—included, as a subgenre, the so-called *Alterslied* (old-age song), a tearful poem in which the poet presents himself as a sadly misunderstood and superannuated plodder—no doubt to goad his public to a generous repentance (and reward!).[7] Thus, many apparently autobiographical elements of William's poems prove on closer inspection to be stock themes of a particular genre, or can at least be partly understood as so much rhetorical convention. It would therefore be rash indeed to attach literal biographical meanings to William's lines: they fit in perfectly with the poetic traditions of his day.

This fact is of capital importance. When a reciter of *sproken* addresses his public at court, he does so in an age-old *role*, one involving a rich store of rhetorical techniques for the subtle advancement of his own cause. Thus we see why these poets expressed modesty so prolifically: by humbling themselves, they evoked the nobles' favors and liberality. It is in this light that we must also read a great many of William of Hildegaersberch's personal formulations. When he bemoans his failures in life, regrets his misspent youth, confesses that he has more often sought fortune than found it, has often ventured on some ill-fated pilgrimage, has suffered shipwreck, has been stricken down with illness, bitten by a dog, or betrayed by a woman, we should not think he was the first reciter to use such methods to ingratiate himself with his public and to do so without the least autobiographical justification.[8]

It is much harder, however, to deny biographical relevance to those passages in which William apologizes for his poor education. These verses, of course, also served as *captatio benevolentiae*; yet their emphasis and frequency are so marked in William's work that some connection with his real situation must be considered fairly probable. True, much here is still unclear, the more so as this problem is causally entangled with another obscure matter: the sources of William's verse. That his poetry was molded on tradition is beyond doubt. The mere use of the "walk" topos to introduce didactic poems (where the poet begins by stating that he once went out walking—an example is given below) proves that the author was thoroughly familiar with the conventions of the *sproken* genre. And how could he not have been? He must at least have heard fellow poets at court festivities. Beyond that, though, it is extremely difficult to determine William's precursors with any precision; the international genre of short, didactic court poetry is as impenetrable as it is widespread, and the role of oral transmission only adds another incalculable factor.

The mere search for possible French antecedents to William's poetry, for example, is extremely laborious. Yet for all that, the effort seems worthwhile: there are, in fact, striking similarities between William's poetry and the moralizing literature associated with the court of Hainaut, exemplified by such authors as Condé *père* and *fils* and Watriquet de Couvin.[9] Some Middle Dutch sources of William's poetry have also been discovered, though these were fairly obvious: Boendale first, and van Maerlant too, of course, against a background of a general literary education and thorough knowledge of the Bible. For medieval writers, this literary baggage seems somewhat meager, but perhaps familiarity with other writings from home and abroad lie concealed beneath. To be sure, much research has yet to be done before we can locate William more confidently on a scale ranging from "well read" (de Vooys) to "illiterate" (Jonckbloet).[10]

Until further information is discovered, we had best go by William's own evidence, which indicates a fairly modest education. This shortcoming seems to have bothered him more than others. As a fervent disciple of Boendale's doctrine of poetic veracity and probity, he must have realized how little he fulfilled Boendale's third poetic demand, namely that the poet be a true "grammarian," or Latin scholar. His lack seems to have thwarted William, particularly when confronting the *inventio materiae*, the search for material, a question that he explored repeatedly.[11] Normally, medieval authors found their material in the writings of others. Hildegaersberch, for his part, must have been an avid collector of the latest news rather than a reader of old books. Always seeking new material, he trusted his eyes and ears, obtaining, as he often explained, matter and allusions through hearsay rather than reflection or inspiration.[12] For his Latin erudition, William tended to rely on educated clerks, of whose scholarship and critical opinion he repeatedly acknowledged himself in awe.[13] Of course, such acknowledgments were but further instances of the diplomatic professions of humility so characteristic of his work; still that does not mean they did not reflect the genuine frustration of a professional poet who knew that, by contemporary standards, he had less learning than befitted a versemaker of high merit.

Probably, both elements—humility and insecurity—were present, and all such quasi-biographical comments were included both for their topical and rhetorical effect as well as because they truly reflected William's personal situation. This is indisputably true of William's repeated references to the "gentleness" of the noble lords, that is, to their liberality. To be sure, such testimonials were habitual in medieval court literature, but they also—and certainly in the way Hildegaersberch used them—reflected the poet's particular relationship to his patrons. Hildegaersberch coupled the feudal ideal of princely largesse toward vassals (also extolled by other *sproken*-tellers)[14] with the Christian ideals of *caritas* and *misericordia*, and usually contrived to relate them as well to the generosity of noblemen toward artists—in the event, the poet himself.[15] According to William, giving, rewarding, thanking, no less so than poetry, were noble arts, and his technique of referring (not by chance, often toward the end of his recitals) to the signal gratitude he hoped to reap with his instructive entertainment was often most ingenious.[16]

Quite possibly, an unmistakable gesture with his hand or hat during the recitation did the rest.

William well realized his dependence on the lords' good will, but he also knew that such subservience need not be shameful; as a poet, he felt free to state quite bluntly that he was out "to earn favor or gain" (gunst te crighen of ghewin; LXXXII/7). He was only too well aware that the lords' favors swayed his fortunes for good or ill, or as he put it more poetically: "still, I find myself at their mercy" (doch bin ics bleven op hem selven an ghenade; LII/4–5).[17] We know from the wide range of payments to poets recorded in the accounts that no fixed tariff existed for literary appearances at court. Hildegaersberch had to please the nobles if he wanted to earn enough for his daily wants, as he himself was quick to confess: "if I speak to anyone's displeasure, then both thanks and board are lost" (spraec ic iemants onghevoech, so waer danck ende cost verloren; XXXI/34–35).

That, however, was just one side of William's character: along with professional humility he also had his professional pride and, indeed, re-markable self-confidence. This paradoxical alloy of dependence and in-dependence, of servility and self-exaltation, of modesty and pretension, is characteristic of Hildegaersberch and all the other writers and poets of whom he was the most memorable Middle Dutch representative: the master speakers.[18]

Within the unofficial guild of itinerant "speakers," the masters set the tone. Although they might arrogate this title to themselves, it was their public who judged its justification by using it—as they did with Hilde-gaersberch—in the accounts (and hence also in common parlance?).[19] Once adorned with such laurels, the masters felt exalted far above the large mass of reciting entertainers who earned their keep at the lords' tables. Their motives in desiring to rise above this motley crew, more-over, were not purely material: strong professional pride was also in-volved. The master speaker sought literary glory and respect in addition to an income.[20]

And William of Hildegaersberch did have literary ambitions. He looked back nostalgically on the good old days, the golden age when "honored was the poet's name, when praised he was and crowned with fame" (waermen doe een dichter kinde, hy wort gheërt, hi wort ghepre-sen, sijn naem ghespreet, sijn lof gheresen; XXIV/10–12; cf. LXXXIII/ 1–12). But in competing for the lords' favors, Hildegaersberch was not prepared to lower himself to providing cheap amusement; he knew that such entertainment all too quickly degenerated into boot-licking, for which William had nothing but contempt.[21] His chief artistic claim was lofty workmanship: he purveyed the *truth*. To Hildegaersberch, indeed, truth was the quintessence of poetry: "the real poet's way is to lay bare the truth" (gherechte dichters zeede, dat is die waerheit bringhen voert; XXIV/6–7).[22] Repeatedly, William insisted that he was telling the truth; the truth was the trademark of this literary traveler—a trademark but not a monopoly, incidentally, because the truth flew high in the banner of many an itinerant poet; by the truth you could tell the master.[23]

But what is truth? Poetic truth was not the superficial, objective sanction of verifiable facts, but the moral, religiously sanctioned and eternal truth of God's order.[24] It was that sacred truth which William strove to convey in the poem entitled "Twisschen wil ende die waerheit" (Between wishes and truth; CXII/21–34):

> Men soud den heren seggen twaer
> Wat oirbair is of zielen vaer,
> Soe mochten si crighen onderscheit,
> Waer die beste baet an leit.
> Eer ende oirbaer leiter an,
> Die den heren gheraden can,
> Dat hi die waerheit gaerne hoert:
> Uter waerheit soe comen voert
> Alle doechdelyke wercken.
> Die waerheit en wil gheen onrecht stercken,
> Want God heeft selve aldus gheseit:
> "Ic bin die wech ende die waerheit,
> Wye mi volghet, hi sel naken
> Den rechten pat ende dbeste raken."

The noble lords should be told the truth about what is useful and what is harmful to the soul; so they may know what is best for them to do. It is an honorable and useful task to win the noble lords for the truth: from truth spring all virtuous acts. Truth cannot bring forth injustice, for hath not God Himself said: "I am the way and the truth; he that followeth me will speedily enter upon the right path."

The first line must be considered a declaration of William's personal poetic mission: "The noble lords should be told the truth," even if—indeed, precisely because—the truth is hard. We shall consider the concrete contents of this truth in later sections; meanwhile, let us pause for a brief comment on the principle. William realized (or rather proclaimed, for here, too, rhetorical strategy was in play) that his love of truth might cost him dear. Truth is not popular with exalted noblemen,

9. Manuscript with poems by Hildegaersberch. (Koninklijke Bibliotheek, The Hague, MS. 128 E 6, fol. 30r)

be they lords spiritual or temporal: "Truth ever has foes 'mongst the cloth, 'mongst the lords" (Die waerheit heeft altoes wedervechten byder clesi, byden heren; XXXI/6–7).[25] Our court poet knew only too well that he was taking a risk when he donned the mantle of the apostle of truth. And remarkably, he often voiced this very problem in his poems. The frequency with which he expounded on the theme of poetry, its practice and nature, probably makes him the most poetical of all Middle Dutch poets; we cannot help but wonder whether his noble audience was that interested in the professional problems of their festive poet. Nevertheless, in his verses and *sproken* he often discussed the risks of his own profession, and particularly the tensions between his dependent position, on the one hand, and his love of the truth, on the other. Did he do this mainly in his prologues, fearing that the noble lords would become incensed if he presented no such introductory apologies?[26] William's professional motto was clearly that defense is the best form of attack.

For all that, he had great difficulty in serving the lords *and* the truth. At their most profound, these two entities were almost irreconcilable: "Who nobles aims to tell the truth, his rhymes must drudge to find" (Die waerheit enter heren wil, dien can niet wel te rime maken; CXII/ 2–3). The prologue to "Opt voersien" (On foresight; CXVIII) is wholly devoted to this problem (1–11):

> Wat ic dichte of wat ic make,
> Dat staet te straffen of te laken;
> Wye die waerheit node horen,
> Dien ist contrari voerden oren.
> Willen dichters segghen twaer
> Daer die waerheit is contraer,
> Soe wert hi thants een onweert gast.
> Sel een dichter staen te last,
> Om dat hi die waerheit seit,
> Daer oerbaer ende baet an leit—
> Wat ghenoecht ist dan te dichten?

No matter what poems I fashion, they earn me censure; to those who do not like to hear the truth they have an unpleasant ring. If a poet wants to tell a truth that goes against the grain, he at once becomes an unwelcome guest. If a poet has trouble whenever he tells a useful and uplifting truth, what then is the pleasure of poetry?

In the face of this dilemma, William seems to prefer watering the wine to running excessive risks (12–14):

Ic mocht mijn woorden liever zwichten
Dan ic sprake dit of dat
Daer mi die luden om worden hat.

I would sooner swallow my words than say this or that which would make
people hate me.

In other words, when the dilemma had finally to be resolved, William
preferred silence to attracting aristocratic hatred to himself. Elsewhere,
too, he states quite explicitly that, if necessary, he is prepared to compromise the truth. An example is the prologue to his "Vanden coninc
van Poertegael" (On the king of Portugal; VII) (12–20):

Nu wil ic gaen ende leren schieten
Naden witte ende niet daer in,
Soe mach ic dichten nuwen sin;
Want ic wil nu smeken leren
Ende twaer ontbinden voerden heren,
Machmen dit ghelycke deelen.
Twe materien te helen,
Dats den heren wel ghenoecht,
Soe ist al te recht ghevoecht.

Now must I learn to hit, not the bull's eye, but the ring around it, thus lending
poetry new meaning; for I must learn to flatter and to reveal the truth to the
noble lords in equal parts. If two cloths are to be joined to please the noble
lords, then they must make a true fit.

The poet's art is thus the art of combining flattery with the truth without displeasing the noble lords. To that end he had best aim at the outer
ring of the bull's eye rather than at the bull's eye itself.[27] Now, to achieve
such a near miss William had an almost inexhaustible arsenal of literary
strategies, all designed to render the shafts of his home truths more
bearable to the noble audience—or at least station the poet himself out
of range. This he did by offering up these truths *indirectly*, a device best
accomplished by *fictionalization*. William would purposefully fire his
critical darts in the form of fables or some other metaphorical guise, or
else place the unpalatable home truths in the mouth of a fictional authority. What we have here is double poetic license: William's method
of presenting his social critique in an obviously fictional framework was
not only aesthetically pleasing but, no doubt, tactically acceptable as
well.

A textbook case was his "Vanden sloetel" (On the key; LXXXI), a
poem running to 504 lines and hence unusually long for William. Prob-

ably commissioned by the city of Leiden, it was meant to change Albert of Bavaria's attitude toward the conflict he had carried on with that city since 1393.[28] In his introduction, William mentions a walk—the usual way of indicating that what follows is fictional.[29] The main protagonist expresses the hope that, on this walk, he might find inspiration for a poem that "without the least argument will be praised by the good; because a poet must ensure that any who hear him do not receive what he says in envy or in anger" (sonder enich argueren ghepresen worde vanden goeden; want een dichter moet hem hoeden voerden ghenen diet sullen horen, dat sijs in nide noch in toorn niet en nemen dat hi maect; 24–29). Thus the atmosphere is set: the poet is about to embark on a risky path. There follows a eulogy of locks and keys, whose biblical venerability and social usefulness the poet proceeds to stress. Do his good listeners already have an inkling that the poet has Leiden in mind? "Ye noble lords, now heed these words I utter for your benefit" (Ghi hoghe heren, nu mint dit woert, Tot uwen baten dat ict meyn; 224–25).

The poetic walker now meets a shield bearer guarding a tent in which a rich and mighty lord peacefully rests. The shield bearer stands sentinel under an argent shield bearing two red keys—the arms of the city of Leiden, which assumed the honor of supplying guards for the count's tent whenever he was encamped in the county of Holland. The words that the shield bearer then addresses to the poet reflect his intense love for Leiden and its lord, though he laments that the latter, misled by jealous third parties, does not appreciate the true worth of his loyal townsmen and wrongfully neglects them. The poet replies that he is convinced the lord will change his mind and will rehabilitate the city fathers, and the two interlocutors take leave of each other. Hildegaersberch ends with a eulogy to Leiden and an attack on those treacherous schemers whose "wiles have injured who have meant no harm" (Lozen waen heeft zere bedroghen Den ghenen die selve gheen archeit en myenen; 494–95). How much worthier are staunch citizens than men like these! Treading cautiously, Hildegaersberch thus tries to deliver his home truths without offending his noble audience. Was the approach effective? All we know is that, on 16 June 1401, Albert of Bavaria reduced the punishment he had meted out to Leiden—ten weeks after, as the accounts tell us, William of Hildegaersberch had recited poetry to him.

In Dutch literary history, Hildegaersberch is invariably depicted as a base flatterer who, because writing verse happened to be his "mystery," his professional craft, constantly and shamefully toadied to the nobility.

That portrait, however, is a caricature; it mistakes William's critical intent as well as the situation in which he was forced to voice it. As the preceding remarks have shown, William had to be very wary in his recitals, and he invariably was so; but he was more a poet who juggled than one who prostituted himself. For, as will emerge more fully, William's truth was anything but mealy-mouthed, and he was not afraid to issue protests wherever he appeared. All in all—particularly considering the dangerous path William trod—it is remarkable how much criticism he was bold enough to press home.

It is this very boldness that defines his true stature in Dutch court literature. Although his work is by no means lacking in lighter touches, his main concern was to instruct his high-born audience; his paramount task remained the revelation of the truth. Thanks to his public appearances at the count's table, William's plaints about the abuses he exposed assumed the character of semiofficial proclamations. The poet was transformed into a kind of public prosecutor, often using words reminiscent of the courts of law.[30] But besides being an unsolicited prosecutor, William also commended himself to the lords as an independent arbiter—an adviser whose words merited greater attention than those of the official counselors, who, according to William, were so often unreliable. Indeed, in addition to issuing plaints and strictures, he himself often referred to his verse as *counsel*: "thus William counsels lib'rally. . . ."[31] And no matter whether his objections were negative (censure) or positive (counsel), William invariably tried to *teach* his audience something.[32] To be sure, in his own and in others' eyes (as his own writings and account references tell us) he was above all else a *poet*.[33] But William of Hildegaersberch was a poet with a message—the nature of which we shall now examine in detail.

3. TRUTH AND DISORDER

Hildegaersberch lived in the late fourteenth century when Europe, ravaged by violence, plague, famine, and a period of bitter cold, was in a state of deep crisis. The papal schism divided church and laity; the Hundred Years' War between England and France at times almost paralyzed political life and wasted money and lives; the plague outbreaks were disastrous on a scale now scarcely imaginable. Despite impressive developments in art and manners, notably in Burgundy and the court of Richard II of England, anyone trying to speak the truth in such times had to wrestle hard to discover glad tidings.

No wonder, then, that William's truth was stamped by the same disorder to which, keen observer that he was, he knew the world at home and abroad had fallen prey. "I see the world is all unhinged" (ic sie die werlt soe verkeren), he wrote in the opening line of his poem "Vanden waghen" (On the cart; XVII); and later he observes disconsolately: "The strangest things take place all round, and fill my heart with deepest grief" (Tgheschiet soe vele nu ten tyden wonders ende ghemelichede buten slants ende binnen mede, dat myn herte ist onthuecht; LII/74–77). Complaints about the evils of the day were a hallmark of William's work, and to emphasize this deplorable state he used an array of metaphors reflecting the alleged destruction of Honor: the temple of "Lady Honor" lies in ruins; her ship has sailed away; the lords have mislaid the key to "Lady Honor's tower"; they have forgotten "Honor's name"; Honor has been cast out from "the lords' court"; "Honor's shield has been broken"; the lords have strayed from "Honor's strait path"; and so on.[34]

These expressions already indicate where, in Hildegaersberch's view, the root of the evil lay: among the lords. True, he did not spare others; thus he let it be known that the social climbing of parvenu peasants (the term used here derogatorily for burghers?) was a terrible social evil.[35] Still, his objections to them were in no proportion to those that he addressed to the aristocracy. Just whom he included as lords he (deliberately?) failed to specify; in fact, it seems doubtful that he had any particular social category in mind. What can, however, be inferred from his countless references to the aristocracy is that his real targets were the lords temporal, the secular rulers: men of noble rank, high and low, up to the sovereign himself. While the name of Duke Albert or of his successor, William VI, is not found in any of William's poems (he never mentions specific individuals in his strictures),[36] nevertheless, his unfailing complaints about conditions at court must have included his most exalted patrons. This fact was and remains remarkable: our poet aimed his social brickbats mainly at the very circles from whom he earned his livelihood! While we normally think of the recipients of patronage as providing lip-service, William of Hildegaersberch appears to have been the exception. His audience could expect no flattery from him, only criticism. In short, the substance of William's poems did not seem to square with the situation in which he recited them; one cannot help but wonder whether he did not repeatedly ruin the mood at the festive table. In any case, he obviously felt no compulsion whatever to raise the festive spirit, preferring instead to voice the somber bass part.

He knew well what he was doing. Such poems as "Vander reken-
inghe" (On the accounts; LXXVI), which dealt with financial administration, and "Hoe deerste partyen in Hollant quamen" (How the first
parties appeared in Holland; LXIII), on the origins of the quarrels between the Hooks and the Cods, prove that William was well informed
about the concerns of the court. Also, as we have seen, he was a permanent guest in The Hague; the name of no other "speaker" appears as
often as his in the county records. And yet, in his poems, William's attitude toward the court was utterly aloof. The leading character in one of
his rhyming fables, for example, offered this bit of advice: "'Eschew the
court, my dearest friends; with lords you should not meddle'" ("Schu-
wet dat hoff, lieve vriende; Menghet u mitten heren niet"; XVIII/48–
49). The character in question is a dog who once upon a time found
favor with a kindly courtier, the master cook of a leading nobleman; he
was even admitted to the kitchen, from which other dogs used to be
chased without mercy. One day, though, when a kitchen boy left a piece
of meat lying out and the dog—"as is a dog's wont" (der honden
aert)—tried to make off with it, he was beaten with sticks and nearly
killed by the undercook. Although he managed to escape, he had to
spend the rest of his life without a tail. Disconsolately, he whined to his
canine friends who had envied him in the past, observing that sooner or
later everyone forfeits the lords' favors. One moment you are held in
high regard at court, the next you are in disgrace. The weak invariably
go to the wall.[37]

Yet it is not solely the lords' fault that their courts are frequently so
lamentable. As in the fable of the dog, the lord may bear the responsibility while not being directly culpable. The true culprits, according to
Hildegaersberch, are certain people in the lord's entourage, whose presence let alone high standing at court can only be deplored. William says
it all quite plainly in the remarkable poem "Vanden coninc van Poertegael" (On the king of Portugal; VII) (98–110):

> Die heren sijn wel soe bedacht
> Dat sy niet dan recht en mienen;
> Mar hoer dienres, die hem dienen,
> Die zuecken thonich uten braem.
>
> Wye sy sijn dat sel ic helen;
> Want ic seide in mijn beghin,
> Woude ic dichten on ghewin,
> Soe most ic lyden mitten brode;
> Want die waerheit hoertmen node,

> Dair die sculdighen sijn voir oghen,
> Die mit ghewelt om tfordeel poghen.

The lords mean nothing but good, but their servants are extortioners. I had best pass over their names in silence, because, as I said at the beginning: if I am to earn my bread and butter by my verse, then I must mind my words; for the truth is unwelcome where villains are in open view and their advantage brutally pursue.

These lines, too, are typical of William. Although he explains at some length that the poet must be on his guard, he nevertheless lets it be known that the villains are in the hall. And these men are not the lords, not men who "mean nothing but good" (niet dan recht); rather, they are the lords' servants, who abuse their position at court for their own monstrous advantage. It might be argued, of course, that these wicked servants were merely safer targets for shafts that William was loath to aim directly at the lords. Moreover, the theme of the erring servant was as old and well known as medieval literature itself, and so much part of the tradition that few texts presented at court would have seemed complete without it.[38]

But here, too, traditional is not the same as meaningless, and certainly not in the way William uttered his strictures. To him the wicked men clustered around the lord were the true villains. He referred to these sly and shifty beings as *schalken*, rogues. While he was certainly not the first, let alone the last, Middle Dutch author to do so, he laid bare their perniciousness as no other.[39] For William, exposing the evils at court meant fulminating against these "rogues." In "Vanden droem" (The dream; XCVI), for instance, he tells with characteristic indirectness that he once dreamed of an encounter with the two virtues, Loyalty and Justice, who were in a pitiful state, having been banished from court (73–92):

> "Wy sijn gheboren van edelen gheslacht,
> Onse ouders waren wel gheacht
> Ende ghemint sonderlinghen
> Beide van keyser ende coninghen,
> Daer toe voer hertoghen ende graven.
> Al schinen wy hier aldus bescaven,
> Tcomt al buten onse scouden.
> Doe wy te hove waren onthouden,
> Doe stontet hof in groter eren,
> Ende wye dat boesheit wilde leren,
> Die en hadde te hove gheen bedrijf.

> Wy letteden archeit ende kijff,
> Die heren warens wel op yen;
> Der schalken macht was also cleyn,
> Datter nyemant of en hilt.
> Men voerde doe der Eren schilt
> Alle die werlt op ende neder;
> Nu is die schalc ghecomen weder,
> Ende heeft der Eren schilt doerhouwen:
> Hier om soe sijn wy dus in rouwen."

"We are of noble birth; our parents were well thought of by emperors, kings, dukes and counts. It is not our fault that we now look so wretched. When we used to live at court, the court was highly respected, and whosoever meant evil had no business there. We averted wrong-doing and strife, the lords were of one mind, the rogues' power was negligible. Everyone held the shield of Honor aloft; but now the rogues have come and cloven the shield of Honor in twain; that is why we are in such a pitiable state."

The "rogues" had clearly raised William's hackles. In "Vander verrisenis" (On the resurrection; LXIX), he even related the Easter miracle to this theme: much as the Lord toppled the stone over his grave in order to achieve resurrection, so the nobles must topple the rogues! Now, we know from the court accounts that William appeared repeatedly before the count and his company at Easter. With a poem such as this he undoubtedly gave the Easter celebrations at court an added dimension. What he advocated, after all, was nothing short of a court purge. Still, he had his doubts about the chances of expelling all the rogues: in his "Vanden meerblade" (On the water lily; XXXIV), he compared them to flowers that, no matter how hard you push them down, invariably float back to the surface.

The rogues succeeded in influencing the lords because they were skilled in wielding a most dangerous weapon: words. William alone still dared to tell the lords the truth; in their daily life, however, they were surrounded by treacherous toadies. Flattering and lying, these men had wormed themselves into the lords' good books, ousting the honest servants.[40] They had even managed to find places in the lords' councils, taking on, if not the role of officials, then at least that of semiofficial advisers. And "where the rogue in council reigns, honor little credit gains" (waer die schalken moghen raden, daer staet eer in crancken bladen; VIII/27–28). In addition, the rogues had succeeded in perverting the law, an institution William held in particularly high regard; to him it was a cornerstone of a good society.[41] Alas, he detected decay even in this sphere (LXII/65–68):

> Die nu ter werlt rechters hieten,
> Die worden Lucifers gheselle.
> Wanneer dat sy hem recht vermeten
> Doen sy onrecht, als ic u telle.

Who now are called the world's judges, have become Lucifer's henchmen. Although they claim the judge's prerogative, they do wrong, as I now tell you.

That justice had been turned into injustice was partly the fault of lawyers, *taelmanne* (wordsmiths) for whom the wordsmith William felt nothing but loathing[42]—although they were far less to blame than the rogues to whom the lords had entrusted the administration of the law. "It cannot but the lords' name flaw, when roguish hands dispense the law" (Dat mindert zere der heren naem, Dat si den schalken trecht bevelen; VII/102–3).

Elsewhere, however, William had this warning for the noble lords and ladies (XXI/138–43):

> Hebdi enen schalken knecht
> Diet volc mit onrecht zeer bescheert,
> Ende ghi dan mede der baten gheert
> Ende laet hem daer om dienre bliven,
> Tonrecht sal an u becliven;
> Men macht op nyemant anders wisen.

If your servant be a rogue, one who fleeces the people, and you seek to share in his ill-gotten gains and hence continue to employ him, then injustice will cleave to you; none other bears the blame.

In short, the injustice of the rogues ultimately redounds to the lords; they must bear public responsibility for the wrongs wrought in their name by their servants.[43] In one of his most hard-hitting poems, "Dit is van beschermen" (On protection; XI), Hildegaersberch puns on the title of the poem: the rogues had turned *beschermen* (protection), which was one of the lords' bounden duties, into *bescheren* (fleecing) by dropping the *m* of *mededogen* (mercy). And fleecing people was the rogues' way. Burning with envy of their neighbors' happiness and filled with sheer love of evil, they were eager to rake in as much money as they could.

Alas, though, the rogues were not alone in this: avarice was the root of all the evils that William saw everywhere around him. Not that this court poet was antimaterialistic on principle. Such a stance would have been very difficult for one of his profession to maintain: the spiritual, after all, seldom pays dividends. While he rarely ceased to stress the transience of worldly possessions, he knew how to appreciate them: "Verily you must refrain from holding riches in disdain, for they have their rightful use" (Doch en willic niemant raden datmen rijcheit sal versmaden diemen bruken mach mit recht; I/27–29).[44] What mattered most to William, however, was the last line—namely, it is important how one uses riches, money being a most treacherous enemy, ever ready to turn men's heads. And that was precisely what William saw happening all about him: men's thirst for money had become unquenchable, and that was the greatest source of social evil.[45] Even in the administration of justice, money was now a nefarious influence. The rich often obtained judgments in their favor, or as William put it so forcefully: "Justice is for coin dispensed" (Men siet trecht om ghelt vercopen; XVII/19). On countless occasions, William fulminated against bribes to law officers, too many of whom were themselves rogues.[46] Yet it was not only on the bench that money debauched virtue. Money meant power throughout society, and it gained admission and respect even at court. With money one could become the "lords' friend" (der heren vrient; LXXIII/58), now that the lords themselves had grown so avaricious and fleeced their poor subjects so thoroughly as to leave them with no pelt to grow new wool on.[47] Ever since the lords' friendship had been up for sale, moreover, loyalty had been hard to find and greed reigned supreme: "Loyalty has fled the land, greed now holds the upper hand" (Trouwe is uten lande ghevaren, ghierichede heeft al tghewelt; XVII/16–17).

In short, everyone was grasping for money, intent on his own well-being, his personal estate. That was William's ultimate reproach to the rogues, but even more so to the noble lords, who ought to know better than to allow personal gain to prevail over the common good. For William, the national interest was the highest social good—a remarkable, almost Platonic, ideal in someone of his age and profession and with the particular audience he addressed. William put private interest second to the "common weal" (gemeyn oerbore), the welfare of the country (Holland?) as a whole and its need for harmony and peace.[48] But such great blessings were hard to find where avarice kept sowing dissent (LXXIII/97–101):

> Aldus maect ghiericheit pertyen
> Ende doet die werlt also castyen,
> Dattet yammer is te schouwen:
> Die een gaet den anderen blouwen
> Doot off lam, dats openbaer.

Thus avarice sows dissent and plagues the world shamefully: one man beats another to death or maims him, as is only too plain to see.

William's attacks on the rogues were equaled in frequency by his poetic complaints about the country's internal divisiveness and his repeated attempts to calm the troubled waves of party dissension.[49] Our idealistic court poet stood aloof from the strife of the contending parties, preaching amity and neighborly love. Unity was strength, and in its absence the country would likely perish. In moving verses he would appeal to the lords to cease their accursed quarrels (LXVI/166–69):

> Ghi heren, nu trect voirwaert;
> Seldi mit eren voeren tzwaert,
> Ghi moetet andersins verweren
> Dan op malcander aldus te stryden.

Ye lords, go out to do battle; [but] if you wish to wield your sword with honor, then you must put it to better use than fighting one another.

Although William names no names in his poems, there is little doubt that such passages referred to the quarrels between the Hooks and the Cods.[50] It is too mild to say that he was emphasizing a serious problem in Holland, for the quarrels proved disastrous for the county. That observation leads to a more general question: Was Hildegaersberch's somber portrayal of social conditions the truth, unembroidered by grievance or poetic exaggeration? Or was he simply grumbling because that was his nature?

The first alternative seems the more likely. Not only were his complaints about the county's internal dissensions warranted, but William was also historically acute when he pilloried the malignancy of money: together with disputes involving family or honor, grossly material disparities were equally at fault in fanning divisions among the nobility.[51] In general, the rise of the money economy had negative as well as positive repercussions. As the sovereign's finances came to depend ever more on the accumulation of capital (a process begun in the twelfth century but not fully felt in Holland until the fourteenth), the feudal system, too, came increasingly under the sway of the politics of wealth. It is small wonder, then, that many won admission to the court of Holland on the basis of their assets, among them William of Duvenvoorde in the first half of the fourteenth century and William Eggert in the second.[52]

The influence of these parvenus did not, of course, necessarily bode ill for the national interest (which seems to have been Hildegaersberch's conviction), but it clearly posed inherent dangers. Holland was not the only country in which money helped to undermine the old feudal relationships, based as they were primarily on hereditary land ownership. To the towns and the incipient bourgeoisie, the new dispensation may have promised emancipation from feudal restrictions and obligations. Hildegaersberch, though, was not of that status—he was, after all, a court poet; and by his own reckoning, he was certainly not wrong to think that money was destabilizing the old order.[53] Moreover, money held out the threat of new corruptions, as William apparently realized only too well. That corruption was widespread in contemporary Holland we do not know from William alone. The law, to give but one example, seems to have thrived on venality.[54] To be sure, this view derives more from inference than from direct proof, but then, it is always exceedingly difficult to establish with the help of official documents matters that were deliberately kept obscure. The same applies to the machinations of the "rogues" William so detested, for by their very nature, official papers or letters are unlikely to cite informal intrigues. Here, too, as William was quick to point out, so-called progress ever has its dark side: the more numerous the parties involved in state affairs, the greater the chance of intervention by those with dubious ambitions.[55]

Before we declare William of Hildegaersberch a trustworthy witness, however, we must remember that on occasion he did exaggerate wildly. For instance, he often declared that everything had been so much better in the past; to him, the word *now* always had negative connotations.[56] A few significant questions aside, such as just when these better days had ended, where the Golden Age had taken place, and how William was so familiar with such topics,[57] we have reason to think that he twisted the truth slightly to suit himself. In matters of art, and especially of poetry, which so concerned William when he inveighed against the inescapable artistic malaise, his comments are easily challenged.[58] William's view, namely, directly contradicted the evidence adduced in Chapter I, sec. 2: it would appear that Middle Dutch poetry prospered more in William's day than it had in any previous century. Thus, when William protests that poets had been made more welcome at court in days gone by, we may be sure that his plaint involved a generous measure of subjectivity. Persuasion weighed more with William than proof; it would therefore be very naive to think that he exaggerated only when his self-interest was directly involved. On many other occasions, too, he clearly felt that the ends justified the means. And those ends were, in essence, to convince his lordly audience of the need for moral and social reform, not by revolution, but by the restoration of God's order.

4. A POET CLOSE TO GOD

When William spoke of God's own institution on earth, his home truths were no different from those he addressed to the mortal world: the church, too, was in a turmoil driven by dissension, with two and eventually three rival popes denouncing each other and appealing for armed support from cynical but ambitious kings. William deplored this situation no less than he did the quarrels between the Hooks and the Cods.[59] Which pope, he asked almost sneeringly in his "Vander wrake Gods" (On God's vengeance; XXXV), would the king of Turkey have to address in the happy event of his wishing to be baptized? Still, although William asserted in his "Van ses articulen der werelt" (On six of the world's articles; LXX) that, historically, the papal seat must remain in Rome, he was careful not to choose sides in the schism but stood aloof from the contending parties. In other words, he adopted the same attitude here as he did toward conflicts more confessedly worldly—though this was hardly surprising, for in his opinion, church and laity shared similar problems. Moreover, whereas quantitatively speaking he proffered many more criticisms of temporal than of spiritual rulers (no doubt because his audience was predominantly the former), qualitatively his strictures on the two realms made no vital distinction. He often referred to abuses in church and state in identical tones: "Pride, tumult, and strife 'mongst priests and lords are rife throughout the world" (Hoveerde, werringhe end strijt die rijst nu inder werlt wijt onder papen ende heren; LXX/75–77).[60]

Clergy and lords were, in William's view, cut of the same cloth. Priests, too, often totally ignored pleas for justice; only for hard cash promptly paid did they have a ready ear (XLVII/51–59):

> Papen, clercken, al ghemien,
> Hoe veel onrechts dat si sien.
> Si worden doeff in hoer verstaen;
> Mar alsmen siet die hant ontdaen
> Om uut te tellen die florine,
> Dan slachten si naden everswine,
> Dat altoes scarper is int horen
> Dan enich dier dat hevet oren
> Off creatuer dat aerde voet.

Priests and other clerics are deaf to no matter how much injustice they find; but if any open his hand to count out money, then they are like wild boars whose hearing is better than that of any other creature on earth.

Still, William condemned the priests even more vehemently than the lords for one thing: the pretension that they could teach others from some superior plane, when their own deeds failed to match their words (XCVII/120–25):[61]

> Oec waen ic dat men hem beval
> Dat sy gheestelijc souden leven
> Opdat si exempel mochten gheven
> Van hoerre woorden mitten wercken,
> Om tghelove voort te stercken
> Onder tfolc, cleyn ende groot.

Yet it is my belief that they were instructed to live in the spirit of our faith so that they might set an example by translating their words into actions, thus fortifying the faith of the people, great and small.

In fact, they did precisely the opposite: they ignored their own precepts. William's "Vander heiligher kercken" (On the holy church; LVIII) may be considered a summary of all his objections to the clergy. The church, he argued, was being throttled with a rope of seven strands that the Devil himself had braided, each strand representing one of the mortal sins so prevalent even among priests. William examined these strands one by one, starting with what was traditionally considered the first sin, pride (89–104):

> Deerste draet dat is Hoveerde,
> Die sinte Pieter niet en gaerde
> Die wijle hi was in sinen tyden.
> Nu willen si hoghe paerden ryden
> Opter heiligher kercken goet,
> Ende verteren der armer bloet
> Gulseliken sonder ontsien.
> Doe God selve den eersten stien
> An sinte Pieter hadde gheset,
> Hi was van hoveerde ombesmet,
> Hine gheerde pellen nochte bont.
> Nu versamen si menich pont
> Die ghierighe vander heiligher kercken,
> Om hoor hoveerde mede te stercken;
> Want sonder rijcheit, mit armoede
> Stonde hoveerde in crancker hoede.

The first strand is Pride, after which Saint Peter did not hanker. But nowadays they ride roughshod over the property of the holy church and squander what the poor have gathered together at terrible cost. When God himself laid the first stone [for his church] through Peter, the latter was free of pride; he wanted no furs or precious coats. Now covetous priests are putting away treasure to shore up their pride; because without wealth, pride would languish.

William proceeded to treat the other strands in comparable manner: the widespread envy of the clergy, their covetousness, their simony, their "lack of charity" and of chastity, and last (but certainly not least), their gluttony and sloth. Yet the title of his poem was "On the holy church"! William saw a paradox here, but no real contradiction. No matter how corrupt the priests might be, their office had been sanctified by God, and so had the doctrine they were appointed to guard. Even if the seed of the doctrine was stored in a spoiled basket, it might still bear good fruit. In the opening lines of the poem, William stated unequivocally what, in his view, really mattered (1–17):

> Ic wil altoes prisen ende loven
> Ende in mijn ghedochte setten boven
> Der heiligher kercken fondament.
> Want God, die alle dinc bekent,
> Fondeerde selve die heilighe kercke
> Entaer toe priesteren ende clercke,
> Die die kercke regieren souden,
> Om onse ghelove daer by te houden.
> Die heilighe kercke is onse moeder
> Ende si is spiegel ende roeder;
> Onse ghelove staet daer mede.
> Onse sacrament ende kerstenhede
> Moeten wy ter heiligher kercken halen,
> Alsmen tghelach sal betalen.
> Die heilighe kerck dats onse begheren;
> Nu macht elken mensche deren
> Dat sy dus verre in dwale is comen.

I shall always extol the foundations of the holy church and place it first in my thoughts; for God himself founded them and also the clerical estate set over the church to strengthen our faith. The holy church is our mother, our example, and our rudder; our faith rests on her. We must seek sacrament and piety in church if we are to settle our [final] accounts. The holy church is our dearly beloved; hence each one of us must feel sorely aggrieved that she has gone so badly astray.

William's criticisms were thus aimed, not at the theoretical foundations of institutions established by God himself, but at the erring human practices found therein. Because clerical rule and behavior had become so lax, William saw reason to fear the severity of God's judgment. The likelihood that he would shoulder man's sins a second time was exceedingly slim, as William put it in words reminiscent of a bookkeeper's (LXX/114–19):

> God en wils niet meer besueren
> Want hi heeft eenwarff al betaelt
> Wat hier voermaels was verdwaelt,
> Daermen hem schulde in mochte manen.
> Soe wye nu treden buten banen,
> Die motent selve al becopen.

God will not shoulder our guilt a second time, having paid for it once before; whosoever sins nowadays, will have to pay the bill himself.

Now that man has grown so heedless after the coming of God's Son, there is good reason to fear Judgment Day (68–74):

> Nu heb ic sint ter werlt vernomen,
> Dat onse ghelove wert soe traghe,
> Ic ducht het naect den doomsdaghe;
> Want wy vergheten altehant
> Die leer die ons Christus selve ontbant,
> Want minne, rust ende caritate
> Die sijn verdreven hoerre strate.

Having seen that faith has grown so weak in this world, I am afraid of Doomsday; for we keep forgetting the lesson Christ himself has taught us, and have driven out love, peace, and charity.

Even more than about the Apocalypse, however, our poet worried about individual death. William's work is suffused with thoughts of death, and especially with its unexpectedness.[62] *Memento mori!* William's concern with this dread theme reflects the widespread late-medieval fixation on death, so graphically depicted in altarpieces, woodcuts, processions, "Dances of Death," and gruesome displays of bones and skulls. More concretely, however, William's concern with death probably relates to the plague, which ravaged Holland as much as any other country, particularly in William's day.[63] But even though much of his work dealt with death, he did not much ponder its causes.

In his "Vanden ghesellen die ommeseylden" (Of the companions who went sailing; XXXVIII), for example, he tells of the (notorious?) adventure trip of "five reckless companions" who set sail from Arnemuiden for the coast of Holland. The wind seemed favorable, and the

weather was fair; but then a sudden storm blew up and the small boat
suffered shipwreck: "Overboard they all were thrown as their little ship
went down" (Doe ghinghen sy hem vanden swete spoelen, al wast qual-
ick hoer begheren; 66–67). William's description of their adventure revealed familiarity with maritime matters, as was only to be expected of
a born Hollander, and his audience was sure to have appreciated the
resulting verse. But as ever, William was less concerned with the events
than with the moral. In the final lines he drew a parallel between the
unpredictable weather at sea and the equally unpredictable descent of
death (90–102):

> Al sijn wy op dit leven coen,
> Alsoe cort macht ommeslaen
> Onse bootkijn, als dat heeft ghedaen
> Daer die ghesellen in misvoeren.
> Laet u reden alsoe beroeren,
> Dat ghi rechte mate kent
> Wanneer u God die doot toesent,
> Dat ghi tevoren sijt bereyt:
> Want nyemant tijt noch stont en weyt,
> Hoe off waert hem sel gheschien.
> Dus ist een wiselic voersien
> Die in weldoen ende in doghen
> Tewighe leven heeft voir oghen.

No matter how much we put our trust in life, our little boat can capsize as
quickly as that of the shipwrecked companions. Hold the rudder of reason
straight so that you are on the right course when God sends you death; for no
one can tell death's time, place, or ways. Hence it is a sign of the wise oarsman
that he keeps eternal life constantly, charitably, and virtuously in sight.

The message is clear: if you seek to go to heaven, you must live a good
life on earth. Man's failure to achieve that life is what William deplores
in nearly every one of his poems. His audience, he implies, are sinners.
Yet his intent was not so much to attack them as to teach them to do
better. Here, too—and regardless of the looming threat of the plague—
the topic of death suited William admirably, for it greatly increased the
persuasiveness of his arguments. Sudden death, above all, demands repentance, and because death can strike at any moment, it is imperative
to repent without delay. In some poems, William urged his listeners to
prepare for death even in the "noon of life" (which was, in fact, their
average age) and to desert the path of sin.[64]

The sinner cannot repent too soon, yet neither is it ever too late to repent, for God's mercy and grace are boundless. It is the responsibility of each individual to prepare himself for this grace—though our poet is happy to provide a little help. In truth, however, that help is more the task of priests than of poets, and however much William may have railed against them, he considered theirs a supreme calling. "Let each man heed the words of his priest" (Elcman volghe sijns priesters woorde), he admonished all hearers in "Vander heiligher kercken" (On the holy church; LVIII/230); nor is it surprising to learn that, among the sacraments, he was ever stressing the importance of confession.[65] But no priest and no poet can force the sinner to repent. True contrition begins with the individual's own conscience (LXXVI/273–79):

> Hier om sel een yghelijc,
> Die wyle hi is in aertrijc,
> Sijn consciencie al te gronde
> Graven doer om elke sonde
> Die der zielen moghen schaden,
> Entaer of mitten priester raden
> Dat hi sijn rekeninghe hoert.

For that reason every individual must, while he is on this earth, search his conscience thoroughly and root out whatsoever sin may harm the soul, and then ask the priest to hear his confession.

The poet can advise, the priest listen and guide, but ultimately it is the sinner himself who must freely choose the strait path of virtue and abandon the broad highway of sin. Thanks to his free will, man bears his fate—salvation or damnation—in his own hands, he and he alone. William again and again, and emphatically, reiterated the Christian's personal accountability.[66] "So mend your ways, all ye who stray" (Soe betert U, sidi misdadich; LVI/247), he enjoined his audience—and indeed, anyone with even the slightest comprehension of William's message would think twice before he numbered himself among the saved. With his repeated appeals to conscience, William belonged to that late-medieval school that demanded a personal faith and expected each believer to shoulder his own burden.[67]

This ideal he displayed not only in attacks on sin (his forte) but also when, more positively, he extolled the benefits of virtue. In pointing to that path, William, almost more so than when he deplored sinfulness, seemed to have the nobles in mind. Nor is that surprising, for they composed the bulk of his audience. But William had theoretical as well as practical reasons for addressing himself to the aristocracy: namely, ordinary folk almost always followed their lords' example—in William's day, alas, for the worse, but after repentance, undoubtedly also for the better (XXXI/83–86):

> Wouden priesters ende heren
> Hem selven eerst ter doghet keren,
> Tghemene volck soude hem schamen,
> Dat si niet ter doecht en quamen.

Were priests and lords to turn to virtue, the common people would be ashamed if they did not become virtuous themselves.

William wanted to improve the ways of mankind, and he thought it best to start at the top. This approach typified his hierarchical view of society, a view almost taken for granted in his day and in the circles in which he moved: social differences were God's will confirmed by biblical precedents; hence, social change was harmful to the social and divine order. Nevertheless, the self-evident nature of social distinctions included noblesse oblige: nobles had at least as many obligations as they had privileges. The poem "Van dominus" (On the lord; XXXIII) may be considered a typical exposition of William's views on this subject. Here the character of the ideal prince is presented by means of subtle wordplay on the seven letters of the Latin word for lord, *dominus*. From the "clerks who have shown me how" (clercken, diet mi duutschen voert; 17), Hildegaersberch, who had no Latin, learned that the letters in *dominus* were the initials of the following princely virtues: *discretio, obedientia, misericordia, iustitia, nobilitas, veritas,* and *sapientia*. Together, they described the nature of the perfect prince, as William explained in appropriately Middle Dutch terms at the end of the poem (111–30):

> Selmen yemant noemen here,
> Dese seven letteren min noch mere
> Moet hi hebben al volcomen,
> Diemen te rechte heer sal noemen.
> *Bescheydenheyt*, dats sijn beghin;
> *Ghehoersamicheit* die brinct hem in
> Dat hi by wisen rade leeft
> Ende sinen wille daer toe gheeft,
> Dat *Ontfarmicheit* gheschiet
> Over al sijn arme diet,
> Die ghenade an hem begheren.
> *Trecht* en machmen niet ontberen,
> Die doet alle dinck bescheiden,
> Al en dars die quade niet verbeiden.
> Een heer sal sijn *Edelheit* toenen,

Den quaden castyen, den goeden lonen,
Warachtich wesen ende *Wijs*.
Men mach mit rechte gheven prijs
Enen heer die desen naem
In eren hout ende sonder blaem.

Before any man can truly be called a lord, he must combine all these seven letters in his person. To begin with, Discretion; then Obedience, which causes him to live in keeping with wise counsel so as to dispense Mercy to any subjects who ask for it. Justice, which helps fair dealing, must not be absent, though evildoers had best not count on it. A lord must also show his Nobility, punish evil, reward the good, and live in Truth and Wisdom. We rightly extol the lord who keeps the name made of these seven letters aloft and in honor.

A lord, according to Hildegaersberch, is not a military leader or autocrat first and foremost. Of course he must be strong: the threat of his firm hand scares off possible usurpers at home and abroad. But even more than strong, the good prince must be wise and just, and preside over orderly government. And if, additionally, he sets a personal example of virtuous living, then God's will, inasmuch as it can be implemented on earth (in medieval terms, "under the moon"), is done, thus ensuring the social peace that was William's social ideal: "Wise is he who loveth peace, For God is peace, without surcease" (Hi is wijs die ruste mint, want God is rust, diet wel versint; LXXXII/47–48).[68]

William considered himself a poet close to God. He knew what God's order was, and this he held up before the lords. In fact, he presented himself as a kind of intermediary between his heavenly and his worldly masters. His view of his calling was more that of a priest than of a poet. Yet in William's conception of literature, poetry and preaching were closely related. Thus William sometimes referred to his work as poetry *and* as sermon.[69] Even if we consider the second a figurative expression, in fact many of his poems were rhyming sermons, particularly those based on biblical material.[70]

Perhaps the clearest example is the poem "Vanden doemsdaghe ende van sterven" (On doomsday and death; XXI), whose prologue is a poetic rendering of God's word, followed by an anecdotal account of a meeting in a church between a "lay poet" (that is, Hildegaersberch himself) and a priest. Their conversation turns to art—"Nought was closer to their heart than talk of poetry and art" (Sy en hadden anders niet to doen, dan si van dichten ende van const spraken; 30–32)—with the priest explaining the meaning of the three Latin lines sung during the requiem mass for dead noblemen. In the subsequent lines, William repeats the priest's interpretation to his audience, his message growing ever more rhetorical. The sermonizing tone is most pronounced at the conclusion, which takes the form of a prayer ("So pray we now the Lord our God . . ." [Soe bidden wy den hoochsten Heer . . .]) and ends with a loud Amen (340–50):

> Ay Heer! nu helpt ons daer verwerven
> Doer dijn grote ontfarmherticheit,
> Inden daghe als is voerseit,
> Dat ghi die quade sult berechten,
> Ende onghelijck ghelijcke slechten,
> Ende hemel ende aerde sult beroeren,
> Soe wilt ons, Heer, dan mede voeren
> In u hemelrijc hierboven,
> Daer die enghelen Gode loven
> Ewelijc ende sonder ghetal;
> Nu spreect Amen over al.

Oh, Lord, help us by thy great mercy, on the foretold day when thou shalt judge the evildoer, abolish iniquity, and move heaven and earth, to be so worthy of thee that thou, Lord, shalt take us into thy blessed kingdom of Heaven where the angels, eternal and countless, sing God's praises; to which let all of us now say Amen.

Here poetry has become religious worship.[71] Does that mean William saw himself as endowed with priestly powers? He seemed anxious to repudiate that idea, as witness the apologetic tone, mentioned earlier, in which he referred to his delicate relationship with the clergy, particularly in his sermonizing poems. Yet he did virtually feel a vocation to deputize for the priests, now that they were so badly, sometimes evilly, neglecting their duty. Like royal and urban councillors, priests must "speak the truth unto the lords" (segghen heren twaer; LXX/211); but because they were so patently remiss, poets must fill the breach.[72] Indeed, William even felt entitled to claim a co-patent, as it were, in God's truth, promising his own flock, if only they heeded his urgent pleas, no less than the Kingdom of Heaven itself: "This William counsels without cease—heed his advice and mark it well, so in God's kingdom you may dwell" (Dit raet u Willem, sonder sparen, van Hildegaersberch—wildijt versinnen, soe moechdi hemelrijc ghewinnen; LXIII/168–70).

William was evidently not the only poet to spread the same message as the clergy. In particular, some of the German didactic poets (Der Teichner, Heinrich von Mügeln) have frequently been singled out for their attempts at *Laienmissionierung*, that is, the preaching of pious sermons to an audience usually of highly placed laymen.[73] Although their links with the mendicant orders—the groups of friars often mentioned in this connection—are easier to deduce than to prove and so should not be exaggerated, their poems, with their passionate call for moral renewal throughout the Western world, did come close to the message preached by the friars. Perhaps the missionaries regarded these poets as competitors; equally likely, though, they saw them as allies for moral rearmament.

This less-than-coherent pattern, however, though it opens up a fascinating trail, leads us in a direction quite opposite to that on which we set out with William of Hildegaersberch. At the close of the last chapter, William was presented as the leading literary entertainer at the Hague court. Later, we came to imagine him standing in the pulpit rather than before the festive boards. But let us take care not to replace one oversimplification with another. William's literary genre straddled an indistinct junction of poetry, sermon, admonition, and diversion. If we rely on those of his texts now extant, the sermonizing obviously dominates—to such an extent that, to modern ears, William sounds unfit for the laurel crown. Yet in his own age and company he bore that honor rightly and nobly: he was the court's choice for entertaining the ducal dinner company with recitations in the Great Hall. What a pity it is that we know so little about William's recitation technique! If only we could sit in on one of his performances—would it, for instance, emerge that he made ample use of stage props, voice effects, improvisation, and music? If so, then poems that now seem inert might come to life and unexpectedly flourish.

Furthermore, although William of Hildegaersberch was probably engaged more often as a serious speaker than as a mere entertainer, that need not always have been the case. For instance, during the main church festivals, when according to the accounts (and especially toward the end of his career?) he made frequent appearances, he may well have recited particularly somber poems, and it may be that especially those more "official" poems were recorded and have come down to us. Yet William's work is full of compensating elements. The clearest examples are probably two farcical poems in which priests are assigned a stereotyped, hypocritical role. One (LXXXV) concerns a confessor who impregnates a beautiful parishioner and then, to confound the gossips, signs a pact with the Devil, who swiftly disposes of the confessor's male equipment. When, at the appropriate moment of his sermon on evil tongues, the priest lifts his gown to demonstrate that he could not possibly have done what he was accused of, the Devil sees his chance and strikes (171–78):

> Doe hijt den luden toghen soude,
> Doe sette hi hem an sijn evenoude
> Weder op die selve stede,
> Stiver ende harder mede
> Dant ye wert tot sinen daghen.
> Men sacht streven ende raghen,
> Eer hijt voelde of vernam
> Hoe sijn ghestelle wederquam.

When he wanted to show it to the people, the Devil put his old member back in the same place, stiffer and harder than ever it had been. It could be seen rising up and jutting out, even before he himself realized that it was back in place.

Such a poem makes it clear that, during William's appearances in The Hague, piety and sedate calm did not invariably prevail in the Great Hall. The second satirical poem starts out in typical Hildegaersberch fashion (XXVI/1–10):

> Eens omt jaer soe comt een tijt,
> Dat over al die werlt wijt
> Elck mensche gaern te biechte gaet,
> Al dairmen kersten ghelove ontfaet,
> Van sonden die hi heeft ghedaen,
> Ende neemt penitencie weder aen,
> Als hem die priester raedt te doen.
> Hierom soe prisic dit sysoen,
> Want men peynst dan om die sonden
> Meer dan anders tenighen stonden.

Once a year there comes a time when, all over the world, everyone likes to go to confession, believers being absolved from the sins they have committed after having agreed to do what penance the priest has enjoined. That is why I praise this season, a time when people are more inclined to think about their sins than at other times.

But then the tale unexpectedly shifts. As his "hero" William introduces a notorious rascal who, during his annual confession, tells his priest of his intention to steal a delicious ham; if the priest promises absolution, he will be handed half the booty. The priest agrees because "such indeed are priestly ways that they dance for him who pays" (tis een deel der papen zeede, datsi hem gaerne laten myeden; 70–71). The next night, the knave steals a most splendid ham—from the priest's own larder. When presented with his half, the good cleric is overjoyed—until he discovers the trick. Nevertheless, afraid that his shameful behavior will become public knowledge, the priest is forced to grant the thief the promised absolution. In the moral we recognize our old friend Hildegaersberch only too clearly (226–29):

> Ic woud mense alle dus verdoerde,
> Waer si quamen tenighen steden,
> Die om miede loesheit deden;
> Die menighe souts hem dan wel hoeden!

I wish everyone were paid back like this who from greed does wrong; most would then leave well alone!

Even when he gave them little cause for laughter, William knew how to entertain his court public. Considering the great stress I have laid on his didacticism, the reader might forget that William also had powerful aesthetic motives. It is with good reason that the accounts for 1409 mention the many "beautiful" poems in the Hildegaersberch manuscript acquired by William VI, the meaning here doubtless encompassing not only their poetic splendor but also (in much the same way as we nowadays speak of a "beautiful sermon") the manner in which he presented his lessons. For William did his best to supply an appealing form, not merely by delivering polished verse and a flowery (often far from simple) style,[74] but above all by constantly changing the framework for his discourses. As he frequently stated, his pampered court audience was forever looking for "something new" (iet nieuwes), even in poetry.[75] To judge by William's surviving poems, their novelty must have resided more in the wrapping than in the content—for William was in the habit of repeating himself. Yet the presentation was often surprising: now a rhymed couplet, now a strophe, now an allegory, now a fable, now an elaborate pun, now a sober, symbolic exposition.

In short, there was much to delight the audience when William appeared at the count's brilliant table, and this delight came from, to use Ezra Pound's phrase, "news that stays news." William himself wanted nothing more (XXIV/–5):[76]

> Een dichter die te dichten pliet,
> Die pijnt hem gaerne te vinden yet
> Dat den luden inden oren
> Wat ghenoechte brenct te voren,
> Ende int verstaen oeck wijsheit mede.

A poet likes to find that what he offers gives his audience pleasure and also adds wisdom to their understanding.

And whenever William's wisdom proved too sententious, threatening the enjoyment of wine and meat, conversation and endearments, other poets were at hand to lighten William's heavy fare with more easily digested tidbits. Yet—and this is now a well-known problem—the words of these light entertainers were set down in writing for future generations much less frequently than those of the master didactic poet. Thus, when in the next chapter I try to convey some notion of their poetic flavor, I shall have to rely on a few fragments and a makeshift construction.

III

The Hague Song Manuscript

1. LOVE SONGS

In his poem "Vanden ouden ende vanden jonghen" (Of old and young; XXXII), William of Hildegaersberch describes his (fictitious) meeting with a merry company of courtiers who had ridden out early one summer's day, "bent on having youthful fun" (spelen in der merghen stont; 29).

> Sy brochten voer hem uutghelesen
> Sanghers ende menestreel,
> Die wel behoirden thoren speel;
> Want sy alle vrolic waren.
> Dat zoete gheluut van horen snaren,
> Die zanck die si mit kelen songhen,
> Die dede den ouden mitten jonghen
> Volghen mede in dat foreest.

Before them rode a select band of singers and minstrels who made fit company because all of them were so merry. The sweet sound of their strings and the song that sprang from their throats made young and old alike follow them into the forest.

A sweet maiden buttonholed the poet and provided him with a favorite theme: the truth about young and old. In what follows William relates that truth in verse form, in his own inimitable style. Here, however, we are not concerned with William's truth; rather, we shall try to discover what kind of songs these minstrels sang. What exactly was the "sweet sound of their strings"? Above all, what was "the song that sprang from their throats"?

The nature and range of the vocal music enjoyed at the court of Holland-Bavaria is much more difficult to assess than the poetry of William Hildegaersberch. William's reputation and the importance of his message led to the recording of over a hundred of his poems; his truth clearly did not obsess him alone but had universal appeal. Yet who at the court of Holland had the least need to write down light songs and ballads? These were held to be of trifling importance and not worth the expensive parchment needed to immortalize them. Not only did the public see little reason to commit these songs to paper, moreover, but neither did their authors; anyone with even the slightest talent carried his repertoire in his head. Hence, it is in fact much less surprising that Holland-Bavarian song left so few traces than that some of these songs actually remain.[1] In Leiden University Library are six badly damaged sheets of parchment, all that remains of a *chansonnier*, a songbook in the French style, that must have been compiled shortly after 1400 in the Utrecht-Holland region.[2] These sheets—as unique as they are battered—contain words and score (in part badly damaged) of twenty-four songs. Five bear the name of what may be assumed to be their author and composer: one is inscribed Hugo Boy *monachus* (see fig. 10), and four name one Martinus Fabri. The monk's surname of Boy suggests possible family links with the Dordrecht area. His colleague, Martinus Fabri, can be placed more precisely, for he is mentioned by name in the county of Holland accounts as a member of Duke Albert's court chapel: in 1395, after a successful probation, "magister Martinus Fabri" from Brabant and two colleagues were officially engaged as professional singers at the Hague court. These facts lend the unsightly Leiden fragments capital importance: they are the oldest known scored songs from the northern Netherlands, the first to be connected to a Dutch composer known by name, and the only surviving record of the song tradition associated with the court of Holland-Bavaria.

The idea of this heritage conveyed by Fabri's four songs matches the portrait drawn in Chapter I. Despite their humbleness, these songs confirm that Duke Albert's court, far from being culturally backward, was able to compete with any other contemporary court in Europe. Musically, Fabri's compositions reflect the influence of the *ars nova*, the rhythmically complex, polyphonic song style that must have quickly migrated from France to The Hague. The textual material of the songs also conveys an international flavor. Like his public at the court in The Hague, Fabri was a polyglot: two of his songs have French words, two are in Middle Dutch. Whatever might have decided his choice of language, it was certainly not the content, which was the same in all four songs: love—and, moreover, the special form of love that by 1400 had been the fashion at European courts for two centuries, commonly referred to as courtly love and made famous by the troubadour poets of Provence who had wandered among small but dazzling courts before the Albigensian crusade.

10. The song of *Hugo Boy monachus* (see upper margin). (University Library, Leiden, MS. BPL 2720, fol. IIv)

The opening stanza of Fabri's first song (L6) is typical of his small oeuvre:

> N'ay je cause d'estre liés et joyeux,
> de bien tenir et loyalement amer
> celle pour qui je me tiens amoureux
> et me tenray jusques au definer?

> Parle qui voelt, malgré tout mal parler
> je l'ameray, car c'est la souverayne,
> qui de mon cuer est vraye castelaine.

Have I not cause to be happy and glad, since I truly love one of whom I am enamored and shall remain so to the end? No matter what people may say and despite all the evil tongues, I shall continue to love her, for she is the sovereign, the true mistress of my heart.

The protagonist is invariably a lover who sings in silver-tongued words of his passion for a distinguished lady. His emotions are in turmoil because as yet there have been few signs that the lady returns his love. Still, he persists, no matter what people may say ("parle qui voelt"); he is grateful and glad that he can place his heart and soul in the service of—as the concluding lines of the poem put it—"sa doucheur mondaine qui de mon cuer est vraye castelaine."

Fabri's Middle Dutch songs are similar, in that they, too, are rather pretentious love songs. The words reflect an exalted courtly idiom, dense with conventional metaphor. A good example is the first stanza of Fabri's first Middle Dutch song (L20):

> Eer ende lof heb d'aventuer
> dat ic gheroepen bin ter muer
> daer Orpheus bewairt den tin;
> al is mi zeer gheworden zuer,
> nochtan verblijd na der natuer
> so is mi beid hert ende sin.

Glory and thanks be to destiny for calling me to a fortress where Orpheus is in command; although I endure much hardship there, I rejoice with all my heart and soul.

Again we hear the lover whose lot is difficult, often complex, but who is nevertheless grateful that fate has cast him within the castle of love (the metaphor comes from the famous *Roman de la rose*). Inside the castle walls and in the service of Orpheus, he voices his happy mood, which is quickened by love "nader natuer"—natural love, a concept to which we shall return.

A courtly lover also has less self-confident moments, however. In Hugo Boy's song (L22), the lover even compares himself to Pygmalion, who long worshipped a stone image. His great hope is that Venus herself, aware that his love has been so long unrequited, will finally grant him mercy:

Genade Venus vrouwe tzart,
want mir op eerden nye en wart
ye pijn so hart
als mir ein reyne wijf an doet;
doch duet sijt, vrou, bi dinen rade,
so neem ix niet in quade,
mer um ghenade
so bid ich dich, dunkt vesen goet.

Mercy, gentle lady Venus; never before have I felt such pain as a noble woman now inflicts on me. Because she does so on your advice, I do not take it amiss, but I pray thee for the mercy I so sorely need.

If Hugo Boy *monachus* not only composed the music of this song but also wrote the words, then we have further proof that even in medieval Holland not all monks were of an ilk. For a poet who probably came from Dordrecht, moreover, he used a somewhat unusual dialect: such words as *tzart* and *ich*, *dich*, *mir*, *ein*, and *duet* are more German than Dutch. Boy's poetic idiom, in fact, seems dictated by literary rather than regional conventions: his was the German-suffused literary language that not only appealed to the court of Holland under Bavarian rule but must also have been considered a more distinguished medium for a genre that bore the German stamp like no other—the minne-song, or song of courtly love. By lending their love poetry a German flavor, our Dutch poets tried, as it were, to join the ranks of the famous minnesingers, "Singers of Love," who included Wolfram von Eschenbach, Gottfried von Strassburg, and the great Walther von der Vogelweide.

The results must have been greatly admired at the ducal court during the Bavarian period. The handful of songs by Fabri and also by Boy (if we can tentatively include him among the court poets) is merely the proverbial tip of the iceberg—in quantitative terms, this type of poetry may well have overshadowed the rest of current court literature. If we go by the accounts, no group of artists appeared as often as the minstrels. Now, it is by no means certain that the performances of these *menestrele* always involved both words and music,[3] or indeed, that minnesongs were invariably presented; nonetheless, several indications alongside less speculative data suggest a flourishing tradition of courtly love poetry in Holland-Bavaria. Duke Albert himself dabbled in the genre: from the account entry mentioned on p. 22 we know that he wrote at least one poem—a May song, a lyric of springtime and love.

Alas, this ducal song has not been preserved, not even in the margins of an official document, where, in another case, the scribe did jot down a short love song:[4]

> God geve u minlic goeden dach,
> Lieff uutvercoren, wijflic schijn;
> Ghi muecht al tselve, dat ic vermach;
> God geve u minlijc goeden dach.

God bless you, chosen love of mine, lovely woman; all I own is at your disposal; may God bless you.

These four lines from the later days of Bavarian rule are not much, however, and even when added to the contributions of Fabri and the duke himself do not really allow us to speak of a flourishing courtly tradition. Yet secondary indications can reflect the existence of a tradition and should not be discounted. Among these are lists of presents to various poets mentioned in the accounts, men whose names reveal the cause of their fame, for instance Jan Vrouwentroest (John Ladies' Solace) and Jonkheer vander Minnen (Squire of Love).[5] In addition, artists recorded in the account books as retainers of noble ladies may well have been chosen for their romantic repertoire; after all, it was chiefly the ladies who encouraged the minnesingers. Perhaps, then, "my lady's minstrels from Hollant" mentioned in the Blois accounts for 1361 were such singer-charmers.[6] Moreover, the accounts of 1408 mention "new poetry books" imported for the countess from France—and what else would these new French collections have been but courtly lyrics? Nor were the many unspecified poets who entertained the diners at the court of Holland all of Hildegaersberch's serious mettle; often they belonged to the much larger guild of itinerant minnesingers. By tradition, love poetry was a pillar of any fashionable or would-be fashionable court. Would that we knew more about the words in which they were presented to the court of Holland-Bavaria!

As it is, we can only offer a compromise solution based on a plausible assumption. Now, there exists a Middle Dutch manuscript of courtly love poetry that, while it cannot strictly be called Holland-Bavarian court literature, is nevertheless so close that it may serve as an acceptable, if not thoroughly reliable, example of that tradition in about 1400. I refer to the famous but not exhaustively researched *Haags liederenhandschrift*—the Hague Song Manuscript. The first part of its title was better chosen than the second, for the book has indeed resided in The Hague since the Stadtholder period (at present it is in the Royal Library). On close inspection, however, it proves to contain few real songs: it is more a book of words than of vocal music. Unlike the Leiden fragments, the manuscript lacks musical notation, and it is questionable whether many of the poems ever possessed a score. Most probably, they were meant to be recited rather than sung, doubtless more or less melodiously; for us, though, they unfortunately remain no more than unaccompanied poems. Their contents, however, show them to be of a piece with the work of Boy and Fabri: all sing of courtly love. The Dutch-German idiom of the manuscript, too, fits nothing better than the luxuriant and sophisticated atmosphere at the court of Holland-Bavaria.

Still, this composite idiom faces the student with a considerable problem: how is one to localize a manuscript whose linguistic characteristics cover almost the entire spectrum from pure Middle Dutch to pure Middle High German? The fact that the *Haags liederenhandschrift* includes poems from regions far apart can be gathered from the inclusion of the work of Augustijnken on the one hand and Walther von der Vogelweide on the other; but at the moment we remain unable to identify the anonymous and greater part of the book, which is in a dialect that may be called a (variable) blend of these two extremes. The most ingenious labels have been attached to it: eastern Middle Dutch, Rhenish, Lower German with a Dutch influence, German-tinged West Middle Dutch, and the like.[7] Pending a closer analysis, the most we can claim is that the *Haags liederenhandschrift* was compiled in the western Netherlands, with the German influence explainable by the political and cultural ties of Holland under Bavarian rule with territories to the east. This view is in keeping with that of modern codicologists who argue, on the basis of external characteristics, that the *Haags liederenhandschrift* must have originated in the northern Netherlands in about 1400.[8] That brings us near to the court of Holland under Albert of Bavaria.

One interesting facet has been ignored thus far. An inscription on the last of the sixty-seven folios of the manuscript reads, "This book belongs to Jonkher Johan, count of Nossou of Vyanden, and Marie of Loen his wife." In other words, during the marriage of Count John IV of Nassau-Dillenburg to the Countess Mary of Loon (1440–75), the *Haags liederenhandschrift* must have been kept in the library of their Breda residence.[9] But how did the book end up there? A number of scholars have adopted Nijland's suggestion that the manuscript was originally commissioned by Joanna of Polanen, the mother of John IV of Nassau.[10] If so, we are back with the circle attending the Hague court: the Polanens were one of the oldest and, after their union with the Duvenvoordes, richest noble families in the county.

Still, we must not press too far, let alone present as certainties what are really conjectures. For in all truth, the connection of the *Haags lie-derenhandschrift* with the court of Holland-Bavaria is less unequivocal than that of other writings discussed in this book. Hence, those who refuse to accept anything but absolute certainties had best ignore the rest of this chapter—though if they do so, they neglect one avenue I did not want to overlook in writing this book: using the *Haags liederen-handschrift* to catch a (far from ideal but relatively undistorted) glimpse of an important literary genre at the court of Holland-Bavaria, and one that has remained hidden more than any other.

2. COURTLY LOVE

Even so apparently simple a question as how many texts the *Haags lie-derenhandschrift* contains cannot at present be answered satisfactorily. Quite apart from the problem of defining what we mean by *text* in that work (should we count as authentic text the many glosses, lamentations, puns, and the like that the copyist has seen fit to place between individual poems?), researchers and scholars still argue where one text stops and the next begins. Even the medieval editor of the manuscript wrestled with this problem, and with equal success (or lack thereof). For example, although he often marked quite explicitly, for the convenience of readers, where he thought a particular poem ended, he does not always appear to have been sure of his own verdicts. Nor could he have been, dependent as he was solely on the source(s) from which he copied his texts—much as we must rely on him. It is easy to sympathize with him, as when he adds "without an ending" after a particular text to emphasize that it is not his fault but that of the original sheets if the reader feels shortchanged by an incomplete poem.

E. F. Kossmann, too, had to make a host of difficult decisions when delimiting the various texts in his edition of the *Haags liederenhand-schrift*, before producing 115 separately numbered poems together with some twenty short aphorisms. In adopting Kossmann's numeration, I do not suggest that his decision is absolutely final: added to many un-equivocal cases, he has left a considerable shadow zone in which his joining or separating of verses is open to challenge. Thus, not so long ago experts argued, and for sound reasons, that the first four verses in Augustijnken's much-discussed "Ridder die waldoen haet" (The knight who hates good works; no. 32) in fact constitute a separate poem.[11] This point is characteristic of the current state of research into the *Haags liederenhandschrift*: the length of even the most thoroughly examined poem is still under discussion. We can only wonder how many more surprises the less well known texts hold in store for us.[12]

Under the circumstances, this section cannot provide more than a preliminary survey of a manuscript still so riddled with mysteries. Even so, an apology is called for: my approach looks suspiciously like that of nineteenth-century archaeologists who, to the despair of later students, instead of uncovering promising sites layer by layer (in our case, line by line) would dig almost at random. Then again, unusual boldness may be required to tempt philologists into the treasure trove of the *Haags liederenhandschrift*. Within the short span (less than fifty years) that the excellent Kossmann edition has been available, its author's plea to continue the fine work has gone almost completely unanswered—although perhaps 1940 was the wrong year to publish a Middle Dutch source with so pronounced a German flavor.

In any case, even in the absence of more detailed introductory studies it is perfectly obvious that this collective manuscript was devoted largely to one subject only: courtly love. Indeed, if we leave aside Hendrik van Veldeke, we may state that courtly love probably found its ripest Middle Dutch expression in the *Haags liederenhandschrift*. A useful example is an anonymous strophic poem (no. 26) that is typical of the manuscript as a whole by virtue of its peculiar mixture of Dutch and German—a mixture that, according to Van Mierlo, renders so much of the *Haags liederenhandschrift* "incomprehensible and disagreeable" but that is easily mastered by any reader willing to take the trouble.[13] One must, so to speak, sniff out the little tricks with which a Middle Dutch poet saw fit to "Germanify" his mother tongue—for example by turning the Middle Dutch *hert ende moet* (heart and courage) into the more German-sounding *hertz unde moyt* [HLH26/1]—no doubt because such "refinements" were considered more elegant and better befitting the noble court. Other forms of "dog Middle High German," too, can be understood by the average Dutch reader with a little practice: *zuesen = soeten* (sweet); *Das hait getan = Des hat gedaen* (This was done); *tsoren = toren* (trouble); and so on.[14]

Poem no. 26, then, reads:

Mir ist ghemeert hertz und moyt
Van zuesen worden met goeder gonst:
Das hait getaen min vrouwe goet,
Die met ire wonnentlicher const
Can alle truren van mir weren,
Ende geven vroem and vruden vil.
Wie zi wil met mir geberen,
Ich dien ir sicher aen zil.

Ich dar se nicht nennen,
Die hertzelieve vrouwe min;
Ich vruchte, si mocht kennen
Som nider, der nu zin.
Si verlicht als der dach
In mins hertzin gronde;
Et wer mer zinne ein doetslach,
Of ich zi in misdaet vonde.

Neyn ich niet, des hoffin ich!
Si is der doegden wortzel;
Der hertzlieve gelijchen ich
Der steden dube tortzyl,
Die engheinen gaden gheert
Wan zi den haren hait verloren.
Goet gelove mich erneert
Und behoet vor allen tsoren.

Danc have die vil zarte, gute,
Das men ir lof geeft over al;
Si can meren min gemuete
Sicher in mins hertzin dal.
Al gezelscaf, die ye gewart,
Ist verbessert zicherlich
Dorch die troute, werde, zart,
Werlich das spreken ich.

Wie mucht ich ze volprisen,
Die alre doegden is aen ende;
Min hertz kan se met vruden spisen.
Vrou, ich biede min hende,
Das ir wilt min dienst ontfaen
Und troesten min elenden lijf.
Was ir wilt, wil ich bestaen,
Suese, reyne, zelich wijf!

My heart is magnified by sweet, benevolent words; this was done by my noble lady, who with her enchanting arts can drive out all sadness before me, to my profit and joy. No matter what she may command me to do, I shall serve her selflessly. // I dare not give her name, that beloved lady of mine, lest one of the enviers identify her. She lights up the bottom of my heart all day long; my heart would be fatally pierced were I to find that she had spoiled our love. // No, that shall not happen, I do hope! She is the root of all virtue; I liken my beloved unto the turtledove who seeks no other husband if she have lost her own. Hope and trust keep me alive and protect me from all troubles. // Thanks be to the gentle, kind [lady], let her everywhere be praised; she uplifts my heart. All the company I keep is surely cheered by her loyalty, worth, and gentleness. // How can I praise her enough, whose virtue is without end? She fills my heart with joy. Lady, I offer you my hands, so that you may accept my homage and console the poor thing that I am. I shall do your every bidding, sweet, pure, blessed lady!

This poem may be considered an example of a great many others in the *Haags liederenhandschrift*. A lover pours out his heart. He adores a lady and sings of his love for her, a love that fills him with happiness, certainly now that she has deigned to address him with kind words. He feels certain he can trust his beloved and knows her to be as faithful as a turtledove (in this respect, the poem is one of the more optimistic in the manuscript); for once, then, he need not fear the ubiquitous figure of jealousy, the envier whose evil tongue might otherwise destroy young happiness. Even so, he must take care: it is best not to disclose the name of his beloved. But because his heart is full to overflowing, his mouth is too impetuous, even reckless; and although it remains unclear whose praises he is singing, we know that the lady must be unique, the source of all virtue. Not until the last stanza does the poet address his beloved directly (until that point he merely listed and extolled her accomplishments): he offers her his hands (a feudal gesture of humble submission) and begs her to accept his homage.[15]

This idea of *minnedienst*, or "service" rendered by the knight to the woman he adores; this semifeudal, semireligious conception of love, is characteristic of the *Haags liederenhandschrift*.[16] The man is the servant, the lady his mistress. She is invariably perfect, not only to behold but also deep in her being. Women, according to the manuscript, are the crown of divine creation. God had an excellent reason for choosing a human mother to bear him a son (no. 95), "For nought better has been born, than a woman pure as morn" (Want niet bessers ist geboren dan ein reyne wijf alleine; 16*/7–8), and "all virtue from them [i.e., women] flows" (alle doghet uut hem spruut; 52/16). The salutary influence that women exert on men is reflected chiefly in the joy that they provoke. Innumerable are the lines in which women, often as so many wishful dreams, remove man's sorrow, allay his suffering, drive away his grief, yield him happiness, make him feel lighthearted, and so on.[17] As the final stanza of one of these German-Dutch paeans to women has it (35/ 18–26):

> Was mach men zagen me van wiven?
> Si sint alles loves wert;
> Ir lovelich lof zu vollen scriven,
> Worde alle meysteren zu hart.
> Du minnentliche reyne vrucht,
> Bis wol behuet in eren tzucht,
> Och God, of ich verwerven mucht
> Das du mich woldes leyt verdriven,
> So wer mich vruden vil bescert!

What more can be said about women? They are worthy of every praise. To sing their praises in full would be beyond the powers of any master writer. You, dearest, pure fruit, be well preserved in honor and virtue; oh, if only God rendered me worthy of your solace, how overjoyed I should be!

Still, man's path to woman and to joy is paved with suffering. But then, courtly love is more than a path; it is a long road, admittance to which is itself a favor. The first milestone is occasion to render homage to the chosen lady: "all my grief would pass away, might I homage to her pay" (al mijns leydes weer verganch, of ich mucht in yrme dienst ringen; 77/103–4).[18] And then the "wrestling" starts: abject servitude, for which just one friendly word, one smile, one glance is sufficient reward. Even that reward may be withheld from the lover, who is left with only a hope that all his service will not have been in vain (18/57–64):

> Eren, werden und loven
> Wil ich das minnentliche wijf
> Want si in min hertz es boven
> Al die of erden haven lijf.
> Si moes ich sin in dit bedrijf,
> Ghesciet mir van ir lief of tzorn;
> Wil zir dar iegen haven kijf,
> Min dienst die is zumal verloren.

I shall honor, love, and exalt the loveliest of them all, for she stands higher in my heart than anyone alive. Hence I must continue in this state no matter whether it gains me love or sorrow from her; if she be against it, my service is utterly in vain.

The lover must give his all if he is to receive even the smallest pittance in return. He must be prepared for total surrender, if need be unto death (no. 49). His emotional fate is entirely in her hands (96/33–41):

> Sus willich hoges muedes leven
> Oph hophe das se noch sal geven
> Vrueden vele sonder getal.
> In yr genade lays ich al,
> Lijf, herts, moyt unde sin,
> Het si verlies, 't si gewin.
> Ich hope, ir wijflich moet
> Sal si keren in oetmoet,
> Unde mir genade doen aenscijn.

And so I shall live on courageously, hoping that she will yet bestow unspeakable joy upon me. To her mercy I commend everything: body, heart, feeling, and soul, no matter if it bring me gain or loss. I hope she will prove to be kindly disposed toward me and will be gracious to me.

Courtly love is based on an unfair division. Woman is the crown of creation, the source of all virtue, exalted in character and demeanor.[19] Compared with her, man, despite his worthy intentions, is but a miserable drudge who can hope for no greater fortune than to be allowed to serve her.[20] Yet we must be careful to distinguish the poets' *presentation* of love from their real *opinion*.[21] That is, if we look past the stylization of love and at its conception as reflected in the *Haags liederenhandschrift*, we discover a more equitable distribution of the partners' roles. Not only does the book advocate social equality between the lovers (some poems even suggest that the lover need not heed every whim of his beloved); but love itself seems to be treated as an essentially commensurate union of hearts.[22] In a somewhat theoretical poem whose choice of words is almost reminiscent of Hadewijch, the famous Brabantine mystic poetess, this view is expressed quite unequivocally: "Love doth make of two one soul, of two stout hearts a single whole" (Minne is één ziele van hem tween ende twee herten, voecht in één; 110/31–32).[23] Elsewhere the harmony of the two hearts seems vouchsafed by their similarity: each loves the one who *by nature* is his or her equal.[24]

In many respects, man's subordinate position thus derives at least as much from a division of roles as from love itself. There is paying homage and there is receiving homage, and it behooves the lady to reciprocate the devotion of a lover who proves his excellence and fidelity, if only by encouraging him to persist in his service to her (79/15–21):

> Wijp, sint du aller mannen lijb
> Tso eeren muges bringen,
> So ne halt keynen wederkijp
> Jo in zommelichen dingen.
> Ghif scune geber unde zuetz woert,

> Dem du van hertzen gunes,
> Unde laes dyr vrolich dienen voert.

Lady, though you can honor any man, you need not keep so aloof. Bestow friendly gestures and sweet words on whom you deign to do so, and let him serve you merrily.

According to the *Haags liederenhandschrift*, however, the reward for courtly love need not be confined to a little smile or a friendly word. Several poems, reaching further, have an unmistakable erotic dimension. In some the lover expresses physical longing: "Dear God, make me succeed, in honor do the deed, clasp to my heart her balm, her life" (Och God, laes mir ghelingen, in eeren das volbringen, an mijn hertse dwingen urym balzem-lijf; 65/64–67); and—addressed directly to the beloved—"Would in your arms I lay" (Ich wolde in uren arme legen; 44/99).

But the most remarkable poem here is probably the couplet announced in the manuscript with: "This is the French [address] of a lady in love . . . This the reply of her lover" (no. 73). (Is it pure chance that this jaunty poem should be in French?) The couplet takes the form of a dialogue, or perhaps of a sort of exchange of letters, between a lady and her admirer. The latter seems to have rendered the lady homage for so long that she, too, at last considers the time due to favor him with her body (73/1–12):

> Amis que j'aym et aymeray tout dis
> tant que poray durer, vous m'aves servi
> de cuer vray si lonc temps, que remunerer
> le vous vuel, et abandonner mon corps
> à faire votre commant—
> Fors que puis le chaynt an avant.
>
> Moy poes toucher vous en ay donné
> baysier et acoler et prendre tant quez
> j'ai desormais et à moi juer:
> je ne le vous quer refuser,
> car votre sui, n'alez doubtant—
> Fors que puis le chaint en avant.

Friend, whom I love and long shall continue to love, you have served me truly for so long that I shall reward you and surrender my body to you—save below the girdle. // You may touch, kiss, and embrace me, caress me in all places and make love to me; I shall not deny you, for know that I am all yours—save below the girdle.

The poet is quite frank: the lover may caress his lady everywhere except below the girdle. The lover's reply directs a sharp light on the real aim of his homage (73/1–6 bis):

> De tant que vous m'abandones, ma douche damme
> De renon, cuer, corps et quanque vous portez
> sus li chaint et le souplus non,
> vous merchi, mays devotion ay trop plus
> —qu'amours me sequere—
> A che desous, qu'à che dessure!

For wanting to reward me, my dear lady, with your heart and your whole body save below the girdle, I thank you—but, may love help me, I feel more devotion for the lower than for the upper part!

Nor, if we can believe this lover, is he the only one whose homage is aimed most particularly at his lady's loins: "chascuns plus labuere à che dessous qu'à che desseure" (73/11–12 bis). Although, in view of the clearly comical "undertone" of the poem, it seems wise not to consider this down-to-earth view of knightly homage typical of the age, it was certainly not unusual: in the *Haags liederenhandschrift*—as in the Provençal of Arnaut Daniel, Bertrand de Born, and Bernard de Ventadour, all celebrated troubadours—courtly homage and sexuality are not mutually exclusive.[25] The hackneyed idea of the courtly lover as a lowly worm crawling in dust before "la belle dame sans merci"—and, moreover, without the least promise of success—simply does not apply, or at least not to this manuscript.

Nevertheless, references to the transports of erotic love are few and far between.[26] As the rather abstract poem no. 10 concludes: "Who devotion will embrace, he must suffer love and woe" (Sowie die min in hem wil husen, die moet dicke liden lief und leet)—and in the concrete "practice" of the *Liederenhandschrift*, this meant woe more often than love. By far the greatest number of poems stresses the trouble courtly love causes the wooer and the suffering he must endure for his lady (although on one occasion, the shoe is on the other foot).[27] In the rather free-and-easy poem no. 62, the lover lets the name of his beloved slip out, but for the rest he has little good to say of her (62/1–8):

> Ich heb Claren opghegeven
> Mijn lijf, mijn goyt, wes ich vermach;
> Van haer is mi nicht weder bliven
> Dan sorghe, toren, nacht ende dach.
> Dorst ich, ich souts haer doen gewach,

> Hoe ich comen byn in sneven;
> Ich moet betalen al 't gelach,
> Om mi gaef si niet twe sceven.

All I have, my money and my life, I have yielded to Clara; I have received
nothing in return save worry and sorrow, day and night. If I dared, I would
tell her how wretched I am; I have to foot a heavy bill, but she does not give
two straws for me.

Love suffers especially when, as here, the courtier's love remains unrequited (for the moment, at least). But even when both the lovers are
willing, their troubles, as listed in the *Haags liederenhandschrift*, are far
from over. The world outside often acts the spoilsport, the enemy of
true love. That wicked world figures (this too is a cliché) chiefly in the
shape of enviers, whose sharp tongues are only too keen to spoil the
lovers' happiness.[28] In the opening lines of poem no. 85, the lady complains of the baneful influence of the enviers' tongues:

> Owe, owe, elende,
> Waer ich mich henen wende!
> Hets gheyt mir al onghelijch,
> Das clagic Gode van hemelrijch.
> Ich hayn eynen werden man ercoren,
> Ich vruchte das ich en hayn verloren.
> Owe das doyn der nider tsongen,
> Dey mennegen ghueten haynt bedwongen,
> Unde gebracht in groser noyt.

Oh, oh, misery, wherever I turn! My unhappiness makes me cry out to God. I
chose me a noble man, but fear that I have lost him. That is the work of the
enviers, tongues that have already thwarted so many, causing them sore dis-
tress.

Closely related to the pernicious role of the enviers are the evil effects of
"boasting," in which case the wagging tongues are not those of outsiders but of the wooers themselves.[29] Quite apart from the fact that their
bragging endangers their ladies' reputations, the boasters lay themselves
open to the enviers, who use the information to blacken both lovers,
particularly the lady. Hence, many poems of courtly love—not least
those included in the *Haags liederenhandschrift*—enjoin the lovers to be
discreet: those who keep quiet about their love or lover are least likely
to set malicious tongues a-flapping.[30]

Thus, as with Hildegaersberch, the word often plays a destructive
role in the *Haags liederenhandschrift*: the "rogues" of the former have

become "enviers" in the latter—two pejorative words for two pejorative roles. Yet words can also render sterling service to love. After all, words are the vessels by which the lover conveys his innermost feelings—"Precious cups of meaning"—to his beloved. No wonder, then, that so many poems in the manuscript are overt professions of amorous devotion, generally culminating in the petitioner's imploring the lady to grant him a willing ear, if not a willing heart or even more.[31] Other, even more interesting examples of verbal wooing, however, are the long dialogue poems, several of which appear in the manuscript (nos. 1, 20, 44, 84). Although the lover protests his despair, the lady refuses to believe him before putting him to the test. The dialogue becomes a kind of verbal tournament in which the lady is greatly superior; she plays a cat-and-mouse game, successively feigning surprise, teasing, resisting, and eventually surrendering. Characteristic is the following extract, in which the man pours out declarations of love while the lady keeps pretending that she is treating her admirer's metaphors literally (20/sts. 4–9):

> Vrou, mins hertzin vruden vont,
> Troestet mich vil zenden man!
> Ir hait mich das hertz *dorwont*,
> Das ich geweren nicht in kan,
> Ich haves mit groeser swere gedragen,
> Nu dwingt mich derzu min moet,
> Nu ich't uch moes gewagen.
>
> Here, ir sprecht vremde wort,
> Das ich have *gewont* ur hertze;
> Ir in hait das nicht gehort,
> Daz ich yeman dede smerze.
> Och solde mich daz nicht wol getzamen,
> Daz ich yeman wonten solde,
> Want ich hain wives namen.
>
> Vrou, ir hebt mir nicht gewont,
> Mit zwerde noch mit metze.
> Nochtan bin ich meer onghezont
> Dan of ich stechin zesse
> Met einen swerde het in den live.
> Das deyt ur minnentlicher dwanc,
> Die mich *dwingt* so stive.
>
> Here, wie mach ich uch *gedwingen*?
> Das solde ich gerne wissen dan,
> Want ich geynre-conne dingen

Uch nye zugesprochen hain.
Darom spricht nit ongelimpes,
Want in kan nicht verdragen wol
Van uch uwz gescimpes.

Vrou, daz ich mit uch scimpe ycht,
[line missing]
Das wer gar ongelijch.
[line missing]
Ir sult mich stede ur *diener* vinden,
Des in mach ich ouch nit laen,
Al solde ich des verzwinden.

Here, ir sult Gode zu *dienste* staen,
Die uwez al mach gewalden,
Ende hem met vlize roefen an,
Das er uch in sin hute halde.
Of ir dient, dar men uch nit lone;
Der arbeyt ist verloren gar,
Daerom so dient al scone!

Lady, let my heart find peace by sending me solace! You have *pierced* my de-
fenceless heart, I have found it hard to bear, but now my courage tells me it is
time to let you know. // Sir, you do speak strange words saying I have *pierced*
your heart; I have never heard it said that I have inflicted pain on anybody.
Nor would it be befitting one who bears a lady's name. // Lady, you did not
pierce me with a sword or a knife, and yet I am less hale than had my body
been cut with a sword. It is your love that *compels* me to do your bidding. //
Sir, how can I *compel* you? I would love to know seeing that I have not bidden
you do anything at all. So do not say such untoward things, for I cannot bear
to listen to your scolding. // Lady, that I should scold you . . . would be improper. . . . You will always find me your *servant* and I should not desist even
were you to banish me from here. // Sir, you should be *serving* God who has
you in His power and implore him ardently to keep you in his care. If you serve
where there is no reward, yours is wasted labor, so you had best serve goodness!

Ten more stanzas written in the same spirit follow: the lover must keep
running the gauntlet of his unapproachable lady. A Middle Dutch tradition beginning with the early-thirteenth-century *Tprieel van Troje*
(The bower of Troy) seems to have been alive and well 150 years later:
man may be champion of the battlefield, but regardless of the feats of
arms he accomplishes there, when it comes to love he sadly fails. Still,
almost less readily even than in the clash of arms does the true knight
allow himself to be beaten in love; he will continue to fight for as long
as it takes to win his fair lady:

> Here, ich haves wol gehoirt,
> Das gher us vry hertzingronde
> Meynet samelike wort,
> Als ghir sprochin hait zu stonde.
> Die wort wil ich gerne ontfangen,
> En conde nicht gehelfen mich,
> Das ich uch meer dete bangen.

Sir, I believe that you would join your heart to mine as you have been telling me. I will heed your plea now, because I cannot help myself any longer and shall no longer make you feel afraid.

This stanza—the thirty-seventh!—at last marks the change in the lady's attitude: she decides that she need no longer make her lover feel uneasy, convinced as she now is (or has she known it throughout?) of his honorable intentions. From then on, the exchanges are transformed into a dialogue of partners more or less equal. The joys of courtly love will now be shared, even though one will predominantly play the giving role while the other will be receiving. In an instant of obvious compassion, the copyist added the following words below the last stanza: "omne principium primum difficile est" (All beginnings are hard) and "verbeyt," which, freely translated, means "keep trying." With the right words, the lover can convince his lady that his feelings are true.

But fair words in courtly love are futile without fair deeds. Much though social accomplishments may have been prized even in this social stratum (a subject we shall return to in section 4), the lover must never forget that he is a knight and that he must prove his love with deeds of valor. Consider, for example, poem no. 66; it tells of a "high-born, rich maid" engaged in amorous conversation with a "well-spoken young companion" (jonch ghesel van hoger tael), dressed in the latest fashion and with his hair combed out in pleasant, ample locks. Then enters an elderly cripple whose appearance bears traces of a chivalrous life: although he is now lame, "many a letter by sword was writ" (met swerden menneghen brieve gescreven) in his face. The young fop scoffs at the other's looks ("the beau did make fun of them" [die moyaert helt sijn spot daermede]), but the maid defends the old knight, speaking of the great honor he has earned, and severely rebukes the insolent young dandy (66/120–24, 157–61, 165–67):

> Doe sprach die maegt: "Hi heeft verdient!
> Hem sullen billich wesen vrient
> Goede maecht ende reyne wijf

> Want hi met wapen sijn lijf
> So recht manlic heeft geneert;
> ....
> Al en kan hi niet wal treden
> Aen den dans, noch even gaen,
> Mit wapen heeft hij 't so gedaen
> Daer emmer die manlijcheyt an leget,
> Spottens heeft hi hem ontseget.
> ....
> Manlic moet, die sal men prisen
> Daer men den man gewapent siet,
> Bi den dans en prijs ichs niet."

The maiden said: "That is his due. All noble ladies and maidens should treat him kindly because he spent his life manfully under arms. . . . Although he cannot dance nimbly or walk straight, he has proved his manhood by dint of arms so well that he is above derision. . . . By his arms you can tell the man, not by his dancing."

At the end of the poem, the author holds this maiden up as an example to all women (66/187–96):

> Het soude der wapen seere baten,
> Waren alle vrouwen so gesint;
> Mennich die wert nu gemint
> Hi ne worde nemmerme so waerde
> Soude hi die minne mitten zwaerde
> Op 't felt onder die vianden winnen,
> Hi ne stonde nemmermeer na minnen.
> Mennich is ghemint nochtan,
> Omdat hi reyen dansen can,
> Mennich omdat hi rike si.

It would greatly foster valor if all women felt the same; many a man is now in favor who could not prove his worth as a lover with his sword against the enemy; instead, men are loved because they can dance well or because they are rich.

In the real world, our poet contends, riches and dancing feet make the good lover, but in the model court of the *Haags liederenhandschrift*, love can spring from courage alone. Chivalry transforms a man into a worthy lover; the honors a knight earns in battle also help him to win his lady's love.[32] Moreover, love is not merely the *result* of chivalrous deeds; it is also their *cause*: to win the favors of his mistress, the courtly lover must woo her not only with words but also with bravery in the field.[33]

This theme presents what may be called the quintessence of the courtly love conception (in the *Haags liederenhandschrift* and elsewhere): love's ennobling effects. Love creates better people. If all is harmonious between two lovers, then "one through the other does his best" (d'een dor d'ander dbeste doet; 13/20). Now, given the (according to these poems) more or less innate and inalienable excellence of the female sex, it is man above all who must work at attaining the "best." And accompanying the set of values upheld by such poetry—the homage rendered by the knight to his mistress—is the necessary and sufficient condition for attaining that end. Love, namely, is life's noblest guide. In poem no. 52, a lover defines courtly love as a man's royal road to a blessed life:

> In steden dienste wil ich bliven,
> Onderdanich goeden wiven
> Emmer waer ich henen vaer.
> Oech so willich openbaer
> Den vrouwen altoes spreken goet.
> Et's reden, want des mannes moet
> Overmids der vrouwen troest
> Uut menneger sorghen wert verloest,
> Men is hem billic daerom hout.
> Men kan ghesteyn, cruut noch gout
> Te volle bi hem gheliken.
> Conde ich yet, ich sout doen bliken
> Altoes tot haren besten.
> Lijf ende moet dat wil ich vesten
> In haren dienste mijn leven uut,
> Want all doghet uut hem spruut.

I shall always render homage to good women; nor will I speak anything but good of women in public. And rightly so, for a man's soul is relieved of much sorrow by the solace that women provide. Precious stones, fine herbs, nor gold can be fully compared to women. If I could, I would let everything redound to their credit. I would place all my heart and life in their service, for all virtue springs from them.

He who pays homage to women and shows them love also does homage to and loves virtue, and vice versa. Such is the conception of love, and indeed of life, enshrined in the *Haags liederenhandschrift*. It would be an exaggeration to call it a creed; rather, it is a coherent system of norms based on the belief that the vital value of life resides in love, the shimmering nuance of civilized desire, because Love opens the gates to Honor and hence to the greatest of earthly treasures: acceptance by the glittering elite and by society at large. In one poem, Venus herself declares (86/37–52):

Wie minre is van rechter aert,
Ich byn altoes t'sinen besten.
Gestedich, reyn sulder uch voegen
Mitter daet; hijrmet volvaert!
Pijnt uch alle duecht te vesten,
Werct hierna, ets baet te lesten!
   Sijt ghetruwe unde warachtich,
Unde hout uwe woerde ghestade!
Dat sint punte van gueter eeren;
Uwer sinnen suldir wesen mechtich.
Ets wijsheyt, das ich uch rade.
Wye si siin, diegene die 't leren,
In duegden sullen sij meren.
   Hier comdi mede in hoger staet,
U lof das sal in eeren risen,
Daer men uch kant onder die guede.

I shall always be on the side of the true lover. Ever be loyal and pure! Do your best to be virtuous; it will redound to your credit! Be true and upright and keep your word! These are matters of honor to which you must give your full attention. I am proffering wise counsel; whosoever heeds it will grow in virtue. Through it you will attain great worth; your praises will be sung wherever good men hear of you.

Viewed thus, love far transcends any particular virtue. Service to one's lady, in the *Haags liederenhandschrift*, is simultaneously service to society.[34] And since the enchanted circle of knights and ladies was also the chief audience to which the manuscript addressed itself, we must now ask the extent to which that audience really embraced the chivalrous doctrine, as the poems allege. Did they truly regard love as the cornerstone of society? Or was love rather a marginal phenomenon, praised to high heaven, sometimes to Olympus, in courtly poetry—but only in courtly poetry? In the final section of this chapter, we shall examine more closely the relationship between court literature and actual conditions at the court of Holland-Bavaria. However, so as better to gauge the reality of the courtly code, let us first scrutinize its literary expression further.

3. POETRY FOR CONNOISSEURS

The many dozens of love poems contained in the *Haags liederenhand-schrift* explore all heights and depths of the emotions covered by courtly love. Male emotions, in particular, are depicted in countless variations, from total hopelessness to utter happiness through a rich scale of nuances: discomposure, rebelliousness, disdain, despair, uncertainty, resignation, hope, desire, adoration, surrender, humility, optimism, jubilation. Sometimes these states are unchanging; more often they are transitory, several poems describing the fusion of partly contradictory emotions, such as those in the lover who agonizes between hope and fear (no. 65). But then, courtly love is a paradoxical complex of sensations: as a copyist put it poignantly in one of his glosses (following no. 64), "ic lide ende ben blide"—I suffer and rejoice.

The emotion most commonly described is probably self-pity: the lover's complaint to (or about) his lady that, despite his faithful service to her, she refuses to heed his plea.[35] A choice example is no. 24, a short poem of three stanzas, in which a lover rebels in a manner unusually vindictive given the precepts of courtly love, and summons Nature herself to punish his hard-hearted mistress:

> Ich clage dir, zure winter calt,
> Das mir ein wijf doyt grois gewalt;
> Ich werde in cortzin ziden alt,
> Helpes mer nicht wenden.
> Ich bidde uch, wilde vogelin,
> Das ir laest uwer singen zin,
> So wer vro das hertze min,
> Mucht ich ir vrude penden.
>
> Tze winde zets ich minen zin,
> Of daz he veye in ir anschin,
> Daz beyde ir wengelin und kin
> Van verwen gar verzwinden,
> Bas an iren roeter mont,
> Die ye so vrintlichen stont
> Midden in mins hertzin gront,
> Ich diende yr ye van kinde.
>
> O du zomergroene plain,
> Du salt van mire vrouwen staen;
> Se hait mer alzo mesdaen,
> Das ich ir scade wil meeren.
> Orlof, vrou min, ho geboren!
> Goet dienst blijft an uch verloren,
> Des moist ir, winter, uren tzorn
> Tze mire vrouwen keren.

I complain to you, bitterly cold winter, because a woman is doing me grave harm; I shall soon be old unless you help me to change things. I ask you, little wild birds, to stop singing, so that my heart can rejoice at seeing her pleasure spoiled. // I ask the wind to blow in her face so that her cheeks and her chin lose their color, and also her red mouth, she who once enjoyed the friendship of my heart, whom I have served since I was a child. // You, summer-green meadow, withdraw from my lady; she has wronged me so much that I wish to increase her sorrow. Farewell, high-born lady! True service is wasted on you; hence, winter, cool your wrath upon my lady.

A woman in love can also complain—about the absence of her lover on a foreign battlefield, or about those enviers whose idle gossip thwarts her love.[36]

Like most courtly poetry, the *Haags liederenhandschrift* usually lets the lovers speak for themselves: in most poems the story is told in the first person singular. And yet genuine personal touches are rare and discreet.[37] It is hardly an exaggeration to claim that, based on the manuscript contents, the lovers appear to be an identical couple throughout, so little individuality is there to glean in successive pictures of their relationship. All these quasi-personal effusions are, in essence, just so many expressions of a *role*, designed not so much to convey lively autobiographical experience as to reflect a general human condition: *the* lover paying ritual homage to *the* beloved lady.[38] Viewed thus, the anthology becomes a kaleidoscope of all the emotions characteristic of courtly love. The narrator's perspective throughout is that of a lyrical individual, an "I" who confesses all: his strength, his weakness, his indecision, his confusion, his sustaining hope come pouring from his heart. Yet his own experiences are never such as to prevent other courtly lovers from identifying themselves with the hero of the poem. Probably there was reason behind this approach. But before we investigate this subject more thoroughly, we would do well to consider the devices by which the poems try to fuse ostensibly individual experience with suprapersonal identification.

A key stylistic feature, at first not very noticeable, nevertheless highly revealing here, is the frequent use of proverbs and related aphorisms bearing on general experiences. Ranging from bon mots to platitudes, many of these have been inserted between the poems. More memorable, though—and for us also more important—are the numerous proverbs that appear *within* the longer poems: that is, the lovers explain their personal situation with the help of an appropriate adage. For the public, this technique (to which, again, we shall return) establishes a link between the amorous transports and rebuffs of the literary characters and those of lovers in more everyday contexts, thus helping the reader and perhaps the author to project his own amorous stirrings.

This device is repeatedly employed, for example, in poem no. 100.[39] A squire relates how, one fine day in May, he happened upon an exquisite maiden, who had chosen solitude in her mysterious sorrow. When the squire asked what the trouble might be, a courtly dialogue ensued in which the maiden freely confessed her plight. Her lover had been unfaithful and broken his pledges; devastated by his infidelity, she decided thenceforth to shun all company, to desert the treacherous world. The animated exchange between squire and maiden that follows is lavish with proverbial rules of conduct (60–89):

> Ic seide: "Joncvrou, et is scade,
> Dat u wil is dus ghestelt;
> *Die mitten goeden hem verzelt,*
> *Daer is goet den tijt mede te liden.*"
> "Cnapen die roemen ende niden,
> Ende meer beloeven dan houden,
> Dier heb ic so vele ontgouden,
> Dan mi, leyder, is te swaer."
> "Joncvrou, het mach wel wesen waer,
> *Doch sal men den goeden minnen.*"
> "Cnape, in kanre niet gekinnen,
> Wie si sijn of hoe gedaen;
> Daerom willic alleene gaen;
> *Het toent hem selc in doechden slecht,*
> *Sijn herte is fel ende onrecht,*
> Cnape, dat wetti selve wel!"
> "Joncvrou, al sijn die boese fel,
> Woudi daer om overgheven
> Goet geselscap al u leven,
> So werdi sekerlic ontweget.
> Die wise aldus seghet,
> *Dat men sal den boesen scuwen,*
> *Sijn archeyt mitter doecht verduwen;*
> *Die niet misdoet, hi ne darf niet boten.*"
> "Cnape, ghi sout mi wel doen soeten,
> Opdat ic waende daerin volstaen."
> "Joncvrou, *gheen mensche heeft ontfaen*
> *Yet sekers te hebben, quaet of goet,*
> *El dan hi emmer sterven moet;*
> *Maer altoes sal men dbeste hopen.*"

I said: "Damsel, 'tis a pity your mind is so disposed, for *nothing is won without pain.*" "I have had my fill of boastful and envious squires who promise more than they keep, sad to say." "Damsel, no doubt you speak the truth, yet *good men ever shall prevail.*" "Squire, I cannot tell who they are or how they are made, hence I would fain walk alone; *be a man e'er so good and just, his will is weak so sin he must,* as you, Squire, know but too well!" "Damsel, though the wicked are bad, keep you but good company all your life, then you are certain to elude them. The rule of the wise is: *Evil evermore eschew, who does right need never rue, virtue is its own reward.*" "Squire, you do speak sweet words but I shall not change my mind." "Damsel, *the reaper does not care, nor good nor bad men does he spare, yet hope we can and always must.*"

The conversation so continues; in 180-odd lines there are sixteen proverbs telling lovers what they ought to know, do, and avoid. And as if the general tenor of this homily were not plain enough, the poet ends with an explicit moral injunction: "Oh, lords and all you ladies, too, be ever virtuous and true!" (Ghi heeren, cnapen, maegden, vrouwen, blijft gestede in rechter trouwen; 187–88).

Nor is this the only poem in which the author projects his own experiences, presented in the first person, into the human arena at large.[40] In fact, the personal testimony of lovers often provided the *Haags liederenhandschrift* with the occasion—or, if we prefer, the excuse—for proffering academic advice on sexual manners. As a result, the manuscript is not merely an anthology of love poems but also a kind of lovers' guidebook. The beginning of poem no. 78 is a case in point:

> Zwer zich wil lieben zu minnentliche vrouwen,
> *der doe das ym lere minen sanch,*
> Unde latz zich in yrme dienste scouwen,
> Zo wirt ym lof, loen, eere unde danch.

Whosoever wishes to endear himself to winsome women, *must do as my song teaches*, and place himself openly at their service, when praise, reward, and thanks will fall to him.

Here, the author's amorous-didactic intent is obvious; more often, however, it remains implicit (if still fairly transparent) because the poem is presented as a general reflection on love.[41] This quality is probably most indisputable in a class of poems well represented in the *Haags liederenhandschrift*—allegorical verse. The precise meaning of allegory (or rather, of what we understand by allegory) is one of the most difficult problems facing the student of literature, in theory no less than in practice.[42] Many students base their definition on the one offered by Quintilian in the first century A.D.: "aliud verbis, aliud sensu"—a word that has a different meaning from the one it expresses. Clearly that definition can cover a host of literary forms: metaphor, fable, irony, and many more—and some authorities even contend that Quintilian's definition is not wide enough!

In the Middle Ages, too, there were many literary forms that qualify as allegory. The *Haags liederenhandschrift*, in particular, presents a large variety of allegorical expressions.[43] For simplicity, they can be divided into two main groups, two prominent subdivisions of allegory found also in other medieval writings: reification and personification.[44] In the first, an abstract concept is represented by something concrete—courtly love by the hunt, for example, the man, of course, being the hunter and the lady the prey. The second type, personification, is probably even more alien to modern literary tastes, and works on the opposite principle: here, abstract characteristics, such as personal qualities or emotions, are represented by individuals whose name, behavior, and attributes correspond to characteristics of the abstract entity presented. Thus Hate might be embodied in a garish green, flame-spewing woman, the mother of the furtive little Gossip who turns his back on us as he maligns our good name. Because they employ such caricatures, personification allegories move the modern reader to laughter or boredom—they seem labored and obscure. Nevertheless, the popularity of personification allegories in the Middle Ages—starting with the *Roman de la rose*, which introduced the genre into vernacular European literature—proves that it once fascinated poets and their public. No doubt, the tangible qualities thus personified were considered both moving and truthful. Until the *Roman de la rose*, medieval epic poetry had largely been confined to the description of external events; personification allegories enlarged this realm, allowing for the inclusion of the inner processes of love, loyalty, ambition, fear, and deceit. In other words, allegory was the best-known means of rendering the invisible visible.[45]

And so the *Haags liederenhandschrift* teems with personifications: Lady Honor (who is also found in the writings of William of Hildegaersberch), Lady Love, Sir Good Companion, Hope, Solace, Care, Worry, Fear, and many more. Several poems simply describe the actions of what are ostensibly individual characters but who actually represent universal and abstract concepts: what Hope does is what hope brings to mankind.[46] A fairly straightforward illustration of this is the following poem, in which King Honor considers abdicating in a fit of depression. His daughter, Love, urges him to retain his crown and to give his son Virtue enough time to earn the attributes of a regent. Meanwhile, Love herself will substitute for the king (19/15–21):

> Vader, dats min hoechste raet;
> Ende enich man, die na U staet,
> Die zal mi wesen onderdaen;
> Want ic hebbe van U ontfaen

Een mechtich, edel conincrike
En kinne nyeman min gelike
Sonder U, heer vader.

Father, this is my best advice; and all who love you must submit to me; for I
have been handed a mighty, noble kingdom by you and consider no one my
equal save you, father, my lord.

Uncle Fidelity, too, is enlisted by Love so that the whole family may
rule the kingdom of Honor in harmony. The intent—or rather, the
moral—of the poem is unmistakable: honor is life's supreme test and
reward. We heard Hildegaersberch voice the same opinion, and we shall
later hear it many times more. In order to preserve honor (or to attain
it or, in this particular history, of a monarch in despair, to restore it),
men must unite under the banners of virtue and love and also (particularly in the field of love) of fidelity. Here we have the familiar courtly
code, but now it is depicted not as the live experience of a (fictitious)
individual but as a generally valid principle of life befitting all. Far more
than the expressive poems written in the first person singular, such allegories have a *normative* purpose: the personifications present the reader
with a moral program. The didactic tendency already mentioned has
reached a climax: love songs have become moral precepts, guides to a
good life. The *Haags liederenhandschrift* tends to treat love as a creed
and to base an ethical dogma on it. It is, moreover, chiefly thanks to a
system of personifications that it succeeds in applying this didactic
"tractate-style":[47] the personifications help to amplify and decorate the
lessons in forms valid and acceptable. Allegory is therefore exploited,
not only as psychology, but also as (moral) philosophy and—in view of
its normative purpose—even as ideology.

Yet allegory is more than normative ethics. And while the last poem
was easy to interpret, other allegorical poems are obscure, almost intrac-
table. We may assume that, though we find them hard to fathom today,
medieval readers must have considered them a most attractive facet of
the genre, relishing their mysteriousness, suggestiveness, dense feats of
allusion and symbolism. The aesthetic appeal of allegory is akin to that
of the riddle: both derive their charm from the tension between mystery
and discovery. What lurks behind the literary façade? How are the
words to be interpreted? It is the perennial fascination of detection.

This mysterious side of allegory is particularly apparent in the other
allegorical subtype, reification, which is as amply represented in the
Haags liederenhandschrift as personification.[48] Allegories based on personification are generally fairly transparent, mainly because the names

of the *dramatis personae* clarify their intention and meaning. Where, however, a concrete object is used to symbolize something else, much ambiguity can follow. Moreover, the poet does not necessarily proffer the solution, in which case his poem will continue to puzzle and can, after he has finished his recitation, provoke a kind of guessing game (see sec. 4).

A telling example is poem no. 51. Here a maiden has spread a net to catch a hawk, planning to clip her prey's wings and then keep him as a pet. But the hawk is wary; hiding away in a tree, he hears the maiden say: "This fine bird I fain would lure, and then restrain him caged secure" (Dat si ne daeromme vanghen wilde dat sij haer spot met hem hilde; 27–28). Now that he knows her intentions, he makes sure that she will at best catch a tame crow, a bird that, unlike the proud hawk, prefers a caged existence to freedom. "Reflect on it" (Bezint), the often highly sympathetic copyist has jotted underneath the poem—which is clearly intended as a literary puzzle. The solution is not too difficult to find: a prospective lover is refusing to fall into the maiden's net like a winged bird. Courtly love and male emancipation are not mutually exclusive.

But how shall we interpret another poem, no. 58? (See fig. 11.) Here the copyist has added, "Think carefully" (Besint wael). Had he failed to unravel the mystery, or did he feel (unlike the present author) that the solution would come to anyone who concentrates on it?

> Gonst ter eeren ghepresenteert
> Op eenen vlinse ghefundeert
> Enen volmaecten sonder ghelijch
> Toern; boven wenschen, consten rijch
> Is hi ghewracht, want calc ende steen
> Is louter gout, ghepureert reen,
> Van arab goud ende dure.
> Om desen gaet eene mure
> Hoghe ende starc, ghemaect wale,
> Ende al ghewracht van harden stale.
> Op desen torn ziet men staen
> Eenen hulseboem, wide ondaen
> Mit menneghen scerpen blade;
> Al den torn gheeft hi scade.
> In den boem te middeweerde
> Staet een bloem van groeter weerde,
> Altoes bloyende ende van verwen rijch,
> Men sach nie bloem haer ghelijch.
> Ses sijn der bloemen blade,

11. The *Haags liederenhandschrift* (Hague Song Manuscript) (including poem 58). (Koninklijke Bibliotheek, The Hague, MS. 128 E 2, fol. 32v)

Vol van doegden ende ghenaden.
Die te recht verstaet dit menen,
So sal men se al in eenen
Vinden, ende in hem duren:
Bloem, boem, cruut ende muren.

Proffered for the good of honor, resting on stone foundations, a perfect tower without equal; it is fashioned finely beyond all dreams, its mortar and stone being of pure, precious Arab gold. Round it runs a strong wall, firmly made of hard steel. On this tower stands a spreading holly tree, with many sharp leaves, providing shade for the entire tower. In the center of the tree is a precious, colorful flower, the like of which no one ever saw, in constant bloom. Six petals has the flower, full of virtue and grace. Whosoever wants to grasp their meaning, must find them all in permanent union: flower, tree, petals, and wall.

To solve this allegorical riddle, one must be familiar with the traditional imagery of the genre. In it, a tower or castle usually represented the perfect woman, and a flower wreathed in thorns had been used to represent feminine purity ever since the *Roman de la rose*. But what (qualities) did the petals represent in this poem, and what the metallic wall surrounding the tower? If we could discover another source with a reference to six feminine attributes used in combination, then we might be near to solving this riddle.[49] For, to repeat, allegorical puzzles become easier to solve the more familiar one is with the underlying tradition. Allegory is an esoteric genre.[50] In poem no. 103, an individual sings the praises of a sumptuous chamber in which he would give his life to dwell—no complex problem of interpretation for anyone conversant with the allegorical mode of representing the beloved's heart as a chamber in which the lover is happily ensconced.[51]

Here we come to a crucial feature of the *Haags liederenhandschrift*: to wit, it is written for connoisseurs. Anyone isolating a particular poem from its context so as to examine it like an independent work of art misses a dimension that, in its day, was essential for proper understanding: the dimension of the genre as such. It is essential that the poems be viewed together against the background of the whole. Each poem plays on a well-known theme, topic, and motif in its own way. The aesthetic fascination for the initiates lay precisely in the attempt to comprehend the subtle interplay of convention and variation. Thus, the poet was concerned not with originality in the modern, more spectacular sense of the word, but rather with originality within small bounds, that is, with finespun variations on a familiar theme. The kaleidoscope simile at the beginning of this section was introduced purposefully: from an artistic standpoint, the charm of the kaleidoscope and of courtly poetry can be considered identical. A fresh turn of the tube—a new poem—produces not a totally new picture but a rearrangement of the pieces in the last figure; the charm of successive views lies in the

exciting sensation of seeing the same pieces reappear in ever new config-
urations.

If, for greater clarity, the reader will permit another, rather quirky
analogy, I would say that the courtly love poetry in the *Haags liederenhandschrift* is reminiscent of figure skating. What is referred to as "free
skating" is not at all what the layman would describe as "free"; as he sees
it, successive skaters perform practically the same set leaps as the ones
who came before. The connoisseur, however, is interested precisely in
how the set movements are executed in detail, how they are combined
in a particular performance, and whether the skater ventures to introduce a fresh nuance—a counterturn, a twist, an unusual flip of the hand.
And whereas the layman may grow bored with the set display, the connoisseur can never get enough of the small, delicate refinements.

The aesthetics of the *Haags liederenhandschrift* must have had a similar effect on its original public, an audience raised on the codes of
courtly love poetry and, so to speak, accustomed to the key in which
such poems had been composed for over two centuries. The audience
knew, and expected to hear, the stock topics of courtly homage to
women, of enviers, of the simple delights of nature, of the urgent lover
and the almost unapproachable lady. Much the same was true of other
themes. The manuscript, indeed, comprises some twenty lovers' plaints,
and although we may assume that the original listeners were much more
aware of the conventional character of the verse than we are, they also
appreciated—and more sharply than we can—how each of those
twenty plaints differed minutely from the rest: a different verse construction, a different meter, a different stress. For a large part of the
audience, I stress again, the main aesthetic pleasure of this verse form
lay in the appreciation of these fine details, which explains why every
attempt (including mine here) to characterize the manuscript on the
evidence of more or less typical quotations is doomed to failure.

Nearly every poem in the *Haags liederenhandschrift* is a diversification
of utterly familiar motifs, sometimes to the point of ridicule.[52] Poem
no. 45, for example, seems to fit perfectly into the routine pattern of
lover's plaints, with the usual allusions (love being represented by a
hunt) and metaphors—until the last verse adds a twist astonishing for
lover and public alike: the relationship between lover and beloved
proves to be unlike anything one might expect even of unrequited love:

> O wee das ich so wael weys
> Der liever zin und haer beheys,

Des volgen ich der liever dan,
Ich arme, zender, trourich man.
Haddich mich selven und haer,
Si har selven ende mi, int war,
So wer 't herde wel gepast!
Mar des in es gheen effen last:
En hebbe mi selven, noch si mi,
Ich heb har, und zi is vri.
Hope und troest na min behagen
Dat loept achter lande jagen
Wildir vele dan enich wilt,
Ich blive leyder ongestilt,
Doe ich har clagede minen noet,
Vragede zi mi: is Brugge groet?

O dear, only too well do I know the disposition of the beloved whom I serve, miserable, pining, and sad man that I am. If I had myself and her as well, while she had herself and me, how well everything would then fit together! But that is not how matters stand: I have myself nor has she me; I have but her, and she is free. Hope and consolation are engaged in a wild and fruitless chase. When I told her my plight, she asked: "Is Bruges a large city?"

Courtly poetry as it appears in the *Haags liederenhandschrift* is an art form based on subtle variation rather than on originality. And because the modern reader finds this aesthetic approach strange, it was not until the middle of the present century that scholars came to appreciate that the monotony (as we see it) of, say, troubadour poetry is precisely what constituted its great attraction in earlier times. Robert Guiette, above all, pioneered this territory, and he applied the term *poésie formelle* to the genre—poetry based largely on minimal variation within a set frame. Guiette's terminology has since excited much analysis of many other types of medieval lyric poetry—including the Middle Dutch variety represented by Hadewijch and Gruuthuse.[53]

Nevertheless, the term "formal poetry" is somewhat misleading, for it suggests that the sole significance of these poems lies in their form and not their content.[54] It is doubtful that this was true of troubadour poetry, and it was certainly not true of German *Minnesang* or the *Haags liederenhandschrift*, even though the latter does reflect intense concern with the formal dimension, containing as it does a mass of varying rhyming and metrical schemes, aside from an almost giddy assortment of acrostics and wordplay.[55] A typical example is the ambiguous verse construction of the well-known poem by Augustijnken titled "Ridder die waldoen haet" (no. 32). Depending whether we read the first line of a pair of verses as a discrete unit or combine it with the beginning of the second line (the remainder of which, then, is read as a unit in itself), we come away with abuse or with praise:[56]

> Mich heeft een ridder die waldoen haet
> *Tot geenre tijt* hi es gemint
> Den trouwen goeden hi versmaet
> *Niet* hi es ter doecht gezint
> Tzu der archeit hi hem geeft
> *Node* ich hem doget wenschen
> Want argelist in hem cleeft
> *Alte zelden* hi eerlic leeft
> Ghelijc den goeden menschen.

I serve a knight who hates good deeds / *at no time* he is loved / the good and loyal he disdains / *not* to virtue he is inclined / to wickedness he gives himself / *never* do I wish him well / for guile can be found in him / *all too rarely* he lives honorably / as good people are wont to do.

Poetical wordplay as an end in itself has a tradition going back to long before the emergence of the chambers of rhetoric; literary critics at court valued formal virtuosity as well. Thus, in the twenty love plaints found in the *Haags liederenhandschrift*, attention was focused less on the substance of the lover's lament than on the various ways in which he voiced it. Still, that does not mean that the contents were of no importance, for the contents, though everchanging in form, conveyed the self-same courtly message. Here we seem to be faced with a contradiction: subtle literary play for its own sake versus the didactic objective discussed above. This contradiction, however, vanishes if we look more closely at the social context and the function of courtly literature as they are manifested in the *Haags liederenhandschrift*, this (as Nijland puts it) "remarkable anthology."[57]

4. THE COURT AT PLAY

In a book concerned with literature as a social phenomenon, it is impossible not to consider how the *Haags liederenhandschrift* related to historical reality. True, the book's courtly significance seems at first utterly remote from real life, according even less than William of Hildegaersberch's didactic poetry with the sordid, complicated, enthralling flow of historical events. No politics, no economics, no strife—just love. Yet even if these courtly poems seem divorced from social reality, the fact that they must have been read or heard in some social context, even if only as an escape from the commonplace, leads us to ask how this formal literature related to the society in which it flourished. At the end of section 3, on connoisseurs of literature, we mentioned in passing the assumed social context of the *Haags liederenhandschrift*. Before we continue with that theme, however, let us recall the preceding section, where an attempt was made to define the conception of love enshrined in the manuscript. The reader may be wondering just how that conception fitted the then customary relations between the sexes.

Significant is the fact that, although the *Haags liederenhandschrift* dwells at such length on wooing, it has little to say about wedding. Marriage is totally ignored; it does not even appear as a lovers' dream or ideal, much less as a genuine prospect. That realization, however, tells us as much about our own morals and customs as it does about the *Haags liederenhandschrift*. The fusion of marriage and love as a social norm was effected by enlightened eighteenth-century bourgeois society (though with beginnings at least a century before). In the Middle Ages, marriage and love—certainly in the exalted circles described here— were distinct. Marriage was, above all, a social contract, entered into for reasons of family politics, dynastic need, and territorial or social advantage, and hence usually arranged by the parents. The feelings of the prospective couple seldom mattered, and even more seldom the question of whether or not they were in love with each other. Joanna of Polanen, whom Nijland considers the original recipient of the *Haags liederenhandschrift*, married Engelbert of Nassau on 1 August 1403; the bridegroom was in his thirties, his little bride eleven.[58] The motive was money, not affection. Bride and groom probably first met at the altar. Much the same concerns prompted the hastily arranged marriage of Duke Albert. Here, too, the motive was not love; it was power. True, such power also entailed a vigorous sexual exchange; as the festive orator Hildegaersberch put it (see Chapter II, sec. 1), the national interest demands children. The groom's impending "lying" with the bride was accordingly entered in the count's ledgers, much like any other administrative business.

Not long before that, in 1385, Holland had witnessed what, by contemporary standards, was a truly magnificent wedding. Seldom had there been such a diplomatic feat: a son and a daughter of Duke Albert both entered into marriage with a daughter and a son of Philip, duke of Burgundy! It was a political masterstroke by Albert and gained Holland a mighty ally (although the Burgundians finally had the best of the bargain). Complicated negotiations had preceded the marriage—about the dowry, the inheritance, the rights of future children upon the death of various family members, the papal dispensation needed for so high a degree of consanguinity, and so forth. Anyone reviewing the moves of this political chess game six centuries after the event is bound to look on the four young newlyweds as little more than pawns, the exchange of which, moreover, led—as desired—to a draw. When the great moment finally arrived, there before the altar in Kamerik stood the twenty-two-year-old Margaret of Bavaria and her twenty-year-old brother, William, together with thirteen-year-old John and ten-year-old Margaret, their Burgundian marriage partners. How the principals felt about that wedding we cannot say; all we know is that on her wedding day the Burgundian bride had only barely recovered from chicken pox and that the mother of the bride from Holland had sent two separate requests for permission to provide, in place of the usual squire, "a maid for my maiden [i.e., the bride] after she had been bedded, as she is delicate and as strangers are not as familiar with her ways as those who are daily with her."[59]

All this does not automatically mean that such arranged marriages were mournful or tragic, even by our standards. Couples then simply worked under a different set of expectations. Mutual respect between the partners sufficed to make a marriage tolerable, even happy—provided, of course, such respect was given concrete expression in the shape of children. Seen in this light, extramarital love did not necessarily cause insuperable problems. That it did not at the court of Holland-Bavaria is most vividly demonstrated by the many illegitimate children fathered by Albert and William, children who figure in the official documents as if nothing could be more natural. Besides seven legal descendants, we know that Albert had as many extramarital ones; William VI's one legitimate daughter, Jacqueline of Bavaria, had to share her father with ten illegitimate siblings. Such facts alone justify the conclusion that adultery was as integral a part of daily life at the court of Holland as elsewhere. This is corroborated by the accounts, which abound with the favors that Duke Albert, in particular, bestowed on ladies at his court, including money, knickknacks, jewels, and other luxuries. The rarest favor, however, must been the duke's instruction to have the court lake emptied for the sake of a lady who had playfully dropped a diamond into it. In Albert's displays of gallantry, it was hard to tell ends from means: to dredge up that diamond, the wall at the sluice had to be breached, later to be hastily replaced with a double dam to prevent half the estate from becoming swamped.[60]

Albert was nearly sixty when he issued this impetuous order—clearly, age had not diminished his sexual vitality and needs. During his second marriage, for example (when he was well past fifty), the accounts record gratuities to Albert's mistress in Hainaut and to "Little Belle and the two children she has had with my lord."[61] In addition, Albert, either accompanied by his son or alone, was in the habit of visiting various *stoven* (dubious bathhouses) in the village of Die Haghe, which must have doubled as "massage parlors" for the noble visitors; after all, if all they wanted was a bath, they did not have to leave the Binnenhof—and certainly not after 1401, when a luxurious bathroom was added under the keen eye of Master Engelbert (builder of Egmont Abbey).[62] Albert also had mistresses within his court: the accounts give us glimpses of amorous relations with (in close succession following the celebrated Adelaide of Poelgeest) Lady Barbara, Lady Catherine of Domburch, Lady Catherine of Hoogstraten, Adelaide of Houthuizen, Lady Agnes of Merensteyn, and Matilda, the noble Walter's daughter. What their possible husbands, brothers, and fathers thought of these affairs the accounts do not tell us. In any case, they apparently caused no particular problems; even if the men concerned did not feel flattered (perhaps hoping for princely favors outside the bedchamber), they were in no position to make trouble.

Yet it cannot be claimed that such liaisons *never* caused trouble. Official morality remained bitterly opposed to adultery. Indeed, it almost seems as if William of Hildegaersberch had the duke himself in mind when he declared that "however great our rank on earth, we may for honor nor for sport usurp another's man's escort" (Hoe veel dat wy ter werlt vermoghen, men sal om wille noch om d'eren nyemants bedde-noot begheren; IV/536–38)—and the emphasis that in this poem (on the Ten Commandments) he gave to adultery in particular suggests he had good cause for doing so.[63] Dirk of Delft's writings point in the same direction, for here pride shares its traditional first place among the deadly sins with unchastity, presented mainly as adultery.[64] Naturally, as court chaplain Dirk was professionally bound to rail against this particular evil. And if we read about the tortures and worse he claims were reserved for adulterers in hell, we can feel some compassion for the expiring Albert, whom Dirk saw fit to terrify with such threats on his deathbed.

Church strictures on lax morals at court cannot be dismissed as routine condemnations by unworldly moralizers, men of whom the aristocracy would otherwise have taken little notice. In fact, solid evidence indicates that the medieval court elite was slowly coming around to what had originally been the exclusive moral preserve of the church and was making attempts to blend marriage with love.[65] In Holland, Dirk Potter was the best-known advocate of this course. As we shall see, however, his disposition toward marriage was rather unusual, possibly because Potter was of the lowest nobility; the chances of finding a partner who was socially as well as emotionally suitable decreased as one advanced up the social ladder.

These remarks seem to have removed us far from the *Haags liederenhandschrift*. In fact, though, the manuscript's attitude toward love shows through in exceptionally vivid relief when examined against this background. At the very least, it is tempting (and probably justified) to view the *Haags liederenhandschrift* partly in terms of the tension between the official and the semiofficial morality. If we do that, we shall find that the manuscript decides squarely in favor of true love—the semiofficial approach, that is. It ignores marriage, but speaks only of *natural* love, entered into freely and without the coercion of third parties. Nevertheless, the hostility of the outside world is explicitly introduced, personified by the ubiquitous enviers determined to ruin simple happiness with their foul tongues. Before they could accomplish their evil, though, they had to discover or concoct fuel for their gossip—but that was not difficult to do, for the "natural" choice of partners almost automatically brought lovers into conflict with their surroundings, specifically with the demand that girls remain virgins until their marriage. The overriding concern with reputation, and in the background, the feud between the Cods and the Hooks, must have combined to create suffocating social constraints. Hatred of the enviers, fear of malicious gossip (*claffen*), and the need to conceal (*helen*) one's true feelings, then, appear as the logical concomitants of a code designed to protect "free" love from outside pressure. Viewed thus, the *Haags liederenhandschrift* champions emotions that must shun the bright light of a love hailed as gentle, innocent, sincere.

If we take that view, however, our interpretation risks becoming one-sided, for it reduces the *Haags liederenhandschrift* to a treatise on adulterous—or at least socially questionable—love. In fact, though, while the major theme of the manuscript is the conflict between the "inner and outer norms" of love, many poems ignore the externals completely and concentrate on love as an independent phenomenon. The role of the enviers can, in fact, be understood just as well from that angle: they bespeak the fear of having pure love sullied by the crude intervention of outsiders. In general, the approach we have been discussing does too little justice to the manuscript's literary function, to the possibility that these poems were popular simply because they belonged to a preferred literary genre—that they were an end in themselves. The idea of "play" introduced in the last section to define the purely literary aesthetics of the *Haags liederenhandschrift* is equally applicable to the extraliterary purpose of the manuscript and of courtly love poetry in general.[66] Courtly culture was, most essentially, playful culture, a culture in which the elite tried to set itself apart from the rest of society, aided by a deliberately cultivated, playful life-style.

That style assumed a variety of forms, all reflecting the attempt to present beauty, luxury, and pleasure as practical possibilities. A central feature was the code of love and of courtly homage to women. Anyone could join in this game who proclaimed himself a lover and acted the gallant, whether he in fact was one or not. Here, fiction and fact were intertwined; private emotions flowered (or withered) in the enactment of a collective role. Although rarely ensconced in formal rules, this role playing was sufficiently well defined in practice, certainly for all participants. For those who, like the modern reader, must remain outsiders, the whole drama may resemble an incomprehensible charade, defined by a jumble of rules and permissible moves. To try to uncover a system behind it at any cost—is courtly love necessarily adulterous? must the lady always be put on a pedestal? is love hopeless by definition?—means misunderstanding the essence of a social phenomenon that derived its vitality precisely from the possibility that each individual might express himself freely in certain courtly pastimes. In this unfolding of the personality, song and poetry—centered on ritual homage to women—were crucial, along with dancing, feasting, cultivated conversation, gentlemanly attentions, discussions of courtly love, up to the most complicated games and plays.

Among these more elaborate games, the famous Parisian Court of Love of 1401 was undoubtedly paramount.[67] Its founding charter declared that on Twelfth Night of that year, Charles VI of France and the dukes Louis of Bourbon and Philip of Burgundy had established a *cour amoureuse*. It was organized along the lines of a genuine court: at its head was a king (*Prince de la cour d'amour*) supported by a council (*amoureux conseil*), three conservators-in-chief (the noble founders themselves), eleven conservators, and twenty-four *ministres*. These latter were obliged on every festival of love—"joieuse feste de puy d'amour"—to offer love poems written by their own hands, and to vie for a

12.   Chess in the garden of love; below: the so-called game of kings? (The Pierpont Morgan Library, New York, MS. 691, fol. 131v)

prize awarded by the other nobles. Such festivals were to be held monthly; in addition, there would be three special annual celebrations: on Lady Day, on a day in May, and—the main festival—on St. Valentine's Day (14 February). During the last celebration, all subjects were obliged to be present for "joieuse recréacion et amoureuse conversacion," at which time poetic courtiers could submit their love songs to the expert opinion of a jury of noble ladies. Every one of these poems had to be "sur sa propre amoureuse, et non sur un autre"; strictly proscribed were all disrespectful references to women. Anyone who had slighted women in real life would be expelled from the court of love.

Historical research suggests that the Parisian Court of Love never actually met; perhaps it was asking too much to summon nearly all the European nobles to a festival of love. Even so, the underlying idea was a true reflection of the aristocratic play culture that enveloped poetry and courtly love. In addition, although this particular *cour d'amour* was to be founded in France, it is significant that two members of the Bavarian aristocracy were singled out for special roles. (By all accounts, the idea came from the then queen of France, Isabella of Bavaria, a niece of Count Albert of Holland.) First, the proposed king of the court was Pierre d'Hauteville, a high Hainaut official in the service of William of Oostervant whose close links with Holland were enshrined in his Dutch motto, "God danc"—thanks be to God. Second, William of Oostervant himself was to serve as a conservator; according to the founding deeds, his enthusiasm for the enterprise was such that he offered to pay his membership fee of one hundred golden crowns to the king of France in hard cash.

In high society, clearly, the House of Holland-Bavaria was of considerable account. Did its members live in appropriate splendor at the court in The Hague? The question is difficult to answer, for the relevant historical sources (the accounts, once again) have not yet been adequately examined. Nevertheless, we have various positive indications, of which the most concrete come from the history of art. A telling document depicting the court of Holland at play is the well-known drawing (fig. 13) of a festive company of courtly anglers, in whose midst we can identify William VI and his daughter, Jacqueline (and probably Duke Albert as well). Their costumes are in the latest (Burgundian) fashion: the ladies wear luxurious dresses tucked in high under the breast, with long trains and wide sleeves; the men are in either long *houppelandes* or half-length *houppelandes à mi-jambe*. While the ladies' hairstyles are varied and ingenious, the men's headgear is at least as fashionable. In short, the company is dressed for courting, not angling. The strict segregation of the sexes on opposite banks of the river tells us the same: what is depicted is, in fact, a metaphorical fishing party, with a sweetheart as the catch.[68]

13.   Group portrait of the House of Holland-Bavaria at a fishing party. The ladies include the Countess Jacqueline (in front) and possibly Margaret of Cleves (second from left); the gentlemen include William VI (front right, wearing the insignia of the Order of the Garter) and perhaps Duke Albert (extreme right). The central figure is John of Bavaria (with falcon and Order of Saint Anthony). Fifteenth-century colored drawing in the style of Jan van Eyck. (Musée du Louvre, Paris, Cabinet des Dessins no. 20674)

The engraving known as "The Great Garden of Love" (fig. 14) probably derives from a slightly later period but the same environment. Here motifs of literary origin such as those with which the *Haags liederen-handschrift* abounds are perpetuated in copper: in a paradise fenced off from enviers and the grosser outside world, fashionable lovers have gathered for song, reading (the man holding a [love] letter), games (here, cards), and a *déjeuner sur l'herbe*. The birds warble; wineflasks have been hung in a brook to be kept cool (much as love grows cool, metaphorically speaking?) by water purified by a unicorn's magical horn. Although the print was not meant to appear realistic, it does have links both with the *gaerde* (garden) in which Dirk Potter liked to set his courting scenes and with the bowers that are known to have graced the court in The Hague (to assist such gallant diversions?).[69] As an idealized fantasy, moreover, it tells us much about how the court of Holland-Bavaria liked to regard itself. The engraving has been sometimes interpreted as illustrating the lovers' paradise of which Jacqueline of Bavaria and Frank of Borselen dreamed; but even if this reading should be mistaken, the print, corroborated by its provenance and date, gives clear

14. The Great Garden of Love of Jacqueline of Bavaria and Frank of Borselen. (Staatliche Museen Preußischer Kulturbesitz, Kupferstichkabinett, Berlin. Photo: Jörg P. Anders)

evidence that the court of Holland-Bavaria had become a player in the international game of courtly love.[70] In a dynastic order so closely interlocked, how could it have been otherwise?

Certain entries in the count of Holland's accounts seem to indicate the same. One of the most relevant is the oft-mentioned reference to a May song written by Duke Albert himself, in which he undoubtedly sang the praises of women and nature. The theme of the court at play was also reflected in Countess Margaret of Cleves's orders to an embroideress to make *caproenen* (caps) for her pages and her masters of the horse on which the words "sal ic niet drinken" (I shall not drink) were to be boldly displayed—a courtly joke, no doubt, but perhaps also a sober warning against drinking while on duty.[71] Purely playful, however, was the same countess's order for seventeen *caproenen* to be embroidered with the words "clinghet niet, so en geldet niet; is 't niet gec, so en doghet niet" (unless it tinkles, it does not count; unless it is silly, it is out of place). Was this a reference to fools' caps (with tinkling bells) as a sort of club badge for a fashionable company playing the fool on Shrove Tuesday?

Carnival, of course, was a grand occasion for Hague courtiers to play the fool in an atmosphere of amorous dalliance. In 1387, Albert organized a large Shrove Tuesday party to which he invited all the noble ladies in Holland "to keep my lord company on this Shrove Tuesday with dancing, feasting, and merrymaking."[72] Apparently the party was a resonant success, because Albert arranged a similar feast two years later, dispatching shield-shaped admission warrants to all those invited (against payment). During the five days of these celebrations, Albert, Adelaide of Poelgeest, and other merrymakers went boating on the court lake, where their boat capsized. Unfortunately, the accounts mention only the costs of this small mishap and not how it happened.

New Year's Day, too, was a festival when love often paraded at court seeking offerings and allegiance. The accounts repeatedly mention gifts made by the count on that occasion—and when it came to presents for ladies, the count's celebrated instincts, those of lover and hunter in one, make it easy to imagine ulterior motives. Here literature again bears witness, for two French rondels in the Leiden manuscript (which also included the songs of Fabri and Boy) describe the custom of handing presents to one's beloved on New Year's Day.[73] With typical courtly hyperbole, the lover in one of the two poems declares that that year he is making a present of himself. In reality, of course, the presents were usually rings or other gleaming baubles, often accompanied by suitable verses.

Small gifts frequently served to stoke the fires of noble love. At the junction of courtly literature and everyday reality are the curious slippers exposed in recent archaeological digs (for example from the well of the Beguine court in Mechelen), which are believed to have been given as presents to lovers in fourteenth- and early-fifteenth-century Holland and Brabant. A scene from the *Roman de Tristan* has been cut into the leather of the slippers, representing concealment, a well-known literary motif of courtly love.[74] (A lover anxious not to awaken sleeping enviers does well to keep his feet in slippers, not in boots.)

One of the most interesting forms of literary court play was the *cour d'amour*.[75] Here, the players asked one another difficult questions about courtly love and tried to compose elegant responses. The *Haags liederenhandschrift* includes several examples, again documenting the close relationship between the manuscript and actual play.[76] Poem no. III, for instance, tells us how "a lovely maid of tender years" asked the company (in an obvious allusion) what one should do who has put her soul and happiness into the building of a lovely castle that nevertheless collapses. "When her question she had asked, each said in turn what he thought best" (Doe si haer vragen had bevraecht, yeghelic sprac dat hem goet dochte)—until the narrator himself intervened: "I asked the fair, good maid for leave to have my say" (ic bad der sueser, werder maecht, of ic dat solveren mochte). His answer: it all depends on what caused the castle to collapse. No castle is so strong that some enemy cannot lay it waste, but if that happens, it can always be rebuilt on the old founda-tions. Things are much worse if the castle simply collapses: in that case the foundations are too weak, and they, too, will have to be rebuilt. "All the good and worthy wives would do well to heed my words" (Alle gueten werden wiven, ghevic hier exempel aen).

Although he does not openly admit it, we may take it that the narra-tor's own answer was acclaimed the best—that, in case of love trouble, ladies (in particular) should try to discover its cause and then act accord-ingly. This lesson may be further evidence of the didactic intention of the manuscript; nevertheless, to all players in this aristocratic contest of question and answer, the game itself was at least as important as the solution, fine company giving every competitor the opportunity to dis-course on some intricacy of love and passion and thus present himself as a true courtly lover. It mattered little whether the riddle, pun, anagram, or metrical complexity could be acted upon or even whether it related to personal experience; the enchantment, the thrill, was to imagine one-self an adored and gallant lover and join in the revelry.

The same applies to the genre most strongly represented in the *Haags liederenhandschrift*—the poetic effusions of a lover speaking in the first person. The intimate tone of many of these poems almost makes one forget that, generally, the author was merely trying to earn his profes-sional bread and butter, not rejoicing over personal good fortunes or lamenting his own woes. Most of the manuscript is, in fact, the work of (anonymous) professionals paid to interpret the role of lovers before a courtly public. Admittedly, real emotions may sometimes have been in-volved as well. We must probably believe Dirk Potter, for instance, a full-blooded courtier who certainly ought to have known, when he de-clares in his moral diatribe against *luxurie* (lust) (*BD* 79/20–24):

Item soe sal men scuwen soeticheit van sanghe, van melodien ende die ghe-noechte van instrumenten, van dansen ende des ghelijcs; want Pictagoras seit, soe die cruden wel wassen ende groyen biden kanten der rivieren, soe groyet luxurie biden instrumenten ende melodien.

One should eschew also mellifluous song, sweet sounds and musical enjoyment, dancing, and the like; for Pythagoras has said: as the grass grows on both river-banks, so lust thrives on music and melody.

Far more important than personal amorous dilemmas, however, is the *collective* surrender to that happiness, that perfumed delirium, which is the cause and effect of courtly love poetry. The true objective of courtly song and dance was *gladness*, not romance.[77] There was thought to be a causal nexus between love and song: the one fosters the other. When everything prospers, universal joy abounds—on the personal level through the bond between lovers, on the collective level through participation in the courtly game. The whole court was absorbed in the festive cult of courtly love, with the court poet, so to speak, leading the rest.

Whether one joined in this cult because of a personal romantic encounter was of secondary importance; nor did it really matter whether the players were young or old, of higher or lower rank—though they would, of course, be confined to courtly society. Indeed, courtly love was primarily a mental attitude, a vision of life shared by all the court— and totally denied to outsiders.[78] The courtly love game had an internally cohesive, and externally exclusive, effect, as several passages from the *Haags liederenhandschrift* explicitly state (here, 95/33–35 and no. 66*, respectively):

> Coningen, vorsten, greve, heren,
> Ritter, knechte, dienstman
> Ziet men in vrouwendienst keren.

Kings, princes, counts, lords, knights, squires, pages are drawn into courtly homage to women.

> Der vrouwen recht is, dat si selen
> Mit ridder onde knechte spelen
> Onde vrulich cortsyn hem den tsijt.
> Al hebben dies die dorpers nijt,
> Daerum en sullen sijs nie laten,
> Goet spel is goet, unde dat te maten.

It is a woman's right to play with knights and squires, and to while her time merrily away in such company. Even though the villagers may envy them, they need not cease: good games are good, provided they are kept within bounds.

The envious *dorpers*, or villeins, were not included in these games; the courtly playing field was reserved for *goede lude*—good society.[79]

Courtly love, with its exclusive literary code and life-style, acted as a cement both of court society and—by no means least—of the sexes.

It is, in fact, reasonable to assume that women had a particular interest in the game, because in day-to-day life they were apt to be treated disdainfully, sometimes cruelly. Courtly literature, in vivid contrast, declared them to be the crown of creation. Not surprisingly, then, there are strong indications that in the heyday of the courtly play culture ladies were its vibrant impulse.[80] It seems no accident, for instance, that the Parisian *cour d'amour* of 1401 appears to have been planned by a woman. Moreover, women seem also to have been involved in the writing of the *Haags liederenhandschrift* (in some passages, indeed, the book's general sympathy for women reads almost like propaganda),[81] and one is all the more tempted to consider some lady like Joanna of Polanen as its original recipient. There is historical corroboration for the notion that such noble ladies in The Hague were collectors and connoisseurs of love poetry, as they were farther south, at the courts of France and, formerly, in Provence. In Chapter I (sec. 4), I mentioned the (now lost) "new poetry books" brought in 1408 to the wife of Count William VI by "a man from France": these were almost certain to have contained courtly poetry. Even more telling is an item from the interesting letters of Margaret of Nassau to her aunt, Countess Matilda of Guelders—namely, a reference to an enclosure (alas, also lost): "I am also sending you three little songs I have newly made and which you might enter in the little book" (Ouch sendde ich dir dry leydergin, de hain ich nuwe gemacht, de saltu in den buechgelgin schrijven).[82] In other words, these two poetry-loving noblewomen exchanged New Year's greetings, one of them enclosing a seasonal present of three new poems (on loose sheets) with the request that the other copy them into what must have been a poetry album. The countess of Nassau, who wrote these poems, was the grandmother of Count John IV (who eventually came into possession of the *Haags liederenhandschrift*) and the mother-in-law of Joanna of Polanen. Was it on the basis of such privately owned "little books" as her aunt's album that professional copyists were later commissioned to produce the *Haags liederenhandschrift*?

Yet here we are in danger of restricting too severely the circle to whom the *Haags liederenhandschrift* appealed. For the essence of this literature was that it addressed itself to court society as a whole; clearly, it could not have flourished as it did had men, too, not fully contributed to the fashion of paying literary homage to love. Now, let me reiterate that the concept of play is crucial to any understanding of this genre. Only that ambivalent idea, with its two facets—fantasy and reality—can help to resolve the contradiction in which the last section threatened to founder. One is quite mistaken to dismiss this literature as fiction divorced from the historical reality of court life; love poetry was as much a part of that reality as the "socially committed" verses of William of Hildegaersberch or, for that matter, the official records of the chancellery clerks. Nevertheless, it would be erroneous to think that the cult of courtly love reflected court culture at its most authentic. It was, after all, mainly on special festive occasions, not on an everyday basis, that the court permitted itself to break from routine, etiquette, and the ritual ceremonies of the theater of power—during May celebrations, on Shrove Tuesday, in a bower, at a feast, or during a tournament.

Of these occasions, too, Hildegaersberch was an acute observer, and his poem quoted at the beginning of this chapter proves much less unrealistic than it may at first have appeared. It shows the court at its merriest: the weather is fair, and a gallant company has assembled to play in the open air, luxuriating in the silken comforts and spirit of court life while being regaled with music and dance. And if their songs included verses recorded in the *Haags liederenhandschrift*, the listeners would have been not only gladdened but also instructed in the elaborate niceties of courtliness. Play helped this highborn community to express, confirm, and constitute itself as if in a single flourish. Play was not really the radical flight from reality that Huizinga considered it to be, but a brief outing, a respite.

The code of courtly love was by no means remote from quotidian reality: a stylized, consciously elitist, amiable, and gallant attitude to worldly pleasure was constantly in place at the court of Holland-Bavaria. Even so, artificial situations had to be created for that attitude to reach fruition: beyond bower and banqueting hall one found few opportunities for such refined expression.

The relatively fictitious nature of courtly poetry is most clearly illustrated by one of the central dogmas of the *Haags liederenhandschrift*: the postulate of a causal link between wooing and fighting. In courtly poetry, these appear as necessary complements—when the knight does battle, he becomes a better lover; and when he loves, he becomes a better fighter. In the actual heat of battle such ideals could at most have been confined to rare champions, because then fighting was a contest of life and death and not merely a proof of one's prowess as a lover. Around the mid–fourteenth century, when Philip of Leiden discussed certain incidents in the war between Holland and Utrecht, he observed regretfully that the knights of Holland were less brave than their reputation had suggested.[83] He blamed this situation on their womanizing: "The bobbin guides the thread but not the sword raised in battle." This lawyer from Leiden will not have been alone in realizing that noble love and feats of arms are more incompatible than courtly poetry liked to pretend. That love and chivalry were anything but inseparable will become amply clear in the next chapter, which examines an author at the court of Holland-Bavaria with unrivaled knowledge of war.

IV

Bavaria Herald

1. A SERVANT WITH AUTHORITY

According to the late-fifteenth-century chronicle by Johannes à Leydis, Count William of Oostervant—the later William VI of Holland—was one of many noble guests to attend a splendid banquet at the French court in 1395. Suddenly an elderly herald entered the festive hall, halted in front of William, and, before the count's astonished eyes, drove a knife into the table, ripping the tablecloth. The noble company was astounded: how had their Dutch guest deserved such provocation? In a loud voice, the herald then gave formal explanation: no nobleman whose ancestors' bones lay unavenged on enemy soil was worthy of sharing the king's table.[1]

The background of this dramatic incident will be examined below. First we must, however, look more closely at the man responsible: the herald. Even if the story of his demonstrative act is untrue (as it probably is), it is a masterly invention. The typecasting, for one, is perfect: only a herald could have taken such liberties with a medieval prince. For, although no more than humble servants, heralds were, so to speak, the final arbiters of chivalry and honor at medieval courts.[2] Originally they had merely constituted a subguild of itinerant performers who passed before medieval nobles or visited their courts in large numbers. It was in their company that minstrels gave voice to song (see Chapter III) and the didactic poets recited their verses (Chapter II), with the heralds themselves declaiming about chivalrous deeds. Yet as interest in heraldry grew during the Middle Ages, heralds gained in importance. Knights from all over flocked to tournaments in ever-increasing numbers; and, being covered in helmets and harness from head to toe, they could not be identified by their peers, let alone by the spectators. Hence there arose new styles of armor with heraldic emblems: a blazon on a shield, a badge on a helmet, and so on. Apart from being functional, such distinctions were also decorative: the glistening display of gules, sable, azure, and other heraldic colors, of symbolic emblems on helmets, horse blankets, flags, banners, and pennons, amply expressed the thirst for greater elegance and resplendent fanfare so typical of the waning Middle Ages. Along with the practical and aesthetic purpose, heraldry also had a broader function: similar armorial bearings reflected links, for instance, between allied families or knights in a particular army. It was mainly as a result of the last that armorial bearings quickly became hereditary attributes rather than remaining purely individual distinctions, and thus marked their bearers as members of a particular group.

The identification of armorial bearings soon became the task of a special profession. While it was relatively easy to recognize local knights, how was one to identify the large number of warriors who toured the international jousting circuit like so many itinerant athletes? (We shall return to jousting as a form of sport in section 4.) Identification was the job of the heralds: their work made them experts on the intricacies of international knighthood. At tournaments, they increasingly acted as masters of ceremony, introducing the various heroes and recalling their earlier feats of arms. Indeed, because they were widely traveled, it was conceivable that the heralds had personally witnessed these momentous achievements. Apart from being tournament reporters, heralds—who by now regularly dressed in smart livery—acted more and more often as officials, supervising the elaborate proceedings on behalf of the noble host. They would discuss rules with the leaders of the various parties, register the participants, ensure fair play on the ground, and see to it that the prizes were properly awarded. And since none of the participants knew as much about jousting as they did, the heralds, judged to be impartial experts, quite often had the further task of declaring the winners.

Heralds flourished from the late thirteenth century on, when they became what may be called the high priests of the chivalrous life. Not surprisingly, a hierarchy soon emerged, ranging from simple pursuivants (attendant heralds) through the actual heralds to the highly respected kings of arms, who often appeared within the immediate entourage of their prince, together with his personal physician, secretary, and confessor. Now, too, heralds came to serve as masters of ceremony at large—not only at tournaments, but also at other important chivalrous occasions, including accolades, weddings, and military funerals. On their masters' behalf, heralds traveled throughout Europe, acting as simple messengers (announcing a tournament, for instance) but also as official envoys. As such they could pass safely to and fro between hostile armies—unless they were suspected of spying (sometimes for good reasons) and put to death. But then, spying was not a job for a proper herald.

Most heralds knew what their office demanded. They enjoyed enormous authority in matters of chivalry, and although their authority was only semiofficial, it extended into a field of critical importance to aristocrats of the late Middle Ages. Here, heralds were the acknowledged specialists; not only did they know the most prominent of foreign knights and how tournaments had ended elsewhere, but they could also recount the chivalrous life of days gone by. Who had been the greatest knights, not just a generation ago, but in antiquity? Had Hector really been a greater fighter than Achilles? What were the foremost feats of arms of Hannibal, Hercules, David, and Alexander? And what was the intricate network representing the relationships between the various princely dynasties and noble families? These were all questions of moment: seniority was of vital concern for the nobility. Did the dukes of Brabant have cause to pride themselves on their descent from the French royal family? Did the pedigree of the English kings really derive from the Trojans? How had the German emperor gained his imperial crown, and why was he elected rather than reigning by right of birth? Was there any truth in the rumor that the House of Blois was descended from the traitor Ganelon? How did Flanders become a county? Heralds were the oracles to be consulted on such questions; it was their business to know the answers.

Hence, it is not surprising that some heralds should have committed their specialized knowledge to paper. After all, words about great deeds had been their profession even when they were merely itinerant performers. The books that flowed from their ranks (needless to say, by the pens of a pioneering minority) covered such subjects as heraldry, genealogy, and chivalry past and present. Many heralds produced so-called armorials: systematically arranged, portable books depicting the largest possible number of coats of arms, with gaps to be filled in later—heraldic stamp albums, one might say. Heralds also wrote texts to accompany these illustrations, chronicles of famous campaigns and *Erenredes*, homiletic verses in honor of famous knights and presented as inspiring examples for posterity.

Heralds were of course no strangers to the court of Holland-Bavaria. The accounts kept in the General State Archives, which usually include a special section for "pipers and heralds," show them arriving in large numbers. Mentioned are such individuals as "Ghenp den yraude die den hof beriep die was tot Nymaghen" (Ghenp herald, who brought an invitation to the court at Nijmegen); Cleves herald, "die den hof van Cleve beriep" (who brought an invitation to the court at Cleves); Jerusalem herald, who, on 2 September 1337, conveyed a message from the king of Cyprus; the heralds Crabbendijck and Keyser, who announced a *boerte*, or comical tourney, to be held in Brussels the Sunday after Whitsun; the herald (from) Apcoude; the herald Jan Dille; and visiting heralds who obviously appealed to the court because of their youth or glittering uniforms, such as "a tiny little herald known as Jan the Hollander" (een cleen hyeraudekijn, gheheten meester Jan die Hollander) and "Little Friend" (Vriendekijn), the duke of Brabant's herald.[3]

The counts of Holland did not only receive heralds from near and far; they also employed heralds of their own. By custom, these men often bore the name of one of the territories over which their authority extended; thus, at the court of Holland there were, in addition to the expected Hollant Herald, a Henau (Hainaut) Herald, a Zeelant Herald, and a Vrieslant Herald. The leading herald at this court was, however, Bavaria Herald. He was a king of arms and, indeed, one of the greatest: ever since being invested with the title of *armoris rex de Ruyris* he had been the most prominent herald in the entire Netherlands, the Rhenish parts included.[4] In keeping with his high office, this court servant, like his colleagues at the courts of England and France, moved in his lord's immediate circle—so much so that Count William VI even challenged him to a game of chess (played for money, naturally).[5]

By the time Bavaria Herald acquired this status at the court of Holland, he had had full experience elsewhere. He had been herald at the court of Guelders, an appointment he obviously recalled with fondness, since, at the end of his life, he still signed himself as "Beyeren quondam Gelre, armorum rex de Ruyris." That signature, in fact, was typical of the man. Nowhere did he mention that his real name was Claes Heynenzoon. By the time he became a herald, that office had become a respected profession, and so he adopted it as his name. Even in his Guelders days, he had risen high as Gelre Herald, for instance accompanying the knights led by his later employer, William of Oostervant, to Prussia in 1386–87, and traveling with William I of Guelders to England in 1390, for which occasion he had been given the task, characteristic of his ceremonial function, of purchasing (heraldic) flags for the fleet. Once in

England, moreover, he did some more spending: he bought bells to attach to the ships' flags. That voyage to England, a kingdom ruled by the sophisticated Richard II, and with a rich heraldic tradition even then, must have been very thrilling for a man of such passionate interests.

As Gelre Herald he had written about his experiences. His *Wapenboek Gelre* (Guelders armorial), now one of the treasures of the Royal Library in Brussels, has rightly been called the most beautiful armorial left to us by medieval Europe. At its heart is a collection of no less than 1,800 arms drawn in the most glorious colors by outstanding artists (presumably the famous Maelwael brothers from Nijmegen—their name meaning Paint Well). The arms are arranged in the hierarchic order of the European dynasties they represent, for, as befitted a herald, Gelre was a traditionalist: first the German emperor and his liegemen in order of rank, then the French king with his liegemen, followed by the English crown, and so on to Scotland and Aragon. The German emperor—in Gelre Herald's eyes, the noblest prince on earth—is also depicted on a full-page miniature, where, as the incarnation of authority, he appears in the midst of the seven electors. Nor did Gelre Herald overlook himself: another full-page miniature shows him in his official dress (fig. 15). It is again typical of the man that on this drawing his face should be less clear than the surcoat with the lion of Guelders.

Yet the *Wapenboek Gelre* is not just a collection of splendid illustrations; it also makes interesting reading. Such, too, one would expect of a herald: a rhymed chronicle on the leading European families and poems about great feats of arms both distant in time and more recent. All in all, the duke of Guelders seems to have had a devoted herald in Claes Heynenzoon. The archives, moreover, make it clear that the duke recognized his servant's value, for in 1400 he made him an annual grant of rye for the "many and various loyal services he has rendered us, continues to render us day after day, and may yet come to render us" (vele ende mennige truwe dienste die [hi] ons gedaen heeft, ende dach bij daghe duedt, ende noch doen mach).

That last hope was to be disappointed, though. It appears that, at most three years after that date, Gelre Herald took service with Holland to become Duke Albert of Bavaria's herald-in-chief. Well traveled as he was, he had previously been to the court of Holland on his official duties: as early as 1386, for example, he had made preparations in The Hague for his journey to Prussia, and in the spring of 1400 he had

15. Bavaria Herald as Guelders Herald. (Bibliothèque royale Albert Ier, Brussels, MS. 15652–56, fol. 122r)

stayed in The Hague for one and a half months before setting sail for Friesland with Duke Albert's fleet. Was it this sojourn that decided him to change masters? As we shall see, he bore the "filthy Frisians" a terrible grudge, and he could not have found a better place to vent his spleen against them than at the court of Holland, still anxious to settle old scores with Friesland. But in putting it so, we probably turn effect into cause. More likely, Claes Heynenzoon came to loathe the Frisians because he had been made Bavaria Herald.

What, then, were his reasons for leaving Guelders for Holland? The literary historian finds it tempting to conjecture (but only that) that the change was inspired in part by the flourishing artistic climate at the court of Holland. In any case, Holland could certainly outmatch Guelders in literature, and there the Herald could settle down to his new task with renewed devotion. He took the *Wapenboek Gelre* with him to continue working on it, even as Bavaria Herald. But he also started a new armorial, the *Wapenboek Beyeren* (Bavaria armorial), which unfortunately is kept under private lock and key and not open to our researches. What we know from earlier publications suggests that it is organized similarly to the *Wapenboek Gelre*: it, too, contains more than a thousand colored illustrations of arms surrounded by texts of historical and chivalric concern (see fig. 16).[6]

While the chief interest of these armorials lies in their illustrations, with the text forming no more than a background, the relationship is reversed in another manuscript that our herald prepared (mainly) in his new surroundings. It has come down to us as an autograph: MS. 131 G 37 in the Royal Library, The Hague.[7] The most striking features of this work are its lovely pen drawings of fifty-five coats of arms, some complete with crest, surcoat, and crown executed in gold leaf, silver leaf, and heraldic colors. These drawings accompany three short chronicles of the respective histories of Brabant (down to its origins in Troy), Holland, and Flanders in verse—thus bearing further testimony of the close bonds between heraldry and local history. Nevertheless, the historical interest of the author stretched far beyond neighboring dynasties, as the rest of the manuscript makes clear, for included as well are poems on the Normans, on the genealogy of Noah, a Latin chronicle of the English kings, and a number of textual fragments about Troy with a rhymed portrait of Achilles and Hector, his rival. At first sight this seems a strange blend of fact and fiction; in fact, though, the mixture was quite typical of the general outlook and historical perspective of our herald-historian—as we shall see.

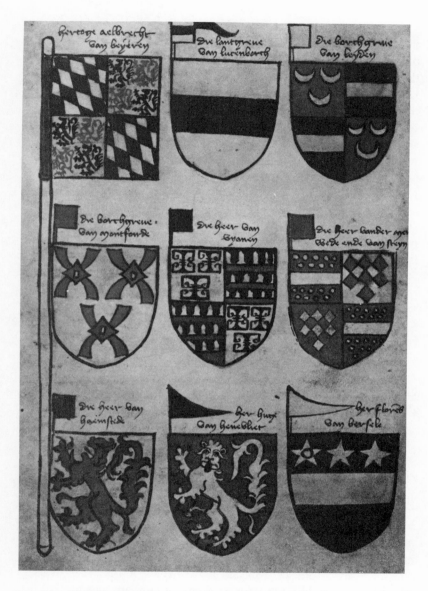

16. The Herald's *Bavaria Armorial*. (Inaccessible manuscript; reproduced from *Bibliothèque Jhr. J.F.L. Coenen van 's Gravesloot* [auction catalogue, 1918])

To examine this aspect more closely, we can probably do no better than look at the two prose chronicles written by Claes Heynenzoon during his time in Holland and dedicated—by "I, Bavaria"—to (by then) Count William VI and Frederic of Blankenheim, bishop of Utrecht. These two contemporaneous chronicles so complement each other that they can almost be described as historiographical twins. I refer to the *Wereldkroniek* (Chronicle of the world), written in 1405–9, and the *Hollandse kroniek* (Chronicle of Holland), the second version of which was completed on 25 May 1409 (thus, the first version must have been finished just after—or perhaps even before?—the *Wereldkroniek*). Neither chronicle has been published in a modern scholarly edition, even though the many surviving manuscripts of each suggest considerable interest in them in their own day, and even though the Brussels manuscript of the *Hollandse kroniek*, written in the Herald's own hand, is something to delight any editor.

It will have become clear by now that Bavaria Herald was extremely productive at the court of Holland: in at most ten years he wrote one armorial, one historical manuscript of heraldic interest, and two chronicles (one of them in two versions); in addition, he did all the necessary research, which is partly recorded in a rough manuscript (also kept in the Royal Library in The Hague; see fig. 17) that may well be the only extant notebook of a Middle Dutch writer. Thus, when this herald declares in his prologues that he wrote merely to keep busy, we must wonder. If he was telling the truth, either he worked day and night or else (the more likely alternative) he had only an undemanding job as a court servant. In any case, his application did not go unnoticed, because he himself came to enjoy the laurels he so ungrudgingly bestowed on his knights—albeit for different reasons.

All this makes it doubly tragic that a man so concerned with good repute should have been so discredited after his death. For while the Herald Beyeren quondam Gelre has been highly honored abroad by modern scholars, who consider him one of the most important of all medieval heralds, his name still suffers at home owing to a devastating attack on his chronicles launched by S. Muller Fz. in 1885.[8] Muller's article concludes with what for academic writers are unusual but, according to the author, "justified apologies . . . for having been so insufferably dull." But then, "two-thirds" of the blame was the Herald's, who, Muller maintains, costs the scholar a great deal of energy and his readers a great deal of boredom. Muller, in fact, saw fit to publish his

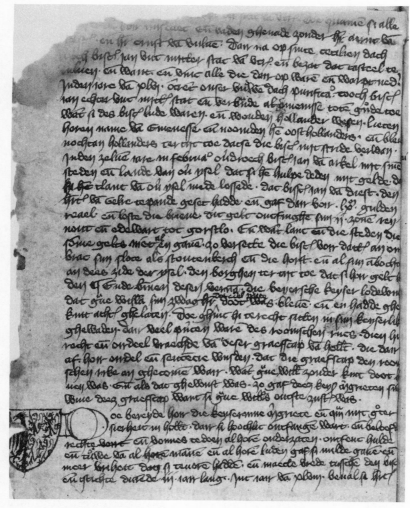

17. The Herald's *Kladboek* (Jotter). (Koninklijke Bibliotheek, The Hague, MS. 71 H 39, fol. 15v)

findings not least because he wished to "dissuade others from dipping into this thick tome." I have chosen to ignore Muller's advice, not so as to bore readers a century later, but because I believe that the chronicles of Bavaria Herald, if judged on their own merits, prove to be anything but dull.

2. THE *CHRONICLE OF THE WORLD*

Anyone writing a world history from the Creation to (almost) his own period has to consult sources. For the medieval historian and his public, this need was an advantage rather than a drawback. Unlike his modern successors, the medieval chronicler had to justify his work not by coming up with as many new discoveries and viewpoints as possible but by choosing the right authorities. Hence, it was a sign not of weakness but of pride that Bavaria Herald freely acknowledged his debt to earlier historians in the prologue to his *Wereldkroniek* (11):

Inden name Ons Heeren Jhesu Christi so hebbic, Beyeren, begonnen zom uten Latine in corten prosen; inden iersten uyt Moyses' boeken, voert van Methodius den marteleer, die God liet weten aldaer hi lach ghevanghen in eenen karker hoe dat die weerelt ierste began. Voert so hebbic uyt Tullius' boeken hier in wat ghetoghen ende uyt Oracius' boeken ende sinen corniken, ende uyt Ysidorus' boeken, ende uyt Homeris den Grieke, ende uten corniken Darijs van Troyen, des philosophs, ende uut Josephus der Joden historien dichter, ende uten corniken Vincent den Jacoppijn, ende uter corniken Martimiaen, ende uten corniken Willems van Malmesberghe, een monick uut Inghelant, ende uten corniken Zegebrechs, een monick van Gembloirs, ende was een die vroetste ende die beste een die men vant of wiste.

In the name of Our Lord Jesus Christ, I, Bavaria, have begun to render this and that from the Latin in short prose passages: firstly from the books of Moses, further from Methodius the martyr, whom, as he lay in a dungeon, God informed how the world began. Further, I drew in some measure on Tully's books and on Horace's books and his chronicles, and on Isidore's books, and on Homer the Greek and on the chronicles of Darius of Troy, the philosopher, and on Josephus, the historian of the Jews, and on the chronicles of Vincent the Jacobin, and on the chronicles of Martimian, and on the chronicles of William of Malmesbury, a monk from England, and on the chronicles of Zegebrech, a monk from Gembloirs who was one of the earliest and best ever known.

In other words, he was writing a world history based on extracts from a reference library ranging from the Bible to Homer. This showy display of sources aroused Muller's suspicions: could anyone really believe that a simple herald had read and digested all these texts?[9] Muller was partly right, but not entirely so. What he forgot was the medieval convention (a practice that would be inexcusable for a modern historian) to acknowledge one's ultimate rather than one's direct sources.[10] Thus, in his prologue the Herald was not pretending to acknowledge his actual authorities; he was simply citing those to which the information conveyed in his book could ultimately be traced back. That in so doing he, for example, erred about "Homer the Greek" is of little moment; he believed in good faith that the history of Troy to which he attached so much importance (see below) was based, *inter alia*, on Homer, because his actual source, Jacob van Maerlant, claimed that he himself had used that poet.

Now, Maerlant was the Herald's great pundit. On this crucial point, too, Muller was mistaken. Solid medieval historian that he was, Muller considered historical sources as almost necessarily being books written in Latin. This explains why he considered Vincent of Beauvais's *Speculum historiale* one of the Herald's possible sources, simply because the Herald (faithful to the principle just outlined) acknowledged his debt to "Vincent the Jacobin."[11] Yet for a herald-historian at the court of Holland in the early fifteenth century, nothing could have been more obvious than to consult Vincent *through* the Middle Dutch verse elaboration of the great Jacob van Maerlant, written a good century earlier. There is little doubt but that a copy of Maerlant's own *Spiegel historiael* (Historical mirror) would have been found at the Hague court, for that work, commissioned in about 1258 by Floris V, the then count of Holland, had been for over a hundred years and still was the only world history written in Middle Dutch.

But even if the *Spiegel historiael* was the main authority for the Herald's *Wereldkroniek* (which, seen in retrospect, seems fairly clear), the Herald did not ignore the rich sources embedded in Maerlant's other work. For biblical history, his *Wereldkroniek* made liberal use of Maerlant's *Rijmbijbel* (Rhymed Bible); for the Trojan war, he referred to the *Historie van Troyen* (History of Troy); for the part of his chronicle devoted to Alexander the Great, he naturally drew on *Alexanders geesten* (Alexander's deeds); and he gleaned plenty of additional information from *Der naturen bloeme* (The flower of nature). These findings transform Bavaria Herald from what until recently was thought to be an obscure disciple of Maerlant into one of the most prominent members of that author's school of Middle Dutch successors. He must, so to speak, have woken up with Maerlant's writings and have gone to sleep with them. To look, as the Herald did, for additional information on centaurs in Maerlant's biology seems fairly obvious, but also to know, as the Herald clearly did, where in the selfsame *Der naturen bloeme* to find Hercules, and to know that Moses appears not only at great length in Maerlant's *Rijmbijbel* but also in a very short passage in *Alexanders geesten*, one had to know Maerlant's works inside out.[12]

Our herald must, in fact, have spent all his days with his nose buried in books, because although the list of his actual sources is quite different from that acknowledged in his prologue, it certainly is no shorter, containing as it does practically everything available in Middle Dutch.[13] Whenever possible, the Herald seems to have preferred sources in his mother tongue. Not that he had failed to master Latin: his autograph 131 G 37 alone proves otherwise. Moreover, the second main source of his *Wereldkroniek* was in Latin and had never been translated into Middle Dutch. This was the *Chronicon pontificum et imperatorum*, the chronicle of popes and emperors by Martinus Polonus (referred to as "Martimian's chronicles" in the Herald's prologue). The *Chronicon* more or less provided the Herald with the background for the second part of his chronicle, much as the *Spiegel historiael* had done for the first, taking us to Octavian, the first Roman emperor. In this second half of the book, the Herald saw fit to introduce subsidiary divisions from additional sources.

Because of his factual approach, and also because he (generally) fails to acknowledge these sources, the work as a whole seems at first to be cut from a single cloth; on closer inspection, however, it turns out to be a patchwork. In fact, nearly all the information in the *Wereldkroniek* appears to have been borrowed from others; nothing essential was added by the Herald himself. Muller, having arrived at this interpretation by a mixture of surmise and analysis, went on to conclude that Bavaria Herald's *Wereldkroniek* was a "commonplace compilation" and hence "deserves little attention."[14] Had not all the facts been culled from elsewhere? But Muller overlooked an equally logical conclusion: the Herald may have borrowed all his data from other sources, but those sources were so numerous and so comprehensive, whereas the *Wereldkroniek* was so succinct, that every act of borrowing must have been offset by at least a hundred deliberate omissions. And yet these many thousands of choices by the Herald are alleged to have yielded a "commonplace" result, a book that, because it followed others so closely, was of small interest! In fact, such a compilation can never be rejected because it lacks originality.[15] No, it was original enough, though its originality was of a special kind.

Every compiler betrays his biases in his selections; and where the selection factor (that is, the percentage of omissions) is as high as it was in our herald's case, clearly the choice of omissions and inclusions cannot be impersonal. Rather, the Herald must have been guided by what, for him, were the essential elements of history—or, more precisely, by the picture of history he saw fit to convey to his public (Count William

VI in particular). Seen in this light, an apparently neutral retelling of history appears to rest on anything but a self-evident conception of the past.

If we compare the compilation with its sources—and in so doing pay attention to the inclusions as well as the omissions—we shall find that the Herald, far from painting a colorless picture of history, was presenting a highly subjective view. The way in which he dealt with his two main sources alone speaks volumes. These authorities sprang from two distinct medieval historiographic traditions: while Maerlant's *Spiegel historiael*, faithful to Vincent of Beauvais, adopted the *heilsgeschichtliche* (the interpretation of history stressing God's saving grace) division of history into six "estates," Martinus Polonus relied for his analysis on the "worldly" (political) framework of imperial succession. The Herald starts out with Maerlant's approach, though in a highly diluted form; upon arriving at the historical climax, the birth of Christ, however, he switches to Martinus Polonus's system. Here, written history begins with Octavian, Caesar Augustus, the first Roman emperor—under whose eventful reign Jesus was born. As a result, the Incarnation becomes but one memorable event among many recorded in Bavaria Herald's *Wereldkroniek*.

It is hardly an exaggeration to say that in the Herald's historical view the first Roman emperor was more important than the Redeemer. The Herald was writing world—that is, profane—history. This fact explains why he so departs from Martinus's account (which, after all, was a chronicle of emperors and popes) in omitting the papal succession, much as, in contrast to the *Spiegel historiael*, he omits nearly all the popes and saints.[16] His history revolves about the succession of secular rulers: he looks on history as a concatenation of royal dynasties to be treated in strict chronological order. In the beginning, that is easy: the first man also ruled over the world, and after Adam there was little more to report for a while than a leadership succession among the Jewish people. But then, in Abraham's day, the first kingdom appeared under Bessus of Babylonia. The Herald goes on to relate how Babylonian rule passed to Persia, which then yielded to Greek supremacy, later to be supplanted by Roman administration and, in turn, by the French crown.

Then came another crucial moment in world history as told by the Herald. The French crown made way for the German "because of the wrongs that Pippin's stock committed against the holy church, thus forfeiting the imperial crown, which fell under German sway" (om misdaet

wille dat Puppijns gheslechte mesdaen hadde jeghen der heiligher kerken, so dat hem hieromme es ontseit die keyserlijcke crone, ende es
gheset inder Duytscher macht; 88v). From that point on, the Herald
keeps his searchlight focused on the German imperial dynasty. He starts
with the three Ottos, until "the great lords in their wisdom no longer
wished the realm to pass on from father to son but that [the emperor]
would in future be elected by seven of them best suited to do so" (die
wijsheit vanden groten heeren des niet langher ghedoghen [wilde] dat
dat keyserrijcke voert meer soude erven vanden vader opten sone, ende
wouden voert meer kiesen van hen sevenen die daer beste toe waren bij
hem selven; 89v). Although usually anything but democratic, the Herald commented favorably on the election of emperors, no doubt because
he knew his own place under "the great lords in their wisdom," but also
because of the end result of such elections: the first elected emperor,
Henry I (known as "the Fowler" and traditionally considered the
founder of the tournament), was an ancestor of the emperor with whom
the Herald concluded his dynastic history. That brought him to 1347
and Emperor Louis of Bavaria. Neither the Herald himself nor his readers would have had to dig deep into the historical record to realize
where they had arrived: at the father of Albert, count of Holland, and
the grandfather of William VI.

The Herald looked at world history quite unashamedly from the van-
tage of his own circle. Starting with the Creation, his history ends in
Holland. Or, viewed another way, history served him as a map of the
present drawn in relief against the past.[17] Thus his patron, William VI,
a liege of the German emperor, could look back on a satisfying past (and
hence also look forward to the future with some confidence): the House
of Holland-Bavaria was a vital part of a mighty dynastic line—God's
own line—in world history, one that joined the greatest of noble
houses, beginning with Adam.

This, then, was the macrohistorical view that the Herald projected
from his sources into world history. Within that projection he unfolded
the rest of his story, though even then his main concern was the rise,
florescence, and decline of dynasties. Among the "second-plane" em-
pires, Troy took particular pride of place. With his great sympathy for
that city—and hence antipathy toward the besieging Greeks—the Herald reflected a common attitude of the Middle Ages. Indeed, he could
not put the word *Troy* to paper without prefixing it with the epithet
noble.[18] It must have been irksome to one so caught up with the idea of
dynastic power to find that glorious Troy did not rule supreme in her

day. But what Troy lacked in supremacy, she made up for in quality; besides, history—and hence God—exalted her posthumously. After all, through Aeneas, her fugitive prince, Troy nourished the infant Roman civilization, which in turn laid the foundation of the German empire in the Herald's own time. Indeed, not only Rome, but England and France, too, were the children of Troy.[19] And so, after "the great loss of Troy" (dat grote verlies van Troyen; 15v) everything turned out for the best—which, happily, rendered that loss more comprehensible.[20] Otherwise it would always have remained a mystery how God could have allowed so glorious a country to be brought down by a wooden horse, by a despicable trick. For although the Herald may not always have been free with his commentaries, all sorts of emotionally loaded words make it clear which side he supported (12v):

Ten lesten wonnen sijt binnen eenen vrede met verradenisse van eenen houten peerde daer 5000 ghewapende in laghen in eender nacht; maer hadde die vrome Hector doen gheleeft, so en ware Troyen op die tijt niet ghewonnen.

At long last, during a peace [i.e., during an official truce] they won victory, treacherously with the aid of a wooden horse in which 5,000 armed men lay hidden for one night [another unchivalrous act?]; but had good Hector been alive, Troy would not have been captured at that time.

This last aside (inspired, incidentally, by Maerlant's *Historie van Troyen*) was characteristic of the Herald's outlook. History may above all be a succession of dynasties, but it is on individuals that these dynasties, and hence the world, rest. In his chronicle, the Herald gives considerable space to the personality of seven (the traditional, quasi-magical number) great princes: Aeneas, the founder of Rome; his brother Brutus, the first king of England; Julius Caesar; Octavian; Arthur; Alexander; and Charlemagne. His otherwise fairly sober and factual history is sprinkled with colorful anecdotes about these great men. As a result, the *Wereldkroniek* is packed with personal tributes. Bavaria Herald was a historian with a weakness for strong men—he admired heroic generals even more than reigning princes. This fact explains his special interest in Hannibal and undoubtedly also in Hercules, whose portrait may be considered a model of the Herald's historical approach.

The Herald first encountered Hercules when, perusing Maerlant's *Rijmbijbel*, he reached the history of the Jewish people under the judge Tola. As usual, our chronicler sets out Tola's rule correctly, but beyond that he mentions the location of his tomb and what was alleged to be a memorable incident from the days of Tola's reign, namely Hercules' defeat of the hero Antaeus: "and was judge over Israel 24 years and Tola died and was buried in Savir 700 and 75 years after Abraham, and in his days Hercules seized Antaeus's sword" (ende was rechter over Israel 24 jaer ende dese Thola starf ende wart begraven in Savir 700 ende 75 jaer na Abraham, ende in sinen tijden so verwan Hercules Antheum den degen; 10v). These items are taken largely from the *Rijmbijbel* and, by themselves, require no further elaboration. What mattered in the end was the dynastic line; since Hercules was no founder of a dynasty, he would not normally have been of particular interest to the Herald. Yet he had performed great feats of arms—so great that by all rights he should be given a more prominent place in world history.

The Herald prepared for this place in dealing with Abraham's sons by Hagar. Of the six sons she bore the patriarch, only one deserved special mention in the Herald's highly personal version of events: "And after the death of Sarray, his wife, Abraham married Agar, his former maid. From her he had 6 sons; one was called Afraim, and from him are descended the Africans" (Item Abraham truwede na Sarray, sijns wijfs doet, Agar voirseit sijn maerte. Daer wan hij bij 6 sonen; die een hiet Affraym, ende van hem quamen die van Affriken; 7v). This Afraim was worth borrowing from the *Rijmbijbel* not only because he was the ancestor of the Africans; he was also, we learn, the father-in-law of Hercules! "This Afraim had a daughter, Chetean by name, whom the great Hercules took for his wife" (Dese Affraym hadde een dochter, hiet Chetean, die creech groet Hercules te wive; 7v). Now, this marriage, by which the great Hercules was joined to a descendant of the patriarch Abraham, was not something the Herald had found in the *Spiegel historiael*, his main source, or in the *Rijmbijbel*, on which this part of his chronicle was chiefly based. To discover it, he had to go back to one of Maerlant's own sources, the *Historia scolastica*—a vast tome from which, moreover, the Herald seems to have taken almost nothing other than that tiny item about Hercules.

Having reached Tola in his story, the Herald seized the chance to unleash his admiration for Hercules to the fullest. Accordingly, before following the *Rijmbijbel* and going on to Tola's successor ("And after Tola died, Jayar was judge in Israel for 22 years, and was born of Manasse . . . [Item na Thola voirseit so wart rechter in Israel Jayar 22 jaer, ende was gheboren van Manassen . . .]; 11v), the Herald decided to interrupt the usual sequence of Jewish judges with a sixty-line biography of the "great Hercules." He raked up his material from various bits and pieces scattered in Maerlant's work:[21] the *Spiegel historiael*, the

Rijmbijbel, the *Historie van Troyen*, *Alexanders geesten*, and even *Der naturen bloeme*, from which he (and his readers) learned, on the authority of Adelinus among others, about the *catus*, that dangerous beast which, according to the combined accounts of the *Historie van Troyen* and *Alexanders geesten*, the "great Hercules" was able to subdue (IIV):

Item in Archadien was een dier hiet Catus ende was gheborstelt als een swijn, alse Adelinis seet, die philosophus. Alst tornich was, so warpt uyt sinen halse vier, ende verberde dicwille die scepe die in de zee waren. Ende het berch hem in holen onder der eerden ende es seer wreet ende snel, ende het et coyen voer alle dinck, maer het en laet hem niet ghenoeghen met eender coyen, maer het neemter 3 of 4 metten steerte ende trecse achter rugghe in sijn hol, om datmense niet soeken en soude waer sij sijn. Dit dier haet zeere den mensche, ende leit hem altoes laghen na hoet den mensche deren mach, omdat den mensche moet ontsien, ende es van vuylre stinckender natueren ghelijc den verken.

Item tot eender tijt quam groet Hercules gaende in eenen beemt voer een gheberchte daer veel coyen weyden, so datter een wart loyende so dat Catus' coyen een hoerden die in sijn hol waren. Nu hadde Hercules horen segghen dattet dier al daer ontrent plach te regneren ende hoe dat ghescapen was, ende hij hadde bij hem Griex vier. Ende dat dier vernam Hercules ende sette hem toe. Nu hadde dit dier veel hoofden op sinen buuck staende, ende als hij hem een hooft af sloech, so wiesser hem 4 weder uten struken. Doen hij sach dat hijs niet verslaen en coste, doen nam hij sijn Griex vier ende verberde dat dier al te aschen.

Item in Arcadia there lived an animal by the name of Catus and was bristled like a swine, as was said by Adelinus, the philosopher. When it was enraged, fire would gush from its throat, often scorching the ships that were in the sea. And it hid in hollows under the earth and was most ferocious and fast-moving, and fed on cows above all else, not leaving it at just one cow but taking 3 or 4 as well as steers and dragging them back into its cave lest men searched and found them. This beast is filled with hatred against man and ever lays traps for him, and envies man the power for which he is respected, and is of a foul stinking nature like the pig.

Item at one time the great Hercules was walking in a meadow before a mountain where many cows were grazing, one of which started to low and was heard by the cows that Catus kept in his cave. Now Hercules had heard the report that this beast held sway hereabouts and how it was fashioned and he had brought Greek fire with him. And the beast heard Hercules and set upon him. Now, this beast had many heads rising up from its back, and when he cut off one head another 4 would grow from the stump that remained. When he saw that he could not defeat the beast [with his sword], he took his Greek fire and burned the beast to cinders.

Such thrilling tales were so much grist to the Herald's historic mill. History to him was not political, economic, or social history, let alone cultural or intellectual history, but military history first and foremost.

Struggle was the motor of world affairs, and that motor ran on chivalry.
As one might expect from a man in his position, the Herald here waxed
lyrical. Of course, he knew enough history to be able to imagine a world
without knights—but that world was far from ideal. Typical of his outlook was his version of the history of Flanders. As a stretch of land Flanders had, of course, always existed, complete with a few towns, but civilization did not reach her until a knight (needless to say, with a coat of
arms) stepped onto her soil (75r–v):[22]

Thien jaer tevoren, eer Grote Karle besat dat keyserrijck, so was in Vlaenderen
op die riviere vander Leyen een stout ridder, ende hiet Liedrijke, ende was ver-
wapent met goude ende lazuer van 10 stucken ghegerrert met eenen schilt van
kele. Dese riddere sach dat alle Vlaenderen zeere woest was ende luttel bewoent,
ende was een wilt foreest, marasche ende onlant, ende daer en stonden inne niet
meer steden dan Ghent ende Cassel, Toerhout ende Cortrijcke ende die borch
tot Oudennaerden. Maer God, daer alle doghet uyt compt, gaf hem gracie dat
hij dat woeste lant begreep ende bewoende, so dat van hem menich edel lants-
heer quam ghelijckerwijs als van Davidt, die een scaepheerde was die daer na
een groet mechtich coninck was ende van hem menich mechtich coninck quam
int rijcke der Joeden; also dat dese Liedrijck den Groten Karle manschap dede
ende swoer hem goet ende ghetrouwe te sijne, ende ontfinc van hem dat woeste
lant dat hij bevrien soude voer allen man, ende so waer hij rovers ende quade
yden wiste, dat hij die vanden weeghe helpen soude.

Ten years before, ere the Great Charles took possession of the empire, there
lived in Flanders upon the River Leye a bold knight, Liedrijck by name, and he
was armed with gold and azure and bore a shield of gules. This knight beheld
that Flanders was very desolate and little inhabited, and was a wild forest,
marsh, and wasteland, and there were in it no other towns than Ghent and
Cassel, Toerhout and Cortrijcke, and the keep at Oudennaerde. But God, from
whom all virtue flows, gave him the grace to conquer and settle the desolate
land so that from him sprang as many noble rulers as from David, who was a
shepherd and later became a great mighty king and from whom sprang many a
mighty king in the land of the Jews; and so this Liedrijck swore allegiance to
the Great Charles and promised to be faithful and loyal to him and received
from him the desolate land which he was to protect for all the people, and
wherever he knew of robbers and evil heathens he was to help rid the country
of them.

Because knights were the guardians of civilization, the ultimate measure of a civilization lay in how it treated its knights. Thus, it was easy
to tell a good ruler by the way he paid his men-at-arms.[23] A fine example
was set by Charles Martel, who appropriated tithes for that very purpose. How a church historian would regard such a practice is not hard
to guess, and the Herald, too, worried about the salvation of Charles

Martel's soul. But so thoroughly did he side with the knights that all he could do was hope for the best (71v; cf. 74v):

Ende doen hij dus zeer gheoerloecht hadde ende den schat van Vranckrijcke daer in ghelegt hadde, doen nam hij den tienden penning der heylegher kerken ende betaelde die ridderen van haren soudien, so dat sinte Eleuterius, biscop te Orlyens, sach daer na zijn ziele inder hellen, in Fulcanus' pot. Ende dat waer alte groten jammer, soude sijn ziele verloren bliven.

And when he had waged a fierce war and had invested the treasure of France in it, then he took the tenth penny of the holy churches and rendered the knights their pay, whereupon Saint Eleuterius, the bishop of Orlyens, had a vision of his soul in hell, in Vulcan's cauldron. Yet it would be a great shame should his soul remain lost there.

In another typical passage, the Herald (this time smartly deviating from his sources)[24] recalled that Octavian's Rome had provided excellently for knights past their prime (37v–38r):

Item in sinen tijden so was te Rome een huys met veel ghemacs; dat was daer toe ghegeven dattie oude, verarbeide ridderscape, die haer leden hadden versleten ende verarmt waren ende niet en hadden af te leevene, so dat die stat hem lieden haer provenen daer inne gaf. Ende daer was toe gheset alles dincs ghenoech van des den daghe tijdich was. Ende daer plachmen in te vertellene van ridderscap ende van striden dat een ieghelijc gedaen hadde; ende dat huys hiet Misericordia, ende in dat huys ontspranc des selves nachs doen Christus gheboren wart een fontayne van olien, ende liep in die Tybar.

Item in his day Rome had a house with many rooms; it was set aside for veteran knights who had worn out their limbs and had become impoverished and lacked the means of subsistence, and the state had them provided with subsidies therein. And there was enough of everything of which they had need. And there they were wont to tell tales of chivalry and of the battles each one had fought; and the house was called Misericordia, and in that house there sprang forth on the very night that Christ was born a fountain of oil that ran into the Tiber.

What other historian bent on telling the full history of the world in 150 pages would have dredged up such details from the unending mass of source material, and then laid them on so thick? But then, our historian was also a herald. His professional outlook was bound, within the broad limits of his extreme selectivity, to mould his worldview. The result was a medieval chronicle that spared Christ no more than three lines and wholly ignored the papacy, but devoted a good sixty lines to Hercules and saw fit to mention that the Emperor Diocletian was the first to embellish his shoes with precious stones (46r). By virtue of his craft, indeed, our author was professionally interested in splendor, and no less so in decorum.[25] As far as the church was concerned, what seemed to fascinate him most (after the Crusades, of course, of which more in the following sections) was the liturgy;[26] as a master of ceremony to noble lords, he clearly found church ceremonial enthralling. And however profound his trust in Maerlant may have been in general, there was one area in which he felt free to improve on his great mentor, the very territory in which, as herald, he himself was the foremost authority: the correct form of address of lords and knights. Anthenor, to be precise, was a *duke*; Carloman was not only a brother of Pippin the Short, father of Charlemagne, but also "prince of Duringhen, of Austria, of Burgundy, and of Provence"; Charles Martel, for his part, was also "swordbearer to the crown of France."[27]

The Herald's bias was not merely reflected in details such as these; it shaped the very framework of his *Wereldkroniek*. He could not, of course, ride roughshod over the historical course of events, nor could he present facts on which his sources were silent. What he could do was shine his spotlight on history so that it fell on what to him, as a herald, were the axes on which the world turned: dynasties, battles, and chivalry.

Much as all heralds were wont to base their armorials on a ranking of European princes, so this one centered his world history on dynasties, as his autograph 131 G 37, with its pedigrees of Carolingians, Capetians, Trojans, and the generations of Noah and of Godefroy de Bouillon, makes clear.[28] The Herald classified the world according to princes and nations, and particularly princes doing battle. Although the prose of his chronicle is fairly flat and prosaic, his vocabulary is richly varied in its descriptions of battle and war; he seems to have had an irresistible need to orchestrate his history with the clash of arms. Thus, whereas the *Rijmbijbel* has Phoenix and Cadmus settle down peacefully in a town, the *Wereldkroniek* depicts them capturing that town.[29] And whereas the *Historie van Troyen* (which was anything but pacifist) has Laomedon ask the Greeks to leave his kingdom, the Herald portrays him driving them out by force.[30] In the midst of all this armed conflict, the full glare of history is allowed to fall on the charismatic generals of the past and on their mighty courage. The absence of heralds in the *Wereldkroniek* is offset by a surfeit of knights. They constitute a group of which Bavaria Herald was not, strictly speaking, a member, but of which he felt a part and a representative. As a herald he identified himself unreservedly with chivalric values.

Among these values, one occupied a lonely height, namely honor. And the place of a man of honor was on the field of honor; indeed, in the Herald's eyes death on the battlefield was almost the natural way of dying for a knight, one, moreover, that earned him a glorious name. In matters of war, the Herald was an idealist; he saw the knight's employment in battle not as a mere job (for pay) but as a true vocation. Knightly ambition was a wonderful challenge, worth living and dying for. But the rules of the game had to be observed. While Hercules might be excused for having been shrewd enough to subdue a mythological monster with Greek fire, a wooden horse in a clash of knights must be rejected as an immoral weapon, the more so when it is used at night and during a truce—hence treacherously. An ignominious victory is a worse disgrace than an honorable defeat. In the same vein, the fact that the French had sullied the glorious memory of ancestral Troy was, in short, contemptible. The founder of their dynasty "was of noble Trojan birth; but they have turned into wretches and are useless and dare not fight; and their kings' names have been reduced to shame and disgrace" (was een edel Troyen gheboren; ende sijn nu worden keytive ende en doghen niet, ende en dorren niet vechten; ende haer coninx namen sijn nu comen te schanden ende t'oneeren).[31]

Whoever brings disgrace upon a knight is asking for vengeance. Why did Hannibal march on Rome? Our herald's sources do not say. But, familiar with battlefields, he himself provides the answer: the Carthaginian Hannibal wanted to avenge Dido's death by punishing Aeneas's Rome![32] In the Herald's world, retribution was not only a respectable but also a rational motive for action. That is why he believed so vehemently that the army of Count William VI of Holland had to hasten back to Friesland. But more on that below.

3. THE *CHRONICLE OF HOLLAND*

The Herald's *Hollandse kroniek*, too, was hard work. True, now that he was dealing with the history of his own part of the world, he needed fewer and less far-flung sources; even so, much material had to be condensed. To this laborious task the Herald's so-called *Kladboek* bears ample witness.[33] This pocket-sized notebook—the only extant jotter of a Middle Dutch author—presents us with a mass of material clearly intended for use in the *Hollandse kroniek* (the majority of which rough scribblings were later copied onto fine parchment for the deluxe Brussels version of the *Kroniek*). The *Kladboek* reflects the Herald's more than purely historical approach: it contains such varied items as a number of rhyming proverbs, the *bispel* (morality poem) of "a herald by the name of Jan Visier," and a strange caricature (?) of a man wearing a fool's cap and identified as Witto Draecksteker (Mudraker—a stage name?) from Delft.

Some of the general sources for the *Hollandse kroniek* were those that served our herald for his world history—Middle Dutch rhyming chronicles (Maerlant's *Spiegel historiael* above all) and Martinus Polonus's Latin chronicle.[34] But for the greater part, the Herald now had to rely on other authorities. Many of his world histories proved of little use when it came to writing about Holland, whereas other works now came into their own, for instance the rhyming history of Holland written for the count's benefit in the late thirteenth century (as a complement to a world history, such as the *Spiegel historiael?*) by Maerlant's younger contemporary Melis Stoke. Of even more fundamental importance to the *Hollandse kroniek* was the whole array of writings ranged around Johannes de Beka's history of the counts of Holland and the bishops of Utrecht, dating back to about 1347. This extremely influential Latin chronicle—dedicated to count and bishop alike and authenticated by the venerable Egmont antecedents of (perhaps) Beka himself, and in any case of his sources—had appeared in a Middle Dutch translation accompanied by a sequel that continued Beka's account to more recent times, that is, to 1393. It was this Middle Dutch version that was to become the main source of the *Hollandse kroniek*. The claim that the Herald also consulted the chronicle of the so-called Clerk from the Low Countries proves on closer inspection to be less certain than many historiographers like to suggest. In fact, it is by no means impossible that the opposite happened, and that the Clerk based his own account on the Herald's. In this field, much spadework remains to be done; North Netherlands historiography is a veritable skein of texts waiting to be unraveled. Yet we must leave this task to others, as our own hands are more than full with the Herald's own writings.

Having all his sources within easy reach, the Herald set to work in his usual manner. In other words, his omissions were both plentiful and, again, typical of his general approach and hence of his historical objectives. Unlike his main source, the Herald decided to reduce the role of Utrecht drastically. Whereas Beka's chronicle had been a history of (in order of priority) the bishopric of Utrecht and the county of Holland, the Herald effected a reversal: his chronicle was a history of Holland first and foremost. And just as in the *Wereldkroniek* history was presented as being synonymous with the history of the ruling house, here, too, the dynastic line served as the backbone of the narrative.

Not only were the omissions again typical of the Herald's technique, but so also were the inclusions. To no scene in Beka does the Herald give so much attention as to the election of Count William II of Holland as king of the Romans and to his prior elevation to the knighthood.[35] Whereas usually he cut Beka drastically, here he deliberately chose to enlarge and embellish the story. To that end he consulted complementary sources (Melis Stoke in particular) for information; but he seems also to have added material of his own. One's view of this contribution, of course, depends on how one interprets the relationship between the Herald and the Clerk, who, like the Herald, differs in certain ways from Beka. If the Clerk was the original source, the Herald clearly went to the trouble of borrowing the material from him—which if nothing else indicates his special interest in this particular episode. Yet it may well be that, at least in this instance, the Herald was the creative author and the Clerk his debtor.[36] In any case, the Herald had a more obvious motive for writing this material. To him, the election of William II must, after all, have been a high point in the history of Holland—the initiation ceremony of a young count followed by his election as king of the Romans. As the Herald saw things, this was an ideal opportunity not only to vent his local patriotism but also to display his familiarity with knighthood protocol.

Elsewhere in the *Hollandse kroniek* the Herald's hand shows in the selection of the material as well; consider the attention given to heraldry, and to the ceremonial grandeur associated with titles and genealogy.[37] In this work the Herald could, in fact, expound at much greater length on heraldic matters than he had in the *Wereldkroniek*. For while in the second he had been handicapped by the silence of his sources (for instance, on the subject of Hercules' coat of arms), in the *Hollandse kroniek* he could rely on his own expertise. After all, it was his job to know the arms of his masters and their kinsmen; and that professional knowledge not only went into his two armorials, but it also markedly affected the *Hollandse kroniek*.

In the autograph preserved to our great fortune in Brussels, heraldry shines forth in no less than 102 colored blazons accompanying the text. Their magnificent execution betrays the expert hand of a herald. Yet it was not only in these illustrations that he displayed his expertise; for he also applied himself to the text. Thus, whereas Beka says of the coat of arms of William II as king of the Romans merely that "in it was found an eagle of black color" (daer een aern van swaerter varwe in ghemaket), our expert dotted the *i*'s of this sparse account with "in which a half-eagle was fashioned in black color, red lions having been applied to his coat with precious embroidery work" (dair een half aerne van zwarter verwen in stont, dair die rode lewe in gemaect waren in sinen wapenroc, costelic van borduren).[38] The most striking feature of the chronicle is the "verbal heraldry," including what was probably the Herald's most "personal" passage, namely his eulogies to fourteen knights killed at the Battle of Stavoren in 1345. Here the Herald was able to quote himself, introducing some of the panegyrics that had been his literary specialty in his Guelders days, before his literary career led him to the writing of chronicles in Holland.[39] It hardly needs pointing out that the arms of our Herald's acclaimed heroes appear in the Brussels manuscript of the *Hollandse kroniek.*

Great heroes, great deeds. In the history of Holland, too, the Herald was fortunate enough to discover a number of famed feats of arms. And those would allow the presentation of a war chronicle—wars to the Herald being golden, not black pages of history. In the *Hollandse kroniek,* then, the author's chivalric heart could again beat triumphantly, and while he felt free to ignore bishops, miracles, and holy relics, he did not fail to record a single war in which Holland was involved. Here the Herald was in his element.[40] Indeed, he was painstaking in listing warriors and casualties: he meticulously checked Beka's list of knights present at a Frisian battle down to the last man, and of one clash he noted that "there were slain 36,596, it was said."[41] To him, an army could be beautiful: John of Diest "assembled a beautiful host of knights" (versamende een alte scoon een ridderscap), and William of Holland drew up "with a beautiful and bold host" (mit enen sconen stoutten here).[42]

But what would armies be without charismatic generals? Although Holland could boast no Hannibal or Alexander, various princes from parts nearer home made quite passable imitations—at least in the Herald's eyes. For example, he took great pains with Charles Martel, "the Hammer," a French prince who, because of his dealings with Utrecht and Friesland, had also been included in Beka's chronicle. Yet that work had failed to pay tribute to his personal qualities—clearly an inexcusable oversight with respect to a king who (as the Herald saw fit to add) was "full of wars" and "victorious" to boot, indeed "the best Christian bastard there ever was." No wonder, then, that we can find a much ampler portrait of Charles Martel in the *Hollandse kroniek*—for which, moreover, the Herald could consult his own *Wereldkroniek*, in which he had already given a longish report of Martel's deeds in a carefully compiled narrative based on the *Spiegel historiael* and the *Korte kroniek van Brabant* (Short chronicle of Brabant). Nevertheless, small differences from the *Wereldkroniek* prove that the Herald returned to the sources once more when writing his second account of Charles Martel. The result of these labors was a portrait of a man who must have been a prince after the Herald's own heart (10r):

In dien tiden regneerde die vroom Kairle Marteel voirscreven, Cleyn Puppijns vader. Het ghesciede tot eenre tijd dat quamen die Sarrasine mit groter moghentheit over die cleyn zee, ende destrueerden al Spangen. Ende dair na over 10 jair quamen si in Gascongen. Die Fransoysen ontboden Kairlen Marteel, horen zwairddragher dat hi quame. Dair quam hi moghentlike mit sinen Duutschen, mit sinen Brabantsoene ende mit sinen Lothrikers, ende zette hem daer jeghen ende streed mit hem; ende sloech hem af 3 kueninghen, also datter heiden bleven 300.000, ende der sijnre bleven 1500. Hi verwan tot eenre tijd den hertooch Lanfreit van Hooch Almangen, ende hi tooch voirt over Rijn ende verwan die Zassen toter Elven toe. Hi verwan die Zwoven ende die Beyeren; hi bedwang al dat volk toter Dunouwen toe. Hi verwan die Vriesen, ende die van Borgongen; hi bedwang Eudon den hertooch van Gasscongen ende den hertooch van Loreyn. Hi bedwang veel Sarrasinen in dat lant van over meer. Ende tot eenre tijd zo quam hi mit groter menichte van volcke in Provincien, ende streed voir Arleblancke jeghen die Provinciale ende versloechse.

Item deez Kairle Marteel die en streed nye, hi en wan; ende hi hadde ten waperie meer eren dan alle sijn ouders, ende hi was die beste cersten bastaerd die ye was. Hi dwang an hem alle die lande van Vrieslant toter Yeronden, zo dat in Vrancrijk in sinen tiden geen coninc en ward, ten moeste bi hem wesen. Ende alsmen hem die crone bood te dragen, zo ontseid hi se, ende sprack het wair meer eren coninc te bedwinghen ende te verjaghen dan coninc te wesen ende croon te draghen.

In those days there reigned the above-mentioned pious and devout Kairle Marteel, father of Cleyn Puppijn [Pippin the Short]. And it happened that the Saracens came across the small sea with a great force and destroyed all Spain. And thence they made for Gascony after more than 10 years had passed. The French sent word to Kairle Marteel, their swordbearer [i.e., high court official], that he come to their aid. And he drew up mightily with his Germans, his Brabanters, and his Lothringians and threw them into battle; and they slew 3 kings, the heathen leaving 300,000, and his own host leaving 1,500. On one occasion, he captured Duke Lanfreit of Hooch Almangen and he continued across the Rhine and took Zassen [Saxony] as far as the Elve [Elbe]. He defeated the Swabians and the Bavarians; he defeated all the people as far as the Danube. He defeated the Frisians, and those of Burgundy; he defeated Eudon, duke of Gascony, and the duke of Lorraine. He defeated many Saracens in the land across the sea [i.e., Palestine]. And at one time he drew up with a large host in Provence and fought at Arleblancke against the Provincials and defeated them.

Item this Kairle Marteel never engaged in battle but he won it; and his arms bore more honor than all his ancestors', and he was the best Christian bastard there ever was. He captured all the lands from Friesland to Yeronden [Gironde], so that in his day there was no king in France but had to side with him. And when he was offered the crown, he refused it, saying it was a greater honor to defeat a king and to drive him out than to wear a crown.

In his own Holland, too, the Herald was able to discover princes of note. As we might expect from a successor of Stoke, for example, he drew a most glowing portrait of Floris V.[43] More remarkable are the sketches he presents of his own lords and masters at the end of the *Hollandse kroniek*: Albert of Bavaria and William VI. Here he is writing history largely unaided: the earliest portraits of these Bavarian rulers of Holland were sketched by the Herald himself.

And that fact is reflected in the writing. At the very beginning of his reign, Duke Albert is shown locked in battle with no less than the Holy Roman Emperor, who had had the impertinence to lay siege to a castle in Bavaria but beat a hasty retreat when the young duke mounted his counterattack. Nor was this the only siege in which the future count of Holland was involved; he captured Hillekersberg (in Bavaria, not the birthplace of William of Hildegaersberch) and took Schaerdingen Castle by storm. Fortunately, a reconciliation with the emperor ensued, whereupon—as if in celebration—the new allies fought a joint campaign in Swabia. Albert's sudden departure for Holland because of "the sickness of his brother, Duke William," was essentially just a shifting of battleground, for in Holland, he proceeded to besiege Heusden and to capture Delft and Middelburg. Later "he was seen in the Eets [i.e., Austria]," but "the great fall of snow and rain" forced him to call off the winter campaign in the Carinthian Mountains. "Item from thence he came to Hainaut," where he joined forces with the king of Auvergne for another successful siege. Then came what for the Herald Beyeren quondam Gelre must have been a most delicate moment: enmity between "the noble prince" Albert and Duke Edward of Guelders. Albert took his fleet up the Lek, fell upon Guelders, "sacking and burning in that country . . . , and after came back home victorious and with great honor" (heerde ende brande in den lande [. . .] ende quam weder thuus mit zeghe ende mit groter eren; 121r).

Duke Albert's road to honor thus seemed paved with war and conflict. The Herald also reports that Albert challenged the duke of Flanders to a duel in Paris; nothing actually ensued, but the count of Holland nonetheless "departed thence with greater honor." And so on and so forth—the siege of Gildenborg in Utrecht; the campaign against Vianen, "with a mighty great host"; the siege of Heulenstein and Velu-wehorst; the putting of Hermalen to the torch. "Then this mighty prince returned home." The chronicle goes on to record the only peace-ful incident in Albert's life that the Herald thought worthy of attention: the marriage of his daughter to the king of the Romans, Wenceslaus of Bohemia, which enriched the Holland-Bavarian line with royal blood. Shortly afterward, however, it was back to the battlefield again. Fi-nally—just after the successful conclusion of the Arkel campaigns, dur-ing which the "lord's banner jutted above the housetops"—the "noble lord departed this earth in God," to be buried in The Hague beside his first wife, Margaret of Brieg (of whom, needless to say, the Herald did not forget to report that she was "of the royal race of the crown of Behem [i.e., Bohemia]").[44] "God grant that both may dwell with Him, Amen."

Was that meant to be the concluding line of the chronicle, as Muller, on the authority of the *Kladboek*, assumed? Whatever the case may be, the Brussels manuscript continues with a biography of William VI writ-ten in the same style (fig. 18). According to the Herald, William was a stock figure of medieval chivalry: knighted by the duke of Burgundy, a successful besieger, a crusader in Prussia against the pagans, the leader of a campaign against Kuinre "with a stout, strong, handsome, and mighty armada" (mit een alte zwide sconen ende machtighen scipheer), the captor of Loevestein, the reliever of Stavoren, and leader of cam-paigns against Gorinchem (besieged), Hagestein (set on fire), and Ev-erstein (laid waste), as well as against a series of castles and towns in Liège, all honorably burned to ashes or razed to the ground. Count William was still alive when this last chapter of history was recorded; his armed feats excited his court biographer with great hopes for the future.

If we had no other sources than these two passages in the *Hollandse kroniek* to tell us about the reigns of Albert and William of Bavaria, we might think that these counts of Holland did nothing but wage war. But from other records and, above all, from what we know of our Herald, we know that his historical vision was merely a projection of his own bias. Not that he ascribed imaginary wars to his masters; but by omit-ting practically everything else and focusing strictly on their feats of arms, he turned these Bavarian counts of Holland into no more than swashbucklers.

Such a portrait was amply justified, the Herald must have thought, in that they had to face such dangerous foes as the Frisians. For while

18.   The *Hollandse kroniek* (Chronicle of Holland). Passage devoted to William VI in the dedication copy. (Bibliothèque royale Albert Ier, Brussels, MS. 17914, fol. 123r)

he treated most of their other battles as relatively minor conflicts, their differences with Friesland he saw as part of a bitter and unending feud. In particular, the *Hollandse kroniek* mentions at some length that many counts of Holland had previously clashed with (West) Friesland. Just before Duke Albert came to power, Count William IV had been killed in Friesland, and the Hollanders had been unable to return with his body. Such a fate was almost worse than death itself for someone like the Herald, to whom honor and hence honorable burials mattered as desperately as in the ages of Achilles and Antigone.

It was this subject that he broached when, as we saw at the beginning of the chapter, he ripped the tablecloth with his knife. The body of his lord was well worth a battle. Indeed, such a campaign of revenge was a debt of devotion that his lord's kinsmen should pay, being honor bound to cleanse the besmirched blazon of their sovereign and country. For such was the chivalric code, of which heralds were the most vociferous upholders and in matters of which it was their duty to guide their noble audience. It follows that, in the campaigns unleashed by Albert and William on Friesland, vengeance for sullied honor was a much weightier motive than it is now possible to imagine. A century earlier, Count Floris V had staked everything to avenge the death of his father, who, being a king of the Romans and hence the pearl in Holland's dynastic crown, had been killed in Friesland.[45] In a similar manner, too, Count Dirk had taken revenge on the Frisians for his father Arnold. "Death to the Frisians" was the Herald's constant battle cry.

But although vengeance was *his* main motive, it was not the primary cause for Holland's war against the Frisians. Their hereditary enmity, rather, was rooted in Holland's claim to sovereignty over Friesland and the Frisians' refusal to accept that claim. The Herald knew, of course, that the Frisians, no less than the Hollanders, were standing on their historic rights, but with this essential difference: whereas he considered the Hollanders' claims legitimate, he summarily dismissed the Frisians'. In particular, the *Hollandse kroniek* (12v) deemed the Frisian claim that Charlemagne had granted them independence a complete fabrication, and in his *Wereldkroniek* he (following Maerlant in some passages, even to the extent of copying his verses) had gone one step further: "And they say that they hold sound privileges from the Emperor Charles that they might enjoy their freedom and be without overlords, but their privileges are sealed with butter, for they cannot bear the sunlight, else they would have been displayed" (Ende zij segghen dat zij goede privilegien hebben vanden keyser Karle, dat zij vrye souden wesen sonder heere, maer haer privilegien sijn beseghelt met botteren, want zij en mogen gheen sonne ghedoghen, anders hadden sijse moghen toghen; 76r).

In judging the Frisians' refusal to submit to their lawful lords the Herald blamed their proverbially contrary and disobedient character.[46] This trait, in fact, had thrown them into armed conflict even before the advent of the counts of Holland—with Holy Roman Emperors and with such French nobles as Charles the Young, Pippin of Herstal, and (of course) Charles Martel, whose heroism found its logical expression in his war against Friesland. As always, Charles Martel emerged victorious, but the sequel to his subjugation of Friesland convincingly demonstrated the ignoble character of this godless people once again—at least according to the Herald (9r):

Ende hi streed enen groten strijd jeghens den onghehoirsam coninc Rabold van Vrieslant, dair hi veel der Vriesen versloech ende bedwang den coninc mit crafte; ende als hi den coninc verwonnen hadde, zo nam hine in ghenaden, op sijn belofte zonder twivel cersten te werden.

Cort hierna zo wert vermaent in enen godliken visoen Wolfranus, een aartsbisschop uut Zwoven dat hi varen zoude in Vrieslant ende helpen die goede priesteren die Vriesen te bekeren. Doe hi dair quam mit sijnre heiligen leer, dattie coninc Raboldus ward gheleerd toten heilighen ghelove ende hi zouden dopen; ende als deez zelve tyran quam ende zette sinen enen voet in der vonten ende der heiliger gheloven wair ghelofte zoude doen, doen zende hem die viand in dat hi vraechde weder die meeste hoop van sinen Vriesen waren ghevaren in hemelrijc of in die ewighe verdoemenisse. Die heilighe bisscop antwoirde hem, dat alle die Vriesen die in voirtiden niet ghedoopt en waren, die waren alle ghevaren ten duvelvolen. Ende als die coninc dat hoirde, tooch hi sinen voet na hem uter heiligen vonten ende zeide: "Ic wil liever mit veel gheselscaps die mijns vaders waren ende heiden ghestorven sijn inder hellen wesen, dan mit luttel dunre kersten die mi niet en bestaen in hemelrijc!" Ende tooch sinen voet na hem.

And he [Charles Martel] waged a great struggle against the rebellious King Rabold of Friesland, slaying a great many Frisians and subduing the king by might; and when he had defeated the king, he showed him mercy against the promise that he would become a Christian beyond all doubt.

Soon after, Wolfranus, an archbishop from Zwoven [Swabia], was told in a divine vision to repair to Friesland and help the good priests convert the Frisians. And he repaired thither with his holy doctrine, to instruct King Raboldus in the holy faith and to baptize him; and when that said tyrant came and placed his one foot in the font and was about to embrace the holy faith, the devil inspired him to ask whether the greater host of his Frisians had been taken to the heavenly kingdom or to eternal damnation. The holy bishop answered him that all Frisians who had not been baptized had gone to the devil. And when the king heard that, he withdrew his foot from the holy water and said: "I would rather be with the great company that were my father's and died as heathens in hell, than dwell in heaven with a small band of Christians that are nothing to me!" And withdrew his foot.

As the Herald saw it, the Frisians' reluctance to bow to authority (that is, to Holland) was a clear sign of disobedience to God's commands. Not surprisingly, he expatiated on the hard work needed to convert them to Christianity. Little could be achieved with kindness, not even by such men of God as Willibrord and Boniface, the second of whom, for instance, never ceased to "preach the word of eternal salvation to the unbelievers" (prediken den onghelovighen volk mit dat woird der ewigher zalicheit) in Dokkum. "Yet those wild butchers stopped up their ears like deaf serpents and would not hear the paternal teaching but with pikes and swords set upon the servants of God and killed them with many wounds" (Mer die verwoede vleishouwers stopten hoir oren als een doof serpent, ende wouden niet horen die vaderlike leer, mer met peken ende mit zwairden versloeghen si die knechten Goods, ende dodense mit menigherande wonden; 9v). Now, if the Herald knew anything, it was that those who would not freely listen to the preaching of the Holy Gospel must be compelled to do so by force, and not least those "wild butchers" from Friesland. By emphasizing their fatal inclination to godlessness, the Herald was able to magnify Holland's war against the Frisians into little short of a full-blooded crusade. Mostly this was done implicitly, but he did once openly describe the conflict so. In his account of the expedition led by Count Floris IV against Stedum, he explained that these Frisians had been guilty of heresy, incest, the murder of priests, and idolatry (64v):[47]

Ten inden jare ons heren 1234, deez grave Florens van Hollant tooch mitten hertogen Heinric van Brabant (die derde Heinric) ende mit grave Diederic van Cleve bi gheheite des paeus Gregorius die IXde also ghenoomt, voeren in die Stedinc Friesen lant bi Bremen, ende verjaechden dair uut ende versloeghen manne, wijf ende kindren; want si dreven katterie, ende die broeder sliep bider zuster, ende en hilden van den paeus noch van niement, ende doden papen ende clerken ende waren omme ghekeerd toter oeffeninghe der afgode.

And in the year of our Lord 1234, Count Florens of Holland went forth with Duke Heinric of Brabant (the third Heinric) and Count Diederic of Cleves at the behest of the pope named Gregorius IX into the Frisian land of Stedum near Bremen and drove from there men, women, and children; for they practiced heresy, and brother slept with sister, and they heeded neither the pope nor any other, and killed priests and clerks, nor were they averse to offering sacrifices to idols.

That the Herald was an enthusiastic champion of crusades is seen clearly in both his chronicles and should not surprise us: fighting heathens, after all, was the surest way of gaining honor and salvation. What is surprising is that in both chronicles he should hint (and this is understating it) that Holland's conflict with Friesland, too, was a holy war against a people who cared for neither God nor his commandments.

Defiance of earthly and heavenly authority ran, according to Bavaria Herald, in the Frisians' very blood. Even when forced to submit to Holland and the church, they could never be trusted not to break their sworn promises. As a recent example, the Herald mentioned one of William of Oostervant's expeditions against Friesland, which culminated in the (militarily imposed) installation of his father, Albert, as overlord of Friesland: "And all the Frisians paid homage and swore an oath to him as their rightful lord, which they kept ill" (Ende alle die Vriesen hulden ende zwoeren hem voir horen rechten heer, dat si qualiken hilden; 121v). Fresh punitive expeditions were thus deemed necessary, but so long as the Herald lived the outcome was inconclusive. Hence he was unable, in his *Hollandse kroniek*, to end the Frisian story on a happy note.

It is probably no exaggeration to say that the Herald's work was a clarion call for fresh campaigns against Friesland—if only reading between the lines. Here we must also consider the dates of his chronicles, and their dedications. Shortly before the two chronicles were completed, Count William VI and the bishop of Utrecht, Frederic of Blankenheim, had successfully joined forces in the so-called Arkel campaigns. Was it the Herald's wish that these lords might also bring their alliance to bear upon Friesland? After all, the history of Utrecht, too, had been full of conflicts with Friesland—something the *Hollandse kroniek* was unlikely to ignore. Nor was it an accident that the Herald should have paid particular attention to Utrecht's most militant bishops.[48] Quite possibly he did so on the instructions of his employer, William VI, at whose behest, too, the *Wereldkroniek* and the second version of the *Hollandse kroniek* may well have received the additional dedication to Frederic of Blankenheim.

But if the Herald did indeed intend to fan the embers of war against Friesland with his chronicles, he must have been sorely disappointed, and his work was written in vain. No doubt his *Hollandse kroniek*, which the prologue tells us was offered as a New Year's present to William VI (and later presented to Frederic of Blankenheim as well?), did help his sovereign to "pass the time"; and William may well also have derived martial inspiration from the many references to his brave ancestors. But the Herald's dream of breathing new life into the Frisian war, in which he had fought in 1400 under the banner of Holland, came to nothing. From the time he finished his chronicles to his death toward the end of 1414, the Frisians were left in peace. The champion had outlived the cause for which he had stood. Seen in this light he becomes a tragic figure, one who lived just long enough to see the Frisian fire die but not quite long enough to witness Agincourt in 1415, a battle that would certainly have uplifted his heart. In the end, fifteenth-century Holland was not ready to find in the Herald's great ideal, the clash of knights, venerable though it was, the inspiration he thought so essential. But before we declare the Herald a lone voice, we must first place him in a wider context.

4. THE WANING OF CHIVALRY?

According to a widespread view, medieval chivalry had passed its prime after the thirteenth and certainly after the first half of the fourteenth century. The Crusades had ended in a series of fiascoes, and tales of knightly exploits were no longer in fashion. In short, chivalry had had its day, in literature no less than in the real world. The cult of the knight had no future and, indeed, no genuine present; it had given way to the burgher and to trade. At best the chivalric ideal might linger as a haunting pipe dream, fed by nostalgia rather than conviction, the object of a melancholy little game that had lost its inspiration along with its reality. The sacred fire had been doused; attempts at revival produced at best an artificial glow by which a played-out class tried without conviction to warm itself.

This account of a decadent late-medieval knighthood—nowhere more masterfully detailed than in Huizinga's *The Waning of the Middle Ages*—has recently been thoroughly retouched, with various scholars stepping out of the shadow cast by that celebrated work to take a less blinkered look at late-medieval chivalry.[49] All, moreover, come to surprisingly similar conclusions and suggest that the prevailing picture of chivalry in decline must, at the very least, be revised. Even in its glory, the claim these days goes, the world of knighthood involved a considerable disparity between dream and fact—in which case the gulf between chivalric ideals and reality could hardly be a characteristic, let alone a proof, of the "decadence" of the late Middle Ages. Quite apart from their views on the period preceding the time studied by Huizinga, these investigators call for a thorough revision of Huizinga's thesis. The general tenor is clear: in the fourteenth and fifteenth centuries, the ideals of the chivalric class were far from dead. The knights may, on the social scene, have had to contend with growing opposition, but they had not abdicated. Old chivalric traditions survived or were infused with new meaning; and the very versatility and intensity of these new forms show that the chivalric ideal still largely dominated the upper reaches of society.

There is much to be said for writing a history of chivalry at the court of Holland-Bavaria in these terms. Indeed, it can be shown that the very phenomena that are nowadays considered signs of the vitality of late-medieval chivalry were in clear evidence at The Hague. To the first of these phenomena we owe the present chapter: heraldry, which could never have flourished without a flourishing knighthood. Or, to put it another way, heralds served to underpin the knights' social and military standing; the survival of the chivalric tradition was best served by men whose professional business it was to guard that tradition, something that heralds did preeminently well thanks to their knowledge of her-aldry, genealogy, and history. Heralds held the past up to their present employers, with armorials, chronicles, eulogies, and so forth. Knowl-edge of the splendid past must be an inspiration for a noble present, must serve as a good example.

In the late Middle Ages, one such example was set by the Nine Wor-thies. This nonet comprised the three greatest heroes from each of the three great cultures, Jewish, heathen, and Christian: David, Joshua, and Judas Maccabaeus; Hector, Julius Caesar, and Alexander; Arthur, Char-lemagne, and Godfrey of Bouillon, the first crusading king of Jerusalem. At the court of Holland-Bavaria, too, the tradition of the Nine Worthies was well known. We read, for example, in the accounts for the year 1396 that the count's council chamber contained "small painted hangings in which are shown the Nine Worthies"—the council's business, after all, was to recommend knighthoods.[50]

Needless to say, Bavaria Herald, too, had the Nine Worthies at his fingertips.[51] In his eulogy to the duke of Gulik, he mentions them ex-plicitly. And not only could he reel off their names and titles, but he also commented on them. In his *Wereldkroniek*, for instance, he expresses surprise that Octavian (the first emperor!) is missing from this exalted company; in his view, Octavian should have been offered Caesar's place. Unfortunately, by then the nonet was too entrenched to be reformed. What the Herald could do instead was set up a list of honor of his own: his Bavarian armorial extols the three worthiest Adolfs, Henrys, and Williams in world history, as well as the three worthiest Jans, Gerrits, Klaases, and Wijnands.[52] Fascination with such chivalric tables of honor was a characteristic of the spirit of late-medieval knights, who conceived the past as one long striving for excellence—not least thanks to the teachings of their heralds. The great heroes of the past were meant to be discussed, admired, emulated, and, if possible, excelled. Tradition creates obligations.

Medieval knights thus took it upon themselves to excel, to shine by their past no less than in the present, and for that nothing served them better than the tournament. When mentioning two jousts in his *Hollandse kroniek* in passing, Bavaria Herald had few doubts about the participants' motives: the tournament was an occasion for gaining "praise and thanks" by distinguishing oneself in the lists.[53] And "praise"—the respect of other knights—was what the aristocracy valued most. The rich history of an institution so dominant in chivalric routine as the tournament clearly is still waiting for exhaustive treatment;[54] but when that history is written, the late Middle Ages will certainly be privileged with the place of honor. For it was then that the jousting cult attained its most spectacular heights, in Holland as much as elsewhere.

We know from our history books that Count Floris V liked to "tourney," while Count William IV owed his title of "knight of honor" not least to his jousting prowess. And had the court of Holland ever witnessed so showy a tournament as the one Duke Albert organized in 1395?[55] In his name, Cleves Herald summoned knights from all over the German Empire to take part. Meanwhile, neither money nor trouble was spared on the preparations. Helmets, velvet, and gold ribbon were ordered from Paris; a servant was sent to Hainaut for pennants and trimmings. Extra swords and mail were struck for the occasion. The host's robe was embroidered in "golden letters." The steel-and-iron lists were draped in precious materials; sashes of gold silk were ordered, red frills for the helmets, sequins, stitchery adornments, gold thread, and damask, the latest from Florence. The tournament itself included not only jousting on horseback, but also a clash on the water, with the contending knights attempting to fling their opponents into the lake from the prow of passing boats. Their efforts no doubt caused much hilarity—appropriately enough, because the event occurred on Shrove Tuesday.

The duke himself took part. Although he was nearly fifty-nine in February 1395, a messenger was sent to Hainaut to fetch "my lord's tilting harness." In view of Albert's age, we may take it that he did not join the main competitions and, in fact, did little more than put in an appearance. But then, Albert's role as a jouster would have been insignificant compared with his importance as organizer of the splendid ceremonies and contests. To the "ordinary" participants, as Bavaria Herald put it, tournaments were merely a "board game" for measuring their strength and enhancing their reputation. For the lords who organized tournaments, however, much more was at stake. For them tournaments were public displays of valor and power and a means of gathering the elite around their throne. Anyone holding a festival placed the guests in his debt.

Closely related to the tournament cult were the orders of knighthood that mushroomed during the later Middle Ages.[56] These might also be mistaken for mere tourneying associations, their members, bedecked with badges ranging from stars to porcupines, seeking diversion behind a façade of high-flown statutes—chivalric rotary clubs, one might say; Round Tables without a Holy Grail, Templars without Jerusalem. But once again, appearances are deceptive, for their games, too, were played in deadly earnest. The main object of the orders of chivalry was to forge both legal ties in the unstable world of international feudal relationships and coalitions based on personal alliances. And such bonds were in fact effected by the orders, membership in which was personal and non-transferable, expressed internally by what were sometimes very carefully stipulated mutual assistance pacts (often sealed with elaborate rituals) and externally by the wearing of what were frequently the weirdest insignia and emblems. The leading nobles, in particular, were avid to establish such exclusive associations, with themselves at the center of honor. Thus, to mention the most famous, the duke of Burgundy created the Order of the Golden Fleece, and, much earlier, the king of England founded the Order of the Garter, which numbered both Albert and his son William among its few continental members—further evidence of the high regard in which the counts of Holland-Bavaria were held abroad. (Thus we see that it was not purely by chance that, in the famous drawing of the fishing party [discussed briefly in Chapter III, sec. 4; and see fig. 13], Count William should have exposed his left knee.)

Holland also had orders of her own. Duke Albert of Bavaria was presumably the founder of the Order of Saint Anthony, mentioned after 1382, especially in Hainaut sources.[57] His son William VI was a member; on the well-known miniature of the Turin cavalcade (see frontispiece), William is shown wearing the ribbon of the order round his neck: the *tau* of the patron saint with a small silver bell attached. Subsequent members of the Bavarian dynasty and their kin also belonged to the (mixed-sex) order: Jacqueline of Bavaria, Frank of Borselen, John of Wassenaar, and Margaret of Burgundy. Secondary founding charters of this order (the originals have been lost) reflect the mixture of elitism, idealism, and sociability so characteristic of all such groups. To join one it was necessary to be of old noble stock on both the father's and mother's side (later these conditions were relaxed, and the paternal line was sufficient). Moreover, although descent from the high nobility was a necessary preliminary, it was not sufficient for admittance; the hereditary predisposition to excellence had to be complemented by personal acts of valor—to be judged by the existing members.

The Order of Saint Anthony had its seat in the chapel of Barbefosse, a valley in the Hainaut forests near Bergen. Members' portraits and coats of arms graced the walls; the tombs of deceased members, adorned with heraldic emblems, enjoined unity beyond death. And although we have no concrete evidence, it is not hard to imagine that Bavaria Herald and his colleagues delivered many a eulogy within these walls. It was here, also, that new members were initiated in lengthy rituals with strong sacral overtones. After a series of prayers and hymns, the new member's badge was blessed by a priest and sprinkled with holy water and then placed around the candidate's neck by the head of the order.[58] The main responsibility of membership was to uphold one another's honor; but upon joining, members also swore to defend the church, to uphold justice, and to protect widows and orphans. Albert certainly knew how to sustain the ancient chivalric virtues.

In addition to being a member of the Order of Saint Anthony, Albert's son, William of Oostervant, was dominant in an order that he himself founded.[59] From 1390 on, entries in the accounts mention the chivalric Order of the Garden—membership in which Count William offered to John of Gaunt, duke of Lancaster, during a visit to England. Extant sources tell us little about the statutes and activities of this order, although the young count used its badge at least twice as a pledge for his debts on the tennis court (an order of chivalry plainly had many uses). Still, the Order of the Garden must have had nobler aims; no order of chivalry was thinkable without an ideal and, if possible, a practical aim to boot. Now, the practical aim was obviously combat, for despite noble and sacred phrases, combat was the very soul of chivalry. But combat with whom? There were no better foes than collective enemies, and heathens were the ideal candidates. Thus the Order of the Sword was founded to effect the reconquest of Palestine—an ancient dream but, not surprisingly, a burning ambition of the king of Cyprus, master of the order. Other masters more removed from the Mediterranean chose to seek out the heathen nearer to home, either because they

19. Knights attacking the heathens. (Koninklijke Bibliotheek, The Hague, MS. 130 B 21, fol. 88r)

had been taught their lesson in far distant lands, or to be able to return home quickly if the Hundred Years' War continued to play havoc, or perhaps for economic reasons.

Economically speaking, the costs of late-medieval crusades seem to have greatly outweighed their benefits—in the eyes of modern historians no less than in those of many contemporaries. But for true lovers of chivalry, the enormous costs were an advantage rather than a drawback: what more obvious way was there of demonstrating one's care for the grand objective of knightly honor and the cause of Mother Church? In defense of this holy cause, then, many a knight "journeyed forth," as they euphemistically put it even then. The "journey" generally led to Prussia, which bordered on lands inhabited by Lithuanian heathens.[60] To win these savage tribes to Christianity (together, of course, with their lands) was the main objective of the Teutonic Order, which organized expeditions east and north from its headquarters in Königsberg. The warriors were recruited in the west (Chaucer's "gentil parfit knight" was one of them). European knights loved nothing better than journeys intended to teach heathens of what stuff the defenders of the true faith were made.

Yet conversion was not a sine qua non of their endeavors: the participants much preferred waving their swords to preaching the Gospel. For most, the religious justification was no more than a post hoc rationalization. Their true inspiration was the good fight that could here be fought without danger to the salvation of one's soul, which indeed the crusade was thought to ensure. And so they would round up their hapless opponents, peasants more often than soldiers, dragging them not very chivalrously from their tubs or beds. Our West European knights enjoyed themselves wonderfully, and when we read accounts of their expeditions to Prussia, it is not just the word *journey* that recalls tourism; the whole enterprise seemed like some kind of chivalric (winter) sport, the sportsmen assembling in Königsberg whence they proceeded—circumstances permitting—to a world wreathed in white. It was a welcome challenge, for in addition to Lithuanians, who often resisted, the knights had to wrestle with bitter cold and difficult terrain. These were ideal circumstances for reaping honor, and all the Prussian campaigns were fought with that goal in mind. In its Festival Hall in Königsberg, the Teutonic Order had even set up a special "table of honor" with seats reserved for knights who had distinguished themselves in these battles. The choice of that elect band naturally rested with the heralds.

In late-fourteenth-century Europe, it had become almost normal for a young man of noble blood to make at least one journey to Prussia as part of his education. Quite often such travelers turned into regular visitors, for instance the young master of Boucicaut who thrice made the journey because there happened to be no fighting going on in France and also because of rumors of a *bele guerre* in Prussia *ceste saison*. Knights from the Low Countries often joined in the bloody revels. Many of the warriors extolled by Gelre (later Bavaria) Herald could boast of a glorious journey to Prussia—and the Herald knew what that meant, since he himself had been to Prussia four times in eight years!

Counts of Holland, too, liked to be seen in Prussia. We know that William IV went on three campaigns, having first been briefed (as we learn from entries in the accounts) by John of Vlodorp, who, as a herald, might be expected to have had intimate personal knowledge of the "state of Prussia."[61] Nor would Bavaria Herald have warranted the title herald had he not made special mention of the count's journeys to Prussia (96v–98r). According to him, the first was made at the behest of William's father, who, having dubbed him a knight from his sickbed, "sent him straightway to Prussia with great honor and at great expense" (ende zande rechtevoirt in Prusen mit groter eren ende cost). William's second journey, the Herald wrote, was something of a disappointment: on his arrival in Prussia, he discovered that "there was to be no journey; and took his leave of the master of Prussia" (that is, the master of the Teutonic Order there) (dair en vel gheen reise; ende nam oirlof anden meister van Prusen). His third venture, however, was a spirited affair. Having returned from a (peaceful) pilgrimage to Jerusalem, "he learned that many knights had set out for Prussia that winter; and he repaired thither for his third journey, and lay there all winter at great expense" (vernam hi datter veel ridderscaps tooch dien winter in Prusen; ende reed dair heen sijn derde reyse, ende lach dien winter dair mit groter cost). The extravagant cost of William's expeditions to Prussia was clearly money the Herald considered well spent.

Because of the perilous beginnings of his reign and also because of his early mental illness, Count William V never reached Prussia, nor, apparently, did Duke Albert of Bavaria. Albert did, however, fight against the Moors in Spain; and according to one story (probably false, but not entirely unlikely), he founded the Order of Saint Anthony for the express purpose of furthering the Prussian campaigns. His son William of Oostervant did go to Prussia, and we can tell from the account books that Bavaria Herald (then still Gelre Herald) was there at the same time. But although they got as far as Prussia, they were unable to do what they had set out for; the weather was simply too bad for fighting chivalric battles. There was great expense, of course, but little honor in the field. Nevertheless, the *Hollandse kroniek* tried to make the best of it: "Item soon thereafter, the noble lord set out for Prussia with many knights and squires from his own country, where he wintered at great expense. But there being no journeys from there, he came back home" (Item cort dair na zo tooch deez edel vurste in Prusen mit veel riddren ende knechte uut sinen lande, dair hi dien winter lach mit groter cost. Meer dair en ghing gheen reyse uut, ende quam tot huus; 123v). After that, he confined himself to briefer journeys to Friesland.

As far as Holland was concerned, in fact, the campaigns against Friesland were even more attractive than the journeys to Prussia. Friesland was nearer; it could also get very cold there, and there was no lack of opponents. And while the Lithuanians were relatively unknown foes, Holland's feud with Friesland was highly personal—and whenever there was the slightest danger of this being forgotten, the heralds made sure to rekindle the old enmity in people's minds. In his chronicles, Bavaria Herald did just that and, moreover, did all he could to belittle what small "advantages" Prussia might have had over Friesland. After all, the Frisians, too, were heathens of a kind. Throughout history, they had been on the wrong side, not least in matters of religion. Hollanders thus had the historic task of serving the good cause on their own doorsteps and of teaching the Frisians manners.

With his attempt to whip up anti-Frisian fervor, Bavaria Herald was rehashing sentiments expressed by earlier men of letters. Stoke, for example, had made a concerted effort to pillory the (inherent) godlessness of the Frisians, and Froissart had branded them (through the mouth of William of Oostervant) "gens sans loi et sans foi."[62] The feud with the Frisians was therefore long standing, and knights seized on it with rare intensity in the late fourteenth century. Part of the explanation for their zeal may be that Holland needed an external enemy. This may sound rather cynical, but the county was in danger of succumbing to the internal tensions of the Hook and Cod dispute. William of Hildegaersberch could not have been the only one to fear that outcome—certainly not when, after the murder of Adelaide of Poelgeest, Duke Albert and his heir apparent quarreled. It might thus easily have been for the sake of restoring peace at home that the eyes of the court of Holland turned to Friesland, the old enemy.[63] To medieval nobles war was a proven means of ensuring internal cohesion. Fighting side by side forges close bonds—bonds that were desperately needed in late-fourteenth-century Holland.

And so Friesland came under attack. The full arsenal of chivalric props was thrown into the Frisian campaigns. It was no coincidence that Duke Albert's tournament referred to earlier was called for February 1395: the date was not only the eve of Carnival but also—and much more significantly—that of the first great Frisian expedition. As training in battle and a show of solidarity, a grand tournament was *the* obvious prelude to real warfare.[64] Heraldry and appeals to the orders of chivalry were used to cement further unity. An entry in the 1399 accounts mentions a payment to "Dirk the painter," a specialist in heraldic design, for six great blazons with the insignia of the Order of the Garden, which William of Oostervant dispatched (together with another three hundred heraldic shields) to his field quarters in North Friesland.[65] And books went along as well. An entry in the accounts during the first Frisian war mentions the acquisition of "a small chest wherein a great many of my lord's books were carried." What might the contents of that chest have been? No doubt the *Boec van den oerloge* (The book of war) was included (which was also mentioned during the siege of Hagestein), and perhaps some legal or historical texts that his lordship could consult every now and then to make certain his cause remained as just as ever it had been.[66] In 1396, the Hollanders were still without the chronicles of their future herald, but that lack was more than made up for in 1400, when he went to Friesland in person.

By then, Friesland was teeming with heralds. The accounts indicate that at least twenty attended Albert's first Frisian campaign.[67] Nor is this surprising, for on such occasions Friesland was a happy hunting ground for them. Here, after all, knights' honor was not just an ideal. And in Friesland, heralds were able to inspire the knights with old tales of honor and vengeance, and in turn gain fresh inspiration for future eulogies. It was not by chance that Bavaria Herald included a complete version of his heraldic poems about the 1345 Battle of Stavoren when he came to write his *Hollandse kroniek*. Other poets who waxed lyrical about Friesland were likewise assured of interest and reward at the Hague court in those days, among them "a speaker from Monickedam who conveyed to my lord a poem about the Frisians," "a speaker who recited a poem about the Frisian journey for my lord," and no doubt many more.[68] All these poems, and in a sense also the prestigious chronicles written afterward, used words calculated to incite the knights to perform valiant deeds in Friesland. Their message was unequivocal: for the knights of Holland, the road to honor led through Friesland.

And honor undoubtedly was garnered in Friesland, though we have few hard facts on the matter except where, in addition to glory, hard cash was involved; here, then, the accounts provide tangible corroboration of what we might find hard to believe on the sole authority of such chivalric idealists (and hence romancers?) as Bavaria Herald. In the cashbook covering the campaign of 1400, for example, we read about a young knight in the lord of Brederode's ranks who used a *buss* (a modern firearm—not very chivalrous but nonetheless highly effective) to dispatch nine Frisians into a better world with four shots, for which feat he was paid a not inconsiderable gratuity of eight guilders.[69] (However high-flying the verbiage, the lower ranks found it impossible to live on honor alone.)

These, though, were spectacular exceptions. Often there was much less fighting than honor demanded—not least because the Frisian campaign turned increasingly into a war of attrition, especially round the beleaguered Stavoren, and armed clashes in the open field grew ever more rare. And while by its very nature the conflict provided few chances for chivalric action, its outcome, too, was much less honorable than the Herald and his kind would have wished. The successes that Holland notched up in Friesland were, despite courtly praises, extremely thin; indeed, the Herald's then employer, the duke of Guelders, saw things quite clearly when he opined (in Froissart's words), "que Frise n'étoit pas terre de conquête."[70] Eventually, Holland's dreams of conquest were reduced to the very modest wish to sustain the stronghold of Stavoren, which remained under constant attack, the Frisians being no less bitterly opposed to the Hollanders than the Hollanders were to them. Nor were the Frisians lacking in heroes: after all, many of their knights had fought the heathens in Prussia as well.[71]

The Hollanders had started the Frisian wars to gain greater honor; in the end their honor could barely be saved. Friesland, in fact, ended up a disaster for Duke Albert and his son. Their exaggerated chivalric ideals proved inapplicable in practice, not only in Friesland but elsewhere as well. Thus they found it increasingly difficult to convince their subjects to fulfil their *heervaart*, their obligation to do military service: either the ranks deserted at the earliest opportunity—as at Stavoren—or else they simply refused to arrive, if necessary buying a release. The lords saw an advantage to this latter course, namely that they could use the money to pay mercenaries instead of being saddled with such recruits as the "cooper from Voorschoten, an old, poor man and lame in both legs; a young squire by the name of John and was scarce 14 years old and poor to boot, or Gerard Cleves, a poor man from Zoeterwoude and he was maimed."[72]

Although most men called up for military service in about 1400 had no alternative but to heed the call, the view that all soldiers fighting in Friesland in the service of Holland—some fifteen thousand in all—were as fired with zeal as Bavaria Herald and his colleagues can be rejected out of hand. Instead, the historical records suggest that the lords found it increasingly difficult to recruit the troops they needed for winning greater honor and wreaking vengeance in Friesland. After 1400, when the failure of the first three great campaigns was still fresh in people's minds, the old anti-Frisian enthusiasm seems to have reached a low ebb. The towns in particular, exhausted by what they considered a waste of good money and human lives, refused to rally behind the count. At court, too, the failure was obvious: when Albert died in December

1404, his estate was so encumbered by Frisian war debts that his widow, the Duchess Margaret of Cleves, was forced to appear at the funeral in borrowed weeds and cast a blade of grass on the grave as a sign of her renunciation of all but her strictly personal hereditary rights.[73] Greater humiliation could hardly be imagined in a circle so attached to prestige that their dearest wish was, not only to live, but also, and perhaps above all, to die, in great style.[74]

No wonder, then, that the Frisian fire should have begun to burn itself out even at court. William of Hildegaersberch may not have openly inveighed *against* the Frisian wars, but neither did he speak up for them—and considering the date and social implications of his work, this omission is highly significant.[75] Dirk Potter, a courtier born and bred, wrote his books after 1410, but that is probably not the only reason why he wasted no words on Friesland. Rather, that conflict must have left him completely apathetic, an attitude seen also in his disdainful dismissal of revenge as fit only for those "who daily ride about in armor and play at war."[76]

Bavaria Herald, however, was unforgiving and never ceased his anti-Frisian propaganda; and if his drive came from the courage of despair, he certainly did not betray that fact in his chronicles. Of the wholly abortive last Frisian campaign he said no more than that William VI found it to be "an anxious journey, for the Frisians beleaguered him, and fired at him with their stone busses in the field; whence he nevertheless came away victorious and with great honor, and took their busses and arms from them" (een sorghelike reyse was, want die Vriesen hem int velt bestalt hadden ende scoten tot hem in mit horen steenbussen; dair hi nochtan mit zeghe ende mit groter eren van hem quam, ende nam hem hoir bussen ende hoir ghetoch).[77] More obliquely, the Herald went on to plead for a fresh punitive campaign. Even while diplomatic missions (Dirk Potter serving on one) were engaged in peace negotiations with the Frisians in the name of the count of Holland,[78] the Herald kept fanning the smoldering embers of hatred. So far as Friesland was concerned, he was nothing if not a hawk. Perhaps it was partly for that reason that he went to such pains to stress that the Frisians were semiheathens: he must have realized that, after so much disgrace and damage, appeals to honor and vengeance no longer sufficed.

But as we now know, even this quasi-religious opportunism failed to rally support for the Herald's anti-Frisian crusade. Not the least explanation of that failure must have been the church's lack of enthusiasm for a "holy" war against Friesland. Whereas the more genuine crusades of earlier times had elicited a passionate response from church and knight-hood alike, now the only people who could be aroused for a potential crusade against Friesland were such fanatic champions of chivalry as heralds. Perhaps something might still have come of the anti-Frisian cause had Bavaria Herald enjoyed the support of Dirk of Delft. But as we shall see, that court chaplain had completely different ideas about what a knight of God was meant to do.

V

Dirk of Delft

1. A MONK AT COURT

The turn of the fifteenth century brought with it a turn in the fortunes of Brother Dirk of Delft as well.[1] Until the last month of 1399, church and cloister had dominated his life. Born in Delft in about 1365 and doubtless recognized as a gifted youth even in his native town, Dirk joined the Utrecht Dominicans at an early age, enjoying the usual education the Jacobins provided for young monks. But while many a monk made do with an elementary monastic education, Dirk continued his studies for at least another ten years, immersing himself not only in innumerable religious texts but also in works of Aristotelian logic (known in the Middle Ages chiefly through Latin adaptations) and other learned tomes. In his day and circle, all learning led naturally to theology, and vice versa. Dirk's studies comprised, in addition to theory, a thorough practical training, especially in strenuous disputations by which pupils had to demonstrate (in Latin, of course) that they had not merely absorbed much book knowledge but also assimilated it sufficiently to formulate arguments of their own. All this went hand in hand with strict discipline and a rigid work schedule, a system of education as sweeping as it was demanding—in short, one that helped turn the best pupils into scholars.

Dirk of Delft was plainly one of the very few brothers with the talent and ambition needed for the highest education, which, since the thirteenth century, had been understood to entail attending a university. This education, too, called for many years of dedication to advanced theoretical and practical studies. And here again, Brother Dirk persevered to the end. He took the highest degree, that of *sacrae theologicae doctor*, seemingly a unique distinction for a Hollander in his day. Doctors of theology were, in the language of the time, so many radiant stars in the human firmament, experts on that ultimate pinnacle which was the knowledge of God.[2] They were highly respected by princes, nation, and church, and—illumined as they were said to be by special grace—

were thought to have a special gift of imparting knowledge of faith and salvation.

It is not clear at which university Dirk of Delft obtained his doctorate; perhaps at the highly respected Sorbonne, but more probably at one of the newer German universities such as Cologne or Erfurt. Yet it is not impossible that his alma mater was still farther from home, in England or even Italy. In 1400, a man from Delft with a bent for learning had to journey far afield. If we can believe Dirk's later declaration, he experienced his extensive travels more as an advantage than as a handicap. In the tone of a man of the world, which coupled well with his characteristically vivid imagery, he explained that the gift of self-knowledge is most highly developed in those "who travel and set forth across mountains and seas where they have to suffer many hardships. Had they stayed at home, they would have been like unto otters and moles" (die reysen ende trecken over berghen ende over meer, want hem veel lidens wedervaert. Hadden si thuus ghebleven, si souden recht als otteren ende mollen gheweest hebben; "S" XL/249–52).

But spiritually beneficial though Dirk's educational travels may have been, in material terms they required considerable sums of money. While these costs would normally have been borne at least in part by the Dominican order, for Dirk financial assistance was also rendered by no less a personage than Albert of Bavaria. How it happened that this ruler of Holland subsidized the education of young Dirk we do not know. What we do know is that on 17 December 1399, Albert decided that the time had come to draw some interest on the capital he had invested. In a letter of that date (fig. 20), the sovereign, using the customary *pluralis majestatis*, pointed out that "over the years we have helped Master Dirk of Delft of the Jacobin preaching order at Utrecht to attend many schools until such time as he became a *doctor in theologia*, meaning master of divinity; which pleases us most particularly because, as we have heard, there is no other in our lands" (wij meester Dirc van Delf, vander predicaren oerde ter Jacopinen t'Utrecht, jaerlix tot veel scholen geholpen hebben, also lange dat hi doctoer in theologia geworden is, datmen hiet: meester inder godheit; daer ons sonderlinghe lieve toe is, want gheen ander in onsen lande en is, als wi vernomen hebben). In the further course of this letter, the duke granted his protégé, in return for the "initial services he has rendered us" (ontfangeliken dienst die hi ons gedaen heeft), an annuity of twenty écus and an appointment at his court—with an eye to the services he may continue to render, "God willing, every day" (oft God wil, alle dagen doen mach).[3]

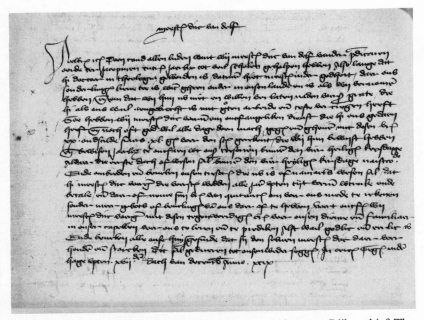

20. Master Dirk of Delft's letter of appointment. (Algemeen Rijksarchief, The Hague, MS. AGH 200, fol. 73v)

Voert ontfaen wij meester Dirc voergenoemt mit desen tegenwoerdigen brieve voer onsen dienre ende familiaer in onser capellen voer ons te leren ende te prediken, alst wail godlic ende eerlic is. Ende bevelen alle onse huysgesinde, dat sij denselven meester Dirc daer voer houden ende starcken. Dit sal gedueren tot onsen wedersegghen.

Further do we, by this present letter, admit the above-named Master Dirk to teach and to preach in our chapels to our servants and familiars all that is godly and upright. And we command all in our household to respect the said Master Dirk accordingly and to render him assistance. This they shall do until countermanded by us.

Was Dirk's exceptional learning the main reason why Albert sought to keep him permanently at his side? Did he wish to enhance the standing of his court with the presence in The Hague of the most learned man in all Holland? Or did he consider it advisable, after the latest Frisian fiasco (and on the eve of the next one),[4] to raise court morale not only with the winged words of a Hildegaersberch but also with the pious sermons of the learned Dirk of Delft? It is possible, too, that Albert's second wife made her influence felt, for Margaret apparently had a strong religious bent.[5] In any event, Dirk's letter of appointment does not specify Albert's real motives; rather, they are set out vaguely and yet with sovereign authority: Dirk must be present at the court "because we have no wish to relinquish him consequent upon the above-said degree which he (if we have been informed aright) did obtain with much labor and expense" (dat we hem nu niet en willen verlaten na den voerseiden grate, die hi [als ons wail aengebrocht is] met groten arbeide ende coste vercregen heeft).

It seems unlikely that the duke's wish, however diplomatically phrased, met Dirk's own needs. After all, by the end of December 1399 he had barely served three months as inspector of Dominican discipline in Flanders, a responsible post which proved that the Dominicans, too, appreciated his worth. Clearly, though, Albert's wishes were Dirk's commands, for Dirk did repair to The Hague. The position awaiting him there can best be described as court chaplain—provided it is understood that a chaplaincy was not an official post, let alone a formal court appointment with a clearly defined task, comparable to that of the clerics who served Albert as clerks.[6] In medieval times, the court chaplain was expected to concern himself largely with the liturgy, but might extend his work to such more or less related activities as preaching, hearing confession, reading the lessons, and rendering general assistance not only in spiritual but also in official or diplomatic matters.[7]

In this role, one quite new to him, Dirk of Delft had colleagues as well as predecessors at the Hague court. During his engagement, for instance, the court accounts mention "Henry, my wife's chaplain" (Heynric, mijnre vrouwen cappelaen), while "Brother William, my lord's confessor" (broeder Willem, mijns heren biechtvader) had played a prominent role at court many years before—not least because Margaret had charged him to make her a book (which, unfortunately, has not come down to us).[8] Thus, clerics at the court of Holland-Bavaria performed a variety of services for a variety of persons. In Dirk's case, too, the sphere of activity was wide and even included a kind of extraordinary professorship (in the language of the day, the post of "regent") at various German universities. A unique diary kept by a medieval student thus tells us that one Narcissus Pfister, a young Dominican, disputed on 24 January 1404 in Cologne before "magistro Dietrico Delf" whether or not a God-fearing man, living a pious life and meditating day and night, might be said to have reached human perfection even in this life.[9]

Although Dirk's presence in The Hague was not as regular as the formula "every day" in his letter of appointment may have suggested, we can nevertheless assume that this most learned Dominican was a permanent guest there, certainly after 1400. As such he is also mentioned in the court accounts. They do not record payment for his services in any particular position, but refer to him only by his title: "Brother Dirk, master of divinity," or simply "Brother Dirk the monk" or "Master Dirk the monk." [10] Especially on the great days of the Christian calendar, he (like William of Hildegaersberch) regularly made his presence felt, no doubt preaching in the court chapel. From behind the special lattice window through which one could look out but nobody could look in, the noble family would have watched their learned protégé celebrating mass, joined by all the "servants and familiars" who observed from the more exposed parts of the chapel.

If the "teaching" that Dirk was expected to do at court was not confined to the preaching of sermons, it is quite likely that he also catechized the courtiers (young and old?) and perhaps even served as their general instructor. For the rest, Dirk probably bestowed pastoral care on Albert and his family. Because such services were administered orally, we can do little more than guess at their nature and scope. Fortunately, though, Dirk did not confine his educational mission at court to verbal instructions. What he had apparently neglected to do at university he made good at The Hague: he immortalized his knowledge of the divine truth in writing. Here again we are able to fill in the picture with the help of the invaluable court accounts. As early as 10 January 1401—that is, just one year after Dirk's appointment—the records mention a payment to "Master Dirk the monk" for costs incurred by him in the preparation of "a book for my lady, that he made for her and brought to her all complete" (om een boeck voir mynre vrouwen, dat hi hoir gemaict ende gebrocht hadde al bereit). [11] Unfortunately, that book has not survived (or, to be optimistic, it has not yet been identified). [12] But another book by Master Dirk's learned hand has been preserved. It is the *Tafel vanden kersten ghelove* (Table of the Christian faith), which, obviously written soon after the one for her ladyship, was handed to the duke just before his death.

The *Tafel* is a masterpiece in the fullest sense of the word. As the reader will see below, particularly in section 3, with this large tome consisting of some thousand pages of prose, divided into "Winter Piece" and "Summer Piece," Dirk succeeded in unfolding a sweeping theological panorama of God's creation. As a religious encyclopedia, the *Tafel*, besides being a reverent and learned tribute to Albert, is also a tribute to God. But it is not only its wide sweep that makes the book seem a cathedral-in-words; Dirk's magnificent style also contributes hugely to the edifice. He writes not facilely, but in a powerful form of Middle Dutch, his compact prose deliberately reaching out for beauty and proving—almost ironically—how much could be done with the medieval vernacular by one schooled in Latin and rhetoric. In his clerical education Dirk is likely to have relied, actively as well as passively, on Latin; but when he wrote for the Hague courtiers, he was forced to exchange that learned language for his mother tongue. That adaptation was symbolic of a much more fundamental shift: on 17 December 1399, Dirk of Delft had abandoned the studious hush of university and monastery for the bustle of the court, where his audience was no longer ecclesiastical but worldly. The noble courtiers were as much Dirk's intellectual inferiors as they were his social superiors; moreover, they were destined by birth and circumstance for a pattern of life and thought quite distinct from Dirk's, but on which the "master of divinity" was nevertheless expected to allow his "magisterial" light to shine.

2. THE STATE OF THE WORLD

The preceding chapters will have told enough about life at the court of Holland-Bavaria to show that a court chaplain had more than enough opportunities for doing good work. If, like Dirk of Delft, one judged life at a medieval court by the norms of Christian morality, one would be forced to conclude that the court was severely at fault. Not surprisingly, then, those passages of the *Tafel* in which Dirk inveighs against what he termed "*appetitus huius seculi*, which means to say: worldly desire" (appetitus huius seculi, dat hiet: begheert deser werelt; "W" XXV/ 240–41) are neither the least numerous nor yet the least inspired. Thus he applied even the first of the Ten Commandments to worldly desire, albeit metaphorically. Much as heathens worship idols, so some Christians, according to Dirk of Delft, bow to avarice, gluttony, and unchastity—which is, if anything, even worse. Dirk took the basic idea and the appropriate quotations from biblical and classical sources; but the finishing touches were his own and reflect our court chaplain's deep personal commitment ("W" XXXII/110–31):

Dit sijn die serpent ende die beeste mit drien hoofde, daer in Apocalipsi staet of gescreven: Vermaledijt is die den beest aenbiddet ende sijn beelde. Dat eerste is ghiericheit, die aenbedet den penninc geliken dat een heyden doet sinen afgod; want die en wil sinen afgod niet breken, dese en wil sinen scat niet mynren; die settet hoep inden molock, dese heeft groten toeverlaet tot sinen blaeuwen sack. Seneca seit: aldus is dat ghelt een godinne geworden.

Dat ander is gulsicheit, die aenbedet sinen buuck; die tempel is die coken, dat altaer is die tafel, die dyaken is die cokenmeester, gesoden ende gebraden is die offerhande, die choorsanck is kyven, striden, afterspraken inder warscap. Paulus seit: Dese eer ende glorien comt hem te scanden, die alleen aerdsche dingen smaken.

Dat derde is oncuusheit; den aenbeden out ende jonc, rijck ende arm, die wijse ende die domme, si willen al Venus-dochter aenbeden ende ommevanghen. Mer die heyden aenbedet sinen god openbaerlic, dese haer godinne heymelick; die bi daghe, dese bi nachte; die en weet niet dan vander vrouwen Venus die overspel dede; mer dese kersten gelovet an enen joncfrouwen ende haer kint, die nye sonde en dede. Hier om seit Cristus onse heer: juwe sonden sijn veel meer.

Of the serpent and the beast with three heads, it is written in the Apocalypse: cursed is he who worships that monster and its likeness. The first [head] is avarice and worships money as the heathen does his idol; for much as the one does not want to break his idol, so the other does not want to subtract from his treasure; one puts his trust in Moloch, the other has great faith in his blue bag. Seneca says: so has money become a goddess.

The other [head] is gluttony and worships his belly; his temple is the kitchen, his altar the table, his deacon the head cook; boiled and roast meat his offering; scolding, squabbling, and backbiting at table his anthem. Paul says: honor and glory do not avail any who savor none but worldly things.

The third [head] is unchastity; it is worshipped by old and young, rich and poor, sage and fool, all wanting to worship and embrace the daughters of Venus. But while the heathen worships his god in public, these revere their goddesses in secret; these by day, those by night; these know no better than to commit adultery with Lady Venus; but those Christians believe in a virgin and her child who are without sin. Therefore saith Christ, our Lord: your sins are much greater.

Of the three-headed monster—avarice, gluttony, and unchastity— the author of the *Tafel* held the last two in particular loathing. Unlike Hildegaersberch, he seemed less distressed by the accumulation of worldly treasures than by worldly excess and carnality.[13] In his systematic treatment of the seven mortal sins, therefore, Dirk made heavy work of "*gula*, which is to say gluttony, and [which] stands revealed in excessive eating and drinking and intemperate living beyond all that is needful" (gula, dat hiet gulsicheit, ende is als sijn ghenuechte staet in overvloedicheit van eten ende drincken ende onmatelic leeft sonder sijn noturft; "W" XXV/180–82). This sin, too, had "many daughters or sprigs" (dese sonde heeft veel dochteren of telghen; 182–83). Dirk knew of a good ten, for which the courtiers at The Hague might not have been able to supply the Latin names, though they were intimately acquainted with the substance. Dirk seems to have based the classification of the first five forms of gluttony, in particular, directly on life at court as he knew it (183–200):

Die eerste hiet *crapula sive ebrietas*, dat is onghevoelicheit in eten of in drincken, als dat een sijns lijfs ghien mate en wete, mer als in enen trechter doer ghiet daer sijn lijf ende sinnen mede werden verswaert. Die ander hiet *castrimergia*, dat hiet verdroncken van alre suverheit, als wanneer hi van gulsichede alle hovescheit, tucht, zede, wijs gebaer ende guet gelaet verliest ende sijn sinnen warden vernevelt, dat hi ghien cuuscheit en hantiert. Die derde is *inmoderancia*, dat hiet onmaticheit, als dat een so verre inder gulsicheit raect, dat hi hem mit ghemeenre spijs tot seker maeltide niet en can genoeghen laten. Die vierde is *leccacitas*, dat hiet leckernye, als dat hi boven ghemeen spijs suect sonderlinge leckernye van wiltbraet, pannemoes mit sonderlinge const van cokenscaep, ende mit alre ghenuechten des ghebruuct. Die vijfte is *prodigalitas*, dat hiet verspildinge, als een mit onghemanierde miltheit ende cost sijn guet overbrengt ende niet toe behoeften, mer tot warscappen verteert.

The first is called *crapula sive ebrietas*, that is intemperance in eating and drinking, one's body knowing no restraint but pouring down a funnel, so to speak, what serves to oppress body and soul. The second is *castrimergia*, that is being devoid of purity, as when, through greed, one forfeits politeness, restraint, morality, good sense, and good manners and allows one's senses to become so befogged as to be utterly lost to chastity. The third is *inmoderancia*, that is lack of moderation, when one has so surrendered to gluttony that one is no longer content with taking one's daily fare at set mealtimes. The fourth is *leccacitas*, that is gormandizing, when over and above one's normal fare one craves such tidbits as venison and trifles prepared with unusual refinement, and feasts on them to the full. The fifth is *prodigalitas*, that is dissipation, when one wastes one's substance with utter extravagance and consumes food to satisfy whims, not real needs.

What courtier could deny that this cap fitted him? Even though Dirk of Delft did not say so expressly, passages like the above must have driven it home to his audience at the court of Holland that, by church standards, they were all outrageously steeped in sin. And our author left nothing to the imagination when, in the *Tafel*, he defined the first principle of the good Christian life as: "Thou shalt hate the world and with a willing heart abandon all that is hers, for whosoever does so hankers after God" (du salte die werelt haten ende al dat hoor is willichlic van herten laten, want wie dat doet die soect God; "S" XLVIII/254–56).

Still, Dirk of Delft was no ascetic, at least not in his *Tafel*. A degree of luxury was, in his view, not only a privilege but even an essential for anyone of rank. That category excluded peasants, for whom fine clothes or sumptuous wedding feasts were clear signs of a most reprehensible

21.   Sin dressed as a courtier (*TKG* "W" XXIII, dedication copy). (Walters Art Gallery, Baltimore, MS. W 171, fol. 90r)

lack of humility: an ostentatious wedding brings such people "expenditure without honor" (scade sonder eer), he wrote; and "costly clothes are intended for lords" (costelike cleder horen den heren toe).[14] In the case of nobles, however, such expenditure was no more than expected. A husband must furnish his spouse with "the clothes, jewels, and ornaments that befit her state and are becoming to her sex" (clederen, juwelen ende cleynoden die horen staet toe behoren ende hoer gheslachte betaemt te draghen). A great man must give feasts and parties "to keep his relatives content and to magnify his name with gladness, goodness, and honor" (houden die vrienden ende maghen te samen ende meren sinen name mit vroechden, guet ende eer). After the coronation of a prince, a grand feast should be held "befitting his great estate" (na eysch sijns groten staets), with a tournament and all the trappings and "whereat are found such great pomp, courtliness, and neatness as does not behoove me here to relate, for these the noble courtiers and lords know better" (groote singerie, hovescheit ende tucht ghescien, die mi niet hier en bueren te vertellen, want dat bet weten die curiael hofluden ende heren).[15]

In such passages, Dirk, notwithstanding his skeptical attitude toward the world's vanities, reveals his sympathy for the exaltation of status and rank that was so rife among the medieval aristocracy. Nothing in Dirk's origins suggests that he had acquired this attitude in his own home; nor would such views have been handed down to him as part of the moral teachings of Dominican mendicants. We may therefore assume that Dirk's view of the hierarchical life was inspired mainly by the court circles in which he moved from 1400. If he wanted to be respected as a preacher there, he had to have some grasp of the basic rules of courtly life. In Dirk of Delft, Duke Albert of Bavaria had a sympathetic court chaplain who, though somewhat detached from this world, certainly did not reject it.

On one delicate point, however, Dirk was and remained unyielding, and that was in his rejection of adultery.[16] Nowhere in the *Tafel* does he make the least concession to the fact that, at court, marriages were political arrangements, and love something altogether different. Thus he mentions the great example of Yba, a Roman noblewoman who thought that the entire male sex suffered from bad breath, and for no better reason than that her husband had halitosis: throughout her life she had not been near another man's mouth.[17] As spokesman for the Catholic church, Dirk zealously upheld marriage as a sacrament of love and fidelity and utterly opposed any form of extramarital love. Although that attitude would inevitably bring him into conflict with what was virtually normal behavior at the court of Holland, nothing apparently could persuade him to dilute his convictions; rather, he continued repeatedly and with gusto to inveigh against adultery.

Hence, when dealing with the sacrament of marriage in his *Tafel*, he amplifies his sources by asking an extra question, namely: "How great a sin is adultery, and what penalty and penance are appropriate to it?" (Hoe grote sonde dat overspul mach wesen ende wat boete ende penitencie dat daertoe behoort?; "S" XXXVII/207–8). Here Dirk seizes his chance to argue at length a question that he in fact took more or less for granted: that adultery is a gruesome sin. First, it is a sin that, like murder, cries out for (God's) vengeance. Second, besides resembling murder, adultery is theft, as witness the fact that, in the Ten Commandments, God placed his injunction against adultery between the injunctions not to steal and not to kill, as if to emphasize that adultery, too, deserved punishment by the gallows or the wheel. Third, the adulterer breaks a universal human law, inasmuch as "all nations and all countries, all centuries, all leagues and all sects have upheld marriage as a most worthy and sacred union and have sealed it with great promises, assurances and oaths. And if any commit adultery, he has broken his

oath and the law" (alle volc ende alle lande, alle eewen, loyen ende secten houden echtscap voir een hoech wairdich heilich dinck ende verga-
deren die mit groter loften, sekeringe ende eeden. Ende als een dan
overspel doet, soe heeft hi eede ende ewe ghebroken; 217–21).

Luckily, though, there is hope even for the adulterer: salvation
through repentance, confession, and penance. Since we know something about that subject from Chapter III, we can understand why Dirk
thought it useful to dwell on the penances appropriate to adultery in
such meticulous detail ("S" XXXVII/222–36):

Dit sijn die penitencien ende boeten die die overspeelre moet doen, sal hi hem
beteren. Eerstwerf soe sal hi vasten, peregrimaedse gaen, haren clederen draghen ende mit roeden hem gheescelen. Want hi in sinen lichaem ghesondicht
heeft, soe moet hijt weder mit sinen liven beteren. Anderwarf soe sal hi aelmissen gheven ende die wercken der ontfermhherticheit hantieren an arme menschen ende gheestelike personen. Want hi teghen sinen evenmensche misdaen
heeft, soe moet hijt weder daer teghen beteren. Derdewarf so sal hi heilighe
steden versoecken, in godsdiensten dicwijl wesen, veel ghebeden spreken, ende
ander gheestelike oeffeninghe pleghen. Want hi teghen die heilighe kerck ghebroken heeft, soe moet hijt mit gheestelike dinghen beteren, opdat God hem
ghenadich si ende voor plaghe ende pijn hoeden ende beschermen ende sijn
sonden vergheven. Amen.

These are the penances and penalties the adulterer must undergo if he is to
better himself. To begin with he shall fast, set out on a pilgrimage, wear hair
clothes, and chastise himself with rods. When he has been healed in his body,
then must he mend his ways. Secondly he shall give alms and do works of charity to poor people and clerics. As he has harmed his fellow men, so shall he now
make restitution. Thirdly he shall seek out holy places, frequently attend divine
service, say many prayers, and engage in other spiritual exercises. As he has
committed offenses against the holy church, he shall now offer spiritual compensation, so that God may show him mercy and save him from affliction and
pain and forgive his sins. Amen.

The reader of the *Tafel* is assumed to be a sinner and is enjoined to
repent the error of his ways and to enter upon the path of virtue. From
an author who in addition to being a theologian was also a chaplain, we
are not surprised to learn that this narrow path leads through the sacraments, and that the priest is there to guide men along it. Repeatedly, the
Tafel commends confession and penance as the sinner's surest road to
salvation. Penance is "the most blessed and finest of jewels our Lord has
left on this earth after his death" (dat salichste ende dat beste cleinoet,
dat God onse heer opter aerden liet na Sijnre doot; "S" XXXV/1–2).[18]
The keeper of this treasure is the priest, to whom the sinner must turn
because he will help to "transform the torture of hell into purgatory,

and to assuage the pain of purgatory by the penance he imposes; and also—and this above all—as, unless the priest grants absolution from them [sins], they will not be forgiven, inasmuch as the priest alone holds the keys to where God consigns all sinners" (die pijn der hellen inden veghevier verwandelt, ende in dien dat hi die pijn des vegheviers mindert mitten penitencien die hi settet; ende oec—dat alre meest is— tensi datse die priester absolveert, soe en werden se niet vergheven, want hi alleen die slotelen daer of hevet, tot welken God alle sondaren wiset; "S" XVI/475–80).[19]

Dirk was here describing an ideal, well aware that the world usually follows a different path. In effect, why should a courtier bother to go to confession? Dirk knew the answer and refused to listen to excuses, toppling them with his sharp intellect and keen pen. In an almost sarcastic outburst, not based on any known source, he drew a sharp caricature of the average Christian with his arsenal of dodges and excuses designed to justify his laxity in confessing his sins. Here Dirk of Delft showed himself to be a pastor only too familiar with his flock ("S" XXXV/91– 118):

Die scrift wijst uut vele sticken, die die ghewarige penitencie pleghen te hinderen. Dat eerste is: wemoedicheit enighe duecht te bestaen, recht als een scuwe paert, dat voor een schim vliet. Dat ander is: scaemte te biechten. Datsi hem niet en scameden voor Gode te doen, dat scamen si hem voer enen mensche te segghen! Dat derde is: dat hem voer die scarpe penitencie scroemt: hoe soude ic vasten, want ic teder bin . . . , hoe soude ic aelmissen gheven, want ic behoeftich bin . . . , hoe soude ic mijn ghebet spreken, want ic cranc van herten bin. . . . Dat vierde is: ghenoecht inden sonden, als aldus: ic moet spelen ende ic moet lachen, sal ic die werlt behaghen; ic moet in minnarschap leven, sal ic minen boel behouden. Dat vijfte is: hoep langhe te leven, als aldus: ick bin jonc, God sal mi sparen, als ic riper werde, so sal ic mi beteren; ic en sal, of God wil, niet cort sterven, want mijn ouders plaghen lang te leven. . . .

Dat seste is: anxt weder in sonden te vallen, als aldus: ic heb mi eens ghebiecht ende ic sondichde weder, ende eer ic mijn penitencie mochte doen, so viel ic weder in sonden; ic en vinde ghien beteringe. Dat sevende is: exempel van enen anderen te nemen, als aldus: die wise man doet dit; die heilige man die misdede dat; dat guede wijf is oec berucht; ic sie, dat wi alte samen sonden doen. Dat achtende is: mistroost Gods ghenade te crighen, als aldus: is dat waer dat ons die predikers segghen, wie mach dan behouden bliven? Is God also wraeckachtich alsmen scrijft, wie mach ymmermeer sijn sonden beteren? Ic wilt laten heen op die riem driven; ic en heb mar een siel te verliesen.

The Scriptures list many hurdles that are wont to prevent true penitence. The first is: infirmity before virtue, which is alike unto a shying horse that flees before a shadow. Another is: shame to confess. What they were not ashamed to do before God, they are ashamed to tell to a human being! The third is: that they shrink from strict penance: how can I fast when I am so delicate . . . , how can I give alms when I am so needy . . . , how can I say my prayers when I am sick at heart. . . . The fourth is: delight in sinning [justified] with: if I am to please the world then I must play and make merry; I must court if I am to keep my beloved. The fifth is: anticipation of a long life, thus: I am young, God will spare me, when I grow older I will improve; I shall not, if it please God, die young since my ancestors enjoyed a long life. . . .

The sixth is: fear of relapsing into sin, thus: I confessed and yet I sinned again, yea, before I could do penance I relapsed into sin; I can find no betterment. The seventh is: to mention the example of another, thus: the wise man did thus; the saintly man strayed thus; even the good wife has strayed; I can see that all alike lapse into sin. The eighth is: despairing of God's mercy, thus: if what the priests say is true than which of us shall be saved? If God is as vengeful as is written, then who need bother to sin no more? I shall let myself drift with the current; I have but one soul to lose.

Any who, ignoring Dirk's forceful plea, nevertheless put their salvation at risk by persisting in sin and ignoring their priest can also discover in the *Tafel* just what looms ahead of them. When Dirk describes hell, he paints a compelling picture of the eternal damnation awaiting lost souls. Indeed, Lucifer and his henchmen seem to have reserved a special punishment for every mortal sin ("S" LI/176–99):

Die *hovaerdighen* werden opghehanghen hoghe ende laghe, op ende neder laten schieten, want die hovaerdighe is altijt mit hoecheit sijns moets an verkeertheit sijns willens verhanghen. Die *ghierighen* wert pick, zwavel, tarre inden live ghegoten; want hem na aertscher haven so onmateliken dorstede, daerom moeten si den kelck der pinen weder overvloedich drincken. Die *nidighen* die doersteken hem selven mit groven strenghen, wantsi van haet ende van avegunsticheit hem selven pleghen te verteren. Die *toornighen* trecken hem selven die oghen uut ende willen hem selven verscoeren, wantsi in haer woedicheit so verblint werden, datsi ghien onderscheit der waerheden en connen bekennen. Die *traechen* legghen onder alle die voeten die hem pijn aendoen of doghen, ende werden van hem allen vertreden, wantsi die salighe tijt so onnutteliken overbrachten ende so die ghenade versuymden. Die *gulsighe* liden overgroten hongher ende dorst datsi daerof sterven willen, wantsi hoer lichaem so wel spijsden mit overaet ende dranc, ende haer lichaem daermede was verswaert, datsi den armen niet en spijsden. Die *oncuuschen* werden doer horen buuck ghesteken, recht als braden diemen specket, ende die wormen crupen doer haer ghemacht, wantsi hoir lichaem mit vulre, onnaerdigher ende onreyne begheerten reysden tot onsuverheden.

The *proud* will be hanged up high to be dropped down hard, for they are ever tied by the haughtiness of their spirit to the perversity of their will. The *greedy* will have pitch, sulphur, and tar poured into them, for they thirsted so avidly for worldly goods that they have to drain the cup of pain to the full. The *envious* will be transfixed with thick cables, for they were wont to tear themselves apart with hatred and spite. The *angry* will pluck out their own eyes and rip them-selves apart, for their anger rendered them blind to the truth. The *slothful* will be trampled underfoot most painfully, for they used to trample on blessed time and so forfeited salvation. The *gluttonous* will suffer deadly hunger and thirst, for they used to fill their body with excess of food and drink and let it grow heavy rather than feed the poor. The *unchaste* will have their bellies pierced, like larded roasts, and worms will crawl through their private parts, for they were wont to whip their body into impurity with indecent and foul desires.

For all that, threats were not Dirk's essential style. Particularly in the pulpit he seemed to trust persuasion more than force, mild words more than descriptions of hell. It is not that Dirk never preached harsh ser-mons, but he certainly preferred to avoid them, as we see in a chapter entitled "How preachers should preach" ("S" XXI), where he pleaded for the soft approach rather than the hard. In a manner revealing of Dirk's attitude to his lord, moreover, he supported this view with the explanation that a fierce tone can infuriate the nobleman to whom it is addressed[20]—and that benefits nobody. This fact the *Tafel* illustrates with the case of the philosopher who read Alexander the Great a "sharp" lesson about his extravagant wardrobe: "And the emperor fell into a rage and had the man's tongue cut off" (Ende die keyser wert toornich ende dede hem die tonghe of sniden; "S" XXI/66–67). Dirk's advice for those who preached to noblemen was therefore: "Let them approach their masters and convey to them the error of their ways by parables, with gentle speech rather than harsh words, for these will not be heard and so they do more harm than good" (Si sullen totten heren gaen ende gheven hem haer misdaet in parabolen te kennen mit suverliken reden, niet mit hardicheden, want dat en hoort niet ende het mochte meer sca-den dan baten; "S" XXI/58–61). Plainly, Dirk was a court chaplain who knew not only his public but his own place as well.[21]

True, it took no great effort for Dirk to express such mildness. Ha-rangues such as those delivered by Hildegaersberch, who never tired of declaring that he was practicing restraint only because he was forced to do so by his circumstances, were foreign to Dirk; the softness of his words, hence, was merely in keeping with his nature. For Dirk was a preacher of love from deep conviction, and not only where his sinful audience was concerned, but even in his treatment of the enemies of Christianity. Naturally, Christians, as the standard-bearers of the only true faith, were in his view superior to Jews and heathens, but that did not mean that he despised the latter two groups; rather, he felt sorry for them.[22] In discussing the Crucifixion, for example, although he did dwell on the torments involved, he—unlike so many other medieval authors—did not betray even the slightest sign of anti-Semitism, laying all the stress instead on the forgiveness that Jesus extended to his executioners.[23] Toward heathens, too, Dirk was remarkably mild. Naturally he hoped for their conversion, but to effect it he looked more to kindness than to harsh penalties.

Nowhere in the *Tafel* do we find the least trace of what might be called the crusader spirit. True, God gave Judas Maccabaeus a sword to defend the good cause, but ultimately Judas (one of the Nine Worthies) attained his ends "with charitable words and sermons rather than with shield or spear" (mitten gueden woirden ende sermoen, dan mit schilde of mit speer; "W" XVIII/246–48).[24] Dirk naturally found support for this stance in the Gospels, which also advocated spreading righteousness on earth not "by the sword" (mitten zwaerde) but by the "remission and forgiveness of sins" (mit oflaet ende verghifnis der sonden; "W" XXXIV/123–25). The *Tafel* grants that it may be necessary to resort to "just wars"—that is, resistance to an aggressor—as a last resort; but it never speaks of holy wars.[25] Dirk wasted no words on the conquest of Palestine or Prussia, let alone of Friesland. Bavaria Herald received little assistance from the court chaplain. Dirk's call from the chancel was "Love your enemies," not "Make war upon them."[26]

Yet neither did Dirk advocate the broken sword, at least not in his writings, which seems odd in so pacific a soul. Indeed, the *Tafel* fairly teems with images from warfare; knights, wars, arms, and battles occur with great frequency.[27] The metaphorical use of physical force to represent Christian spiritual strength is, of course, as old as the Bible itself and occurs in ample measure in the writings of the church fathers and of the theologians with whom Dirk had grown familiar through his long studies. That his use of imagery was traditional, however, does not automatically explain why Dirk should have drawn on just this tradition for his *Tafel*, and certainly not why he should have embraced its militant metaphors. Rather, the harnessing of this extensive arsenal of courtly images must probably be seen as a deliberate attempt to reach out to his audience of courtiers. While the deeper meaning of Dirk's message may have been beyond them, they were only too familiar with the various martial phrases found in the *Tafel*.

One telling example among many is the long chapter in "Summer Piece" (XIV) in which Dirk explains the significance of the great litany that at that time was chanted on the eve of Easter. Here the *Tafel* is on ground—the liturgy—that our court chaplain knew intimately, which alone was reason enough for him to discuss it at length. Dirk's sources referred to the litany as that of the sevenfold procession or of the black crosses, descriptions that provided all the explanatory material Dirk could have wanted. Not content to leave it there, though, he added a third explanation, which, unless it was written by his own hand, he must have borrowed precisely for its power to quicken the hearts of his courtly audiences (to which end, too, he even trotted out the idea of a crusade, though in his case for defensive purposes) ("S" XIV/170–78):

Derdewerf hiet dese letanie jaerlixe heervaert, want wi dan alle der heilighen reliquien ende heilichdom opnemen, ende mitten priesteren in haren ghewade te striden trecken, als mit Gods help teghen die heyden die der kersten lant verstoren, teghen onsen openbare, ontseide vianden, die roven, moorden ende branden, ende oeck teghen die bose gheesten, die ons van Gods verhenghen dat water, onweder, brant, aerdbevinghe, sterft, plaghen, pestilencie, siecte toe- brenghen, ende oec die beeste des veldes, die vruchts opter aerden verderven.

Thirdly this litany is named the annual campaign, for we then shoulder all the saints' holy relics and, with the priests dressed in their robes, stride out with God's help to do battle against the heathens who lay waste to Christian lands, against our common, declared enemies who pillage, murder, and burn, and also against those evil spirits who, at God's behest, threaten us with floods, storms, fire, earthquakes, death, plagues, pestilence, and sickness and also assail the beasts of the fields and the fruits of the earth.

Presented thus, not only the liturgy, but all Christian life becomes a struggle against the mortal enemy, sin—or, as Dirk puts it, paraphras- ing Job: "All man's life is like unto a clash of knights or a battle upon the earth" ("W" XX/450–51). For Bavaria Herald, wars such as those waged by the Maccabees may have served as models for bloody battles against the heathens, including the Frisians; for Dirk of Delft, however, they were moral symbols of "our spiritual war" (onse gheesteliken oor- loch; "S" XL/83).

Dirk bases another chapter ("S" XLIII) on this inner war that rages in the human spirit. He describes the seven deadly sins as "truly hellish murderers, who besiege man's every limb and bind his senses with strong spells and oppress, weigh down, afflict, violate and ensnare, de- feat and kill his conscience" (als rechte helsche mordenaers, die den mensche an al sijn lede belegghen ende mit swairre becoringhen die sin- nen stormen ende die consciencie beclymmen, persen ende pinighen, schenden ende vanghen, verwerpen ende doden; 32–36). Similarly, human virtue is beset by the seven "hellish horsemen" (helsce riddren) of the seven mortal sins, together with their followers, their "sergeants and supporters" (sarjanten [en] wapenturen). In that situation, is there anything a man can do beyond hoping that God will spare his citadel the worst? For Dirk's public at court, the answer was obvious: fight back. Luckily, as Dirk explains elsewhere, "a noble man of virtue" (een edele man van deuchden) is protected by the armor of a "knight of God" (ridder Gods) ("S" XLVI/361–74):[28]

Die vrede is sijn beenharnasch, want op die vrede machmen vast staen; doechtsamicheit sijn sijn sporen, want die verdiende duecht maect menigen man dat hi willigher is ende snelre dan van vresen of heren ghebot; guedertierenheit is sijn panser, want eens mans leven moet als een panser van menichvoudigher guedertierenhede ghebreit wesen; die wijsheit is der duecht helm, want die siet verre over; wairachtich ghelove is sijn scutte ende sijn boghe; reden is sijn zwaert; stantafticheit is sijn scilt; vaste hoep is sijn paert; vrese is sijn breidel; eendrachticheit is sijn wapentuer; guet gherucht is sijn araut. Die sijn die wapenen des lichts, want man die dese wapenen heeft anghedaen is starcker dan die die burgen beclymt, hi is scoenre dan die van verwen glymt.

Peace is his greave [i.e., leg armor], for on peace a man can take a firm stand; virtue his spur, for virtue renders many a man abler and fleeter than would fear or command; mercy his armor, for a man's life must be knit like a coat of mail but of compassion; wisdom the helmet of his virtue, for it overlooks all else; true faith his bow and arrow; reason his sword; steadfastness his shield; confidence his mount; fear his bridle; harmony his squire; a good name his herald. These are the arms of the light, for a man who has donned them is stronger than he who storms castles, and more radiant than he who dazzles with colors.

Such imagery the court public understood.

The simile of God's knight reaches its climax in Dirk's chapter on confirmation ("S" XXXIII). This sacrament for children had been instituted by Christ himself, "for he wanted to strengthen them in the pious virtues of the faith and make of them knights spiritual who under his banner of the gospels would fight against the flesh, the world, and the evil spirit" (want hise starcken woude in vroemheden der duechden vanden ghelove ende [om hen] gheestelike ridderen te maken, die onder syn bannier der ewangelien souden vechten jeghen vleisch, werelt ende bose gheest; 10–13). And that was just the beginning of a homily that Dirk, relying wholly on his own creative imagination, sustained for an entire chapter. The faithful are "God's warriors" (Gods kempen), champions who, "as God's knights" (als Gods ridderen) and armed "with the power of the Holy Ghost" (mit des Heilighen Gheests craft) "remain steadfast and unflinching in the fight they wage in the name of Jesus" (seker ende duerich bliven inden strijt voer den name Ihesu; 59–60). True, they must first receive baptism, just as "the knight must receive assent to go unto battle before he receives his arms and mail from his lord" (ridder moet ymmer eerst ontfanghen wesen ten heervaert te varen, eer dat hi sijn wapen ende gesmide vanden heer ontfae; "S" 67–69). Confirmation is thus a continuation of an armed race with the Devil; it "invests man with chivalrous virtue so that his spirit may do battle against sin and temptation . . . and places God's helmet upon a man's head" (wapent die mensche in ridderliker duecht gheestelic jeghen die sonden ende becoringhe te striden [. . .] het settet den Gods helm op des menschen hooft; 121–30).

This last bit of symbolism forms a prelude to an even ampler exposition on the weapons of light. Here Dirk saw fit to expand five verses of Saint Paul (Ephesians 6:13–17) into a good 170 lines of militant prose. The true knight of God appears fully armed for his fight with the three hosts of the Devil, the world, and the flesh, respectively. He wears the armor of righteousness, forged and held together by chain mail and buckles of truth, love, and succor; leg armor fashioned of benevolence; God's name and faith as a shield with three charges (Dirk, too, was familiar with heraldry), namely God's power, wisdom, and mercy. On his head gleams the helmet of hope; in his hand he carries the sword of God's word, which cuts down lust, pride, avarice, sloth, and spiritual error; he wears the cuirass of intense belief and is seated on the mount that is his undefiled body, shod with godly examples, and saddled with reason. And so on, and so forth. That is how the "knight of God" rides into battle.

Chivalrous battle itself is inseparable from honor. That honor among men is a worthy attribute Dirk of Delft never denied.[29] He was, however (and understandably so), reserved about men thirsting after worldly honors, a twice-vain pursuit in that it is a self-satisfied hankering after transitory glory; at its best it constitutes the chaff that, in purgatory, is separated from the grain of the good soul. Dirk contrasts this "worldly honor" (eer der werelt) with the vastly more exalted "everlasting honor" (eeuwige eer) reserved for Christ's knights in the hereafter: "Christ is the king of kings and lord of hosts, a prince of peace, a father of the world to come, a righteous rewarder of all knights who fight for God's righteous cause; he will crown them with crowns set with everlasting and precious stones of glory and honor, for he hath awaited their victory with close attention" (Cristus is coninc der coninghen ende heer der heerscappien, een vorst des vreden, een vader der toecomender werelt, een gherechtich loener sijnre ridderen die witachtelic striden; hi cronetse mit cronen, duerbaer gesteenten der glorien ende der eren, want hi verbeyt heeft opsiende horen zeghe; "W" XX/451–56).

Needless to say, such honor is not of this world. The beauty of eternal life close to God's divine presence rebukes all worldly glory, which explains why mortal existence can never be other than what it is "in this dark and sorrowful world" (dese besloten duuster verdrietlike werelt; "W" XXXV/10). Even the choicest delights of the courtier's life are meaningless in the end, "for all the world's joys are false and inconstant, short and delusive" (want alle der werelt vroechde valsch is ende onstedich, cort ende bedriechlic; "W" LII/160–61). Moreover, although it may seem to be the "highest end for a man to be at one with the world" (het schijnt nu wel die meeste const te wesen, dat nu een man mitter werelt can leven; "S" XLI/135–36), that is not the real significance of life according to our court chaplain. The aim of earthly existence is rather to prepare us for the true life, the life beyond—not the most inviting prospect for the courtiers whom Dirk addressed, surrounded as they were with every kind of worldly temptation. To live a good life on earth calls for the utmost self-discipline; he who is master of his own soul is many times stronger than he who "storms castles or subdues the heathen" (burghen bestormt [of] heydenen verwinnet).[30]

Dirk of Delft hoped by means of his *Tafel* to change the outlook of his readers radically enough to bring about a change in their behavior as well. The path he displayed to courtiers was one of utmost, rather than least, resistance. Yet for those who were willing to follow their chaplain to become God's knights, Dirk of Delft, in the final chapter of his *Tafel*, held out the promise of a reward unequaled by anything on earth: admission to God's own radiant court. And this, of all courts the most beautiful, is clearly not of this world ("S" LIII/288–301):[31]

So sal in hemelrijc vruechde van buten omme groteliken werden ontfanghen overmits grote gunste ende vrientscap, die ons dan God sal betoghen. Hi sal ons een tafel decken der werscappen ende der eren inden palaes der scoenheden ende vruechden; dairop rechten spijs veel lones ende salicheit; dienstluden ons setten vol lieften ende eerbaricheit; tafelghenoten vol edelheit ende wairdicheit; seydenspul vol ghenuechten ende sueticheit; scone lichte ontsteken vol schinens ende claerheit. In deser hoechtijt te bliven boven tijt in ewicheit, daer salmen clinghen alle heil ende salicheit. Aldus so sel wi sitten in truwen ende in sekerheit, toevloet van allen guede, invloet van alre weelden, omvloet van alle der gaven, overvloet van allen wunschen.

Then shall in the kingdom of heaven the uttermost joy be imparted in abundance thanks to the great favors and friendship God will bestow upon us. He shall set us a table of glory and honor in his palace of splendors and joys; treat us to much reward and bliss; surround us with servants abounding with love and courtesy, table companions of nobility and merit, string music filled with delight and sweetness, shining lights sparkling with brightness. Oh, to abide in this blessed state beyond time, in an eternity of salvation and bliss! There shall we dwell in hope and certainty, awash with possessions, flooded with abundant treasure, drenched with gifts, inundated by the fulfillment of all our wishes.

3. CREATION AND SCHOLASTICISM

No author at the court of Holland, and probably no courtier either, was more aware of the relativity of earthly affairs (life at court included) than Master Dirk of Delft. Our court chaplain's perception spanned time and space as far as Eternity, and with his *Tafel vanden kersten ghelove* he tried to make the courtiers privy to his sweeping vision. His encyclopedic work covers the whole of Creation, from the ore under the ground to the swooping eagle in the sky, from the first day of Creation to the Day of Judgment. The universe is laid bare from its greatest down to its most trivial detail, from God's essence to a man's sneeze, passing through reflections on the soul, the Fall, the nature and hierarchy of the angels, the life of Jesus and of the Antichrist, as well as spiritual and temporal justice, the liturgy, the role of the pope, the rules and mystique of chivalry, and the duties of peasants. Strict attention is paid to what we would nowadays call natural science in its broadest sense, for included are the planets, the four elements, the zodiac, the correspondence between human features and human character, the nature of blood, and much else. The *Tafel* also dwells at length on such subjects as usury, class differences, education, lies, and greetings, all woven into one great ethical system. Few topics are not discussed in one paragraph or another of Dirk's masterpiece.

In view of this curious jumble, Dirk's *Tafel* might easily have turned into a kind of almanac, some Middle Dutch *vade mecum*. But it is nothing of the kind. For the *Tafel* not only explores a vast field, but it also reflects a masterful grasp of the niceties of medieval thought, possible only because Dirk's intellect matched the majestic range of his arguments. That he kept the reins of his exposition firmly in hand is obvious from the careful design of the *Tafel*, probably devised by Dirk himself. Although every chapter is self-contained, so that on superficial inspection the work may appear to be a compendium of fifty-seven ("Winter

Piece") and forty-three ("Summer Piece") independent sections, respectively, on closer examination the sequence of these chapters proves to be part of a very carefully structured plan.[32]

Axiomatically, the *Tafel* starts with God himself, the first chapter being devoted to his nature, his name, and his triune essence. Dirk passes on to God's creative powers and his work of creation in this world, which later is examined in its material composition (the four elements). Next comes man, the focus of the "Winter Piece," with his soul and material aspects (character, physiognomy, seven ages) and—above all—his moral essence. Successive chapters present the human virtues in systematic order, an account that is logically followed by the equally systematic treatment of man's sins, the discussion of which is introduced by a disquisition on sin, the Devil, evil spirits, and the Fall.

Having thus reached the middle of his "Winter Piece," Dirk proceeds to explain how a man should confess his sins and obtain absolution from his priest, bishop, or even, for the most serious lapses, the pope. That brings the author to God's mercy, as revealed in the incarnation of his Son. A series of chapters is then devoted to the life of Jesus, from Joseph's marriage to Mary to the mission of the apostles. The central section of the *Tafel* (introduced by a discussion of the four evangelists and their sacred books) bridges "Winter Piece" to "Summer Piece" with an account of the Redemption.[33] The chapters devoted to the work of the apostles are followed by (quite logically) three chapters on the triune "state of the holy church," seven chapters on the seven works of charity, seven chapters on the seven divine offices and the liturgy, and seven chapters on the seven sacraments.

From that point on, the book follows a looser, though still far from haphazard, organization. The reader is now treated to a series of chapters on outstanding examples of virtue and vice in human history, together with a lengthy exposition in which the social order is described in terms of the rules and pieces of chess. After man's past and present, Dirk goes on to discuss the future, with chapters on death, the Antichrist, and eschatology.

Just as this scheme reflects a careful design, so also do the many cross-references in Dirk's text, with the references to subjects still to be discussed bearing even better witness to his compositional mastery than the (more numerous) references back to questions previously examined. Thus, in his description of the Holy Land, he mentions in passing that he will be returning to Christ's baptism in the Jordan—and in so doing points a good sixteen chapters ahead.[34] And during his account of

Christ's ascension, he adds: "Of the joy and bliss in heaven shall I still speak toward the end when I write of life eternal" (vander vroechden ende salicheit des hemels sal ic na segghen, als ic vanden ewighen leven sel int eynde scriven; "S" XV/247–49). Dirk kept his word, but not until 440 pages of prose later. Even though he may have added these cross-references after the work was completed, this rather academic reservation does not affect the crux of the matter: Dirk of Delft set out to make his *Tafel* a coherent whole, while still allowing the reader to pick at it chapter by chapter, reading each passage separately with profit and enjoyment.

This point can be exemplified by a look at chapter 3 of the "Summer Piece," which examines the Sunday in mid-Lent known as *dominica in rosa*, so called because on that day the pope consecrates a golden rose. The "greater sacrament" associated with this ritual must have been of particular interest to Dirk's courtier audience: after carrying the rose in procession, the pope handed it to "the bravest knight present at his court. And that knight is seated in his saddle with great pomp amid lords and princes and the populace and carries it [the rose] past all who are assembled. And thereafter, that knight is held in even greater respect and renown throughout the court" (den vroemsten ridder die teghenwoordich in sijn hof is. Ende die ridder sit up sijn ghereyd mit alle sijnre cierheit mitten heerscappen ende vorsten ende volck ende voirtse om alle die stat. Ende van dier tijt so is die ridder in alle den hove te eerliker ende te waerdigher; 11–15). After this outward description of the ceremony, Master Dirk proceeds to an elaborate symbolic interpretation. The rose represents not only Christ (the Rose of Jericho) but also the sinful believer to whom are attached, like thorns on a rosebush, all the sins of the flesh, "such as adultery, impurity, defilement, unchastity, lack of humility and impure greed, idolatry, enmity, dissension, envy, anger, partiality, scolding, manslaughter, drunkenness, dissipation" (als overspul, onreinicheit, onsuverheit, oncuusheit, onscamelheit ende onreinige ghiericheit, aenbeden der afgoden, viantscap, kijf, aefgunsticheit, toorne, secten, scelden, dootslaen, dronckenscap, werscap; 134–37). And, as if his meaning were not already clear enough, Dirk added this ominous rejoinder: "And whosoever doeth any of these things, shall not enter the kingdom of God" (Ende die deser ghelike dinghen doet, die en sel dat rike Gods niet besitten; 137–38). What member of the court of Holland could entertain the least hope for eternal life after so authoritative a pronouncement?

Yet Dirk would not have been the court chaplain he was had he not also pointed to the path of salvation, which, as we saw in Section 2, passes through repentance and penance. Here, too, Dirk could apply the metaphor of the rose ("S" III/138–48):

Van desen doornen sel werden rose-bladen inden hof der penitencien ende inden acker ons herten gronts, als wi die omkeren willen ende graven mitten grave der ware bekennisse onser misdaet ende mitten grave ware berouwe van alle onse quaet, mitten derden grave der ware scaemte van al onse wercken. Ende als die wint die comt van zuden, die Gods ghenade doer onse ghedachten dringhet, soe beghinnet te vlieten die meyereghen onser tranen, die een guede lenten beghint te kundighen, dat alle sijn doorne der sonden beghinnen in doechts bladen verwandelt te werden.

These thorns shall become rose petals in the penitent's head and in the garden of our hearts, if only we make a fresh start and dig up our misdeeds with the spade of true confession, and all our sins with the spade of true repentance, and all our works with the third spade of true shame. And like the wind that cometh from the south, and bloweth God's mercy through our thoughts, so the May rain of our tears beginneth to flow, heralding a good spring in which all the thorns of sin shall be changed into the petals of virtue.

Nor was Dirk's store of flowery metaphor exhausted with this tactful rejoinder. The rosebud was also the symbol of the "truly devoted and believing soul" (ighelic innich ghelovich gheest) and, as Dirk went on to show, was constructed of twelve concentric whorls. Upon examining that complicated bud, he was able to say of every one of its whorls that he had either devoted a chapter to it already or would do so later. Because his exposition is typical of the structure of Dirk's thought no less than of his writing, we can do no better than follow it step by step.

Dirk's description of the rosebud begins with the outer, twelve-leaved whorl representing the twelve apostles: "And thereon shall I yet write a chapter." There follow whorls with progressively fewer petals, successively symbolizing the eleven disciples who hearkened unto Jesus in Galilee ("And of these . . . have I before written a chapter"), the Ten Commandments ("of these . . . I before wrote a chapter"), the nine angelic choirs ("of which have I before spoken in a short chapter"), the eight blessings ("of which have I before written a chapter"), the seven gifts of the Holy Ghost ("upon which I wrote a chapter before"), the six works of mercy ("of these works shall I yet write a chapter"), the five stigmata ("of these I shall yet speak when I write of our dear Lord's passion"), the four evangelists and the four cardinal virtues ("of which I wrote in two chapters before"), the trinity ("of which I spoke before"), the two testaments, and, finally, the "shiny golden bud found toward the center of this rose, which is the overflowing love of God . . . and it bestoweth strength and life upon all the aforesaid petals" ("S" III/158–285).[35]

There is as much system to the *Tafel* as there is to the Creation itself. The former is the work of Dirk of Delft, the latter of God. Dirk's familiarity with the system underlying the Creation and his ability to bring it home to his Dutch readers derived from his excellent education and above all his extensive reading. Once again, superlatives are warranted: no other writer at the court of Holland-Bavaria was even remotely as well read as Dirk of Delft. It was certainly not from intellectual vainglory, but for reasons we shall explore below, that Dirk allowed this extensive knowledge of literature to radiate from every part of the *Tafel*. He was extremely liberal with acknowledgment. Often these were presented in general terms, such as "the teachers say . . ." or "the masters ask . . ." (by which Dirk was in a sense referring back to his student days), but he also mentions his sources by name. Among these, the Bible (naturally) takes pride of place, followed by the fathers of the church and by classical authors, the latter being introduced in particular as authorities on questions of practical conduct.[36]

It is largely thanks to the Dominican father L. M. Daniëls, who devoted his academic career to the study of the *Tafel*, that we know so much about Dirk's sources. For not only did he locate most of the sources mentioned by Dirk specifically, but he also uncovered others that were used without open acknowledgment.[37] As a result of this scrupulous and time-consuming investigation, in the thousand pages of prose that constitute the modern edition of the *Tafel* (which Daniëls edited), hardly a page lacks a link to some source. And for many of those cases in which no link has thus far been found, further research may well succeed in bringing a source to light. Is it by chance, incidentally, that such lacunae are generally associated with the "worldly dimension" of the *Tafel*, that part least influenced by the Latin sources for which Father Daniëls looked so painstakingly? In other words, is it possible that vernacular sources may be hiding behind some of these passages?[38]

But regardless of how many new sources may yet be discovered, it is unlikely that their number will rival that of Dirk's gleanings from the Latin tradition. Thanks to his education, Dirk probably read (and wrote?) Latin as easily as he did Middle Dutch, and since the former was deemed more authoritative in matters of religion, our doctor of theology—unlike Bavaria Herald—preferred to use the original sources, even when a popular Middle Dutch translation of the Latin text was available. Thus he worked from the *De natura rerum* rather than the vernacular *Der naturen bloeme*, the *Historia scolastica* instead of the *Rijmbijbel*, the *Elucidarium* rather than the *Lucidarius*, the *Ludum scaccorum* instead of the *Scaecspel*, and the *Legenda aurea* and Beka in the Latin.[39] The popularizing translations by Maerlant and his school were no more appreciated by Dirk than they were intended for him.[40] Indeed, he may not always have realized that a translation was available; such renderings did not usually circulate in the colleges. But even if Dirk had encountered some Middle Dutch translation or elaboration, he would have refrained from using it for reasons of philological scruple, suspect as popular writings on theology must have appeared to his learned eyes. Thus, when he did feel impelled to mention one popular text in the vernacular, namely *Dat boek van den houte* (The book of the wood), which dealt with the wood of which the Cross was made, he hastened to explain that it was an "apocryphal book, by teachers not greatly esteemed" (dat is apocrifum, want men daer of niet veel onder den lerars en hout; "S" V/117–18). And of that his parishioners must have been convinced.

But let us return to Dirk's more general sources. As I said earlier, almost all the wisdom contained in the *Tafel* is borrowed wisdom. In that sense, Dirk's *Tafel* was no less a compendium than Bavaria Herald's *Wereldkroniek*, and its originality, too, resided mainly in the selections its author made from a vast number of sources. A crucial difference, however, is that whereas Bavaria Herald, except in his own rather narrow and specialized field, copied his sources almost word for word, Dirk's method of quotation may be called very active: he regrouped, reconsidered, and reformulated the data from start to finish. Hence, although the *Tafel* was based on scores of original writings, the result was Dirk's very own, highly personal work. That Dirk—who must have known better than anyone else how free he had made with his sources— should nevertheless have found it necessary to name his authorities so often was not due (I must reiterate) to a desire to parade his learning or to an inferiority complex. Rather, he wanted to leave readers in no doubt but that the knowledge his *Tafel* dispensed had the most authoritative origins, that it bore not merely the imprint of his highly esteemed doctor's title, but also of all the learning this doctor had imbibed. The multitude of authorities was not introduced to compensate for what knowledge Dirk lacked, but to add additional merit to what he had to convey. In this connection, it was also characteristic of the man that he invariably quoted authorities in a positive way, as corroboration and support of his own view, and never for polemical reasons or in refutation.[41]

In fact, the respect for authorities that such thinkers as Dirk of Delft displayed was anything but a sign that they could not produce arguments of their own. On the contrary, it was precisely in wrestling with the intellectual work of others that their own intellects had been sharpened; Dirk's exemplification of the process was thus strictly in keeping with the best scholastic tradition. The *Tafel* is filled with argument and discussion, for Dirk not only explains *how* the Creation is a unity but also *why* it should be so. Indeed, the explanatory clause introduced with the conjunction *because* to set out the reasons underlying a particular teaching is one of the most common sentence constructions in the *Tafel*. Here, then, we have a fundamental difference from the work of Hildegaersberch: for although both men occasionally presented the same view of God's order, it was the *doctor in theologia* alone who knew why that order held together as it did.[42] To arrive at that understanding, a true Schoolman had to do more than digest the authorities; he had also to study the subject at first hand and preferably dispute upon it in public. It was in this area—the development of arguments rooted in the fusion of *auctoritas* and *ratio*—that the scholastic education which Dirk of Delft had so thoroughly enjoyed was at its most effective.[43] In this enterprise, a leading role was reserved for teaching based on the fusion of *lectio* with *questio*, a biblical passage serving as introduction for arguments generated by a series of questions. The object was to clarify the passage in question by systematic investigation and, if possible, to discover God's underlying intention. The Bible thus served as revelation, thanks to which the Creation could be shown to follow God's path without detour. In the Schoolmen's view, book and path lay open in principle to anyone versed in scholastic methodology.

And with that methodology Dirk of Delft was familiar as no other Hollander of his day. We cannot tell whether he used the scholastic method to teach at court; but we do know that he wrote many parts of the *Tafel* in that spirit. In the long section he devoted to the life of Christ, particularly, Dirk often slackened the narrative pace, the better to set off the text in the sharp light of the scholastic *modus legendi cum questionibus*—that is, to expose the deeper meaning behind Christ's life and passion by question and answer.[44] Often the answer was in three parts. The first, "according to the letter," was based on the literal interpretation of the biblical story; the second, "according to the faith," was based on the doctrine; the third, "according to the spirit or to virtue," showed what moral the reader could glean from the biblical story.

Let us consider, for example, the passage in which Dirk, discussing the story of doubting Thomas, asked "whether Saint Thomas did err in casting such great doubt on our Lord's resurrection" (of sinte Thomas daer an misdede, dat hi an ons Heren verrisenis soe seer twivelde).[45] Master Dirk's answer was that "the teachers" exonerated Thomas "with three splendid reasons" (mit drie scone reden). The first reason, which Dirk tells us came from that mighty medieval thinker Albertus Magnus, was according to the letter: the apostle Thomas had seen so many signs of Christ's weakness, Christ having been "apprehended, beaten, condemned, and crucified, that he was the tardier to believe in the power of his divinity" (als dat Hi ghevanghen, gheslaghen, veroordelt, ghecruust was, dat hi te lancsamer te gheloven was vander macht sijnre Godheit). Hence he was unable to accept Christ's resurrection there and then, which made Thomas not so much a skeptic as one of tardy faith.

Die ander reden is naden gheloef, ende gheeft sinte Gregorius uut daer hi seit aldus: Mi heeft veel min ghebaet Maria Magdalena, die rasch gheloofde, dan Thomas, die lang twivelde. Thomas in sinen twivel betastede die wonden Cristi ende heeft van ons die wonden twivels ende onghelove ofghesneden. Des ghelijcs vinden wi, dat Pharao, coninc van Egypten, bleef verhart in onghelove ende starf. Petrus viel vanden gelove ende beterde hem. Thomas was traech ende lancsom ende hem twivelde. Dit ondersceit is al vander voirsichticheit ons gheschict ter leer.

Die derde reden is nader duecht [om] ons te troosten ende gheeft uut Crisostomus, daer hi seit aldus: Hoe groot schijnt an desen ons heren Ihesus guedertierenheit, die om éénre sielen wil te behouden, coemt self ende betoecht hem dat hi self die gheen is, die om haren wil ghecruust is, ende sijn wonden laet betasten ende handelen, ende woude hem waer sekere teyken gheven. Want niement an hem en sal werden bedroghen; ende dits dat woort, dat onse heer Ihesus seide totten heilighen man Carpus: Ic ben bereet noch om ééns menschen wil anderwarf ghecruust te werden. Seide hi niet tot sinte Peter: Ic gae te Romen noch eens ghecruust te werden?—of hi segghen woude: waer dat niet ghedaen, noch waer ic bereit om des menschen wil den doot te liden.

("S" XIII/213–35)

The other reason is according to the faith, and was given by Saint Gregory when he said: I was moved much less strongly by Mary Magdalene, who was quick to believe, than by Thomas, who doubted for so long. Thomas in his doubt touched Christ's wounds and so excised the wounds of doubt and disbelief in us. Pharaoh, king of Egypt, for his part, remained steeped in unbelief and died. Peter fell from faith but recovered. Thomas was slow and tardy and filled with doubt. These differences were sent us by Providence as a lesson.

The third reason is according to virtue and is meant for our consolation and was given by Saint Chrysostom when he said: How bright doth our Lord's mercy shine forth, who to save one man's soul came himself to testify that he was crucified for his sake and allowed his wounds to be touched, wishing to give him a certain sign. For no one shall be deceived in him; and this is the word our Lord Jesus spoke to Carpus, the holy man: I am ready to be crucified all over again for one man's sake. For did he not say to Saint Peter: I shall go up to Rome to be crucified once more?—as if to say: had it not happened already, I should have been willing to suffer death for one man's sake.

These were superior Bible lessons, under a master who knew why the Scriptures contained just what they did. The above passage was characteristic of Dirk's approach, in that he asked no less than three questions about the manifestations of the risen Christ, each the subject of three arguments. Similarly, he subdivided his discussion of Christ's ascension ("S" XV) into nine "articles," elucidating who did the ascending, whence he came, in what manner, for what reward, whither, in what company, to what end, why then and not later (for instance on the Day of Judgment), and how the apostles reacted. (The system of dialectical reasoning used by Aristotle in his *Topics*, in brief, was taken over by the scholastic exegetes as a gift from the pagan heaven!) In the treatment of these nine questions, one question raises another, with the complete treatment of all these "articles" rendering over 540 lines of majestic and compelling prose.

No subject was too demanding for our Schoolman when facing arguments about the Bible. If in the above quotation he used such relatively "obvious" arguments as Thomas's disbelief in Christ's ascension, many other questions broached in the *Tafel* are of the kind that have earned Schoolmen the (generally unjustified) epithet of hairsplitters. Six successive "questions" concerning why the child Jesus, though not saddled with original sin, was nevertheless circumcised ("W" XLI), for example, may be considered an exaggerated and unnecessary elaboration. Imbued with the same argumentative passion were Dirk's seven questions concerning the arrival of the three kings at Christ's crib ("W" XLII), including the possibly quite logical but to us rather farfetched question of how, having come from so far away, they were able to discover the newborn infant with such dispatch. Needless to say, there were three reasons, the literal one being that "as Hierome hath said they were seated upon three dromedaries, which are the fleetest of animals, for they can cover more of the way in one day than a good horse can in three" (als Iheronimus seit, datsi saten op dromedarios, dat die snelste

22. William VI (hat with fur rim) and John of Bavaria (long staff) at the Feast of Finding the Cross (3 May). (Museo Civico di Torin, fol. 118r)

dieren sijn, wantsi meer weghes mogen lopen in enen dage dan een goet paert in drien dagen).

Some of Dirk's "questions" are reminiscent of those asked by Frits Droogstoppel, the tedious candidate for communion, of his distraught instructor Parson Blatherer in Multatuli's famous novel *Max Havelaar*. Dirk's intention, however, was neither to plague the reader nor to treat him to anticlerical irony. He was sincerely earnest, and he gave his best in the discussion of such questions precisely because, to Schoolmen, they were the very essence of theology. After all, at stake was the correct interpretation of God's intentions. Nothing in his Creation was without sense or reason.

That fact was obvious to such brilliant Schoolmen as Dirk, who saw it in the overall "coherence" of God's system, a coherence that in turn was apparent from the "analogies" with which the Creation is filled to overflowing. Repetition, namely, is the hallmark of the Master. Sometimes the resulting symmetry is obvious—night and day, winter and summer, Old and New Testament, and the time before and after the incarnation of Christ. But often the discovery of an analogy (in its literal sense, that is, as the unveiling of a hidden meaning) demands the utmost intellectual ingenuity. That is because the interconnections found in the Creation are rarely obvious and can, moreover, be most varied. In the scholastic view, they were not links needing construction, for instance, by a poet; rather, they had to be revealed by a thinker. A connection is not a sign of some meaning created for a particular occasion, but of one intended for all time by God. The greater the number of connections we grasp, the better; the brilliance of the Creation then becomes ever more clear. Thus, for ever-changing reasons of subtle correspondence, the *Tafel* proffers a great variety of symbolic representations of Christ: the eagle, the lion, the phoenix, the pelican, the seed corn, the grape, the white lily, the red and the golden rose, flowers in general, the mirror, the blood that causes dry twigs to come back into blossom, and so on. In addition to their appearances, things also have an inner meaning, which, according to the Schoolmen, was the essential cause of their existence. In his Creation, God has given man millions of signs of his omnipresence.

To Dirk of Delft and other scholastic thinkers, this fact was most plainly reflected in the endless series of numerical correspondences found in Creation and in history. The Bible and the world, for example, fairly teem with meaningful threes and sevens. Yet other numerical correspondences can be found as well. Thus Dirk dwelled at some length on the number forty when explaining (necessarily by threes) why Christ had to fast in the desert for forty days ("W" XLVIII/18–58):[46]

Theologici, die meesters inder godheit, seggen datse heilich is omdatse die Gods soon Cristus mit menigen exempel sijns levens wyede: eerst in sijnre ontfange- nis, want hi 40 weken in sijnre joncfrouweliker moder lyve was; daerna in sijnre predicaedse, doe hi 40 maende lange den volck den wech Gods lerende was; daerna in sijnre passien ende gecruusten doot, doe hi 40 uren lanc inden grave lach; daerna in sijn verrisenge, doe hi 40 dage lanck voer sijn jongheren op aertrijck bleef. Aldus schijntet billick te wesen, dat onse heer Cristus 40 dage inder woestinen penitenci van vasten woude aennemen.

Die ander sake is naden gelove, want dat getal 40 inden ouden testament in menigher figuren den gelove voer ghinc. Want 40 dage ende 40 nachte regende God op aertrijck, doe die werelt in water verghinck; 40 dage ende 40 nachte was Moyses inden berch Synai bi Gode dat hi dranck noch at eer hi ontfangen mochte die ewe ende gebode; 40 jaer lanc waren die kinder van Ysrael van Moy- ses inder woestinen geleyt, doese God spijsde mitten hemelschen broede, eer si quamen inden lande van beloften; 40 jaer lanc was vrede inden lande van Ysra- hel; 40 jaer lanc regnierde David over dat lant; 40 uren lanck was Jonas, die propheet, in des walvischs buuc ende 40 dage lanck sette hi den volck van Ni- niven penitencie te doen; 40 dage ende 40 nachte was Helyas mit eenre spise, eer hi totten berch Gods quam Oreb; 40 sulveren voeten waren inden tempel gegoten; 40 ellen lanck was die tempel wijt; 40 jaer out was Abraham, doe hi Saram sijn wijf nam; in 40 jaren comen om der sonden plagen; om 40 gueder lude spaert God die werelt; om 40 scicten si die stride: daerom was Cristus 40 dage ende 40 nachte mitten duvel in kyve.

Die derde sake is nader duecht ende na gheestelick verstaen. Die werelt wert in vier eynden gemeten; dat jaer in vier tiden begrepen; die ziel van vier elemen- ten beseten, dat gelove in vier evangelien gelegen. Sou woude onse heer Cristus 40 dagen wesen inder wildernis opdat wi mitten getal van tienen alle dese vier voerseit souden verhogen; omdat wi vander werelt ende der tijt ons levens tien- den Gode souden gheven ende dat gelove mitten tien geboden souden houden, hierom so sijn dese voerseide vier op viertigen mit tien verhoghet.

Theologians, masters of divinity, say that it [the number forty] is sacred because God's son Christ honored it with many examples during his life: firstly during his conception, because for forty weeks he remained in his virgin mother's body; then in his preaching when for forty months he taught God's way to the people; thereafter in his passion and death by crucifixion when he lay for 40 hours in his grave; thereafter in his resurrection when he remained on earth for forty days for the sake of his disciples. Hence it seemed meet that our Lord Christ should have chosen 40 days of penitential fasting in the desert.

The second reason is according to the faith, inasmuch as the number 40 prefigured the faith in the Old Testament in diverse ways. For God rained down upon the earth for 40 days and 40 nights so that the world perished in the water; for 40 days and 40 nights Moses dwelled on Mount Sinai before God, neither drinking nor eating ere he was handed the law and the commandments; for 40 years Moses guided the children of Israel through the desert, when God

fed them on heavenly bread ere they reached the promised land; for 40 years
was there peace in the land of Israel; for 40 years David reigned over the land;
for 40 hours Jonas, the prophet, abode in the belly of the whale, and for 40 days
he commanded the people of Nineveh to do penance; for 40 days and 40 nights
Elias was bereft of food ere he came to God's mount Horeb; 40 silver feet were
cast in the temple; 40 ells was the temple wide; 40 years old was Abraham when
he took Sarah to be his wife; in 40 years' time the plagues sent for our sins will
have passed; for the sake of 40 good men God spared the world; for the sake of
40 was the peace concluded: wherefore Christ fought the devil 40 days and 40
nights without cease.

The third reason is according to virtue and spiritual understanding. The
world is measured from four corners; the year is divided into four seasons; the
soul is invested with four elements, the faith enshrined in four gospels. Thus
our lord Christ dwelled for 40 days in the wilderness so that with the aid of the
number ten we may multiply all these aforesaid fours; so that of our worldly
possessions we may all our lives offer tithes to God and keep the faith by the
Ten Commandments, the abovesaid four having been increased to forty by [a
factor of] ten.

In scholastic circles, a demonstration such as this was almost tanta-
mount to a proof of God's existence. For did it not establish beyond all
doubt that there was a system in the Creation, one of such grand perfection, moreover, as could only have sprung from a divine plan? Indeed,
the more closely one inspected it, the more perfect that plan seemed to
become. This mode of analysis and "unriddling" of the Creation was the
task of learned theologians, men who stored the fruits of their thoughts
in a *summa*. The *summa* was the crown of scholastic science: an encyclopedic work in which (like a small-scale cosmos) the entire Creation
was presented in a systematic nutshell.[47] This field was tilled largely by
learned Dominicans—by Saint Thomas Aquinas above all and by Hugh
Ripelin of Strassburg, whose *Compendium theologicae veritatis* was based
on Saint Thomas's *Summa theologiae*. The *Compendium* was the main
source of Dirk's *Tafel*, and it is no exaggeration to state that with the
Tafel a Dutch Dominican had presented a unique *summa*, one written in
the vernacular, not for learned colleagues but for laymen at the court.

What these courtiers made of Dirk's Dutch *summa* we shall consider
in the next section; meanwhile, let us try to determine what it meant to
its author. Dirk of Delft had undertaken a formidable task, not only in
collecting material for his *summa* but also, and above all, in translating
into the popular language what had always been the preserve of Latin
scholars. What was Dirk, for instance, to do about the symbolic interpretation of Latin names? Dirk's main source, Hugh of Strassburg's
Compendium, contained an explanation of Jesus' name that was too sug-

gestive not to be included—but how was it possible to convey in Middle Dutch what Hugh meant when he explained that the name *Jesus* was an acronym of *Jucunditas, Eternitas, Sanitas, Ubertas*, and *Satietas*? In the event, Dirk of Delft was inventive enough to produce his own interpretation. He stated that the Middle Dutch name *Ihesus* was composed of the initials of the words *Innicheyt* (fervor), *Heerlicheit* (splendor), *Edelheit* (nobility), *Scoenheid* (beauty), *Urede* (peace),[48] and *Slot* (stronghold)—each of which he honored with a commentary ("W" XLI/186–221).

Dirk's *Tafel* was a huge project, and even today anyone delving into that magnum opus, whether religious or not, is bound to fall under the spell, as he might in a cathedral, of the sweep of its creator's imagination. In the humble, pious eyes of the author, of course, that meant being overawed by the splendor of God's Creation. God, indeed, seemed to have intended a system even in sin. Thus, the seven main virtues not only correspond to the seven gifts of the Holy Ghost and the seven sacraments, but they also have their mirror images in the seven mortal sins, which are related to seven corresponding parts of the body and are symbolized by seven beasts, in their turn symbols of seven devils who plague the sinner in appropriate ways but were subdued by Jesus at seven moments of his life.[49] Even apparently absurd phenomena have explanations. Unlike William of Hildegaersberch and Dirk Potter, who were incensed to discover that villains often grew fat on worldly flesh-pots, Dirk of Delft knew why that should be so: because evildoers will receive nothing but punishment in the hereafter, they are allowed to collect whatever rewards they have earned on earth for the few good deeds they have wrought.[50]

He has, in fact, an elegant theological retort for everything—elegant meaning that each answer "squares" with others, thus increasing its validity. For related reasons Dirk quite often tries to change arrangements by fours into arrangements by threes, or to turn sixes into more meaningful sevens.[51] Triplets are his particular favorites, for God himself works mainly by threes. Thus, apart from the innumerable matters having three explanations, the "Winter Piece," for example, expands on the Trinity, the three heavenly hierarchies each with three choirs of angels, the three trees in the earthly paradise, the three garments of the soul, the three rules of physiognomy, the three divine virtues, the three main categories of sin, and the three estates.

This last trio derived from the eleventh century, when Adalbert of Laon subdivided mankind into warriors (the nobility), worshippers (the clergy), and workers (the peasantry). Once the bourgeoisie came to the fore as an "independent" group, however, the old trio became outdated. And how was the new system to be reconciled with the old? Did one have to be a realist and cease to speak of a division into three? Or should the new estate be considered an extension of one of the old, namely the peasantry, which would help to maintain the old tripartition? Depending on their own status, time, and circumstance, different people came up with different answers.[52] Yet no matter what they thought, the whole discussion grew increasingly academic with the inexorable rise of cities and the middle class. This was particularly true of Holland, where urban power blossomed later than it had in the southern Netherlands, but where the powerful combination of town, middle class, and trade still had to be reckoned with from the fourteenth century, even by the court, which was increasingly forced to gear its policies to urban demands. Certainly in about 1400, when Dirk was at The Hague, the court saw much toing and froing not only by individual burghers but also by spokesmen for the towns; by then, the bourgeoisie had become at least as important in the administration of Holland as the nobility.

Nevertheless, when Dirk of Delft discussed God's social order in his *Tafel*, he clung resolutely to the traditional tripartite division and excluded the burghers from his picture. Elsewhere in the *Tafel*, too, he did his utmost to spirit the new element away, often going much further than his sources, who generally devoted only the occasional word to towns and merchants.[53] It is inconceivable that Dirk did so out of unworldly ignorance; after all, he had visited such cities as Delft, Utrecht, and Cologne. Nor is there the slightest indication that he had personal motives for denying the burgher his place under God's sun—except that this place was likely to upset what Dirk considered a happy and God-ordained state of affairs: the three-part division of society. That was probably reason enough. For Dirk of Delft, God's order outbid everything else. He was therefore loath to surrender the tripartition: reality had to take second place to the Schoolmen's systematic urge. But did Dirk render Duke Albert and his courtiers a service by giving in to that urge?

4. PIETY AT COURT

Dirk of Delft took a courageous step when he decided to write a Middle Dutch *summa*, a tradition too deeply mired in the combination of

church, Latin, and scholasticism to lend itself readily to populariza-
tion.[54] Worse, academic specialization had to be abandoned if one
wanted to appeal to laymen. Dirk must have been the first to heed the
advice he offered teachers in the *Tafel*, namely "that their lessons be neither too subtle nor too hard. Nor shall they keep them on their own
high level—for then they would be writing for themselves—but rather
match them to the simplicity and callowness of their pupils" (dat sijn
lessen te subtijl noch te swair niet en sullen wesen. Ende niet en sal hi
lesen naden hoghen sinnen die hi wel verstaet—want dan lase hi hem
selven—mer nae simpelheit ende grofheit sijnre jongheren; "S" XX/79–
82). However exalted his court audience at The Hague may have been
socially, theologically they were undoubtedly as "simple and callow" as
Dirk's university pupils. As a result, our "master in divinity" had to
pitch his lessons deliberately low.

Dirk succeeded. A careful comparison of his own text with his many
sources reveals just how much learned material he omitted—not, of
course, because he judged it uninteresting, but because he must have
felt that it would bore his worldly readers. This would explain why the
Tafel totally neglected mysticism, a spiritual approach, as intense as it
was demanding, with no appeal at all for most courtiers.[55] Similarly,
Dirk declared that he would refrain from detailed discussions, spiritual,
social, or political, of the position of the clergy: "for since I desire to
instruct worldly persons with this book, whom I would love dearly to
fill with respect for the Christian religion and reverence for the church,
so shall I write nothing more about the priesthood and the clergy"
(want ic nu mit desen boec wairlike lude leren wil, die ic tot ontsich der
kersten ghelove ende reverencie der kercken gaerne woude brenghen,
so en wil ic vander paepscap ende clergie niet meer scriven; "S" XIX/
256–59). We find him applying the same principles repeatedly in his
Tafel, omitting what will probably prove too difficult or counterproduc-
tive and greatly simplifying the carefully chosen remainder, the better to
render it comprehensible to his readers.

In this connection, Dirk's ingenious use of simile and metaphor deserves special mention. Apart from theological and ethical (and hence
learned and stylistic) objectives, this particular use of language also had
a didactic aim: by referring to the familiar, Dirk tried to explain facts
both unfamiliar or complex. Many of his metaphors were traditional,
but others (by no means just a few) were apparently of his own making,
intended to make religious themes more accessible through worldly il-

lustrations. We have seen this already in his frequent use of martial images (sec. 2 above), and an even greater number of illustrations seems to have been culled from the more serene world of castle, chancellery, and court.

Such examples must have forced Dirk to think very hard, for here his academic sources were unlikely to prove of much use. That *liberum arbitrium*, free will, was the third subdivision of the human soul, for instance, was something Ripelin's *Compendium* could argue with conviction, but it needed Dirk's ingenuity to clarify that abstract concept with the help of a castle gatekeeper: "The third is *liberum arbitrium*, that is a free will, which God gave unto man in the beginning so that he may do what he wills to do and omit what he wills not to do; and may be likened to a keeper posted inside the castle, whom no one can force to open up if it please him not" (Dat derde is *liberum arbitrium*, dat hiet een vrijghemoet, dien God den mensche ghegheven heeft inden beghin te doen dat hi wil ende te laten dat hi niet en wil; ende mach wel gelijc wesen een poortyer die binnen den casteel is, dien men niet dwinghen en mach op te doen sonder sijn behaghen; "W" XII/167–71).

Likewise, the *Tafel* compares the relationship between speech and spirit to a drawbridge; the virtues of obedience and helpfulness to messengers and envoys; the apostles to knights; the poor clothed by charitable persons to heralds clad in their masters' coats of arms; soul and reason to twin counselors; the senses to watchmen on the battlements; fantasy to an imperial hall; the sacred fire that radiated from the apostles after Whitsun to a coat of many colors "cut to the measure of great princes and lords" (wel te maten na haer recht alse groten heren ende vorsten); and teachers of religion (such as Dirk himself) to stewards who feed the soul with spiritual fare.[56] And much as a king's host is equipped with a banner and trumpets, so the spiritual army of Christ the King bears a cross and church bells; the priest serves a bishop as the knight serves his duke; the bishop in procession resembles a prince departing for battle; Mary Magdalene stood by Christ's grave like a sentry; the archangel Gabriel knelt before the Virgin "like a young knight" (als een jonc ridder) and proclaimed his message "most courteously and in princely manner" (seer hoveschelick ende princelick); the pope was Christ's *ruwaard*, bailiff, stadtholder, and steward all in one.[57]

No less illustrative were the miniatures in the *Tafel*, which, though absent from the modern edition, brilliantly illuminated the early manuscripts.[58] They are particularly numerous and beautiful in the earliest version of all, now in Baltimore, where the first thirty-one chapters of the "Winter Piece" contain thirty-five miniatures considered among the greatest of North Netherlandish book illustrations (see figs. 23–24). Manuscript and miniatures were probably produced under Dirk's personal supervision in a Utrecht studio, much as was the first book that Dirk wrote for the Hague court, presumably (unfortunately, this work is known from the accounts only). Almost every chapter of the Baltimore manuscript includes a miniature, a concrete illustration that breathes life into the abstract ideas under discussion—an inclusion that must have greatly stimulated courtiers reading the text. For example, Dirk's rather symbolic deliberations on the soul are accompanied by a picture of a man lying lifeless on the ground, while God, holding the world, hovers over him and the soul, in the shape of a child, passes into man from God's mouth (fig. 23).

The glorious miniatures found in the manuscript do not, however, have a purely didactic function. They are aesthetic first and foremost, princely illustrations in a princely work. For that manuscript was the personal property of Duke Albert of Bavaria, whose arms grace the righthand edge of the dedication page. The marvelous quality of the manuscript apparently rendered it desirable enough to later generations (in our day it is beyond the financial reach of all but a few) that they were careful to preserve it—just as only the illustrated versions of the many manuscripts of Bavaria Herald have survived. These latter manuscripts, of course, were autographs, that is, books written in the author's own hand; the Baltimore manuscript of the *Tafel*, by contrast, is a showpiece probably produced from Dirk's original autograph by professional copyists and illuminators, barely in time to be presented (possibly by the author himself) to Albert before his death.[59]

Unfortunately, the prologue to this dedication manuscript is missing; other copies of the *Tafel*, however, do contain prologues with what appears to be Dirk's own dedication. In keeping with the rules of the *ars praedicandi*, the one in the "Winter Piece" starts with a biblical passage: "The fear of the Lord, saith Solomon, is the beginning of wisdom." In this context, *fear* of course means awe or respect: the respect that man owes the Creator and that makes him (as the text then explains) eager to discover what is pleasing in God's eyes and what is not. Next, the prologue sets out Dirk's reason for dedicating the manuscript to Albert:

Daerom, waerdige lieve here, opdat ic iu moghe wisen ende leren dat ghi uwen God ende Scepper mede salt leren kennen ende oefenen ende oic bet te hoeden

23.   Man receiving his soul from God (*TKG* "W" XII, dedication copy). (Walters Art Gallery, Baltimore, MS. W 171, fol. 25r)

van sonden, so heb ic iuwer eren ghemaect een tafel van den kersten ghelove ende der ewen; ende also als ic gaern woude iu willich te dienst staen. Dat ghi desen tafel hebben somwijl in uwer hant, opdat ghi voir die oghen der moghentheit Gods, die ghi vruchten, bedencken ende ghehoeghen selt, hoe ghi Hem te wille moghen leven ende in kersten ewe ende ghelove houden—opdat ghi alle hinder ende quaet iuwer zielen moghen voorbicomen an dat anschijn der ewigher eren, daer ghi salich ende heilich an ziel ende an live mit alle iuwe vrienden ewelic moet leven ende regnieren. Amen.

So that, worthy and beloved lord, I might show and teach you how to know and revere your God and Creator, the better to eschew sin, I have prepared Your Honor a table of the Christian faith and law; and also because I would fain be of service to you. May you hold this table in your hand from time to time, thus keeping God's power before your eyes, allowing it to come to fruit in you and to make you reflect and recall how to live for his sake and preserve the Christian law and faith—so that you might overcome all impediments and evils in your soul in the light of eternal honor and so that you shall live and reign evermore with God's blessings and hale in body and soul amidst all your friends. Amen.

This passage merits closer examination, for it gives concise expression to several important aspects of Dirk's book. The *Tafel* was written partly "in honor of" Albert; and the very fact that it was prepared by someone in the duke's service redounds further to its patron's honor. But the magnification of Albert's name was certainly not the ruling purpose of the *Tafel*; rather, the objective was to influence Albert himself, to acquaint the duke with his God and Creator and also the "better" to keep him from sin. Compared with this noble aim, Dirk's wishes are modest: that his master might "from time to time" pick up the book and reflect on how he might live in accordance with God's will.[60] A reasonable hope, indeed, and certainly when set against the reward Dirk could promise his distinguished reader if he heeded the *Tafel*'s advice: that he would overcome "all impediments and evils" in his soul by the light of "eternal honor" and continue to reign in heaven surrounded by all his friends. The last clause was highly significant. Dirk was fully aware of what was due his lord, and Albert's might was such that Dirk could hardly proclaim that, in the hereafter, the last will be the first. Provided the duke read the *Tafel* carefully and took it to heart, he would enjoy not only the temporal honor of ruling over Holland, but also the eternal glory of making his authority felt in heaven.

This, as the prologue to the "Summer Piece" put it, was the courteous advice of "a humble preacher, by the name of Brother Dirk of Delft, master in Holy Writ and regent [i.e., professor] in the universities of Arfordia [Erfurt] and Colonia [Cologne] in the year of our Lord one thousand four hundred and four" (enen oetmoedighen prediker, ghehieten broeder Dirc van Delf, meister inder heiligher scrift ende regent inder universitaten van Arfordia ende van Colonia, int jair ons Heren dusent vierhondert ende vier). On the lower left edge of the authentic dedication copy, Duke Albert, wearing a monk's habit, is shown kneeling in prayer beside a banderole with the inscription "Give me true faith, oh Lord" (Ghif mi, Heer, ware ghelove; fig. 24). We may take it that this prayer was meant to sway the book's influential reader. Was this wish ever satisfied? Or, more plainly, did Dirk succeed in persuading his illustrious patron to take the path he had mapped out for him? That question is more easily asked than answered. It would be a grave mistake to take the effectiveness of Dirk's lessons for granted. No matter how forcefully the court chaplain inveighed against adultery, for example, everything suggests that during Dirk's stay at court marriage vows continued to be broken as a matter of course. At best, some courtiers may have undergone the penances Dirk deemed fitting for this sin, though their penances were probably softened into almsgiving and other charitable deeds, rather than heightened into what Dirk had actually prescribed—self-flagellation and the wearing of hairshirts.

Still, if we probe no further and so conclude that courtiers were largely indifferent to Dirk's teachings, then we should be dismissing the matter all too easily. The problem is, we simply lack enough solid evidence for a deeper analysis. What, in the end, do we really know about the piety of the dukes of Holland-Bavaria? Moreover, even if we could measure their piety, what value should we attach to it? We might well be projecting modern ideas of "genuine" versus "superficial" faith into the medieval situation, with all the concomitant pitfalls. In our strongly secularized century, piety is practically synonymous with intense religious experience, and we tend to expect much the same of the Catholic Middle Ages, dismissing everything else as lukewarm. To take a case in point: to us it is (to say the least) surprising that Duke Albert should, at set times, have visited the abbey at Rijnsburg in order to dance with and "pay court to" the nuns or to disport himself with his recently acquired leopard.[61] Such frivolity makes it hard for us to reckon the protection that this sovereign lord extended to the abbey as a token of unmitigated piety.

Even though Dirk of Delft is unlikely to have welcomed these contacts between court and abbey, we must remember that what now seems downright incongruous was normal enough in the Middle Ages. Huizinga called the coexistence in one person of devotion and worldliness "a kind of reconciliation between two moral extremes hardly conceivable to the modern mind." He went on to illustrate the point with portraits of a number of "devout worldlings," late-medieval aristocrats who combined piety and worldliness in equal abundance. As he put it in the *Herfsttij der middeleeuwen* (the unabridged original version of *The Wan-*

24. The dedication manuscript of the *Tafel vanden kersten ghelove* (Table of the Christian faith). (Walters Art Gallery, Baltimore, MS. W 171, fol. 1r)

ing of the Middle Ages): "In the medieval consciousness, two conceptions of life appeared side by side: while the pious, ascetic conception attracted all moral feelings, wordliness asserted itself all the more remorselessly, wholly abandoned as it was to the Devil. If one of these two becomes dominant, then we see the saint or the unbridled sinner; as a rule, though, they are in a widely fluctuating, unstable equilibrium, and we are presented with passionate people whose red-blooming sins may cause their overflowing piety to burst out all the more fiercely."[62]

Eruptions of "overflowing piety" by counts of Holland-Bavaria are unknown. Is it their sobriety or Huizinga's predilection for the extraordinary that makes their faith seem rather tepid, even commonplace? Unfortunately, we have no means of looking into the heads and hearts of the counts themselves—as distinct from those of their authors'. Restricted as we are by the very nature of our sources, we must rely wholly on the actions of the counts and their family, with the underlying motives remaining largely hidden from us. Was it, for instance, from exaggerated veneration of the Virgin Mary or purely for the sake of appearances that Duke Albert paid a speaker in the service of the margrave of Hessen "who spoke of Our Lady" the excessively high sum of ten guilders in 1386?[63]

In short, the danger of our getting bogged down in speculation is certainly not farfetched. If we nevertheless insist on a firm answer to our question, we find a wide variety of indications that the court of Holland was indeed active in pursuit of piety. Thus, even though, unlike Count John IV of Nassau and his wife, the Hague nobles apparently did not keep the mystical writings of the Blessed Henry Suso (1296–1366) in their library,[64] they nevertheless bought breviaries and prayer books at regular intervals. Also, they doubtless had a sound knowledge of the Bible, for in order to understand, say, a lecture by Dirk of Delft on the significance of the number forty, they had to be familiar with both the Old Testament and the New.[65] That the court precincts contained a church and several chapels hardly needs to be mentioned; indeed, numerous favors and gifts were bestowed upon these buildings by the counts, and frequent attendance of mass seems to have been normal.[66] Would the court, moreover, have employed a man such as Dirk if the nobles had not had a genuine pious strain? Again, the *Tafel* was not the only pious book Dirk wrote for the count's family; previously he had composed a book for Margaret, to whom William the Confessor had earlier still handed a devout text written on priceless parchment. Even more telling, perhaps, was the court's insistence on religious decorum in the temporal sphere. No other European knightly order is known to have used religious initiation rites of the kind associated with Albert's Order of Saint Anthony, including long prayers and chants and the blessing of the order's badge.[67]

We could expatiate even further on this subject, but it might be more opportune to scrutinize the reverse case. For the skeptic, nothing could be easier than to dismiss this devotion (and with some reason) as mere lip service to religion. In the Middle Ages, it was virtually impossible to ignore religion completely; certainly the nobility could not admit indifference to the church, not even in their innermost thoughts. Nonetheless, the skeptic will detect many symptoms of a less elevated standard of piety at the court of Holland-Bavaria. First, of course, there were the numerous and widespread violations of church rules, for breaches of promise, adultery, worldliness, crime, corruption, and deception were ever rife at courts. Then there was the unquestioning, almost matter-of-fact way in which people attempted to square minor faults with their religious consciences. The accounts make us privy to this side of things when money was involved—for the count's impropriety of dancing on Fridays, for instance, and for William VI's lapse in wearing his spurs in church.[68] Such minor indiscretions show that, although the court regarded church precepts seriously enough to offer penance, their piety was insufficient to enforce obedience.

The counts seemed possessed of at least a strong inclination (to put it baldly) toward the irregular and dissolute life; afterward, if necessary, they could contrive to settle their accumulated debts to God. It often appeared that, when faced with the salvation of their souls, these men lived in a permanent state of negotiation with the Almighty. Their good works seem often to have been mere atonement for inordinate behavior. As early as 1367, for example, Albert elevated the court chapel (in which Dirk of Delft would perform his priestly duties from 1400) into a capitular church, "the better to augment the service to our Lord . . . in remission of our sins and to augment the salvation of our souls" (om te meerren den dienst ons Heren [. . .] in aflate onser sonden ende in meerringhe der salicheiden onser zielen).[69] Albert's act was a pious one, no doubt—but our appreciation is somewhat modified by the realization that it in fact constituted Albert's penance for having beheaded the lord of Adingen without a trial when he heard the (false) rumor that the nobleman had been storing arms in his castle in order to launch an attack on Hainaut. Here, piety had followed fast upon cruelty. Such practice, moreover, was all too common. Were good works, then, a medieval form of striking a spiritual balance—as Huizinga put it—or, rather, a more down-to-earth form of haggling?

In general, it is remarkable to what extent piety at court seems to have been dominated by *external* forms. Piety was thought to reside in deeds and gestures. True, the reader will recall an earlier reservation: in that we have no records of the count's feelings, let alone his unconscious, we must perforce concentrate on the historical facts. But even so, we cannot but conclude that at court (and not only there) religious observance was largely a matter of outward show.[70] Thus, the count and his family attended mass (Margaret of Cleves even daily), bestowed favors, gave alms (on high church holidays, usually double the normal amount), clothed the poor, and fulfilled the customary dues of their position. Their pious works extended all the way to distant Friesland: in 1398, a deanery staffed with twelve canons was founded in memory of those who had fallen there. The establishment was provided with a guest house where "in God's honor and for the salvation of souls" thirteen poor people could find free shelter for three days "under the supervision of one or two ladies." Similarly, once churches had been founded, their upkeep and embellishment were further signs of piety, visible to God, unmistakable to man. At the count's expense, the angels in the main court chapel were restored, the tabernacles gilded, stained glass installed, and a Madonna ordered from a master in Aachen.[71]

Court chaplain Dirk of Delft certainly did not oppose such outward expressions of piety;[72] in all honesty, what other form of piety could be expected from a flock so deeply rooted in this world? Alms to men and generosity to the church were the most obvious and undemanding means by which the wealthy could display their faith, and the resulting good works served God, donor, and recipient simultaneously.[73] In general, Dirk (as we saw also in section 2) was a warm champion of ritual displays of piety; orthodox Catholic priest that he was, he considered good works and the sacraments central to Christian observance. The *Tafel*, significantly, did not yet reflect the more inward religious attitude of the *devotio moderna*, a contemporary movement then spreading fast in Holland (but not at court?).[74] To Dirk, a nobleman could express piety most usefully by lavishing financial support on religious establishments; we need not be surprised, then, to find the *Tafel* lingering on this aspect of loyalty to the church.[75] Here, too, Dirk's influence at court can be demonstrated: there is reason to think that our Dominican friar from Utrecht and sometime professor of divinity from Erfurt went to exceptional efforts to persuade Albert and Margaret to fund the establishment of a Dominican convent in Voorhout, associated with the Utrecht Chapter and approved in 1403 by the Chapter General in Erfurt.[76] Perhaps Dirk was later satisfied to learn that the Dominican convent in The Hague continued to enjoy the court's favor, as reflected for example in presents of turf, of barrels of herring during Lent, and of a stallion to the prior.

Yet even Dirk did not see faith as a mere panoply of gestures. As the banderole on the dedication page of the *Tafel* teaches, by praying to the Lord for "true faith," it is the spirit that most counts, and the spirit means inwardness. Besides a good Christian life, true faith, in Dirk's view, also involves a thirst for divine knowledge. The true Christian must not only believe and obey, he must also, as Plato once taught his own disciples, learn and comprehend. As we saw, the *Tafel* seems designed to foster the second goal more than the first. In the words of Daniëls, its author was "more the doctor wanting to instruct than the preacher wishing to inspire his congregation".[77]

Alas, in pursuing this aim Dirk demanded too much of the court. As a priest he seems to have done precisely what was expected of him; but as a teacher he exceeded his mission. His *Tafel vanden kersten ghelove* was, in the end, a more searching and difficult catechism than all other Middle Dutch writings of its kind; perhaps it was even the most learned catechistic study in the vernacular literature of all Europe.[78] Impenetrability was the price to be paid for keeping within the tradition of the scholastic *summa*; although his contribution admittedly enriched the literary heritage of the Netherlands as no other, readers at court were clearly overburdened. Or can we really believe that Duke Albert and his circle were genuinely interested in Dirk's twelve reasons for Christ's circumcision, or in his subtle arguments connected with such questions as why God did not become a man at the beginning of the world, why he should have appeared on earth as the Son and not as the Father or the Holy Ghost, why Christ ascended to heaven precisely when he did, why the Holy Ghost should have appeared as a dove and not in some other guise, and whether the star of Bethlehem was a real star (on which subject there were of course three conflicting scientific "conceptions and opinions").[79] Did the court really appreciate all Dirk's efforts to enrich the Middle Dutch vocabulary with countless neologisms designed to render scholastic jargon more comprehensible to his noble readers?[80] From what we know of the court of Holland-Bavaria (and of medieval courts in general), we can be sure of the answers.

In short, despite Dirk's judicious attempts to produce an instructive handbook for the court, his *Tafel* was too learned for its noble readers, even if we suppose that the author was occasionally at hand to provide extra glosses in person. Dirk's outstanding literary contribution, finally, is unlikely to have appealed to the count and his court. His scholastic reflections must have been so many proverbial pearls cast before animals most uncourtly. Although his contemporaries loved allegories, Dirk's symbolic language must have seemed to them farfetched and abstruse. Of course, even they must have appreciated his comparisons, in the second chapter of "Summer Piece," of Christ to a grain of corn, the Virgin to a field, the Father to a sower, and God's love to a plow—all the more so when he continued by likening wisdom to the coulter on a plow; love of God and of one's neighbors to the plow's two wheels; angels, prophets, and patriarchs to the draft animals; God's mercy to the plowshare; and the archangel Gabriel to the plowman. All in all, however, while Dirk's *Tafel* was greatly respected and admired, it remains debatable whether its real message was understood, let alone heeded.

He cannot have been happy about that result; intellectually (and hence emotionally, since to him the two were virtually synonymous), he must have felt a lone voice crying in the wilderness of The Hague. Perhaps this helps to explain why Dirk was seen at court far less often than his letter of employment would have led Albert to expect.[81] It is also the most plausible reason why, after 1404, the accounts make no more mention of Dirk of Delft—after Albert's death in December 1404, Dirk probably turned his back on The Hague. Such a step would in any case have been expected: he had, after all, joined the court for the solemn purpose of serving his protector, and his relationship with Albert's son and successor was undoubtedly less personal. William VI was much more interested in chivalry than in theology—he was, in fact, the type of nobleman who would find more appeal in a Bavaria Herald than a Dirk of Delft. For his religious reading, indeed, William VI would probably have been quite satisfied with the writings of William of Hildegaersberch, from whom he is known to have bought a manuscript. He would, moreover, expect his chaplain to accompany him to Prussia or to go on secret missions to Friesland[82]—which certainly were not tasks for the learned Master Dirk of Delft.

Dirk presumably left The Hague, vanishing out of sight. Nowhere do we find the slightest trace of him after 1404—unless Axters's (tentative) supposition is correct and the sermons in a Bruges manuscript attributed to "a notable doctor, master in divinity, and monk in the same [i.e., Dominican] order" were actually by Dirk of Delft.[83] That supposition has considerable support. Not only is Axters's opinion (to use a favorite argument of Dirk of Delft himself) authoritative in this field, but the sermons are also followed by a chapter taken directly from the *Tafel* ("W" XI). Additionally, in the sermons themselves we can hear strains that could easily have been struck by Dirk: the carefully argued reflections on the nature of angels, for example, betray the hand of a Schoolman of mark. Still, some characteristic features of the *Tafel* are missing: there are no knights of God, no everlasting honor, no illustrations drawn from court life. Then, too, there is an (uncharacteristically) intense concern with the mystical nature of the soul.

Still, these differences do not necessarily disqualify Dirk of Delft from authorship of the sermons; more appropriately, they simply reflect the fact that the respective audiences of the *Tafel* and of the sermons were dissimilar. The sermons, for instance, appeal repeatedly to an audience of "beloved sisters"; that is, they were obviously addressed by a Dominican guest preacher to a congregation of nuns. Now, Dirk undoubtedly felt as much at home in such company as he had at the court in The Hague—not that the nuns measured up to his scholarship, but they would have been more receptive than the court nobles to his spiritual message and religious knowledge. And once again, the teacher seems to have matched his words to his pupils; the reception of his discourse by the Flemish nuns will have been less princely but probably more grateful.

Much the same is true of the *Tafel* itself. From the extant manuscripts we know that, after its initial appearance in aristocratic circles, the work received an enthusiastic welcome from Beguine and other convents.[84] In these groups, the book undoubtedly filled a need: it provided a catechesis written in the vernacular and in a style to match the spiritual profile of a devout audience of nuns lacking the Schoolman's education. At the court of Holland, meanwhile, Dirk Potter had begun to give voice to an entirely different tune.

VI

Dirk Potter

1. A COURTIER WITH A CRIMINAL RECORD?

For a man who was to become a staunch advocate of calm and reason, Dirk Potter's biography had a violent beginning.[1] In August 1400, he and a gang of friends and relatives (including several women) trounced another party of courtiers (clerics among them) so viciously that two were left dead and at least three others badly wounded. The cause of this fray, as of so many like it, can only be inferred from the bare bones of the known facts, but it must have been grounded in the feud between the Hooks and the Cods. Courtiers quite understood that settling such disputes might involve manslaughter, but so long as the enemy was not ambushed and was finished off in honest hand-to-hand fighting, people were generally prepared to forgive and forget. In this instance, however, the Potter brothers and their friends did not go free; on the contrary, the authority—in the person of Albert of Bavaria—saw fit to make an example of them in an effort to restore dignity and order.

An open letter followed, dated 30 November 1400, in which Albert declared that, the council having failed to persuade the two parties to settle their differences, a settlement was to be imposed. Albert obviously considered Dirk Potter and his associates guilty, because he awarded Dirk no damages for his wounds and ordered his party to pay a heavy fine, in what amounted to a typical combination of material and spiritual redress. The Potter party had first to pay a fine of 600 écus (easily thirty times Dirk of Delft's annual pay), a third of which would go to the count and the remainder to the victims' kin. Nor was the spiritual aspect of penance ignored. The Potters were further ordered to have a thousand requiem masses read for the men they had killed, to buy their victims (posthumous) membership in a monastic order, and to go on a pilgrimage—in person, and not by paying a deputy—to Our Lady of Rocamadour in Quercy, southwestern France. Finally—and as severe— two hundred of their number were ordered to prostrate themselves in public in the church at The Hague. Merely paying and praying did not always satisfy the medieval sense of justice; often the guilty were expected to humiliate themselves in public as well. From the exceptional importance that courtiers attached to honor, name, and prestige, it is probable that the last punishment was the bitterest of all.

Such medieval sentences were far from light. Yet once the debt to society had been paid, the matter was forgotten; the guilty did not have to suffer from a criminal record or even a heavy conscience for the rest of their lives. Dirk Potter's subsequent career demonstrates this fact clearly. Barely three weeks after Dirk had paid the count's share of the fine, Albert rewarded him for services rendered. And that was only a foretaste of favors. Nowadays, in most (though not all) societies, a man with Dirk's record is unlikely to rise to high legal office. Dirk and his brother Peter (very possibly the ringleader of the gang), by contrast, were apparently both appointed bailiffs at The Hague and Haagambacht (the trade district that grew up round the court) under Albert's successor, William VI. In that capacity, Dirk Potter would have had to apprehend criminals in the count's name and hear their pleas before a bench of "well-born men."[2] The crimes over which he had jurisdiction included manslaughter and instigating violent brawls. Thus, any person accused of these misdemeanors in Haagambacht had the consolation of being brought to justice by a bailiff with personal experience of such clashes.

Being a bailiff was probably no more than a subsidiary duty for Dirk Potter, for we know that while he held that office (from 1408 to 1416) he also served the count in other capacities. From the importance of these various services, we can see once again how great a favorite he was, not only of Albert but even more so of William VI. Dirk Potter started his court career before 1400 as a humble treasury and chancellery clerk, but he eventually served the county of Holland as a diplomat. On behalf of his sovereign lord, but no doubt also of the countess and of the council, he traveled widely at home and abroad. His last journey took him to Rome, where, in 1411–12, he was engaged on a confidential mission, the aim of which has never been revealed—which shows that Dirk Potter knew how to keep state secrets.[3] When necessary, though, he also had a ready tongue, and it was doubtless for his skill with words that he was included in the county's peace mission to Friesland.[4]

In addition to discretion and eloquence, Dirk Potter had a gift even more remarkable: he could write. Writing was, in fact, part of his inheritance. His father had been a clerk in the count's service, and his brothers held similar positions, as, in due course, would his own son Gerard.

25. Account signed by T(heodoricus) Potter de Loo. (Algemeen Rijksarchief, The Hague, MS. AGH 1269, fol. 84r)

Yet no matter how crucial his heredity and upbringing were to his literary development, Dirk Potter had to learn to read and write for himself, and for that he had to go to school.

There is little doubt but that the schooling he enjoyed (at court or in the village of The Hague?) was more than elementary, for in later years Dirk Potter proved to be exceptionally well educated for a layman. In part he must have acquired some grounding from the rough-and-tumble of practical life, but reading, writing, arithmetic, and Latin he certainly learned at school. In other areas, young Potter probably learned the rudiments in class and then rounded them off with practical experience: in jurisprudence, for instance, and government; in his skillful use of his mother tongue (which the modern Dutch reader may be unable to follow without glosses), and in gaining fluency in French, and probably in Italian and perhaps also in English. His remarkable linguistic gifts are borne out not only by his having been entrusted with so many foreign missions but even more so by his writings. For although his school education was intended to prepare him for an administrative career, it also taught him to appreciate fine writing. From his later works, we can tell that school gave him a particular taste for classical Roman writers, a taste he continued to cultivate in later life. Thus he immersed himself in Ovid, in pseudo-Ovidiana, and in the many commentaries on Ovid's work that abounded in the Middle Ages.

Still, he did not rest content with reading; he also started to write—literature as well as official documents. When he first surfaced on the literary scene, he had already ascended some way up the social ladder: his first work, *Der minnen loep* (The course of love), was published after his visit to Rome in about 1411–12. In Italy, he seems not only to have been outraged by the lax (homophile) behavior he encountered, but also to have conceived his first poetic work.[5] Was it perhaps fashionable in Roman diplomatic circles to write in one's spare time, or did the envoy from The Hague wish to surprise friends at home by returning as a cultured man of the world?

Whatever his reasons, the end result was unmistakable. He wrote literature to please himself and not to anyone's orders. None of his writings can be considered paid work done for some noble sponsor or anyone else. The only readers Potter addressed directly were members of his private circle: a "lovable and fair lady," a "dear son," "my friends."[6] It would, of course, be naive to conclude that these were the only readers Dirk Potter had in mind; yet there is nothing in his life or work to suggest that his writing had any aim other than to offer his literary skills to a small group of friends and relatives—for whom, in effect, he would not only have fought feuds but also have wielded a quill. Thus, while he wrote his official papers on instructions from superiors, in writing literature he submitted to no one. In that realm he worked neither to order nor for money, and perhaps not even in the hope of currying (further) favors, but simply because he had the inclination and the intellect to fulfill his cultural potential.[7] Common as that attitude may be among twentieth-century writers, it was most unusual at a medieval court. If my assessment of Potter is correct, he must have been one of the first "independent" writers in Dutch literary history.

Independence seems also to have determined his attitude to his sources, which modern students have found exceedingly difficult to trace. His last work causes the least trouble: the *Mellibeus* seems to have been a fairly literal translation from the French.[8] More problematical, however, are the sources of Potter's other works. The *Blome der doechden* (Flower of virtue) has close affinities with the Italian *Fiore di virtú*, but also differs widely from it in many respects. Much the same is true of *Der minnen loep*, which, though based largely on Ovid and on medieval Ovidian commentaries, nevertheless has an independent flavor.[9] Of course, unsuspected new sources could come to light at any time; indeed, literary history is thick with instructive examples of such discoveries. In particular, spectacular finds may be expected in the immense (and hence poorly explored) medieval genre of morality tales, to which the sources of the *Blome* must be assigned. But there are also haystacks without any needles, as *Der minnen loep* amply attests: courtly love poetry has been explored like few other facets of medieval literature, and still Potter's firstling continues to stand more or less on its own.

Perhaps, then, it is time to recognize that Dirk Potter was, if you will, a complete outsider. His independence (though mark well—from the literary tradition alone), which in a sense may be considered a sign of modernity, runs like a red thread through this chapter. For although (or because?) Dirk Potter was the perfect courtier, he differed from all other writers at the court of Holland in many respects. Sometimes—as in his best work—he reminds one of his older contemporary, Chaucer, who also made extremely free with his medieval and classical sources, and of whom it is also believed that he started writing as a hobby while employed as a court official and a diplomat, not to curry favor with this noble or that but simply to entertain a small circle of friends and acquaintances at the court of Edward III and Richard II.[10] Odious though comparisons may be, Dirk Potter appears to have started his literary career for much the same reasons. In any case, he, too, was not only a moralist (especially in his first book) but also a natural storyteller and, moreover, one who wrote about what was certain to appeal to intimate friends: namely love, in both its acceptable and its forbidden form.

2. LESSONS IN LOVE

In the four books of *Der minnen loep* (The course of love), Dirk Potter presents the reader with tales of famous and less famous lovers, all encapsulated in what may grandly be called a theory of love. That theory also explained what love ought *not* to be: neither the "crazy" (gecke) infatuation Potter deals with in the first book nor the "illicit" (ongheoerloefde) love for, say, blood relatives, Jews, and heathens that he discusses in the third book, for example. The remaining two books are devoted to "true love" (goede minne). In book two, Potter pays fulsome tribute to it, setting out its ideal growth in four stages (thus doing full justice to his title): the dawn of love upon first glimpsing the beloved at a social occasion; further meetings in the intimate surroundings of garden or bower; frolicking in the bedroom, which leads to intercourse; and, finally, married or "permitted" (gheoerloefde) love—to which the fourth and last book is devoted.

At first sight, Potter's conception of love seems as homely as it is traditional. In particular, the idea of love as a slow development toward the ultimate (physical) union in the marriage bed would now be considered rather old-fashioned. Yet old-fashioned is not necessarily medieval, and if we hold up Potter's view of love not to our own mirror but to that of his period—and, moreover, read his book very carefully—*Der minnen loep* emerges much less conventional and trivial than we anticipated. To appreciate that fact, we need only recall earlier chapters of the present book. In particular, in Chapter II we saw that the (to us) familiar bracketing of marriage with love was anything but taken for granted at the medieval court of Holland. Nevertheless, Dirk Potter posited a strong connection between bedding and wedding: in his eyes, if all went well, true love would be crowned with marriage. That view explains why the whole of the fourth book is devoted to conjugal love; and even if later a wily snake proves to be hiding in the grass of marriage, and though we may differ about the extent to which *Der minnen loep* is dedicated to married love,[11] it is obvious that its author devoutly desired the "true lovers" of the second book to have a long and happy marriage.[12]

Dirk Potter was of course not alone in this "romantic" view of wedded bliss. Court chaplain Dirk of Delft, for instance, took the same view (naturally); and as an ideal, married love had more than once been extolled in the chivalrous romances so beloved of medieval aristocrats. But the more or less self-evident way in which Potter associated marriage

with love, while almost completely ignoring marriage as a social ar-
rangement (made by dynastic and propertied families), rendered his
conception of love rather unusual, the more so in that Potter was a
(married) man of the world and not a cleric.[13] When William of Hildegaersberch wrote verses on marriage, he made no mention of love;
when the *Haags liederenhandschrift* sang the praises of love, it omitted
marriage. *Der minnen loep*, by contrast, was a paean to the union of the
two.

Because Potter's view of love seems so familiar, we are inclined to
forget that it might have seemed "modern" in the past. Perhaps "modern" was not its most signal feature, though; if we insist on a label,
"bourgeois" might be more appropriate. Marriage as a social contract
was, after all, primarily (and in historical terms, understandably) an instrument used by the aristocracy to expand, or at least to consolidate,
their lands, authority, and wealth. But what of the attitude toward marriage on the part of medieval social sectors less concerned with power
and riches, simply because they had little to lose?

Here we are brought up against a very complex question, one to
which we cannot possibly hope to do justice within the scope of this
book.[14] As a considerable oversimplification, however, we can suggest
that modern historians tend to think that these emerging classes (no
doubt to the delight of the church) were willing to give greater leeway
to the private feelings of young people in the selection of marriage partners—though naturally in the devout hope that the children's choice
would not clash with the parents' class interests or with other social or
family concerns. In macrohistorical respects, this "Christian-bourgeois"
conception of love, and the class with which it was associated, were to
set the tone in later centuries for even the highest social circles—a very
rare example of the "upward mobility of culture."[15] The resulting vision
left its traces in *Der minnen loep*; for in his conception of love and marriage, Dirk Potter was already something of a bourgeois. It may seem
rather daring to attribute bourgeois ideas to this man, a courtier
through and through, a secretary to a succession of counts, and, at the
end of his career, the holder of a patent of nobility, a landed estate, and
a double-barreled name, but that paradox cannot be brushed aside; indeed, it will continue to hold our attention for the rest of this chapter.

Meanwhile, if we remain with the *Der minnen loep* and thus confine
ourselves to Potter's conception of love, we can maintain that, although
the book and the ideas expressed in it were not wholly aristocratic, they
were no less elitist because of that. Potter declares, for instance, that love

can influence noble spirits only, not "callow youths" (huusbacken jonghe) whose "unpolished tongues" (ongheslepenre tonghe) can destroy love as quickly as they can arouse it, an eventuality that leaves these unlicked cubs quite unconcerned: "The skin is too thick to pierce . . . A swine would not notice the casting of lilies in the mud" (Tfel is dicke, 't en mach niet doer [. . .] een zwijn soude des weynich achten, datmen lelyen trade int slijck; I, 1321, 1342–43). And when Potter says elsewhere that tradesmen know nothing of true love, he shows himself to be a thorough and unabashed snob (I, 215–20):

> Ledighe luden moghen minnen;
> Maer die sijn lijftocht moet winnen
> Mit aernste ende mit hantarbeyde,
> Wil die volghen der minnen zede,
> So blijft hi slechs daer by verloren.
> Arme luden, wacht u daer voren!

Leisured people can indulge in love; but if those who must earn their bread by hard manual labor want to devote themselves to love, they are bound to come to grief. Poor people, beware!

Potter refers to those made for true love as "leisured people," that is, a class distinguished not so much by birth as by ease and wealth; those earning their bread by manual labor, in contrast, cannot be good lovers. Later in the poem, he even goes so far as to specify their unfit occupations; and when he proceeds to consider who *is* qualified for (true) love, he is very careful to stipulate that, rather than noble blood, a noble heart is a sufficient (and, indeed, a primary) qualification. The relevant quotation is long but instructive—if only because "wisdom" and "cunning" are central to his moral philosophy (II, 665–95):

> Want rude menschen van grover aert,
> Die sommighe volghen des ploeghes staert,
> Die ten water varen visschen,
> Die tvleysch houden opten disschen,
> Smede die dat yser bluffen,
> Spitter, delver mit horen muffen,
> Monick, schipper, waghenaren,
> Timmerluyden, molenaren,
> Plackers ende die vetten die huden,
> Ende anders vele der ambochtsluden,
> Van sulken en heb ic nye ghehoert
> Dat se die minne ye heeft ghemoert
> Als sy die edel luden doet.
> Daeromme seg ic uut minen moet,

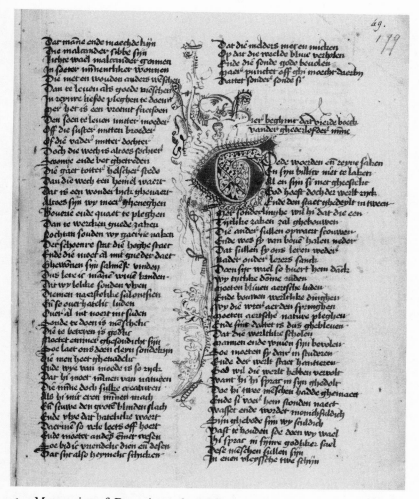

26. Manuscript of *Der minnen loep* (The course of love). (Koninklijke Bibliotheek, The Hague, MS. 128 E 6, fol. 179r)

Dat minne daer wy dus off lesen,
Moet een edel zake wesen,
Wantsy mit nyemant ghemeen en heeft,
Dan mitten ghenen die edelic leeft
Off daermen guede daden off hoirt
Off die is van goeder gheboort,
Off die van naturen edel sijn
Ende van duechtdentliken schijn;
Reyn, cuysch, subtijl van sinnen,

> Die eerbaer sijn ende tru van binnen,
> Lustelic, guet, van finen aerde,
> Off betemelijc sijn ten zwaerde
> Ende der wapen gaerne behaghen,
> Off die hoir liefde heymelic draghen
> Ende huefsch sijn in horen manieren
> Ende die hem zedelic regieren
> Mit wijsheit ende mit zueter list.

Of common folk, coarse of character, such as walk behind the plough, fish in the sea, serve food on plates, smiths who forge iron, gardeners who dig the soil, monks, boatmen, coachmen, carpenters, millers, plasterers, tanners, and many other tradesmen like them—of such I have never heard it said that they were touched by love as noble people are. And so I make bold to declare confidently that the kind of love we are discussing is a noble thing; befitting only those who live nobly, or whose noble deeds are widely known or who are of noble birth, or are noble by nature and virtuous; pure and chaste and refined, honorable and true, merry and gracious, who wield their swords nimbly and gladly, or who conceal their love and are of courtly manner and permit their actions to be guided by wisdom and sweet cunning.

In other words, Dirk Potter had a class-prejudiced view of love, though not in a formal or legal sense. To him, young members of the upper middle class were as qualified for courtly love as the nobility. Amon was "rich, noble, and of courtly speech" (rijck, edel ende van huefscher tonghe; II, 3924); Floridamas was "not rich, but well born" (niet rijck, mair wail gheboren; II, 1838); Astenborch was "a rich burgher's child" (eens rijckes burghers kint; II, 3306)—yet they all figure in *Der minnen loep* as models of "true love." Nor do class differences have to obstruct true lovers—on the contrary, Dirk Potter has a special sympathy for lovers from different estates (the man being invariably of lowlier origins than the woman). Thus we are told that Anazaretes, a maiden "of nobler descent" (van edelre stam), was wrong to spurn her admirer Isis, who was "of lowlier burgher stock" (van slechter burgher aert gheboren), for his humble origins; and we are given to understand that the relationship between Cydippe (noble descent) and Aconsius (noble character) or between Quintilianus (rich, lower nobility) and the royal Penella were models of "true love."[16] Hence, while the theme of love and class difference—one that in later centuries would cause so much ink to flow—does occur in *Der minnen loep*, it is introduced only so there will be no doubt as to Dirk Potter's own opinion: provided the lovers belong to the elite of "leisured folk," class differences need not impede their love or marriage.[17] Like the nobleman Orphaen in the fourth book, Dirk Potter prefers "virtue to birth" (duecht voer die gheboerte) in the choice of a marriage partner (IV, 1131). Indeed, he even sees advantages in the man's being of lesser birth, for then the husband will be more likely to do his best for the woman, and all the less likely to indulge in the faithlessness to which other men so easily succumb.[18] What matters is that the lovers' hearts beat in unison; when that happens, the woman, as far as Potter is concerned, could as well be of royal blood and the young man a "merchant's son" (eens coopmans soon; II, 73–74).

Thus, while Dirk Potter may not have been democratic in matters of love, he took a liberal enough view of it, as he did also of other spheres of life—which brings us not only to the relativity of his traditionalism, but also to the promised examination of his apparent "respectability." That Dirk Potter was not at all the strict moralist for which he might be mistaken, given what was said at the beginning of this section, becomes apparent when we reach his ideas of forbidden love, as outlined in the third book of *Der minnen loep*. Particularly arresting is the way he deals with incest—a subject on which he not only holds forth at great length but toward which he displays a degree of tolerance that the modern reader might find excessive.[19]

Naturally, he considers incest a violation of God's commandments and deems it "weird" (een vreemt faetsoen) that mother and son, brother and sister, or father and daughter should want to cohabit. Moreover (as he then illustrates with several examples), it is too rare (!) that any good comes of it. Still, "although it were better out of one's mind than in it, yet is it love for all that" (al waersi beter uuten sinne dan daer in, 't is doch lieft; III, 322–23)—a form of love, additionally, that can "spring from a pure brook" (vloeyen uut een reyne beke; 631) and that "follows the course of nature" (volghet der naturen; 311). In short, even though incest is a sin and best avoided, "one may indulge in it" (men macher wat off maken; 310)—provided it does not go beyond the "third degree" (derde graet; 312–16), which, according to book two, means that one can have a good romp *on* the bed, while exchanging endearments, caresses, and fondling of breasts that are "not too firmly encased" (niet te vast besloten; II, 1299–1323), but must not get *between* the sheets for sexual intercourse.

Incest is not the only theme in which Potter starts with a list of theoretical objections only to end up interpreting the rules rather freely. Fourth-degree sexual relations fall in this category as well. Officially, intercourse is reserved for marriage; only within wedlock can there be "permitted love" in the full sense of the words. Moreover, the pleasures of marriage, so *Der minnen loep* contends, are greatly enhanced if congress is postponed until after the wedding. But book two knows only too well that the flesh is weak, and several of its illustrative examples show premarital "true love" culminating in the fourth degree of physical contact. As far as Potter is concerned, however, such cases still constitute exemplary love—or, as he remarks when telling the story of Sabina and Floridamas (II, 2045–49):[20]

> Daer was trouwe ende trouwe was daer,
> De minne was guet ende vreuchden baer.
> Al was sy inden vierden graet,
> So ghedaen en was niet quaet.

There was troth and troth there was, the love was good and fruit it bore. Albeit of the fourth degree, it did no harm to anyone.

Dirk Potter's liberal attitude becomes even more patent in book four. The central pillar of married love, he explains there at some length, is absolute fidelity; "however oft true love may stray, troth must have the final say" (202–3). But that permissive clause about "straying," and hence the possible emergence of "new" desire, is a mere prelude to all the infidelities that Potter then lays bare. Quite bluntly, while he condemns adultery in theory, he does not exaggerate its enormity in practice—it being understood, of course, that it is the *husband* who does the straying. That qualification is significant, for if the husband's adulterous union were to produce issue, the children would have no claim to his estate, whereas the illegitimate offspring of an adulterous wife, because the father would be, practically speaking, unknown, would be free to claim the full share of their patrimony.[21]

But as far as Potter is concerned, more important by far than the legal justification of the disparate treatment of adulterous men and women is the difference between the two partners in respect of *honor*. If a married woman commits adultery, both she and her husband lose their good name; if, by contrast, the husband strays, no one's honor is compromised: at most he has committed a sin for which he will have to answer to God, but not to his fellow men—and certainly not to his spouse.[22] For that reason alone, Dirk Potter thinks that a woman should contain her anger if her husband's fidelity appears doubtful, and not try to repay him in the same (let alone double) coin. Nor should she heed the gossips, "for to believe them lightly is more often than not a great pity and causes much harm" (want sulck gheloven lichtelick is duck ende menichfoudelic groet jammer ende schade gheschiet; IV, 1681–83). Above all, a woman must not spy on her husband; spying inevitably leads to frustration and often backfires on the woman (1843–1960).

To demonstrate the truth of that remark, Potter tells various stories about suspicious wives forced to pay dearly for their mistrust. For example, it once happened in Schiedam—"as several people can still recall" (dat weten noch wel sommighe lyede)—that the master of the house had an affair with the maid (IV, 1971–2032). The maid confided in her mistress, who decided to catch her husband in the act; to that end she changed beds with the maid one night when the husband was expected to pay his unwelcome attentions. The husband, believing he was lying with the maid, "merrily made love; then retired to his own chamber" (vrolic mede leeft; hi ghinc weder in sijn ghelach). Immediately afterward (Potter does not tell us how he managed this remarkable feat) the husband reported his nocturnal adventure to his best friend, whom he invited to come round to the maid's quarters: "'Repair thither and claim your rights as if you were I; you will find that the door [literally or allegorically?] still stands open'" ("Gaet ghi mede aldair, ende veinst u recht off icket waer; ghi vint die dure noch open staen"). No sooner said than done; the friend repaired to the same couch and lay with the woman. "Her husband she mistook him for, and gave her body as before" (Ende was oick der vrouwen bi; se meende twaer hair man gheweest, so dat hoir lief was totter feest). Potter had a good laugh at this erotic comedy of errors, but when the truth came out, Schiedam society laid the blame not on the husband, but on the woman: "Her honor she has forfeited. . . . To trap her husband she did try, but with another man did lie, so people looked at her awry" (Eerlois is sy nu gheworden [. . .] Si waende verschalken horen man, mer si bleef selve in die pan ende wort gheschent in horen daghen, dat seker billicx is te beclaghen). In short, the wife would have done far better to stay in her own bed and let her husband have his way with the maid. Still, the husband was not fully absolved: the Schiedammers thought it most unbecoming of him to have passed his paramour on to his friend so unceremoniously.

Clearly, the author is not overly worried about adulterous males as such, as we see in the advice he offers their wives: "And should your husband go astray, or should he falter on the way, do not with anger him reproach, but show him kindness if you can" (Ist dat u man ontruwelic leeft, als u deynct in uwen sinne, bewiset hem dair om ghene onminne; verwint mit goetheit, off ghi moecht; IV, 2216–19). Indeed, he reminds his readers very soberly that many men lived with more than one woman and did nobody the least harm. In support of this claim, too, Potter cites a battalion of precedents, beginning with the patriarch Jacob and going on to several unknown men: pagan princes "and many others" had a round twenty, thirty, forty, a hundred, or even two hundred wives, "ever ready to bestow their love" (altoes bereyt te haren live; IV, 970), "surprised though you may be" (hoet u verwondert; IV, 2240); and many a Christian, too, was allowed to consort with two or three women.[23]

These ideas force some change in our original view of Dirk Potter's moral philosophy. In fact, he shows himself to be rather a libertine and a liberal, especially as regards male behavior. Yet not even he is prepared to sanction such grievous lapses as love for a Jewess or homosexuality— these are wholly outrageous. One should never be tempted to stoop to the level of Italians, who, though their country teems with the most beautiful women, know no greater delight than to seek the love of other men.[24] For the rest, true lovers, particularly widespread in the German Empire (and hence also in Holland; II, 721–22), can do whatever they like. Dirk Potter would of course prefer them to embrace virtue and eschew sin; but if they could not refrain from the latter—enticing as it so often is—than they had best venture no more than minor, pardonable sins and—if they cannot do that—hold their tongues (III, 1245–64):

> Sonde te doen is menschelic,
> Die te beteren is godlic.
> Moetet emmer ghesondicht sijn,
> Soe laet ons doen cleyn sondekijn,
> Diemen heet ghenadelic.
> Ende wye van moede is so rijck,
> Dat hi moet minnen van naturen,
> Die minne doch sulke creaturen
> Als hi mit eren minnen mach
> Ende scuwe den groten blinden slach,
> Ende vlye dat hatelicke woert,
> Daermen so vele leets off hoert.
> Ende moetet anders emmer wesen,
> Soe bid ic vriendelic dien ende desen,
> Dat sijt also heymelic schicken,
> Dat die melders niet en micken,
> Op dat die weelde blive verholen
> Ende die sonde Gode bevolen;

Maer punctet, off ghi moecht, daerbij,
Dattet sonder sonde si.

To sin is human; to undo sin divine. But if sin we must, then let our sins be petty and pardonable. And any so rich in passion that they must needs love by nature, let them choose such as they can love with honor, and not allow themselves to be blinded and avoid the evil tongues which cause so much misery. And if any must needs stray, then my friendly advice to them is that they manage things in such manner that the gossips do not notice, that their happiness remain hidden and their sin known to God alone; still, if you can, you had best eschew sin altogether.

This quotation (which ends book three) sums up Dirk Potter's moral outlook. Of course, it is best to avoid sin altogether; and Potter does not forget to close on this pious note. Yet he realizes that man cannot help lapsing into sin every so often, and even into mortal sin. In that case, what matters most is to keep all evidence of his weakness from the outside world. *Secrecy* is Dirk Potter's all-purpose watchword; it presides over the entire *Der minnen loep*.[25] For when all is done, secrecy guarantees that the sinner remains of good repute, even though he has broken the official code. If lovers take such care—with the woman's honor deserving as much protection as the man's—they can, as far as Dirk Potter is concerned, do much as they please.

In fact, *Der minnen loep* goes one step further still, giving advice to lovers who are determined to have their way with reluctant partners. True, even Dirk Potter draws the line at physical force; still, clever stratagems are part of the game of love, if not of true love, and without them no lover can hope to triumph.[26] Many of these stratagems are variants of the "concealing" game so beloved of Potter: by concealing lapses from prying neighbors, they avert dishonor. But ruses can also be used to talk the woman (for invariably it is she who must be persuaded) into compliance and, above all, to get her into bed.

Potter presents these ruses as the lover's last resort; yet the unmistakable pleasure with which he tells long stories about such trickery in book two only confirms our suspicion that he considers them not just ultimate expedients but almost indispensable, and in any case highly diverting, ingredients of "true love." Here the crown must go to his story of Neptanabus and Olympia (II, 3067–91). Neptanabus was "in the black arts more skilled than any other known to man" (in swarten consten vroeder dan yemant anders diemen wiste). When he arrived in Macedonia from Libya, he fell in love with the queen of that country, the famous beauty Olympia. In the seductive tones of a great seer, for which his renown spread quickly, Neptanabus told the queen what the future held for her husband, King Philip. Her predictable reaction was to ask whether the sage might not know what lay in store for her as well. Needless to say, Neptanabus was ready with his answer (II, 3098–3119:

> "Vrouwe," sprac hi, "mit groter eeren
> Suldi uwen tijt toe bringhen.
> Die Goden hebben vreemde dinghen
> Mit u te schaffen inder tijt,
> Ic wil dat ghy des seker sijt.
> Een God heeft u hert ende sin ghegheven
> Ende wil natuerlic mit u leven,
> Ende hi sal in wonderliker formen
> Te nacht in dese camer stormen;
> Mer weest sonder anxt ende blijde.
> Hij sal comen bij uwer zijde
> Ende winnen an u een kint,
> Dat vanden Goden sal sijn ghemint
> Ende sal alle die werlt dwinghen
> Datmenre ewelic off sal singhen.
> Wanneer hi coomt, so swijcht al stille
> Ende laten doen al sinen wille.
> Die Goeden willen dattet ghescie;
> Want sulck wonder en gheschiede nye."
> Die vrouwe sprac in soeten schijn:
> "Der Goden wille, dat is die mijn,
> Dier en can ich niet weder staen."

"Madam," said he, "a great honor lies in store for you. The gods have singled you out for a special task, as I hasten to assure you. One god has fallen in love with you head over heels and he naturally wants to lie with you, and he will rush into your chamber this night having assumed a strange form; but fear not and be glad. He shall come and lie by your side and give you a child that will be loved by the gods and will conquer the whole world, so that people will sing its praises for evermore. When he comes, keep perfectly still and let him have his will of you. The gods want it to happen, for such a miracle has never yet been." The queen replied sweetly: "The will of the gods is mine as well; I cannot deny them."

The rest of the story is not hard to guess. Neptanabus the magician turned himself into a magnificent dragon with a most beautiful, crowned human head; that night he flew through the window of the queen's bedchamber (II, 3137–46):

Daer ghinc hi bijder schoenre legghen
Ende dede des ic en can ghesegghen.
Sij waende dattet was een God;
Maer neen, hi hilt mit haer sijn spot.
. . . .
Hadde hijt mit consten niet ghemaect,
Hi en hadder nymmermeer an gheraect!

And so he lay beside the beautiful lady and did what I may not say in full. She thought he was a god but no, he was playing a trick on her. . . . Had he not used it, he would never have succeeded!

The child born of the union of Neptanabus and Olympia was to prove famous indeed (in keeping with his father's prophecy): he became Alexander the Great. But Neptanabus's deceptions did not end there. When rumors began to spread that Queen Olympia was with child, he let it be known that "God himself had done the deed; and what the gods deign to decree, fills one and all with joy and glee" (dattet God selve dede; ende wes die goden plaghen te voegen, daer liet hem een yghelic mede ghenoegen; II, 3158–60). Hence, her extramarital fall greatly enhanced the queen's reputation—as Dirk Potter put it, "her honor flourished all the more!" (hoer eer floreerde veel te meer). True, King Philip was furious at first, but "the more about the gods he learned, the less by fortune he felt spurned; he thought that God had honored him" (mer doe hi vanden Goden vernam, die zake hem doe wail bequam; hi dochte, God deet hem te eren; II, 3163–65). And so Neptanabus could continue to do as he pleased, "visiting" Olympia under the benevolent eye of her spouse. What moral did Potter draw from this story (II, 3192–3206)?

Dustanighe saken, wilt versinnen,
Sijn der vrouwen eer mede ghesterket,
Off ghi yet zwackes werct.
Eert die vrouwen, waerde man,
Ende die sulker konsten niet en can
—Als nyemant huden sdaghes en doet—
Die werde bedacht in sinen moet
Dat hi der vrouwen ere wachte
Mit anderen liste ende ghescachte,
Als men vele wel heeft ghevonden
Noch huden ende in ouden stonden,
Dier ic u een deel wil saghen.
Want zuete woirden doen behagen,
Daer wy rade uut nemen moeghen,
Die te schimpe ende te aernste doghen.

With these arts can you a woman's honor protect, should ever you go too far. Respect woman's honor, oh worthy man, and any who do not command these arts—as none seems to do these days—let him protect a woman's honor with other stratagems and ruses, of which quite a few have been devised, in the present and in the past, and of which I shall now list several. For pleasant words are agreeable provided they contain advice that is useful in earnest and in play.

Dirk Potter's counsel to lovers, therefore, is to use sweet words in "earnest and in play" (te schimpe ende te aernste doghen). The "play" in *Der minnen loep* hardly seems less important than the "earnest," as such roguish tales as this make clear. Dirk Potter seems at least as concerned with serving up erotic tales as with teaching useful lessons; throughout *Der minnen loep* one senses the author's delight in a titillating story. As a result Potter is, by modern standards, the most "literary" of all writers at the court of Holland, and certainly the most humorous. For while Hildegaersberch, too, could be witty, and although the *Haags liederenhandschrift* contains several comic poems, no other work provokes as many laughs as *Der minnen loep*. True, in it, we cannot always tell what is fun and what is not; to appreciate the book's humor to the full, after all, one would have to have been present at court when it was first read out aloud, catching the author's winks, grasping all the contemporary allusions, having a keen ear for contemporary linguistic nuances, and being surer about the precise meaning of the more difficult passages.[27] It is true of all medieval Dutch writers that their humorous passages are often harder for us to grasp than their serious ones. And there is little doubt but that Dirk Potter was one of the wittiest of them all, certainly in the county of Holland.[28]

The author of *Der minnen loep* took a highly ironic view of his characters and their actions. But then, as we have just seen, his moral philosophy was rather broad: a ruse, a little white lie, a peccadillo here and there—he forgave them all. Or rather, he seasoned his moral philosophy with a strong pinch of wit; he did not expect his readers to take all his lessons to heart—far from it. He tended to laugh at man's busy to-and-froing, especially in the byways of love.[29] In so doing, moreover, he would often indulge in self-mockery, particularly when presenting himself as a man grown wise in the ways of love, having tried in vain to win the favors of women and been sent packing (by their husbands perhaps?). Such passages are quite devoid of self-pity, unlike so many of Hildegaersberch's lines.[30]

All this was doubtless a literary device, and we would be rash to mistake Potter for a gay blade *tout court*. His opinion that all who make love to Jews should be consigned to the flames, no less than the incident with which we opened this chapter, suffice to show that, though he could jest, he could also be serious, even denunciatory. Yet *Der minnen loep* is so steeped in irony (however hard it is to discern) that we have some reason to regard its author as one who took love, if not all life, as it came, a man who distilled Ovid, church doctrine, chivalry, and practical experience into an amorous and sophisticated code that could be applied in practice and taught to others—certainly if one was prepared to accept some inconsistencies and act on one's own discretion. Those who look to Dirk Potter to preach as coherent a doctrine as Dirk of Delft do him an injustice. Unlike Dirk of Delft, Potter did not consider consistency an end in itself; on the contrary, we may put it, with only slight exaggeration, that for him consistency, inflexibility, and dogma often paved the road to hell. Potter embraced incongruities without much forethought and in so doing dug a chasm between theory and practice, adding a pungent aroma of ambivalence.

This attitude is clearest in his view of women.[31] On the one hand, he reverently placed them on a pedestal, as witness many passages of *Der minnen loep*: while men may enjoy greater freedom, woman is the crown of Creation. Indeed, Potter even seemed to pride himself on the high esteem in which he held the weaker sex. On the other hand, though, he could also condemn their behavior and complain of their innate tendency to order men about. Dirk Potter would teach them better, those *vroukijn* (little women), as he was wont to call them. With its ambivalent view of women, *Der minnen loep* not only expresses the idealistic and exalted vision of women that is enshrined in the chivalrous code, but also (and here we see that Potter knew his Ovid) a form of misogynist cynicism—much as the book as a whole presents love as an ideal but also elaborates on its less beautiful aspects, right down to forbidden love. Potter himself realized full well that he had stressed this shadowy aspect, so much so that he was at pains to apologize for his frankness in various passages—especially to the ladies.[32] Nor was he necessarily being hypocritical when, in later works, he offered something like an apology for *Der minnen loep* itself.

3. VIRTUE AND REASON

It is not known how much later than *Der minnen loep* Dirk Potter wrote his other work. He himself gives the impression that the interval was considerable, for in the first chapter of his second book, the *Blome der doechden* (Flower of virtue), he seems to dismiss *Der minnen loep* as a youthful lapse: "Of worldly and vain human love rooted in carnal temptation, I did write much in a book which I penned during my youth in Rome, more, I am afraid, than it pleased God. And should I have sinned thereby, I now beg God in his loving kindness to forgive me" (Van werltlijker mynnen ende van menschelijker ijdel liefde die uut vleyschelijker becoringhen hoeren oerspronc nempt, daer heb ic in een boec dat ic in jonghen tijden maecte te Rome veel aff ghescreven, ende meer dan Gode, als ic duchte, bequaem is. Ende off ich daer aen ghesondicht hebbe, soe bid ic der ontfermherticheit Gods dat sij mij dat wille vergheven).

Still, it would be naive to take him wholly at his word. For how is it possible to reconcile this claim with the fact that, in *Der minnen loep*, Potter presents himself as an experienced man of mature years, anxious to pass on his knowledge to young lovers? In fact, in both books Potter plays a rhetorical game with both his readers and himself. In *Der minnen loep*, he acts the seasoned sophisticate, the better to lend his lessons the authority of practical experience; in the *Blome der doechden*, he distances himself from his first work, the better to commend his new, obviously superior, book.

It follows that we can place little weight on Potter's autobiographical comments.[33] What does seem fairly certain is that his two later works, the *Blome der doechden* and the *Mellibeus* (which accompanies the *Blome* in the so-called Rekem manuscript of 1485), appeared in quick succession. This we deduce from the fact that the initial letters of each chapter of the first work form an acrostic with those of the second, which indicates that the two texts formed a diptych from the outset and not only in the Rekem manuscript. The complete acrostic reads: DIRIC POTTER VAN DER LOO UTEN HAGE HEEFT MI GEMAECT; GOD SI ES GHELOEFT ENDE GHEBENEDIJT VAN ALS, AMEN (Dirk Potter van der Loo from The Hague has made me; God be praised and blessed for everything, Amen).[34] Potter's two-part name sets a *terminus post quem* to both works: they must have been written after 25 March 1415, when the count of Holland invested Potter with the fief of Ter Loo (near Voorburg), whereupon our author hastened to style himself Dirk Potter vander Loo, no doubt because it sounded more impressive. In addition, we also have an obvious *terminus ante quem*: 30 April 1428, the date on which our author died. In other words, we can tell that Potter's later works were written at least four and at most sixteen years after *Der minnen loep*, which itself dates back to the years 1411–12.[35]

But no matter whether the period of Potter's literary silence was long or short, the change in style is inescapable. Not only did he write his later works in prose and replace the predominantly Latin sources of *Der minnen loep* with Italian (*Fiore di virtú*) and Old French (*Livre de Mellibee*) ones, but, at least as remarkably, he used a new approach as well.[36] Thus, in the very first chapter of the *Blome der doechden*, he discloses a change of heart: he no longer pays exclusive attention to love but presents his readers with a complete doctrine of virtue and vice; in addition, he adopts a much more pious perspective.

The aim of *Der minnen loep* was to teach the meaning of courtly love (I, 134), to help readers become adept lovers versed in the esoteric code. The *Blome*, by contrast, dwells on the difference between good and evil and aims to guide the seeker into the Kingdom of Heaven. To that end, the *Blome* (in keeping with the Italian *Fiore* and related texts) is divided into successive pairs of mutually opposed virtues and vices: Love and Hatred, followed by Joy and Sadness, Tranquillity and Anger, and so on—twenty pairs in all, including Honesty and Deceit, Humility and Arrogance, Purity and Unchastity, and Remembrance and Forgetfulness. Only the last chapter, on Sobriety, lacks a negative counterpart; perhaps Potter wanted to end his book, like *Der minnen loep*, on a major key. Within the chapters themselves, too, Potter's approach is fairly systematic: he invariably starts with a brief outline of the idea to be discussed, proceeds to paraphrase relevant opinions by Christian and classical authorities, introduces an animal symbolizing the virtue or vice under discussion, gives one or several examples illustrating the central idea of the chapter, and ends with a (sometimes fatuous) four-line poem that enjoins the reader to practice the virtue or avoid the sin.

Thus we find a different Dirk Potter from the one we met earlier, and one who, again, seems to betray a change of heart. That change is reflected elsewhere in the *Blome* as well. *Der minnen loep*, as we saw, looked favorably enough on lovers' stratagems and even considered them indispensable to courtly love, allowing lovers, in addition to gaining wisdom (about which more in section 4), to journey through life with "sweet deceit" (*zoeter list*); the *Blome*, in contrast, castigates such ruses as "false coin" (*valscher const*), as so many tissues of lies and bad faith.[37] Potter's attitude toward adultery, too, points in the same direction: nothing remains of the tolerant understanding, not to say sympathy, evinced by the (married) author of the *Der minnen loep*.[38] And while Venus appeared in the prologue to *Der minnen loep* as a kind of poetic patron, the *Blome der doechden* simply states: "Venus is full of deceit . . . so let everyone be resolute and watchful lest he be caught in her girdle" (Venus is vol valscheit [. . .] een yeghelick sy stercmodich ende wacht hem dat hij in horen gordel niet ommevanghen en werde; 82/11–13).

Nevertheless, a closer examination reveals a number of parallels (and not trivial ones, either) between Potter's earlier work and the *Blome*. In particular, both books use the same heuristic approach of making their point with the help of opposites. In *Der minnen loep*, love is divided into two antithetical pairs: good and evil, permitted and forbidden.[39] And although the number of opposite pairs is expanded in the *Blome* with the extension of the moral range, the underlying principle remains. In the prologue, Potter describes his meeting a gardener (undoubtedly no less fictitious a scene than the meeting with Venus in the prologue to *Der minnen loep*) who is busy filling a basket indiscriminately with weeds and lovely flowers (fig. 27). Potter, the expert on what fine blooms a (moral) garden can bring forth, goes on to separate good from evil generally—again with the help of opposites, his lengthy discourse on sin serving the urgent purpose of allowing virtue to emerge all the more victorious.[40]

Another feature that both books have in common is the failure of their systematic approach to stand firm in practice. In fact, Potter's approach serves merely as a rough frame, allowing him to present his lessons in some kind of order; yet if we look closely, we discover that he deviates quite widely from his main design, not only because he is continually associating ideas, but also because he so often blurs the distinction between chapters ostensibly devoted to opposites.[41] Recalling his earlier work, we are tempted to think that the real Potter's thoughts did not run closely enough along black-and-white lines to enable him to construct black-and-white schemes. In any case, even in the *Blome* he felt free to relinquish the strict systematic approach from time to time. Nor did he feel in the least compelled to keep all his chapters the same length; while some were rounded off in accord with the *Fiore* tradition (definition, authorities, animal symbol, example, verse), others reflect Potter's own hand.[42]

This independence of spirit also informs Potter's attitude toward religion. In contrast with Dirk of Delft and even with Hildegaersberch, he shows little interest in priests, the traditional intermediaries between faithful Catholics and God. It almost seems as if he thought that believ-

27. Author and gardener. From the prologue to the *Blome der doechden* (Flower of virtue). (Franciskanenklooster, Vaalbeek, MS. A 22, reproduced from *BD*, frontispiece)

ers could dispense with the clergy—indeed, as if he disliked them. It is a remarkable fact (and one that places our earlier remarks in quite a different light) that while in *Der minnen loep* he presented the spiritual and temporal states of mind as two alternative ways of life (never disguising which he himself preferred),[43] he seemed to go one step further in the *Blome*, dispensing, whenever possible, with the spiritual side altogether.

Yet despite its crabbed view of the clerical estate, the *Blome* clearly belongs to the genre of spiritual literature. Thus, Dirk Potter declares in the prologue with some self-assurance (8/22–9/5):

Hoe wael ic ken dat ic gheen doctoer en ben, noch gradeert in godlijken scriften, soe salmen doech mijn leer ontfanghen daer sij doecht ende waerheit in hebben [. . .] Hierom wilt van eenen stompen man die wereltlijc is also vriendelijc die worde van saligher leeringhe ontfaen, als ghij bij wilen van eenen hoghen gheleerden gheestelijken man ontfaet wijslijke exempel van cleijnre salicheit [. . .] Nu en houde ic mij doch niet voer eenen gheleerden, mer voer eenen leerenden man, die gherne als ic den tijt hebben moechte uut mijnre daghelijcscher hanteringen der cancelrien van Hollant, daer ic die minste in was, plach te oeffenen boeke der heiliger scrifften, ende oec mede der poeten. Ende off een mensche wat goets wiste dat den ghemeynen luden verhoelen were, soude hij dat sijnen lieven vrienden niet op doen, die den wech der salicheit daer bij vinden mochten?

Although I know I am not a doctor, nor have graduated in Holy Writ, yet does my teaching deserve to be heeded, since it contains virtue and truth. . . . Hence I pray you to take from a simple man the words of the blessed doctrine as you would take prudent advice on salvation from a most learned of priests. . . . For I do not take myself for a learned man, but rather for a learner, who, had he had time to spare from his daily duties in the chancellery of Holland, where he was the lowliest, would fain have studied the books of the Holy Writ and also of the poets. And if any had good tidings hidden from the common man, would he not want to make them known to his dear friends, who might discover the path to salvation thereby?

By setting out what he was not—doctor, learned priest, or graduate in Holy Writ—was Potter perhaps referring to the only person who, so far as we can tell, was all these things at the court of Holland, namely Dirk of Delft? That is a tempting assumption, even though that learned theologian had departed from the court at least ten years before Potter wrote these lines.[44] In *Der minnen loep*, too, is a passage that might be taken as a reference to Dirk of Delft: declaring that there was much in the practice of love that shunned the fresh light of day, Potter went on to say, "and not all of them [are] known to those from Delft" (en weten die van Delf niet al; I, 943). P. J. Leendertz, the editor of the 1845 edition, did not know what to make of that line: "I think it must have been a common saying, although I have not met it anywhere else."[45] But viewed against the background of Potter's life at court, one could read the line as a reference not to the naiveté of the people of Delft in general, but of one of them in particular.

In any event, Potter felt that the cultured layman had something of value to say on religious matters. That view was also given full expression further on in the *Blome*—for although that book dealt with the Christian life and aimed at nothing less than illuminating the earthly path to the Kingdom of Heaven, it barely referred to the sacraments of priesthood. It follows, then, that Potter completely ignored what, to Dirk of Delft and Hildegaersberch, was the chief—if not the sole—path to salvation. Indeed, when the *Blome* does introduce the occasional cleric, it invariably assigns him a negative role.

To appreciate this point fully, we cannot rely on the only published edition of the *Blome*, because its editor, the Franciscan Stephanus Schoutens, omitted the greater part of Potter's critique of the clergy without comment. If, however, we consult the (sole) extant manuscript of the text, we find that the *Blome* is larded with anticlerical references. Moreover, we find as well that the twentieth-century Schoutens had a medieval predecessor—for in the margin of the manuscript, these critical passages are often accompanied with such "directions" as "disregard" and "as far as here." The intention, clearly, was that anyone reading the text out loud in the refectory of the Maastricht Franciscan monastery (to which that manuscript eventually found its way) should skip all slurs on the clergy.

For Potter's part, however, it seems evident that he wrote passages such as the following with deliberate intent:[46]

[. . .] ende namelijc boven al die gheestelijke staet daer ons hoeft aen staet; daer uut coempt alle boesheit ende ontrouwe ende boverie diemen ter werelt hantieren mach. Want die grote clergie ende subtilheit der sinnen die sij ghebruyken, en wil niet lijden dat sij simpel sijn, mer vol alre loesheit ende cloecheit ende listicheit.

[Infidelity, falsehood, and wickedness have infected all mankind] and above all those clerics who wield authority over us; from them comes all the wickedness and infidelity and villainy there is in the world. For the senior clergy use subtle ways . . . and are full of wiles and shrewdness and cunning.

Ende die biechtvaders smeeken oec mede om goede provien te hebben ende groet te werden, alsoe die gheestelijke lude int ghemeyn ghierich sijn; ende mitsdien vallen sij allen te samen, heer ende bichtvaders ende die smeekers, in des duvels hof, daer sij langhe na ghestaen ende ghearbeit hebben.

And the confessors hanker after good prebends and advancement, because the clergy at large is avaricious; and in this all of them, lords and confessors and supplicants, are as one in the Devil's court, having long since taken up residence and work there.

Ich duchte dat menich priester snachs bij wijven is, ende gaet dan smorghens te biechten ende te missen.

I believe that many a priest lies with women at night, and in the morning goes forth to hear confession and to say mass.

[. . .] haerre vele eens wolfs herte draghen onder een lamshuyt, als decke onder-vonden is dat sij heymelijc des vrijdaghes vleesch aten ende vuyle, oncuysche vergaderinghe plaghen te hebben mitten susteren ende beghijnen.

[There are many hypocritical priests] who carry a wolf's heart under a sheep's fleece, and have often been found to eat meat in secret on Friday and are wont to attend vile and unchaste gatherings in the company of nuns and Be-guines.

While Dirk Potter may have been a staunch upholder of Christian virtue, he seems to have had little respect for the clergy. In that sense, too, he was perhaps the most "modern" author at the court of Holland. For whether or not we may justly apply the suggestive term *devotio mo-derna* to his approach, we do know that the late Middle Ages witnessed the emergence of an attitude toward religious life and practice that dis-pensed with the absolute necessity for priests as mediators, performers of ritual, and exemplars of morality.⁴⁷ The causes of this important de-velopment (which continued until the Reformation) were, as in all such processes, complex and varied. They included a growing revulsion at the dubious life-style of some clerics (to whom religious doctrine and personal life seemed to be completely separate issues), and also the widespread complaint that the priests' lessons were too difficult for the ordinary believer to comprehend, not to mention inapplicable in daily practice.⁴⁸ Laymen, then, Potter included, became increasingly con-vinced that professional Christianity should be shorn of its priestly trap-pings and replaced by a more individual (and hence also a more inward) union with God. The late-medieval layman dared and wanted to stand more firmly on his own feet in matters of faith.

Which brings us back to Dirk Potter, the independent spirit. Still, the reader would do well to keep a sense of proportion when judging him. When Dirk Potter wrote his books, the true cult of the individual lay five centuries ahead. Like almost everyone else in the Middle Ages, Dirk Potter was firmly wedded to tradition, and he was proud of, rather than frustrated by, that bond. Nor did any book he wrote lack orthodox precursors; the *Blome*, for instance, abounds with quotations from, and paraphrases of, Christian and classical authorities.

For all that, Potter was keen to be accepted as a new authority by his friends and readers, and to that end he had only to expand what he had begun in *Der minnen loep*—except that in the *Blome*, our layman and courtier presented himself as an expert on matters of religion rather than on love. Again, the prologue serves as the writing on the wall, inasmuch as Potter, despite frank avowals of his own limitations (no university degree, . . . a learner rather than a man of learning, . . . a simple layman, . . . a humble clerk of chancery), put himself forward as one who knew what was good for others. This self-confidence was something that Potter, in the *Blome* even more so than in *Der minnen loep*, justified by his intimate knowledge of "Holy Writ and also of the poets" (boeke der heiliger scrifften ende oec mede der poeten). Yet if we look more closely at his treatment of these sources, we find that he not only adapted them very freely but also added his own opinions when he saw fit to do so.[49] Thus, in the chapter on disobedience, he paraphrased Saints Gregory, Chrysostom, and Augustine, arguing that disobedience may well be a moral duty, inasmuch as what a man does reluctantly and with a bad conscience, he rarely does well. Nor was Potter prepared to leave it at that, for he went on to say: "But correcting and improving upon these learned doctors, it strikes me that, if a man does good even though it be against his will and albeit he do it reluctantly, he cannot be doing wrong" (Doch soe dunct mij op die correctie ende verbeteren mijnre doctoren, hoe een minsche wel doet ende goet, al ist teghen sijnen wille ende hij oec daer al strumende toe gaet, ten can ymmer niet quait wesen; *BD* 120/7–9).[50]

Even when it came to a field grazed more intensely than most, namely the history of Troy, Potter had an independent opinion. He did not, of course, reinterpret the events of the distant past: for those he, like Bavaria Herald, was fully prepared to trust Maerlant's *History of Troy*.[51] Yet his views of some of the leading characters in the Trojan drama differed radically from Maerlant's. Queen Hecuba of Troy attracted most of his scorn, joining Nero and Herod as a model of "wickedness."[52] The more traditional accounts, in contrast, had nothing but good to say of her, the chaste wife of the noble Priam, king of Troy; for them, the only blot on Hecuba's reputation was that she lured

Achilles into the Trojan palace—on the pretext of arranging his marriage to the Trojan princess Polyxena—thus allowing Paris, who lay in ambush, to pierce Achilles' vulnerable heel with an arrow and kill him. That act was, of course, anything but chivalrous, but Maerlant had deliberately glossed over Hecuba's part in this deception: since Hecuba had lost her beloved Hector, the bulwark of Troy, shortly before at Achilles' own hand, Maerlant thought it only fitting that she should thus revenge Hector's death:[53]

> Al wast dat sy hem verriet
> Dies en wondert my recht niet,
> Noch en sprekes haer niet te scande.

Although she betrayed him, I am not surprised by that, nor does it redound to her discredit.

Potter, however, thought differently. That by her underhanded attack on Achilles Hecuba had transgressed the immunity of those engaged in negotiations was to him, a lawyer and a diplomat, an unforgivable sin and the height of wickedness: "Truly, if that was not wickedness, then I know not what wickedness is" (Seker: was dat ghene quaethede, soe en weet ic niet wat quaetheyt es; *ML* I, 3116–17). Hecuba may have been a chaste woman, but it would have been far better had she taken a lover and not broken the diplomatic code (I, 3175–88):

> Boesheit nyemant en is bequaem.
> Noch prisic bet een vrouwen naem
> Die zedich waer ende goederhande
> Ende truwelic droech der minnen bande
> Ende van nyemant arch en sprake,
> Maer saghe an hoirs selfs zake
> Ende hadde een weynich overghetreden
> Der eren pat in menschelicheden
> Mit enen vrunde ende niet meer,
> Dan datmen bewisen soude eer
> Eenre valscher lozer verraderinne
> Die wreet ende nydich waer van sinne
> Ende oick soe hatelic waer ende wanschapen
> Dat nyemant en begheerde bij haer te slapen!

Evil is not becoming to anybody; yet I would sooner praise a woman who was modest and true in her affections and spoke ill of no one, but had strayed a little from the path of human virtue with a friend and no more than that, than show respect to a false traitress who is evil and envious of character and filled with hatred and so ugly that no one would want to sleep with her!

And so Dirk Potter vented his detestation of the queen of Troy, fully aware that in so doing he was going against revered tradition: "Though a good woman she was said to be; that view does not appeal to me" (Doch heet sij goet onder den wiven; maer daer en willix niet bi bliven; I, 3107–8). He was capable of settling his own convictions, and he let that be known.

He also differed from Maerlant in his assessment of another paladin in the Trojan drama, Odysseus—or Ulixes, as he was called in Middle Dutch. Here, however, the roles were reversed: whereas Maerlant spoke ill of Ulixes, Potter held him in high regard.[54] In his version of Ovid's story of Achilles and Deidamia, for example, he extolled Ulixes (here again, most likely using the *History of Troy* as his source) for his cleverness in exposing Achilles' female disguise. As Potter tells it, when Odysseus introduced himself as a traveling merchant and displayed his wares to the ladies, one broad-shouldered maiden had eyes only for the beautiful sword lying among the knickknacks. . . .[55] It says much for Potter's independent outlook that he, despite having read Maerlant's pitch-black portrait of Ulixes, was able to cast him in so positive a role. It is also quite clear what Potter so valued in Odysseus: his cleverness. To Maerlant—who was anything but an antirationalist—that cleverness was nothing short of slyness, a stealthy and cowardly attribute unworthy of a real knight; to Potter, by contrast, the fact that Ulixes was "the most subtle" of all Greek fighters was a recommendation.

With that small digression through *Der minnen loep* we return to the main characteristic of the *Blome*: its author's special concern with, and appreciation of, "reason." That concern becomes obvious only on careful reading, for "reason," while it is the subject of one special chapter, subtly informs most chapters of the *Blome*.[56] In general, whenever Potter feels the need to justify a particular opinion or act, he does so by appealing to "reason"; indeed, in worldly matters the *Blome* knows no greater praise than to assert that a particular view "is based on sound reasons" (mach wel op reden staen; 102/29). Thus it is reason that, beside God, ensures that evil cannot ultimately prevail: injustice "may and does exist, but it cannot endure inasmuch as it is against both God and against reason" (mach ene wile staen, mer sij en mach niet dueren, want sij is tegen Gode ende teghen reden; 76/18–19). Moreover, reason helps man to look after himself: "He is wise who guards what is his with reason" (hi is wijs die tsijne mit reden bescut; 41/35). Reason is, on the one hand, the guardian of the good and of the status quo and, on the other, a guide to (self-)improvement: "Who employs reason will be saved; and who does not employ reason will be stripped of honor" (wie der reden ghebruyct, sal ghesalicht worden; ende wie gheen reden ge-bruict die en heeft gheen eere; 94/19–21). Reason, honor (on earth), and bliss (in heaven) thus constitute the three pillars of Potter's moral phi-losophy: the last two are the ends, the first the means to attain them. The good man can therefore be called an adept of "reason": "the good man founds all things on reason and moderation" (die goede set sijn dinghen al op reden ende mate; 94/19).

The last quotation emphasizes the close links Potter sees between "reason" and "moderation." We might put it that, to him, moderation is inherent in reason: the second entails the first. Moderation, of course, was already an established ingredient of the courtly system of values; to appreciate that point we need only look at the *Haags liederenhand-schrift*.[57] Yet Dirk Potter (and he was not alone) assigned moderation a pivotal role in all human actions, in a sense harking back to its classical origins: the Hellenic idea of the golden mean. The most reasonable course to anything, according to the *Blome*, is invariably the middle course: between two such extremes as prodigality and thrift, "it is best to keep a reasonable mean" (soe is best een redelijc middel ghehouden; 84/25–26). Conversely, immoderation is as good as synonymous with unreasonableness. Dirk Potter was averse to all extremes, and desired all men to keep themselves and their impulses under "reasonable" control.

This sensibility was clearly reflected in his attitude toward violence and such concomitant emotions as vengefulness and anger. Though not, of course, a champion of pacifism, which was then virtually un-known, he was extremely wary of these emotions, as the *Blome* diptych on "peace" and "anger" make abundantly clear.[58] In it Potter warns al-most continuously against sudden outbursts of anger and preaches the greater efficacy of forbearance. True, in some cases war may be waged with "reason . . . and with honor," but whenever possible it is far better to forgo revenge, anger, and violence. The main argument for that view has less to do with Christian love or the preservation of domestic peace than (and this too is characteristic of Dirk Potter) with the fact that anger generally turns against the angry party, who, in his wrath, may commit ill-considered and hence unreasonable acts that he will later re-gret: "It has hurt many deep to vent their ire" (Het heeft die menige quaet gedaen hem selven in erren moede; 27/13). A wise man—and for Potter, the wise man was the perfect man—is able to "check his angry mood; for he can never pursue with anger or revenge all who have done him injustice" (hij is wijs die sijnen tornighen moet bedwinghen can; hi

en condt doch nummer meer soe vele in toerne verbolghen noch ver-
crighen mit wraeke als u mit onrecht aff ghetoghen is; 27/30–32).

As a staunch advocate of reason, Potter had always voiced his opposition to violence. The reader may remember that violence was almost
the only means of getting a woman into bed that Potter rejected in *Der
minnen loep*: a little white lie or a ruse (in short, cunning) might pass,
but violence was evil and unforgivable. Moreover, quite apart from such
(punishable) acts of molestation, Dirk Potter (in sharp contrast to, say,
the *Haags liederenhandschrift*) was convinced that courtly lovers had no
call to use physical force. Here, too, the doctrine of love he had
preached in *Der minnen loep* grew into a complete philosophy of life in
the *Blome*, where Potter's watchword throughout was "thinking, not
fighting."

This facet of Potter's moral doctrine was even more marked in Potter's third book, the *Mellibeus*. He based this work on the influential
Liber consolationis et consilii (The book of solace and good counsel) by
the thirteenth-century jurist Albertanus of Brescia. (Translated into
French soon after it was written, this work in its French translation
served not only Potter, but also Chaucer.) Mellibeus, the eponymous
hero of that book (which is really a succession of monologues and conversations), is bitterly aggrieved because his enemies have sacked his
home and violated his daughter. His immediate reaction is to seek vengeance, but his wife, Prudentia, pleads with him to take friendly advice
first. His counselors' opinion, though not unanimous, is that violent
reprisals are required; but again Mellibeus's wife urges him to reflect.
Remonstrating with him at length, she succeeds in convincing him that
he would do far better to negotiate with his enemies and, instead of
seeking bloody satisfaction, ask for restitution. No sooner said than
done. Prudentia engages in quiet diplomacy, Mellibeus starts peace
talks, the vendetta is settled, and everyone is satisfied.

Mellibeus is a book written on two planes. The first, the literal plane,
concerns the justice (or better, though not in the modern sense, the
rationality) of violent retribution—an important topic during the
Middle Ages, not only in the context of the so-called *Fürstenspiegel*,
works outlining the rules for princely behavior, to which Albertanus's
book was closely related, but also in discussions of the individual's ability to choose between a life of conflict and one of harmony. The second
plane of the *Mellibeus* had a special bearing on this individual dimension, for on that plane the work symbolized the inner conflict between
the temptations of evil and the power of goodness that is played out in

everyone's mind. Read thus, the book is a plea for inner harmony, for the tempering of one's emotions and spirit with "moderation, counsel, and reason." By viewing the *Mellibeus* against the background of Potter's other writings, we are not surprised to find that in this area he remained constant to his source. For the (French version of the) book written by the Italian bailiff Albertanus was most congenial to Dirk Potter's beliefs. Where it preached peaceful negotiation rather than bloody revenge, it fitted in perfectly with Potter's own views on war and peace; where it pleaded for stoical calm and reasonableness, it was at one with Potter's "moderation" and "reason." The spiritual kinship of the two works is further illustrated by the fact that the heroine of *Mellibeus* bears the name of the crux of Potter's ethics: Prudentia, wisdom.

4. WISDOM AND SUCCESS

In Dirk Potter's moral program for man, wisdom headed the list. Wisdom is, in the person of Lady Prudentia, the patron saint of his *Mellibeus*; the whole tractate was a defence of rational behavior. In the *Blome der doechden*, too, prudence was portrayed as a paramount virtue. The chapter on wisdom (together with its counterpart, foolishness) is one of the finest in that book.[59] Indeed, everything suggests that, for Potter, wisdom was not merely one virtue among many; it was, rather, of supreme importance, the one virtue that should control all mortal actions. In the first sentence of that chapter, Potter (using the allegory on which the *Blome* is based) calls wisdom a flower "redolent with every spice, excelling many a less wholesome flower" (39/35–36). The overriding importance of wisdom was thrust even further forward later in the same chapter, in a litany to virtue unequaled in the entire *Blome*. Here, the wise man appears no less than perfect (41–29–45):

Hi es wijs die wijslijck leeft; hi es wijs die Gode boven al mint; hi es wijs die quaet gheselscap haet; hi es wijs die Gode ontsiet ende Sijne gebode hout, want ontsiech van Gode is beghinsel alre wijsheit. Hi es wijs die hem ghenoeghen laet; hi es wijs die sonden haetet; hi es wijs die hem niet alte vele en onderwint; hi es wijs die sijnen vrient inder noot bijstaet; hi es wijs die den quaden casteyet; hi es wijs die den goeden stercket, want hi doet Gode lieve. Hi es wijs die tsijne mit reden bescut. Hi es wijs die sijnen heer tot doechden raet, want die contrari doet, die blijft verloren hier ende ginder, ende wat quaet die heer bij sinen rade doet, compt up sijnre sielen. Hi es wijs die in sijnen dinghen mate hout; hi es wijs die hem selve niet te vele en beroempt; hi es wijs die Gode sijnen scepper danct van alle dat Hij hem verleent hevet. Hi es wijs die hem selven wel besiet ende hi es wijs die dij toecomende dinghen besorghet. Hi es wijs die ghene ijdel worde spreket, want bijden worden merct men den man ende verneempt wat hij in heeft. Hi es wijs die die heilighe kerck eert; hi es wijs die doecht van goeden luden segget, want een man worter bi ghemint ende liefghetael. Hi es wijs ende wel gheleert, die alle dinck ten besten keert.

Wise is he who wisely lives; wise is he who loves God above everything; wise is he who hates bad company; wise is he who stands in awe of God and keeps his commandments, for the fear of the Lord is the beginning of wisdom. Wise is he who is content; wise is he who hates sin; wise is he who does not shoulder more than he can bear; wise is he who hastens to his needy friend's aid; wise is he who castigates the wicked; wise is he who fortifies the good, for he testifies to his love for God. Wise is he who prudently looks after his own. Wise is he who counsels his master to be virtuous, for any who does otherwise is lost here and beyond, and what evil his master does on his advice will be held against his own soul. Wise is he who is temperate in all things; wise is he who does not trumpet forth his own virtues; wise is he who gives thanks to God his creator for everything he has bestowed upon him. Wise is he who bethinks himself and wise is he who looks to his future. Wise is he who utters no vain words, for from his words you can tell the man and gather what there is to him. Wise is he who honors the holy church; wise is he who speaks well of good people, for any who does so is held in high regard. Wise is he and learned who makes the best of all things.

Wisdom is extolled even in *Der minnen loep*, a book devoted to love. "Wheresoever love is cornered, cunning and wisdom are ready to help," Potter explains (Waer liefte staet in enighen hoecken, daer sullen list ende wijsheit altoes in hulpe sijn bereyt; II, 3796–98); and elsewhere he shows us wisdom allied with sweet cunning, the mark of the good lover: true love is confined to those who "are seemly and show wisdom and sweet cunning" (hem zedelic regieren mit wijsheit ende mit zueter list; II, 694–95).[60] And since, as the practical Dirk Potter knew only too well, "not all people are equally wise" (die luden en sijn niet even wijs; II, 1233), he urges his readers to steer an even course, to "make sure that you wisely live" (syet dat gy wijslick leeft; I, 1244). Without wisdom one cannot hope to prosper in love: one will either destroy that which held the promise of good love or else succumb to "forbidden" or "foolish" love.[61] Had a fourth book not been in preparation, Potter would undoubtedly have named "wise" love as the counterpart of stupid love in book one of *Der minnen loep*, with "wise" love (if it is good) comprising both the "good" love of book two and the "permitted" love of book four. Wisdom, thus, was the crowning virtue even in *Der minnen loep*.

This approach strongly suggests bourgeois morality. And indeed, in the extensive literature on the subject, wisdom is often portrayed as a shibboleth of bourgeois ethics.[62] Needless to say, this generalization needs qualifying, and here not all scholars are agreed. What is agreed is that wisdom, as *sapientia*, is a virtue rooted in biblical, classical, and medieval-aristocratic ethics, and thus anything but a bourgeois creation. Even so, there is little doubt but that the classical conception of wisdom received a boost from the rising bourgeoisie, and with a different stress than medieval aristocrats, in particular, customarily placed on it. This development was reflected in a change in the Latin, for soon *prudentia*, as opposed to *sapientia*, came to set the tone—that is, wisdom as a pragmatic rather than a philosophical concept. In modern terms, the emotional dimension of *prudentia* is common sense—not to say slyness or craftiness—rather than wisdom. "Wisdom," in brief, seemed to have become a collective name for the ability to act appropriately in the daily round. And although (Christian) virtue remained paramount, worldly prosperity was close behind.[63]

It was precisely in this spirit that Dirk Potter treated "wisdom." He had early ceased to consider it the *donum sapiencie* that Dirk of Delft had presented as one of the seven gifts of the Holy Ghost,[64] portraying it instead as worldly wisdom: the *prudentia* of the *Mellibeus*, the *const* (artfulness) and good sense of the *Blome*, and even the "sweet cunning" of *Der minnen loep*—in short, the kind of wisdom with which the typical burgher tries to make his way in the world. Perhaps "prudent living" is the best paraphrase of Potter's approach: a way of life that wholly depends on such related qualities as foresight, temperance, reflection, and good sense. By now the reader will have little doubt about the extent to which reason dominated Potter's moral philosophy: reason provides man, if not with a passport to heaven, then at least with a guide to worldly success.

I have chosen the last term deliberately. For the new wisdom was, by and large, a pushy morality, a pragmatic ethics designed to procure one a better position (whether in the amorous, material, or social sphere). This quality underlines the close links between the new morality and bourgeois aspirations, the aspirations of a class poised to gain a whole world in the late Middle Ages. Unlike the old nobility, the bourgeoisie was not out to consolidate or strengthen an established position; rather, it aimed to conquer a "new" place in society. In this struggle, neither birth nor military strength could help: these were to remain exclusively "noble" attributes for at least a few generations. Instead the burgher had to rely on his own ability, on his "bourgeois wits": for him good sense was the most reliable tool of personal advancement.

Yet the familiar character of the ambitious merchant was not alone in depending on *ratio*. Some courtiers were in a similar situation, especially those who had not been designated for high office by birth (or by exceptional military talents) but who nevertheless hoped to make their mark. For them, the most effective method was to arrive at court with a fortune and use it to curry favor with the high and mighty—a method deplored by many a writer but effective for all that, as seen in the case of William Eggert, an immensely rich and successful merchant from Amsterdam who made himself indispensable to the count of Holland-Bavaria by helping to meet the costs of the administration.[65] But what was an ambitious boy to do who could flaunt neither money nor ancestors but nevertheless aspired to rise high at court? If we are to believe Dirk Potter, all he had to do was harness the powers of his reason to the furtherance of his career.

Understandably, Potter advanced this view mainly in the *Blome der doechden*. Whereas in *Der minnen loep* cleverness was offered as the surest road to sexual success (particularly in bed), in his second book Potter seemed more concerned with material triumphs. True, he abominated those who used their money to toady to the nobility: "If a man of low estate appear at a lord's court and he be rich in possessions, then the lords want to dine with him . . . , for the rich usually wield power and influence thanks to their possessions, and hence are received and exalted by the lords" (coempt een man van cleynen state ter heren hove ende hij rijck van haven is, soe willen die heren mit hem eten [. . .], want die rijke hebben ghemeynlijken macht ende moet om haers goets wille, ende sijn ghesien ende ghehoecht bijden heren). They would do far better, he adds, to stay home and not come to court for the express purpose of "climbing higher" (om hogher to rijsen).[66] Yet Dirk Potter was anything but content to leave power entirely in the old and seasoned hands of the nobility, thereby excluding all newcomers. Rather, making one's name and improving one's position—often at a prince's court—is the central theme of many of his moral tales and examples. For example, according to Potter, the (rational) faculty of "recollection" has helped many a poor man to improve his competence (was Potter perhaps referring to the power of recalling administrative and legal precedents?) and hence to attain a "great position, dignity, and honor." By their "modesty," too, many "have risen to a great position and greater dignity" (opghetoghen geweest tot groten stade ende hoger werdicheit). Thus "humility has helped to raise up many of lowly estate" (onderdanicheit heeft menigen man van cleynen state groet gemaect), and the same is true of competence: "We find daily and everywhere that those well versed in clerical or other temporal skills are raised up, and that they attain great positions and dignity" (wij sient alle dagen in allen eynden, dat die constenaren van cleercgien of van anderen tijtlijken dinghen verheven worden, ende sij tot groten state ende weerdicheit comen).[67]

As one emphatic though typical example of a successful (court) career, Potter mentions the case of a Roman philosopher who withdrew to a lonely and barren desert to reflect on the meaning of wisdom.[68] When the emperor passed by and asked for his conclusions, the philosopher handed him a scrawled note that said: "Whatsoever thou doest, do it wisely—and foresee the outcome" (Wat du doen sulste, dat doe wijslijck—ende voersie dat eynde). Back home, the emperor had this philosophical scrawl "copied out in large, elegant letters" and displayed in his palace. The emperor continued to prosper, so much so that envious nobles conspired to assassinate him. They went to his barber, who proved willing for hard cash to cut the emperor's throat as well as his beard; yet when the barber saw the philosopher's pronouncement displayed in the royal chambers, he reflected on the "outcome" of his foul deed and confessed everything. The culprits were punished, the barber was acquitted, and the emperor had the philosopher "brought before the court with a great show of honor and kept him his whole life long by his side in such dignity as he might have bestowed upon his own brother, which he had well deserved with his sound precepts. Thus he obtained by wisdom what he would never have been able to obtain by great wealth" (werdelijken te hove halen, ende verhief hem in groeter eren; ende hielten bij hem sijn leven lanc in alsulker werdicheit als sijn broeder, des hij wael verdient hadde mit sijnre goeder leeren. Dus vercreech hij mit wijsheit dat hij mit groten goede nummermeer vercreeghen en soude hebben; 42/36–40).

Those who live wisely are sure to prosper, even at court—that is what Potter seems to tell his readers here and elsewhere. Still, the example of an ascetic temporarily brooding in a desert and of a Roman emperor is hardly sufficient to demonstrate that wisdom will also further a man's career in the sandy soil of the early-fifteenth-century Hague court. That demonstration is provided far more convincingly not by any words that Dirk Potter ever wrote, but by his life itself, for his experience exemplifies the successful application of his own theory.[69]

True, Dirk Potter was a courtier by birth (his father had reached the rank of secretary to Duke Albert), but his origins were not such as to guarantee a successful career at court. Normally, official posts were not hereditary; if Dirk Potter wanted to follow in his father's footsteps, he had to prove his own worth. Possibly with a (paternal) eye to this goal, Dirk Potter had been sent to school very early, and, if we are to believe his later testimony, he was a diligent pupil. The practical school of court life provided much additional knowledge, hard to gain from books, including official procedure and terminology. By no later than 1385, then, Dirk had become an official in the count's service, and such he remained until his death forty years later.

Dirk Potter started out as a simple treasury clerk. His name is first mentioned on 12 November 1385, when he was paid for copying out that year's accounts. He must have continued to perform such rather unspectacular duties in the treasury until 1400—that is, until the violent act described at the beginning of this chapter. As the reader will recall, the consequent death of several courtiers—for which Potter could not deny responsibility—did anything but thwart his career. Less than six months later, the treasury clerk received a special reward for his services. Another eighteen months later, on 14 November 1402, Duke Albert presented Potter with the Noordeinde estate on which Dirk had been living, "in recognition of the services . . . he has rendered us on many past occasions . . . and will continue to render us." Nor was Duke Albert mistaken in Dirk. In January 1403 Potter apparently rose to become master clerk, a position that entitled him to sign documents in the count of Holland's name, a duty he performed for the first time during that year. Shortly afterward, his official range must have been extended to include the administration of justice, though he remained attached to the treasury and the chancellery. On 29 August 1408, he was appointed to the highly responsible post of bailiff at The Hague, to mete out punishments, make appointments, and collect fines on his sovereign's behalf. In his day, bailiffs were already notorious for their openness to corruption, though we cannot tell whether Dirk Potter, too, abused his office—bribes were not something one entered in the books even then.[70]

Whatever the truth, Dirk Potter's star continued to rise during the early decades of the fifteenth century. It was then, too, that he started to travel widely, visiting many places at home and abroad as the count's envoy. As such, he held peace talks with Friesland, negotiated the construction of dikes with villages in Holland, discussed trading rights with the city of Dordrecht, and stayed for over a year in Rome on a mission that, as we have seen, still remains secret. Moreover, in the name of the count of Holland (William IV, after Albert's death in 1404), he called on the German emperor, probably to arrange for Jacqueline's succession.

He also appeared before the English king, Henry IV, attending court in London in 1404 on behalf of "my dear lady of Holland" and again in 1413, this time as the count of Holland's official secretary who had come to demand compensation for the seizure of Dutch ships by English privateers. In short, Dirk Potter had risen from lowly clerk to his count's trusted servant and confidant. He received his reward in about 1410–15, when he was raised to the (lower) nobility and enfeoffed with the sizable estate of Ter Loo. Perhaps his marriage helped his smooth progress: if the (all too rare) signs do not deceive us, Dirk Potter's marriage to Elizabeth, Lady Van der Does, bound him to the Hook nobility even before he wrote *Der minnen loep*.[71]

Still, it must have been his personal qualities, devotion, and application that, in sum, allowed him the life of the nobleman Dirk Potter van der Loo after 1415. His main strength lay in his common sense and loyalty, and there is little reason to doubt that the virtues the *Blome* commends to the ambitious—a reliable memory, humility, "artfulness," wisdom, and the associated attributes of temperance and rationality—also belonged to the author and, moreover, in ample measure. He seems to have been able to take good care of himself, not only in matters of religion, but also in his social life—"care," no doubt, in the sense given by the *Blome* itself in its chapter on wisdom, where it is stated that the man "who goes to sleep without caring . . . will rise without honor" (40/11–12). Honor, after all, was the courtier's paramount concern, and Dirk Potter knew what he was talking about.

His personal background provides a special gloss on what is a unique passage in the *Blome*, one where Potter enlarges more freely than most other Middle Dutch authors on what constitutes true nobility.[72] He does so by means of a plea, as emotional as it is rational, in the chapter on nobility, which (with its counterpart, baseness) he probably included in deference to the *Fiore* tradition. Now that we are more familiar with Potter's work and life, we find it easier to assume that, in this field, our author had no need to consult outside sources. Admittedly, the crux of his argument is traditional: true nobility is nobility of the soul, and blue blood is worthless without a noble heart.[73] But very quickly the argument takes flight, betraying Potter's personal involvement. This is best illustrated by his own presentation, beginning with a long but revealing quotation (88/31–89/20):

Die luyde heiten wel edel omme dat sij van edelen gheslechte ghecomen sijn; al sijn sij onedel van natueren ende van wercken, des en sien sij niet aen. Och, het scilt alte veel: edel te *wesen* ende wel *gheboren*! Dat heiten welgheboren luyde die vanden scilde gheboren sijn, ende hebbent van horen ouderen ende niet van hem selven. Het is die menighe van edelen ouderen gheboren die een edel ader niet en heeft aen sijnen lijve, ende is soe rechte onedel als hij wesen mach: van onghenade, van oneerbarheit, van ghiericheit, van onscamelheit, van bloedicheit, van onwetentheit, van onbequaemheit, van vuylen seden, van quaden regimente, van onkuysheit, van vuylen onnutten worden, ende wreet, lelic, onsinnich, vol verraderie, moerdadich ende alre boesheit vol.

Hoe sal die minsche edel moeghen heiten die niet edelen is in gheenen poenten, noch manlijc in daden van wapen? Hij sal daer omme edel heiten om dat sijn ouders edel waren? Trouwen, het is wel menich heilich man gheweest die kinder liet die niet wijs en waren noch heilich; menich scoen man die kinder liet die niet scoen en waren; menich goedertieren man die kinder liet die wreet ende boes waren; menich manlijc heelt die kinder liet die saghen waren, ende vele des ghelijcs soe dat die kinder niet altijt der ouder natuere hadden, noch die doecht ende dat vordel die hoer ouders plaghen te hebben. Ende hoe coempt dan die edelheit meer te eerven dan die doecht, of manheit, of scoenheit, of lelicheit of ander sake dier ghelijke?

Sonder twivel, als men die waerheit spreken sal voer Gode ende voer die werelt, soe en is edelheit niet anders dan een ingheboren doecht, daer eer, scamelheit ende manheit mede ghemenghet is. Het en mach niemant edel sijn dan bij sijnen edelen wercken der doechden. [. . .] Ende of een man van slechten ouderen waer, en sal hij dan mit edelen daden niet moeghen verdienen dat hi edel sij? Sonder twivel, jae hij! Hij mach hem des beroemen dat hijt van hemselven heeft ende niet van sijnen ouderen! [. . .] Nu sich: ist dan niet beter ende saligher dat dijn ouders bij dij in eeren gheedelt werden? Also wel machmen nu mit edelen daden op ghetoghen ende gheeert worden als men over 600 jaer moecht! Ende soe machtich is nu die keyser enen man te edelen diet mit edelen daden verdienen, als die keyser die over 1000 jaer was. Mer het coempt al aen die verdienten.

Many are taken for noblemen because they are of noble descent; that they are ignoble by nature and deeds seems to make no difference. Yet there is indeed a world of difference between being *noble* and being *well born*! Well born are they who are born of noble stock and so owe it [i.e., their nobility] to their ancestors and not to themselves. Many are born of noble ancestors who have not one noble vein in their body and are as ignoble as can be: disgraceful, dishonorable, avaricious, unseemly, malevolent, incompetent, immoral, or bad habits, unchaste, foul-mouthed and full of idle chatter, cruel, ugly, senseless, treacherous, murderous, and filled with every wickedness.

How can a man be called noble who is not noble in any way, nor manly in feats of arms? Shall he be called noble because his ancestors were noble? In truth, many a saintly man has begotten children that were neither wise nor saintly; many a good man has begotten children that were cruel and evil; many a hero has begotten children that were cowards, and there are many other examples of children lacking their parents' proven qualities, virtues, and advantages. Why, then, should nobility be more readily inherited than virtue, or manliness, or beauty, or ugliness, or the like?

Indeed, if we are to speak the truth before God and before all the world, nobility is nothing but innate virtue in which modesty and manliness are joined. And so no one can be noble save by his noble works of virtue. . . . And although a man came of simple parents, may he not deserve to be called noble by virtue of his noble deeds? Without a doubt, he does! He may pride himself on owing it to himself and not to his parents! . . . For behold, is it not a better and more blessed thing that your parents should be held in honor thanks to you? Indeed, we may be more exalted and honored by our own noble deeds today than by deeds done 600 years ago! And the emperor is no less able to ennoble a man who has deserved it by his noble deeds, than an emperor was 1,000 years ago. What counts are a man's own deserts.

Clearly, Dirk Potter was no keen supporter of heredity in general, and not at all of the inheritance of noble titles. Rather, he assumed the opposite: people should be ennobled by virtue of their own achievements alone. For how else could it be guaranteed that the patents of nobility were vested in the right people? As an important subsidiary argument, moreover, he stated that "in the good old times," the ancestors of the old nobility were commoners before they were ennobled for their personal prowess. He cites what he thought were pertinent historical precedents: Julius Caesar was the son of a Roman patrician, Charles Martel was a bastard, the English royal family was descended from an exiled Trojan—and there were many similar cases.

For his native Holland, Potter (without acknowledgment) uses the chronicle of the Clerk of the Low Countries to tell the story of the "count of Hollant" (that is, Floris V), who, to fill the reduced ranks of his knights, summoned the forty "richest householders" to appear before him one Whitsun (90/5–13),

daer hij enen hoghen hof mede hielt, ende hij sloechse allen ridder nader maeltijt ende gaff hem scilde ende wapene daer huden daghes sonder twivel veel af sijn die van dien gecomen sijn, ende overmits outheit der tijt soe verre gheleden is dat sij menen alle van coninghen ende greven ghecomen wesen. . . . Ende dit hebben sommighe voertijts benomen mit wil datmens inden croniken niet en heeft moeghen setten, omdat mens hem niet te verwijt segghen en soude— hoewel dattet hem groet eer waer, ende in anderen landen dicke gheschiet is ende noch daghelijx ghesciet.

when he was holding high court, and he dubbed all of them knights after dinner and gave shields and arms to those from whom many members of the present-day nobility are doubtless descended, although the passage of time has persuaded them that they have sprung from kings and counts. . . . And some have deliberately prevented the truth from being written in the chronicles lest people know about it—though it redounds to their honor and was done frequently and continues to be done daily in other countries.

Potter continues in a similar vein for the remainder of the account: true nobility is an inner quality; the outer glitter of noble descent misleads one far too often. And, as so often, he illustrates his thesis with references to animals: sparrowhawks nesting in shrubs are "much more useful for hunting than those dwelling in high castles" (ende veel nutter ten weytspele dan die ander die inden hoghen castelen wonen)—from which it follows that "they are oft better who are of lowly and simple blood than many who have sprung from great families" (sij bij wijlen beter sijn die van laghen, slechten bloede sijn dan vele die uut hoghen gheslechten ghesproten sijn; 90/47–91/3). He concludes with the story of Sallustius, who, though of simple descent, was for his rectitude elevated to the Roman senate. When Tranquillius, a nobleman "who had been humbled and demoted on account of his ruthless and evil ways" (was ghenedert ende ghedaelt overmits roekeloesheit ende quaden regimente des levens; 91/39–40), objected, Sallustius rounded on him (91/ 42–92/2):

"Du, Tranquilli, hebs onrecht ende sprekes op mij onbillik ende sonder reden. Ic ben gheboren van enen oetmoedighen armen gheslechte, ende ben gheedelt bij gunste der goden om mijn lieflijke weldaden ende om der doecht die mij ingheboren is, soe dat allen die van mij comen hem verhogen sullen der edelheit ende vordele die hem van mij comen sal wesen. Ende du, mitter oneerbarheit dijns lijfs ende mitter vuyler onnutticheit dijns levens, hebste dijselve onedel ende oneerbar gemaect, ende allen die van dij comen sullen voertaen besmet ende onsuver wesen bij dij, omder lelicheit dijnre onedelre daden, soedat sij hem ewelijck bedroeven sullen als sij dijnre ghedencken."

"Thou, Tranquilli, art wrong and speaketh ill of me without reason. I was born of a humble and poor family and have been ennobled by the grace of the gods for my good deeds and for the virtue within me, so that any who spring from my loins may increase the nobility and advantage accruing to them from me. And thou, with the ignoble deeds of thy body and the utter uselessness of thy life, have rendered these ignoble and unworthy of respect, and all who spring from thy loins will be infected and rendered unclean by you, by virtue of the vileness of thy ignoble deeds, and they will evermore feel dejected when they call thee to mind."

This answer convinced the other senators that they had chosen well; Sallustius "was highly praised for his retort and was offered an even higher position, while Tranquillius was banished and died poor and unhappy, according to his deserts" (groten lof vander antworde, ende hij wart noch vele hogher verheven. Ende die ander wart versteken ende sterf in armoede ende in onsalicheit, nae sijn verdienten; 92/3–5). Rewards according to one's deserts—the same old strain. Yet however much Potter may have inveighed against the nobility, he nevertheless prized his own noble status. In that sense he was the complete conformist, even though he was but a new recruit to an old club. The result was a fascinating, complex personality, a man in whom ambition and frustration lived side by side, as did self-confidence and humility.

Ambition must have stimulated Potter's own rise, assisted by his supple abilities to conform and adapt—the motor and the grease. As Potter himself seemingly realized only too well, those who want to advance in their master's service must first know their place: "And if thou be a servant in a prince's house, then raise thyself no higher than thy master would have thee do and let thy master himself raise thee up according to thy deserts, as he is bound to do" (Ende bistu oec onthouden totten vorsten huyse, en verheffe dij niet hoegher dan dijn heer dy hebben en wil, ende laet dij die here selver opheffen nae dijn verdiente, als hij doch sculdich is te doen; 58/38–40). That is why fools do not make good servants, "for they know not how to bend their stiff knees, nor how to give civil answers; whence it is best to leave them to tend the beasts, for like flocks to like" (want sy en souden haer styve knyen niet bueghen en connen, noch oec worde gheven die bequaem waren; daerom ist best laten wijse bijden beesten, want ghelijc mynt ghelijc; 125/9–12).[74] So much for stupidity; its opposite, wisdom, for Potter must be matched by adaptability.

Now, adaptability toward his superiors was something Potter himself must often have displayed, not least because during his long career at court he served several masters. Starting under Duke Albert, he (like Bavaria Herald and, in a sense, William of Hildegaersberch, but unlike Dirk of Delft) went on to serve Albert's son, William VI. When the latter was succeeded upon his death by Jacqueline of Bavaria, Dirk Potter continued as her secretary and her faithful strength and support. He departed with the countess's army against her uncle John—but when the latter captured the county of Holland by might and by money, Potter apparently changed masters without much difficulty. Similarly, when John of Bavaria was poisoned, our Dirk proceeded to serve John IV, his last master's archenemy. And in 1425, when Philip of Burgundy was made regent of Holland, Dirk Potter van der Loo ceased to be a Bavarian, became a Burgundian secretary, and received a sizable increase in pay as a reward for aiding and abetting Philip's annexation of Holland.[75]

It has sometimes been said that Dirk Potter served the state rather than any particular person.[76] Little malice is required, however, to assert, partly from Potter's own writings, that he did serve one person with remarkable success—Dirk Potter himself. In a man of his standing, such service called for great flexibility and patience, virtues that Dirk Potter first praised in *Der minnen loep* with words that now seem far less bland than they at first glance appear (I, 1244–46, 1318–20):

> Daerom, syet dat gy wijslijck leeft
> Ende wacht den tijt mit sachten moede:
> Het sal u wael vergaen te goede.

Hence, see to it that you live wisely, and bide your time with gentleness: it will pay you well.

> Laet u gheen wantroest verdoren,
> Ende wacht den tijt mit wijsen sinne.
> Ghi wervet entelijc uwen wille.

Let not distrust destroy you, and bide your time with good sense. You will have your way in the end.

Here we are back with the Potter of the *Mellibeus*. Living wisely implies not only patience, but also resignation, even humility, and that not from weakness but in one's own interest. Potter may well have learned this lesson during his apprenticeship in 1400: striking out at random can hurt the striker as much as it harms the victim. In any case (as we saw in section 3), his writings show him to be a passionate advocate of rational, as against physical, exchanges, a man strongly averse to all forms of aggression.

In the chapter of the *Blome* devoted to the subject, Potter argues that strength can take various guises, some men being considered strong "who daily ride in armor and play the game of war" (die daghelijx in wapene rijden ende orloch speel hanteren) or because of "some victories they may have won in war, in assaulting the enemy, at camps or on the battlefield" (eenighe zeghe die sij ghehadt moghen hebben in strijde, in storme, in campe of in velde; 49/27–30). But that is not what he means by strength. To him, authentic strength is above all strength of mind, as symbolized by the lion, who, though physically as hard as iron, sweeps away all traces of his presence with his tail, the better to avoid confrontations "and not to fight unless he must" (ende niet vechten, ten sij bij noede; 50/2). In short, the strong lion behaves like a cunning fox! And: "there is more wisdom in fleeing when cornered than in trusting in your strength and striking out wildly" (het is meerre wijsheit als het noot is te vlien daer gheen verweren en staet, dan op ghelove dijnre crachten mit wille inder doet te gaen; 50/8–10). Unlike Bavaria Herald, then, Dirk Potter felt that strength lay not in a show of strength but in the use of one's brains. Seen thus, the difference between Dirk Potter and the Herald is no smaller than that between him and Dirk of Delft.

Much as these other two writers appeared "old-fashioned," so Dirk Potter seems exceedingly "modern"—not so much because of his go-ahead attitude (after all, the Herald and the court chaplain also "made good" professionally) as thanks to his pragmatic and rational approach and, more particularly, to the way he, an individualist before his time, tried to walk the middle way—certainly if his life was any reflection of his writings. Devout without feeling the need for priests, an elitist who did not draw too fine a distinction between the nobility and the middle class, an advocate of diplomacy who did not summarily condemn war, a servant who depended on no single master, and a lover who avoided being strictly monogamous—and all that coupled with a readiness to seize what opportunities arose and the conviction that reason was the best guide to a superior life.

The explanation of why Potter seems, all in all, more modern than his idealistic but one-sided and old-fashioned fellow authors at the court of Holland-Bavaria cannot be that he happened to write ten years later than Dirk of Delft, five years later than the Herald, or some seven years after Hildegaersberch's death. His (relative) modernity is the result not of his (relative) youth, but of his personal attitude and background. There must have been others like him—certainly in similar official positions, which, nearly everywhere and certainly at any late-medieval court, were ideal springboards for social advancement.[77] In that respect, Dirk Potter was no more than a representative (though an early and highly placed one in the northern Netherlands) of a whole group of newcomers: lay clerks who became increasingly indispensable as political advisers and who, close as they were to the sovereign's person, were able to rise to positions that, if not spectacular, nevertheless provided them with a comfortable life at court.[78] They admittedly lacked the glamor of the old nobility, the erudition of many a priest, the renown of the most famous of knights, or the riches of certain burghers—but they were undoubtedly as influential and enviable.

Dirk Potter stood out from this new elite because he alone had the time, the talent, and the good sense to commit his ideas to paper, thus giving us precious glimpses of his mentality and of that of men like him.[79] Moreover, he had an unusually "modern" approach to writing: he composed his little books at his leisure and to please himself rather than his masters. Writing to him was a form of cultural self-realization.[80] Last but not least, he seems to have been the first "independent author" to appear at the Hague court.[81]

VII

Court Literature

1. BALANCE AND PERSPECTIVE

This book explores Middle Dutch literature against the background of medieval court life. That sociocultural perspective defines its objective no less than its approach.[1] To begin with the approach: establishing the court as context has value only if we actively interpret the texts against that background, for instance by indicating the extensive links between Dirk Potter's writing and his official position. Yet the more obvious the links are, the greater is the danger that our view of literature will be turned into an exaggerated projection of our assumed knowledge of the historical background, and conversely, that our view of the historical situation will become too deeply etched by what (we think) we can discover in the literature. Neither danger has been entirely avoided in this book.

A similar balance must be struck with regard to the first-named point above, namely the selection of the texts that form the object of our investigation. We have chiefly been looking at texts produced in the confines of the court of Holland-Bavaria—these texts almost alone and virtually no others. As a result, we have combined texts that, given a different literary approach, would have been treated separately. We have, thus, juxtaposed a chronicle with a theological compendium, because both were written at the same court and for the same noble family. This unusual combination produced new insights—for instance revealing that the religious fervor with which Bavaria Herald imbued his war propaganda found little favor with the court chaplain. But then, it is true of most studies that what is gained in breadth tends to be lost in depth. In our case, the sociological approach helped to blur the boundary between distinct genres; or, more concretely, while we compared Dirk of Delft with the Herald, we neglected almost completely to compare him with other authors of Middle Dutch theological handbooks. By placing him exclusively in the context of the court, in other words, we failed to place him in the context of the church.

Now, these are disadvantages, but not debilitating ones. Other studies by other writers can (and I hope will) give sharper contours to what this book has left unclear. Ideally, they may proffer a multidimensional model in which the flat social plane outlined in this book is expanded in space, time, and genre. If that happens, the *Haags liederenhandschrift*, for instance, not only will be held up against the patterns of amorous behavior at the court in The Hague but will also be compared with the contemporary Flemish poetry of Gruuthuse and the much older love poetry of Hendrik van Veldeke—and all this against the background of changing historical circumstances as well as on, say, the independent literary plane of formal rhyming and verse techniques.

Moreover, even in the "two-dimensional" framework of this book, not all the gaps have been filled; and before we try to reach any general conclusions, we had best take stock of these gaps. To begin with, we have confined our attention largely to *new* literary works produced at the court of Holland-Bavaria—important contributions, no doubt, but by no means unique in portraying the contemporary culture. After all, people at court did not just produce new texts: they also read or listened to old ones. To obtain a fuller picture of the literary culture of the court of Holland-Bavaria, we should have to investigate systematically which older (Middle Dutch) texts were available to these circles in manuscript form. Ideally, then, we would have to extend our study from the literature originating at the court to all the literature then in circulation in Holland-Bavaria.

As a first sally in that direction we can point out that in the late fourteenth and early fifteenth centuries interest in the work of Jacob van Maerlant never flagged at the court of Holland. Behind many of the authors mentioned in this book, the authoritative figure of this "father of [medieval] Dutch poets" loomed large; in fact, we may assume (whenever we cannot so prove) that all our authors were familiar with his work. Certainly Bavaria Herald was better versed in Maerlant's writings than any other Middle Dutch author, from *Alexanders geesten* through the *Historie van Troyen*, *Rijmbijbel*, and *Der naturen bloeme* up to and including the *Spiegel historiael*. Yet even Dirk Potter knew his Maerlant—the *Historie van Troyen* almost certainly, and probably other works of Maerlant (*Alexanders geesten, Der naturen bloeme*) as well. William of Hildegaersberch, too, learned his poetic skills from Maerlant— and perhaps more thoroughly so than his obvious gleanings from Maerlant's *Strofische gedichten* (Strophic poems) and *Spiegel historiael* would suggest. Even Dirk of Delft, though undoubtedly superior to Maerlant in learning, probably did not think it beneath him to borrow this or that from his predecessor.[2]

It is of course possible that all these authors acquired their knowledge of Maerlant's work independently and from secondary sources. Still, it is by no means inconceivable that they consulted the same sources (at least in part), namely Maerlant's manuscripts themselves, which were probably to be found at the court of the descendants of Maerlant's chief protector, Count Floris V of Holland. It would be well worth the trouble to find out whether, among the many extant Maerlant manuscripts, there are copies that can be considered the former property of the court of Holland. A representative example is the beautiful manuscript of the *Rijmbijbel* (now kept in the Royal Library at The Hague), which, to judge by the miniatures, must have originated in the same (Utrecht?) *scriptorium* as produced the dedication copy of Dirk of Delft's *Tafel van den kersten ghelove* and the breviary for Albert's second wife. On similar grounds, the stock of books kept at the court of Holland-Bavaria may be surmised to have included manuscripts of the *Sachsenspiegel* (a compendium of medieval law compiled in Middle Low German) and of Beka's *Cronike*, texts that no court could conceivably have done without. Thus, manuscript research in particular is likely to make a considerable contribution to the reconstruction of the reading matter available at court.[3]

Yet even though we have deliberately restricted ourselves to only the most original literary expressions of the court of Holland-Bavaria, our discussion has still been far from complete. This shortfall was not so much chosen as imposed on us: often lacunae in the source material simply allow for no more insights. For example, we know from the court accounts that, before he wrote the *Tafel*, Dirk of Delft composed another book for Albert's (second) wife, but unfortunately this work seems to have vanished irretrievably. No less fascinating and frustrating is our scant knowledge of the contributions of William the Confessor, an author whose writings seem to have been related to those of Dirk of Delft. According to the accounts, this Carmelite *leesmeester* (Bible teacher) from Haarlem served as confessor to Duke Albert and his family shortly before Dirk of Delft appeared at court. Especially on the Christian high holy days, William was a regular guest in The Hague, for instance on Christmas Eve 1388, when he "heard my lord's and his family's confession." Now, this William also wrote for the court: the accounts for 1395–96 mention a substantial gift to "Brother William, my lord's confessor," as a reward for "my lady's book that my lady [Margaret of Cleves] had bid him make," and of which a copy was ordered soon afterward for the Ladies of Kruiningen by the same Margaret.[4] Apparently this book, too, has vanished—unless we accept the recent and plausible suggestion that it must be identified with a Middle Dutch collection of Bible sermons that has come down to us in numerous manuscripts, among them the authentic copies owned by Margaret of Cleves and the Ladies of Kruiningen.[5] What we can say is that the two manuscripts were executed in the same way as the first copies of Dirk's *Tafel*, including the dedication copy of that work—which does not, of course, constitute proof of their origins. Meanwhile, it seems preferable to adopt a reserved attitude—even at the risk that a closer investigation may show that a special chapter on William the Confessor must be added to this book.

While this case may be one of knowing all or nothing, we do know something (though much too little) about a different topic. As we saw in Chapter I, section 4, and Chapter III, section 1, we know much less about light verse at the court than we might wish, and so the literary climate there appears to have been (even) more serious than it probably was. Hence, it is a happy circumstance when we do encounter samples of light-hearted verse of a type that was seemingly quite common. Today, for instance, the parchment of an official register and the humor of a Peter Potter allow us to savor a drinking song such as must have been sung at the court of Holland-Bavaria (see fig. 28).[6] Like his more famous brother, Peter Potter was a clerk in the count's service; but he also dealt in wines and managed a tavern. These two activities—ink and drink—joined hands when Peter Potter, drafting a document for the archives, jotted down a song that counseled the drowning of sorrow in a friendly glass:

> Wir willent vreulich singen "ho!"
> Und vreuwen uns des wijnez train;
> He maicht vil manich hertse vro.
> Dar um wil wirs nicht avelain;
> Scheynck yn, und la diin truren stain!

Let us sing merrily ho! and rejoice in the tears of the vine that gladden so many hearts. Let us not tarry, therefore; pour and let go of your sorrow!

This bit of doggerel was probably typical of a song style popular at the Hague court.[7] In this context, the word *popular* has a double meaning: widespread, and rooted in the people. For no matter how exalted the court may have been and have felt itself to be, that never prevented

28. Peter Potter's drinking song. (Algemeen Rijksarchief, The Hague, MS. AGH 2150, fol. 44v)

its noble members from now and then (indeed, probably more often than the extant texts indicate) indulging in what to us seem rather vulgar frolics. The surviving fragments of the high-spirited compositions of the court musicians Fabri and Boy, for instance, contain a number of French ditties with less pretentious melodies than the usual songs and with verses downright licentious. What else but scabrous can we call the little air about Marion from Arras, whose easily tired boyfriend, Colin, fails to give her armor a long enough rub?[8]

> Marion d'Arras,
>   a fait taluas
>   par Colin frotter.
> Et quant il est las,
>   recreus et mas,
>   il s'en voelt alieer;
> Et celle a plorer
>   et li demander:
>   "Amis, ou t'en vas?
> Il te faut hurter,
>   quoy qu'il doibt couster,
>   encore cha bas."

Marion from Arras had her armor polished by Colin. When he grew tired, worn out, and exhausted, he prepared to leave her. But she began to cry and besought him: "Friend, where are you going? You have to go on polishing down there at any price."

Now, the mere occurrence of this ditty alongside songs by Fabri and Boy in the same Leiden fragments is by no means proof that this air, too, was sung at the court of Holland. But nor should we be too hasty in supposing the opposite simply because of the vulgarity of the theme. In Holland, as elsewhere, the courtly and the ribald were not mutually exclusive. Indeed, the fact that even so earnest a reciter as William of Hildegaersberch wrote two fairly vulgar farces may be considered relevant.[9] A liking for vulgarity beside the sacred was clearly nothing of which the court felt the least bit ashamed: thus, in the splendid initial capitals of one of the accounts, and beneath a pious Latin saw that everything save God is transitory, we discover a drawing of two dogs stirring a pot that is being refilled from between . . . two spreading buttocks (fig. 29).[10]

This scatological sketch takes us to what was evidently the preferred date and venue of the most popular court amusements: Carnival and the Shrove Tuesday celebrations. Closely though these festivities may have been bound, in origin no less than in their subsequent history, to *urban*

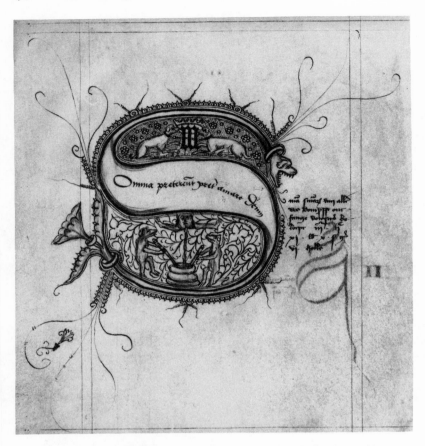

29. Account entry with pious saying and scatological drawing. (Algemeen Rijksarchief, The Hague, MS. AGH 1253, fol. 29v)

culture during the late Middle Ages, the court of Holland-Bavaria was not averse to joining in the revelry. Carnival, in fact, saw the height of pleasure at court:[11] as the accounts indicate, people abandoned their restraints—social, sexual, and religious—in February more than at any other time. (Mock) tourneys were held, sumptuous banquets and receptions given, there was dancing, and, in 1415, "all manner of women and men came to the court to act as monks in the great hall"[12]—which is not to suggest that they stood about in devout silence.

On these evenings of merrymaking, various texts were read, as we know from payments to declaimers of verse entered in the accounts. Regrettably, these texts have not survived, for they would have afforded glimpses of an aspect of "literary" life at court that can scarcely have been negligible. Perhaps the possible relationship between the court of Holland and the simple yet famous short manuscript to which Verwijs, rather romantically, attached the title *Van vrouwen ende van minne* (Of women and of love) in 1876 may prove pertinent to our investigation.[13] Although this pamphlet was discovered in 1821 among various documents from Egmont Abbey, its monastic origins may seem belied by the coarsely amorous contents. Now, it is anything but certain that the little book began its life in Egmont itself; all we can say with fair assurance is that the manuscript must have originated in Holland in about 1440 and that it includes copies of much older writings. If we combine these facts with the strong German linguistic flavor of some of the writing, we find ourselves, at the very least, approaching the sphere of influence that held sway at the court of Holland-Bavaria—a fact corroborated by the contents of the manuscript: several poems of the *cour d'amour* genre; a piece by William of Hildegaersberch; short musings on love in the style of the *Haags liederenhandschrift*; a song lampooning the peasantry that must have been greatly applauded at court; and various Shrove Tuesday pieces, including the famous "Blue Boat." That poem, however, presents us with a ticklish problem: must the triad in the subtitle of Pleij's path-breaking monograph on this text, namely literature, popular entertainment, and bourgeois morality, be extended to include court entertainment at The Hague as well?

But enough of that. Apart from pointing to several concrete perspectives, the above comments are intended mainly to explain that our knowledge of the literature at the court of Holland-Bavaria can still be enlarged and enriched by new studies. Nevertheless, nothing prevents us from offering some conclusions in the meantime. The first of these comes as a pleasant surprise. Without wishing to inflate the results of this study, we feel justified in claiming that the court of the counts of Holland-Bavaria seems, even in its literature, to have had greater luster than was once believed. We might have anticipated or at least suspected this, since detailed studies have already shown that the musical life at that court was considerably more refined than its former reputation suggested, and even the fine arts have been shown to be of greater quality than the experts thought.[14] The court now emerges as a center of literary life that was a match for any other court in its day and age, and not at all the backward swamp that medieval Holland has so often been called, not least by virtue of its soil. But then, what else could be expected of a dynasty allied by marriage to what were then the greatest noble families of Europe?[15] In literature no less in politics and music, the court of Holland-Bavaria occupied a far from insignificant position: it was, after all, influenced by contemporary French and German cultural currents and participated in both.[16] Indeed, the court at The Hague was a vital part of European elite culture, rather than a standard-bearer of a specifically Holland-Bavarian culture molded only by native institutions or native artists and scholars.

Not that there were no cultural contacts between the court and the "provinces": the use of Middle Dutch alone (stripped of its marked German overtones by the people) saw to that. It is also likely that the style and elegance of the court acted as a spur to the cultural life of the lower nobility and of well-to-do burghers in Holland at large. Poets of the stature of William of Hildegaersberch, for instance, appeared before a variety of audiences, which indicates that the court at The Hague, though the literary centre of Holland, was anything but an island, isolated and ignored.

Other circles, too, especially the various municipal authorities, engaged increasingly in cultural activities.[17] Thus Dordrecht had its own musicians, and many towns boasted schools of music during the period under review. Some of the accounts even mention town "speakers," such as "Godekijn [Godwyn], the speaker of Tricht" (1383) and "Bertelmees [Bartholomew], the speaker of Delft" (1404)[18]—who, nevertheless, were a tiny minority by comparison with the reciters employed by the nobility. Moreover, one of the duties of town musicians and "speakers" was to help ingratiate the town administration with the high elite. All in all, there was very little independent cultural life in urban Holland during the late fourteenth century, and certainly so far as literature is concerned. Even dramatic entertainment, which apparently was a pre-dominantly urban phenomenon, seemed to prosper most when Duke Albert and his retinue came to town (though it should be remembered that only performances attended by the count are recorded in our sources). Thus we arrive at about 1400, when there was a turning point and, even in Holland, groups outside the high nobility began to come to the fore. Historically, then, it was under the House of Bavaria that, for the last time, a noble court may be said to have set the tone in Holland, both in politics and in culture.

Even so, courtly leadership continued for a while longer. Even though the imbalance of our sources has distorted the overall picture, it appears that in around 1400 the Bavarian court far outstripped the rest of contemporary Holland as a center of (literary) culture. In so stating, however, we must also acknowledge that, as a literary influence, the court at The Hague was no real match for the other great courts of its day: the English and the French royal courts and the ducal court of Burgundy produced writers far greater.[19] Here too, though, everything must be seen in proper perspective, and Holland, after all, was even then a small country. And in all modesty, the impact that it made in politics and literature (as a center of Middle Dutch literature in particular) placed other contemporary courts in the shade.[20] If, moreover, we compare the culture that prevailed at the Hague court under the Bavarian counts with that of earlier periods, we must conclude that cultural expression there, and perhaps literary activity as well, had never before reached such heights. At the very least, accomplishments in the sphere of literature compared favorably with literary life during its earlier heyday under Floris V and his immediate predecessors.[21]

Admittedly, Dutch court literature at the end of the fourteenth century—to flesh out this internal comparison—was cast in a different mold from that of the late thirteenth century. Above all, it had become more varied; for while Jacob van Maerlant had enjoyed what amounted to a literary monopoly under the reign of Count Floris V, or at least had reached a height solitary in its eminence (and consequently had been asked to serve many masters), in the Bavarian period a host of authors had come to serve a single patron. In particular, it had become possible for men with many different backgrounds to survive as professional authors—which, not surprisingly, produced a more varied textual offering. Whereas writing had still been the prerogative of the clergy in Maerlant's day, more and more layman authors stepped forward during the fourteenth century. In Holland-Bavaria we need only mention the moralizing poet Hildegaersberch (who still seemed doomed to share the layman's frustrations), the historian Bavaria Herald, and, above all, the court official Dirk Potter, a layman who trod the literary stage with towering self-confidence.[22]

Nor did the new simply take its place beside the old, for simultaneously, literary forms that had been in vogue in the thirteenth century suffered a steep decline. This was particularly true of a genre still widely popular in Maerlant's day, one that, in the decades between 1200 and 1250, had had almost the whole literary arena to itself (save for lyric poetry), namely chivalric romance. To many, these epics—an immense complex of stories about such lordly heroes as King Arthur and Charlemagne—represent the crown of medieval literature, and certainly with some justification. Yet that genre was as good as absent from the court of Holland-Bavaria. True, in *Der minnen loep* Dirk Potter referred to Perceval and Tristan in words that suggest his readers were familiar with these heroes; moreover, there were (noble?) retainers at the Hague court with such names as Wailwin (i.e., Gawain), Perchevael, and Lancelot.[23] All in all, though, these traces of chivalrous romance were few; the genre had clearly ceased to appeal.

Of course, such mighty rulers as Arthur and Charlemagne had not been forgotten—as two of the Nine Worthies, they lived on as glorious memories. Yet although they were still revered, they no longer served as pivotal figures. This loss of status was not confined to the court of Holland-Bavaria; rather, here again that court was keeping abreast of developments in the foremost European courts.[24] In trying to suggest a more specific explanation for the decline of chivalrous romance, we are therefore justified in falling back on hypotheses that have proved valuable elsewhere.

Let us begin with a two-pronged supposition involving an approach both intra- and extraliterary. The former is nothing more sensational than the belief that the medieval literary public, too, periodically felt a need for novelty. More precisely: after having dominated literature for two centuries, chivalrous romance began increasingly to pall as the fourteenth century progressed. This "romance fatigue" involved content as well as form, for the court now showed a growing predilection for *short* poems.[25] In Holland, William of Hildegaersberch was aware of this change in taste, as these lines in his "Van feeste van hylic" (On the wedding feast) make clear (LVI/165–67):[26]

> Want goet ghedicht ende niet te langhe,
> Een schoen vertreck van nyewen sanghe,
> Dat heeftmen gaern ter heren hove.

For a good poem and not too long, a lovely snatch of a new song, these are greatly liked at a noble's court.

Thus, even the court of Holland had grown weary of lengthy episodic, casually constructed, and verbose tales and was demanding short and novel offerings. The word *novel* applied to this genre quite literally, and although Dirk Potter did not use the term (let alone admit that he had acquired the style in Italy), there is little doubt but that *Der minnen loep*, consisting as it does of sixty short love stories in eleven thousand verses, was connected with this new trend. The late-medieval court enjoyed tempo and variation, which partly explains why long-winded chivalrous romances were at last being rejected.

The liking for different forms went hand in hand with a liking for different contents: thus, too, the growing aversion to the old stock romances, which may have found appeal among the young but increasingly failed to do so among adult and more sophisticated lovers of literature. Here we encounter the extraliterary explanation for the decline of chivalric romances. That is, important external developments had ensured that court life in the late fourteenth century was no longer what it had been two centuries earlier when these romances were so cherished. In particular, the rise of a money economy and the concomitant increase in the importance of towns, the middle classes, and commerce had thoroughly changed the old balance of social power.

Feudalism was no longer, or at least not everywhere, the backbone of the social system; a prince now had to deal not only with vassals, but also with increasing numbers of men who, though of lesser status, had an active future in government. In Holland, the rising administrative nobility ousted the old landed gentry from the prince's council (thus initiating the quarrels between the Hooks and the Cods), only to be challenged in turn by a professional elite of administrative technocrats (such as Dirk Potter) who made themselves as indispensable to their sovereign as knights had done of old. When the country went to war, urban professional militias were hired; men who in earlier days would have been knighted now often became court officials.[27] In addition, vital political decisions were now made less and less frequently in the prince's council chamber and increasingly at what amounted to state assemblies, in which the towns were the prince's most important interlocutors. Even for his most "chivalrous" campaigns, such as that against Friesland, the count had to enlist the support of the towns.

It is not difficult to see that Arthurian romances—to confine ourselves to these—should have become unfashionable in this new world. Of what possible interest were stories about a perfect and lofty king who presided imperturbably over a Round Table of noble lords? Once upon a time such tales might have entertained a noble company; now that realm had ceased to be even a utopian dream. The social order depicted in the Arthurian legend—a king surrounded by knights, with not a burgher in sight, and the towns, though in the picture, serving mostly as suppliers of arms and clothing to the court—had grown far too unreal to survive except in a static imagination. Only those who went to war in foreign parts, in Friesland or in Prussia, could rescue snatches of the chivalric dream. But even the *Haags liederenhandschrift* makes it clear that that dream had grown stale;[28] and Bavaria Herald had to pull out every stop to maintain chivalry as an important element in world history. By the time Dirk Potter came along, the chivalric cult embodied in Arthurian legend was but a worn-out fantasy.

Those at the center of power now needed to think, write, and negotiate. To prove oneself by arms alone had ceased to be an end in itself. The official had replaced the knight as keeper of the peace, and the count now governed not upon the counsel of his barons but in harness with the towns. The Arthurian legend had become an anachronism, had ceased to serve as the model for an Edenic court. But what was to take its place?

2. CHAOS, TEXT, AND HONOR

The fourteenth century was dynamic and complex, a period of ferment but also one of confusion. In countless publications, historians have called it an age of chaos, often contrasting it sharply with the orderly thirteenth century. Notorious upheavals seem to corroborate their view of fourteenth-century life: the plague, the Great Schism, the Hundred Years' War, and famine, to mention just some of the most appalling. The culmination of this apocalyptic view is Barbara Tuchman's evocation of the calamitous fourteenth century as a distant mirror of our own, no less turbulent, age.[29] Yet anyone with a critical eye cannot accept this perception—of our own age or, for that matter, of the fourteenth century (and that, after all, is our present concern)—without qualification. Indeed, every century could, after suitable selection, be shown to be just one long succession of spectacular tensions, crises, and misfortunes. In fact, the division of the past into chaotic and orderly periods may be said to reflect an attempt by historians to bring some order into their own chaos.

And yet, even though we have no instrument for measuring the tensions of the past, we must grant that the second half of the fourteenth century was an exceptionally checkered period in Western Europe. This was so not least in Holland, where, in addition to all the international calamities we have mentioned, the Hook and Cod conflict (which in turn was connected with the ascendancy of the towns) guaranteed permanent tensions. These tensions, moreover, were felt most strongly at the court, which was both entangled in all the political conflicts raging in Europe and feeling the repercussions of the discord among the nobles as well as the effects of urban expansionism.

That this picture of an alarmed late-fourteenth-century Hollandish nobility is not merely historical projection but fact reflects the spirit of the age we know, at least in part, from the relevant court literature. Once again, it is important to avoid oversimplification: how can so varied a corpus of writings by so many different authors, comprising thousands of pages of prose and many thousands of verses, be reduced to a common denominator without unjustifiable generalization? Yet a hesitant "even so" seems to be called for here. Dangerous though it may be to work with such concepts as *Zeitgeist*, atmosphere, vital consciousness, and the like, there is no doubt that many passages in the literature associated with the Holland-Bavarian court express an unmistakable sense of unease.

Authors repeatedly air their dissatisfaction with abuses that were rife in their own day and circles. William of Hildegaersberch did so expressly—in fact, he did very little else. But others, too, deplored the ills of the age. Their writings continually attack the prevailing spirit: *now* is a word that almost invariably carries a negative connotation. The nobles no longer live by their own laws, complains Dirk of Delft; social relationships (read: social distinctions) have woefully declined, moans the *Haags liederenhandschrift*; these days bragging often sets the tone, Dirk Potter tells us; the strongest now have the greatest influence at court, concludes even the loyal Herald.[30] By contrast, "earlier" usually looks "better" to their eyes: in the olden days, poets were still respected (Hildegaersberch); lovers still knew the meaning of faithfulness (*Haags liederenhandschrift*); a man's word still counted for something (Dirk of Delft); knights still cherished honor (Bavaria Herald); and lords still chose good servants (Potter).[31] It seems that these authors were gripped by feelings of gloom and decay, which, though not always openly expressed, were nevertheless shared by all.

These conclusions can of course be brushed aside with the objection that writers have voiced such criticisms throughout history, that writers are more notorious even than farmers for being full of complaints. Even a man like Jacob van Maerlant, whose age seemed so ideal to our authors, endlessly protested that everything used to be better. And yet, the almost matter-of-fact tone in which the authors at the court of Holland-Bavaria declared that the world was toppling downhill—a tone that in no way suggests their attitude was in the least eccentric—is explicable only on the assumption that their public, too, felt the same deep sense of malaise. Nor is anyone looking at the history books likely to gainsay them.[32] But regardless of how justified their scorn and dismay with contemporary conditions may appear to later observers, one thing is indisputable, and that is that the literature produced at the court of Holland-Bavaria reflected a profound gloom, a haunting unease. This mood is perhaps best illustrated through analysis of a complete poem, "Vanden scepe" (On the ship) by the didactic poet Augustijnken.[33] The poem is included in the *Haags liederenhandschrift*; it is, in fact, startling that this thoroughly Hollandish poem should have tolled so somber a note amid so many ("German-tinted") expressions of courtly happiness.

The setting is entirely Hollandish: in the type of introduction often found in the work of William of Hildegaersberch, the poet describes a walk he once took beside the Merwede River at sunrise. Finding a small boat, he rowed upstream to the most enchanting ship he had ever seen. A lady (who seems always to be present in such poems) tells the amazed visitor that the (of course, allegorical) ship is built of only the best that one can imagine and manned by a full complement of courtly virtues: Modesty, Steadfastness, Morality, Loyalty, Justice, Temperance, and Generosity. But wonderful though everything seems to be, the ship is about to be boarded by the villains Envy, Deceit, Shamelessness, Disloyalty, Evil Intent, and Avarice. Because these villains have the ship's *masters* at their mercy, the crew is forced to put out to sea, desperately hoping that the tide will turn. The lady introduces herself to the poet as Lady Compassion and hopes that her story will reach the masters through his good offices; "for your work brings you before lords and ladies." Then the ship sails away, leaving Holland behind, and the saddened poet follows her with his eyes. The name of the ship is *Certainty. . . .*

But Augustijnken would not have been a medieval writer had he not attempted to steer Certainty to a safe harbor. If only the masters resolved to change tack, the ship of (ideal) state could still return to Holland: "Oh you lords of great renown . . . bestir yourselves to bring her back!" (Och, ghi heeren van hogher aert [. . .] Pijnt u, dat ghi se weder haelt!). Admittedly, our poetic pilot does not seem sure just how the (social) tide is to be turned—but that is no reason for abandoning the attempt. The conviction that it is possible, at least in principle, to bring the ship back safe, no less than the prevailing sense of insecurity, is an important constant in the court literature of Holland. The message of "Vanden scepe," in fact, is a constant of all medieval literature, inasmuch as, the rare exception aside, medieval writing invariably has a didactic objective.

Writers and poets may have been somber, but they were never prepared to leave it at that—they always tried to indicate a way out. This positive approach rarely appeals to the modern reader, who seems to prefer the more cynical and tragic expressions of medieval literature: everything else seems like so much moralizing cant or provincial naiveté. But what we think of that literature today—and how the change in public taste has come about—need not detain us here; for the present purposes it is enough to recognize that the medieval conception of literature was much more idealistic and didactic than our own.

In the Middle Ages, literature (or, more broadly speaking, the written word) saw itself as a guide to the good life, with the author as its guardian. It is not that the art of fine writing was despised, but the ethical role of literature loomed much larger than its aesthetic appeal.[34] Authors taught readers to distinguish good from evil and formulated what they considered the appropriate rules of behavior. That in so doing they recalled forgotten values, advocated new standards, or tried to drive home well-known points was of secondary importance; what mattered was the attempt to guide their readers onto the right road by the (written or spoken) word.

The medieval conception of literature was thus moralistic and didactic—in Holland as elsewhere, and not least so during the decades around the turn of the fourteenth century, decades that may not have inspired great optimism but were thereby suffused all the more with idealism. The ubiquitous confusion demanded an ideological anchor, and writers and poets were ready to provide it. At the court of Holland-Bavaria, all of them wanted to *teach* readers how to improve themselves—be it as lovers, administrators, or Christians.[35] Each in his own way thus presented himself as an ardent world reformer, as a humble but useful signpost to better times.

Each in his own way: for if we compare them, we see that all these artists sought salvation in different directions. The reader might well consider this lack of unity just one more symptom of the uncertainties enveloping the age. Be that as it may, we can—even if we confine ourselves to the ideologies enshrined in the texts already discussed—just as easily speak of a multiplicity of prescriptions, old as well as more modern, for the good life. Such writers as Bavaria Herald and Dirk of Delft, with their glorification of knighthood and orthodoxy, clung to traditional models; the *Haags liederenhandschrift*, too, upheld the old values in its didactic approach. And William of Hildegaersberch, though otherwise cut from more modern cloth, hankered after the good old days as well. The only one of our writers to serve up genuinely novel ideological fare was Dirk Potter; yet even he did not dream up original themes but merely added fresh notes to old tunes. All in all, then, Holland-Bavarian court literature was rather conservative. True, its writers thought a change in outlook essential, but they had far from dismissed the old values. On the contrary: they considered restoration, not revolution, the best cure for sickness, whether social, political, or moral. And how could it have been otherwise, when all these men were at the same court? Huizinga was certainly not wrong to assert that late-medieval court literature tried hard to throw up a dam against the frightening threat of total disintegration.[36] In writing for the old order, our authors (necessarily) clung to the old values.

Now, one shibboleth of that system was *honor*. Honor was synonymous with what we might nowadays call a good name; it involved one's standing among one's peers and—no less important—one's own attitude toward that standing. This preoccupation with status led to a veritable cult in the court literature of Holland, with *honor* appearing thousands of times. As we have seen, it had a key function in the arsenal of concepts used by our authors. To William of Hildegaersberch, social decline could be equated with the loss of honor, which made the restoration of honor (through a general moral revival) of paramount importance. The absolute value of love extolled in the *Haags liederenhandschrift* lay in the honor it bestows on both men and women. To Bavaria Herald, chivalric honor was the alpha and omega of culture and refinement, and to Dirk Potter, too, the preservation (or better still, increase) of honor was something the individual, whether he was in love or not, must never forget, lest he forfeit not only his name but also his soul. In short, all our authors considered honor the highest earthly good. Only heavenly bliss was more desirable still, and it was characteristic that Dirk of Delft should have described the latter as "eternal honor."

On closer inspection, in fact, it appears that the term *honor* had overtones and nuances peculiar to each author. For one (William of Hildegaersberch), honor was inseparable from moral goodness; for another (the Herald), from chivalrous feats of arms; for a third (Dirk Potter), from social aplomb. Like "freedom" in later times, "honor" was a flag under which many different ideas could sail. But no less characteristic than the fine distinctions associated with the term was the fact that honor invariably headed the list of values for all our authors. They might have differed about the means for achieving honor, but the end was always personal repute, a good name; while its definition may not have been crystal clear, none doubted that honor was the quintessence of the virtuous life. Small wonder, then, that the captain of Augustijnken's symbolic ship of state was called Lady Honor. Without honor none could prosper; and the converse was equally true: those who prospered gained honor. Wherever Honor, as a personification or as an abstraction, appears in the literature of the court of Holland-Bavaria, she is the lady (or the king, or the sum) of all earthly virtues, second to only God and salvation. In glorifying honor, each author at the court of Holland-Bavaria, in his own way, upheld the traditional aristocratic values and style.

All this points us in the direction of cultural anthropology, and specifically its distinction between *shame cultures* and *guilt cultures*—that is, societies based on the avoidance of (public) shame or of (private) guilt, respectively.[37] This distinction can also be formulated positively, in terms of honor (public reputation) as opposed to (individual) conscience. The two concepts are not mutually exclusive, of course: there are no pure shame or pure guilt cultures. Nevertheless, the pairing can often be applied to good advantage—not in the sense of diametrical opposites but as covering a broad spectrum between two (theoretical) extremes of cultural preoccupation: honor and shame versus conscience and guilt. And even when we do not wish to translate the lack of one as the dominance of the other (which is indeed not always justified), we are still left with the interesting question of how a particular milieu experiences honor and shame.

If we ask this question about the court of Holland-Bavaria and use its literature as our guide, we are likely to conclude that it was an outstanding example of an intense shame culture. For the attainment of public recognition—honor—was the highest objective for this society, and public shame (loss of honor) a stigma to be avoided at all costs. To be sure, our authors did not ignore conscience or guilt—the term *consciencie* occurs repeatedly, especially in their reflections on Christian morality.[38] Nor is it surprising that the voice of conscience should have been sounded in this context: Christianity, with its stress of man's individual sinfulness in the eyes of God, made an enormous contribution (especially after the Reformation) to the rise of the extreme guilt culture in which we find ourselves today.

For all that, another factor was no less influential in causing the gradual transition from a shame culture to a guilt culture: namely, the gradual emergence of a more open, more mobile society in which the opportunities for self-realization were increasingly divorced from advantages (or disadvantages) either inherited or imposed by politics, religion, tradition, and social change. In a (theoretically) perfect and open society, there are no barriers to self-improvement: there one's progress is independent of one's origins, sex, or external coercion; instead one's inner urges are what drive one's actions. In a tightly bounded society, by contrast, one that insists on strict social limitations and where life is controlled largely by circumstances, the opinion of the outside world is more compelling than one's own, and the question of individual wishes, certainly if they run counter to convention, largely irrelevant. This constriction was probably most obvious in heroic societies, where young men were forced willy-nilly to prove themselves by dint of arms. Any who could not fight (very special cases excepted) were deemed to be devoid of honor, while those who performed great feats on the "field of honor" were revered and applauded even beyond the grave. Such societies hinged on martial ambition; there was simply no place in them for conscientious objection.

Given these considerations, we immediately grasp why Dirk Potter, alone among all the authors at the court of Holland, should have had affinities with a guilt culture.[39] Short of revealing himself as a Calvinist *avant la lettre*, he nevertheless proved less susceptible than the rest to the authority of priests in matters of ethics and morals, relying as much as possible on his own judgment. This incipient individualism informed Dirk Potter's social views no less than it did his practical behavior, thus gaining him an outstanding career at court, his relatively modest birth notwithstanding.

In adopting a critical stance toward the glories of chivalry and war, and, as far as we can tell, fighting for none but his own cause, Potter shrugged off the old chivalric patterns but still prospered at court. Judged by the standards and possibilities of his own age, Potter achieved a remarkable independence, with self-reliance his spur and reason his guide. He had no objection to breaking the social rules, merely advocating trust in reason to help preserve one's good name (generally assisted by cunning and secrecy). In refusing to bow unreservedly to accepted social mores, Dirk Potter may be said to have moved between honor and conscience, his compass perhaps tilting toward the second. His sense of honor was strongly internalized, to use a modern term.[40] Yet no less significantly, reputation continued to matter greatly, even to him. In particular, he fastidiously avoided open breaches of public standards, so that at times he had to go his own way in secret. Whenever he crossed or even approached the line of permissible behavior, fear of public opinion caused him genuine anxiety. While he was apparently able to accept the idea of sinning in God's eyes, the disgrace of public disqualification was a nightmare to him. Not sinning as such, but that others should hear of one's sins, was the fatal lapse. To be found out was earthly hell.

The cult of honor, then, was deep in Dirk Potter's blood as well. And how could it have been otherwise for one who lived at court? That small, exclusive, and closed society, confined to a relatively small area and based on subtle hierarchical distinctions between individuals who knew one another personally, often intimately, was the ideal breeding ground for a dyed-in-the-wool shame culture. Life at court was highly competitive: posts, favors, possessions, titles, mistresses—all went to the most aggressive. The good fortune of one quickly turned into the misfortune of others. This situation explains the (to our minds) near-pathological dread of the gossip and slander so often railed against by our court authors.[41]

Of course, these writers' tirades against "enviers, braggarts, and villains" were so many literary topoi; but they were nevertheless true to life by being rooted in the sociopsychological soil of extreme status consciousness and social constraint—in other words, in a shame (or honor-based) culture. In that type of culture, which depends on sound reputations, a word can make or break a person—the honorific address of a herald no less so than a gossip's evil tongue. Even one's own self-esteem is a function of public opinion; whosoever is mocked must either avenge himself or . . . feel deeply ashamed. Honor is all. Court culture is shame culture—or, as the *Haags liederenhandschrift* puts it (no. 55B):[42]

> Vrou Eere zeghet dus mi:
> Lof of hof daer ich niet en zi,
> Daer moet Vrou Sceemte buten staen.
> Her Erentrijch sprect na mijn verstaen:
> Vrou Eere, Vrou Sceemde moeten hoven,
> Sal men den hof mit eeren loven.

Lady Honor tells me this: from whatever praises and courts I am absent, there Lady Shame is absent as well. Sir Honorful says, if I understand him aright, that Lady Honor and Lady Shame must both attend court before its praises can be sung.

In other words, honor vouches not only for individual excellence, but also for the reputation of the whole court. Everything, in both its literature and the harsh world outside, suggests that the court of Holland-Bavaria cultivated an individual as well as a collective sense of honor.

That combination must have been the driving force (to confine ourselves to just one important example) behind the Frisian expeditions of

Duke Albert and William VI. To our thinking, these campaigns may well have been a senseless waste of money and energy; for the aristocratic imagination, however, no greater cause existed, or could exist, than the pursuit of personal honor on the field of battle. The way the Frisians had been flouting the authority of Holland was an insult to the counts' blazon. Further, that the body of Count William IV, instead of receiving honorable burial, still lay on enemy soil was an almost magical symbol of Holland's collective guilt.

Of course, other considerations were involved in the Frisian war as well. As we saw in Chapter IV, section 4, Holland probably needed an external enemy to close ranks at home; in addition, the towns (as suppliers of money and manpower) were swayed by commercial interests to lend financial support to the count's military campaign against Friesland. Still, the modern system of politics dictated by economics must not blind us to the existence of additional historical compulsions. Not all wars have focused primarily on the pursuit of gain, nor was access to the Hanse towns the main cause for Holland's resumption of the struggle with Friesland. At the heart of the conflict, rather, was an all-pervading sense of honor, and this is reflected particularly in the literature produced at the court of Holland-Bavaria, especially that of Bavaria Herald.

The Frisians, too, knew the meaning of honor and shame. On Sunday, 27 August 1396, when the first warship sailing the flag of Holland appeared off the Frisian coast, a woman ran down to the beach, lifted her skirts, and, shouting "You are welcome here!" bared her buttocks to the Hollanders.[43] Her act caused the attackers to boil with fury; such contempt—and from a woman!—could not go unavenged. A rain of arrows flew at her; soldiers then hacked her to pieces—"en cent mille pièces ou plus," as Froissart, with his love for detail, put it. Such behavior did not seem very chivalrous, but then, honor had to be satisfied before all else, and chivalry seldom had time for the poor, the disobedient, or the nameless.

While an insult can be expunged by armed force, it can also be avenged with words. In a shame culture, even scolding can be a dire weapon: it wounds so sorely because it besmirches the victim's reputation.[44] Let us consider one case. When John of Bavaria, pretender to the throne, set out against Dordrecht in 1419, he was helped by Count John III of Nassau-Dillenburg. To meet the count's expenses, John of Bavaria promised, on his honor, to hand over 5,000 Rhenish guilders—a prom-

30. *Scheldbrief* (scolding letter) attacking John of Bavaria. (Hessisches Hauptstaatsarchiv, Wiesbaden, Sec. 170, no. 1026)

ise he failed to keep. The respective strengths of Nassau and Bavaria were such that the duped count could not take armed revenge; instead he wrote a so-called *scheldbrief* (scolding letter), in which he circulated the story of John of Bavaria's misdemeanor to almost the entire imperial nobility and to all the towns in Holland. The worst aspect of all was no doubt the drawing that accompanied the *scheldbrief*: in it John of Bavaria in full regalia is shown pulling a pig up by its tail and affixing his seal (with the arms of Holland-Bavaria) to the beast's hindquarters (fig. 30). A short verse in the mixed German-Dutch language with which we are now familiar added force to this early-fifteenth-century caricature, for out of John of Bavaria's mouth came the words: "Here I stand before the pig's backside, and press my seal upon it; . . . my word of honor and promise of loyal support are no longer worth anything; and foolish is he who continues to serve me."[45]

As far as we know, John of Nassau never received his 5,000 guilders, but he certainly dented his enemy's honor. While such behavior may seem infantile to us, it was then very serious. In a culture so dominated by tradition, birth, status, and pomp, a man's self-respect was as good as synonymous with his reputation. Hence, the honor of the court at The Hague was less a matter of personal pride for Duke Albert and his successors than a means of shoring up their authority both within and outside the county and of ensuring that their court had status in the world. The court culture of Holland-Bavaria had an important goal: to delineate the fact that, precisely in an age of confusion and decline, the old values of the nobility were still upheld, and would always be so.

Nor did that message go unnoticed. In the poem "Von dem pfen-ning" (On the penny) by the late-fourteenth-century Austrian writer Peter Suchenwirt, we find an ancient nobleman telling a poet which courts continued to honor the arts. First, of course, came the Holy Ro-man Emperor's, but Duke Albert's was not far behind: "Wol auf, mit mir gen Holant, / Tzu hertzog Albrecht, wie der lebt; / Dez mut nach grossen eren strebt, / Wohrhaft und milt, bey mannes mut!" (Off let us go to Holland, to where Duke Albert abides; who strives for great honor, is true and generous, yet imbued with manly courage!)[46] Such-enwirt ought to have known; as the most famous and best traveled of medieval heralds, he had visited nearly every court of standing, from Prague to The Hague. And indeed, as he said, the court of Holland-Bavaria existed for nothing so much as for honor. Thus it assigned to its writers the special obligation of showing how to attain that goal— which explains why Hague court poets, to use Hildegaersberch's expression, were "Vrou eren knechten"—Lady Honor's servants (LXXXIII/32).

But apart from setting an example, Holland-Bavarian court literature also reflected the honor-based culture in which it flourished. By foster-ing literary life, the princes of Holland-Bavaria showed that they knew that such sponsorship could only redound to the court's honor. In "Von dem pfenning," then, Suchenwirt had excellent reason to see a causal connection between an honorable, princely life and artistic patronage. Hildegaersberch, too, realized this clearly (LXXXIII/83–87):

> Waer vrou Eren vriende hoven,
> Daer sietmen dichters conste loven
> Ende ander constenaers daer by.
> Dat doet—het is een melodi
> Die den goeden toebehoert.

Where Lady Honor court does keep, there are the poet's arts extolled, and other artists are acclaimed. That is as it should be—it is a melody that goes with good people.

So said William of Hildegaersberch, not least singing the praises of his own parish. But even so philosophical a mind as Dirk of Delft declared that his *Tafel vanden kersten ghelove* had been written, not only out of love for, but also in honor of Duke Albert, while Bavaria Herald patently wrote his *Hollandse kroniek* to enhance the honor of his prince and province by glorifying their history. Thus an interesting question is raised: how involved were the counts of Holland-Bavaria themselves in the literature written at their court?

3. LORD AND AUTHOR

These last remarks may have caused the reader to ask what justification exists for treating all the texts produced under the Bavarian counts of Holland as a single corpus. Should they not perhaps be considered instead as a series of independent literary initiatives having nothing more in common than the fact that their spiritual fathers—their authors— lived at roughly the same time and place?[47]

I would not mention this alternative if it did not contain a grain of truth. It is tempting to exaggerate the coherence of Holland-Bavarian court literature, both thematically and historically. Yet in no way can its authors be called medieval precursors of the Muider Circle—that is, of a group whose members remained in close personal touch and read their work to one another at regular soirées.[48] (In point of fact, even the Muider Circle was much less of a literary *circle* than was claimed in later centuries.)[49] Even so, the Holland-Bavarian court authors did know one another well.

It would be a hopeless task to retrace all these writers' interrelationships; instead let us examine just one typical case, that of Dirk Potter, the youngest of their company. To begin with, we may safely assume that he knew William of Hildegaersberch.[50] Particularly during his later years, when Hildegaersberch was a regular visitor at The Hague, Potter held a position of trust at the court, which makes it almost inevitable that he was present on several occasions (for instance during Christmas 1407 or Whitsun 1408) when William addressed the count and his company. Dirk of Delft, too, could not have been a stranger to Potter—a rare bird like that learned doctor would not have escaped Potter's eagle

eye, certainly not during his regular court visits in 1399–1404. Moreover, Potter's writings contain passages that seem to refer to Dirk and
his opinions; we may therefore assume that Potter had as many opportunities to listen to Dirk of Delft in the court chapel as he had to hear
Hildegaersberch in the Great Hall.

And Bavaria Herald? Did Potter avoid him because they held vio-
lently opposed views on peace and war? It is certainly hard to imagine
them as close friends; but it does appear from the accounts that, in April
1409, the Herald lent Potter a horse on which the latter repaired to
France.[51] Apparently our dynamic diplomat was in more of a hurry than
the Herald's horse was used to, for the accounts tell us that Potter "wore
the horse out and ruined it on the journey" ([het ros] ofgereden ende
up die reyse verdorven heeft). Now, the loan of a horse does not necessarily imply personal ties, let alone—and this is more important for
us—literary ones. And yet Dirk Potter seems to have borrowed freely
from the Herald's writings. The stories of Semiramis and Lucretia with
her Virgil in *Der minnen loep*, for example, agree in many details with
Bavaria Herald's *Wereldkroniek*, as does the account of Hannibal's spoils
of war in the *Blome*.[52] Nor should this surprise us; indeed, it would have
been most peculiar if a courtier who, in his own words, had his nose
constantly buried in books did not look at chronicles written during approximately the same years that he worked at the same court.
Similarly, we can readily accept that Potter—expert on courtly love life
that he was, and familiar with the "sweetness of song, of melodies and the delights of instruments, dancing and the like" (soeticheit
van sanghe, van melodien ende die genoechten van instrumenten, van
dansen ende des ghelijcs; *BD* 79/20–21), to which he attributed an
aphrodisiac effect—was familiar with the *Haags liederenhandschrift*
(though he did not explicitly refer to any of its poems) as well as with
Fabri and Boy.

All in all, we have good reason to suppose that the authors at the
court of Holland-Bavaria belonged to a single cultural circle, even while
we grant their individuality. But what, the reader might wonder, was
the distance of each one of them from the undisputed center of that
circle, the sovereign—that is, Albert and William VI? All the writers in
question were, of course, formally dependent on the counts of Holland;
yet even on this formal plane, considerable differences can be discerned.
Bavaria Herald and Dirk Potter were wholly in the counts' paid service;
Dirk of Delft's court chaplaincy was presumably a part-time post; while
Hildegaersberch may be described as a "freelance" author.

There must have been even more marked differences in the relationships between these lords and our writers on the (no less important) informal plane.[53] William of Hildegaersberch, it seems, never actually conversed with his sovereign: he appeared at court, performed at the count's table, and left again. While the Holland-Bavarian counts undoubtedly prized William as a poet, they apparently did not deal with him personally. Contacts between Count Albert and Dirk of Delft must have been far closer. Dirk was, after all, the count's protégé, whose education Albert himself had paid for. But in any case, after 1399, when Dirk was appointed "to teach and preach to our servants and familiars" in the court chapel, the count must have engaged him in personal conversation at times; and if Dirk was also Albert's confessor—which cannot be proved but seems reasonable to suppose—his links with the sovereign must have been very close indeed.

Bavaria Herald's contact with the counts also seems to have been close. On 5 December 1405, William VI and the Herald played a game of chess, which the Herald won and which earned him a handsome cash prize. Rather than being exceptional or a coincidence, this game was apparently characteristic of what was only to be expected: a sympathetic relationship between a belligerent count (a fanatical campaigner in Prussia and Friesland) and an expert on chivalric codes. Nor need there be any doubt about the ties between the counts and Dirk Potter: anyone sent by his sovereign on secret missions and serving as that lord's agent and secretary must have been close to his master. And yet Potter did not dedicate any book to Albert or William VI, or to the latter's successors John and Jacqueline—which brings us to the paradox that the most trusted servant among the authors at court may have been the one with whose literary output the counts were least familiar.

In a sense, that impression is symptomatic of the overall picture. No matter how often those with great literary reputations may appear in the administrative records as having rendered some service to their sovereign, they are never described as *authors* in the counts' service (the only exception being William of Hildegaersberch, who is on record as having received payment for reciting his work to the count). Was the counts' interest in the literary products of their servants really so minimal? All we can say is that no Bavarian count of Holland seems ever to have asked about the progress of a literary work, nor has any left records of literary sponsorships as such.[54]

The counts' wives, by contrast, do seem to have patronized authors; indeed, the *grandes dames* of the Hague court were far more actively

31. Margaret of Cleves, patron of literature? Sixteenth-century drawing in the Recueil d'Arras. (Bibliothèque Municipale d'Arras, MS. 266, fol. 29)

involved with books than their husbands ever were. Most of the many
breviaries mentioned in the accounts, for example, were purchased by
ladies. One entry in 1398 mentions "a man from Utrecht who was asked
to illuminate a manuscript for my lady."[55] That lady was Margaret of
Cleves (fig. 31), who became Albert's second wife in 1394, and there are
strong indications of her direct involvement in what we would call literary life in the broader sense—especially in the preparation of pious
texts. As early as 1395, a payment of three guilders was recorded for "a
book my lady had [ordered to be] written." A few weeks later there is a
mention of a (lost?) book by Brother William, who, though he was "my
lord's confessor," nevertheless wrote at the duchess's behest: "Item on

my lady's orders by Brother William, my lord's confessor, for giving her a book that my lady had bid him make, 10 new guilders" (Item bi mijnre vrouwen bevelen by broeder Willem, mijns heren biechtvader, gegeven tot miere vrouwen boec dat mijn vrouwe hem bevolen hadde doen maken, 10 ny gulden).[56] The precise wording of this entry merits close attention: not only was Brother William paid ten new guilders on the instructions of Margaret, but we gather that Margaret had also "bid" him "make" the book (presumably, the text). We know of no such instructions to an author by any male member of the house. For Margaret, however, active intervention in the production of books and texts was apparently not unusual—we know that she commissioned books not only by William the Confessor but also by Dirk of Delft, who was "wont to call on my lord during the high holidays." Even though he was employed by Duke Albert, his first (no longer extant) book "was made for my lady and brought to her all ready made" in 1400.

Nonetheless, the only extant book by Dirk of Delft, the *Tafel vanden kersten ghelove*, was dedicated to Duke Albert of Bavaria in person, the dedication copy bearing the duke's coat-of-arms and its perusal being expressly enjoined upon the sovereign lord: "Hence, worthy and beloved lord, that I might show and teach you how to know and serve your Lord and Creator and also to keep out of sin's way, I have made Your Honor a Table of the Christian faith and age; and also because I would willingly serve you. May you at times take this table into your hand" (Daerom, wairdige, lieve here, opdat ic iu moghe wisen ende leren dat gi uwen God en Schepper mede salt leren kennen ende oefenen, ende oic bet te hoeden van sonden, so heb ic iuwer eren ghemaect een Tafel van den kersten ghelove ende der ewen; ende also als ic gaern woude iu willich te dienst staen. Dat ghi dese tafel hebben somwijl in uwer hant).[57] And it was in a similar manner that Bavaria Herald presented his *Hollandse kroniek* to Albert's successor, William VI, on New Year's Day 1409: "And have compiled this present history as briefly as I knew how; which chronicle I would present to you, Duke William, Count of Holland, upon the New Year so that Your Grace might read it and pass the time with it" (Ende hebbe deez teghenwoirdige historie ghecopeleert zo ict alre cortste mochte; wilcke cronike ic u, hertoge Wilhelm, grave van Hollant, uwer wairdicheit dair in te lesen om dachcortinghe scencken moete tot enen nyen jair).

By and large, then, we have no reason to doubt that the counts of Holland-Bavaria took a personal interest in the literary life of their court, even if we must assign their womenfolk—or at least one of

32.   Prince and author: Duke Albert and Dirk of Delft.
(Bibliothek Darmstadt, MS. 2667, fol. 14)

them—the more active role. The counts may not have commissioned
new literary works, but they are at least thought to have read these
works, if only "at times" (Dirk of Delft) or to "pass the time" (Bavaria
Herald). That they did so need not be questioned; why else would
Duke Albert have ordered a bookcase or his son William VI have purchased a book "with many beautiful sayings that William of Hildegaersberch had made"?

Thus, although the wish that even the highest in the land might read
their books may not have been what drove these authors to produce, it
must certainly have influenced them. We know, for example, that Dirk
of Delft wrote his *Tafel* with Albert of Bavaria in mind.[58] And if William
of Hildegaersberch was only half as aware of his public's wishes as he
claimed he was, nearly all his poems must have been written to please
his masters. Moreover, a main theme of William's repertoire was remarkably in tune with one of the counts' chief concerns; his repeated

call for the restoration of peace and order under a sovereign protected by God must have pleased both Albert and William VI greatly. Similarly, William VI was undoubtedly delighted with Bavaria Herald's *Hollandse kroniek*: not only did its conclusion paint an exceptionally glowing picture of this noble lord and of his father, but the book also spoke of the antiquity and standing of Holland and the line of its counts more admiringly than any book written before or after. No wonder the prologue expressed the author's hope that "Your Grace might read it"; if the Herald did indeed hope to surprise the count with his New Year's gift, he must have surprised him most pleasantly.

On the whole, therefore, the Bavarian princes were true patrons of literature in Holland. Nevertheless, we should keep in mind just what their patronage (mainly) included and what it (mainly) excluded. The counts of Holland-Bavaria were not in the habit of handing out commissions to their court authors, let alone dictating to them; nor do they seem to have pursued a specific literary policy. If the preceding sections have made anything clear, it is the extent to which the authors themselves determined the literary scene, even in this medieval setting. For it can be said of every writer at the court of Holland-Bavaria that he took up the cudgel for his own cause, the Herald glorifying the knighthood, the court chaplain the priesthood, and the court administrator the public service.

Important though this autonomy may have been, however, it did not lead these writers to ignore the concerns of their exalted readers: courtly patronage—albeit indirect—was part of their historical background, and without it their writing cannot be fully understood. It so happened that the counts of Holland-Bavaria employed servants who, in addition to their official duties, had literary talents and aspirations and who (generally) offered their work to their prince and his peers. Whether these nobles knew of a book before it appeared in writing, whether indeed they instructed their servants to write it, may be an interesting question, but it does not alter the fact that, by patronizing some men, they enabled them to write books that, if successful, might occasion further favors. Thus count and writer had a mutual interest that, however vague, was undoubtedly present.

It would therefore be wrong to conclude from the absence of spectacular proof to the contrary that the counts of Holland-Bavaria were of minor significance in the emergence of literature at their court. Far from it—they were of primary importance, inasmuch as they were patrons of the arts in the classical sense. Patronage facilitates. By taking up residence in The Hague, by living there in formal estate, and by assigning literature (Middle Dutch literature, more specifically) a place at their court, the Bavarian counts facilitated the development of Middle Dutch writing. Particularly helpful was the fact that the difficult early years of Bavarian rule were followed by a relatively stable political era under such strong and capable rulers as Duke Albert and William VI, his son and heir. Although peace and quiet were never fully achieved, the Bavarian rulers remained firmly in power for half a century. This, too, helped to foster a climate in which art could flourish, with the counts providing the necessary, if not sufficient, conditions. How great their influence was may be gathered from the fate of court literature when these conditions were no longer satisfied.

4. THE END

"In fact, no more than two princes of this house ruled over Holland," wrote W. G. Brill more than a century ago: Albert and William VI of Bavaria.[59] His formulation may be slightly exaggerated, but it is nevertheless cogent. Neither William V, Albert's Bavarian predecessor in Holland, nor the later successors of William VI ruled the county in a way that boded well for the future. Thus, much as the beginnings of Bavarian rule had been beset with problems, so its end was turbulent. As early as 31 May 1417, the day of William VI's death, his daughter and heiress, Jacqueline, had to face the threat of Burgundian annexation.[60] Not the least of her troubles was the fact that, although a woman was entitled to wield authority over the county, she had great difficulty in actually doing so. A marriage to a strong man had been the obvious answer, but Jacqueline's father could hardly have made a worse choice than Count John IV of Brabant. At just fourteen years of age, John hardly represented the outward embodiment of authority that Holland needed, and his inner qualities seem only to have underscored rather than offset this weakness. To aggravate a situation already tense, John and Jacqueline could conceive no children, so the complicated diplomatic wrangle originally needed to obtain a papal dispensation for marriage between cousins (in which, needless to say, Dirk Potter was involved) turned out to have been a total waste of time.

Scarcely had Jacqueline of Bavaria become countess of Holland than her uncle, John of Bavaria, Duke Albert's younger son, established himself as *ruwaard* (thereby relinquishing his bishopric of Liège) and raised an army against Jacqueline. The county of Holland was, understand-

33. John of Bavaria. Sixteenth-century drawing in the Recueil d'Arras. (Bibliothèque Municipale d'Arras, MS. 266, fol. 30)

ably, deeply divided, the Cod towns believing that the pretender's reign would be to their advantage, the Hook party remaining loyal to its sovereign. Ultimately, John of Bavaria had his way: by the treaty of 1419, arranged from Burgundy, he was to share authority over Holland with Jacqueline's husband, John IV. In fact, though, John did no power sharing; the weak John IV was fully occupied in his own Brabant, and Jacqueline, disappointed in Holland and in her husband, sought exile in England.

The erstwhile countess's hopes rose anew when John of Bavaria died in 1425, his prayerbook having been rubbed with poison.[61] Was Jacqueline behind the attempt? All we can say for sure is that the murder was planned in England. Still, if Jacqueline had hoped to regain Holland in this way, she was disappointed, for she was summarily incarcerated in 's Gravensteen Castle, Ghent, by the mighty Duke Philip of Burgundy, who then vested authority over Holland in John IV of Brabant, by now a Burgundian puppet. Later, after having fled from Ghent in male disguise, Jacqueline was able to muster an army against Philip; but the unequal match ended in 1428 with the so-called Peace Offering of Delft, a discomfiting settlement for Jacqueline. The duke of Burgundy became *ruwaard* of Holland, and Jacqueline, now a countess in name only, withdrew to Teylingen Castle. There, in 1433, she renounced all her claims to Holland, whereupon the county was officially incorporated into the wealthy and sizable duchy of Burgundy, the old "Middle Kingdom." The delay in effecting this annexation during the years since 1417 had been no more than a stay of execution.

With this tumultuous background, it was only natural that literary life should have ceased to flourish at the court in The Hague. In this respect, too, it would seem that only two Bavarian counts had in fact reigned over Holland. Jacqueline no doubt wished matters to be different, but she was helpless; she had grown up in Hainaut, and had spent almost no time at The Hague, not even as countess of Holland. We do know that, at Teylingen Castle, she had a considerable library, English works included, on history and medicine[62]—but reading them during her (quasi-)banishment, or having her companions help ease her sorrow with the help of the "three descant song books" in her possession, was not the same as supporting a radiant center of literary court culture.

In that regard, John of Bavaria accomplished more during the brief period (1419–25) of his reign in The Hague. Unfortunately, the times were not propitious for court literature; even when the political situation was relatively stable, economic recession, inflation, and natural disasters (such as St. Elizabeth's flood in 1421, when the dikes near Werkendam were breached) forced attention elsewhere. John of Bavaria knew, however, that it was a matter of honor not to let his cultural reputation lapse, and so his court did not become a complete cultural desert.[63] Indeed, among the artists who remained there under John's patronage was no less famous a painter than Jan van Eyck.[64] Unfortunately, although in the three years (1422–24) that he and his companions worked at the Hague court "master Jan the painter" is unlikely to have left his brush idle, no evidence of his work at the Binnenhof has come down to us. The belief that he may have painted a hall or a chapel at the count's palace is thus as justified as the absence of concrete evidence is disappointing.

As to the interface of art and literature, we know of a book (of un-known contents) illuminated with golden initials for John of Bavaria's wife by Van Eyck's fellow artist, Henry the Painter (*Heynrich melre*); although this book is mentioned in the accounts, it, too, seems to have been lost.[65] In addition, the accounts mention a poet in the employ of the last Bavarian count of Holland at The Hague; his name is given as "Barthelemi," presumably the same Bartholomew who figured as "Bertelmeus de spreker" (Bartholomew the speaker) in the account books of Albert and William VI.[66]

Despite these names, however, literary and cultural life at The Hague seems to have declined steeply. In particular, visits by traveling artists from east of the border had become rare.[67] After having propelled Middle Dutch literature and literary appreciation so effectively under the great counts, such vital impulses simply ebbed away. Perhaps this decline was symptomatic of the growing French influence in The Hague under John of Bavaria—a development that later, under the Burgundians, was to keep an almost throttling grip on Middle Dutch literature.

This new French influence is reflected in the only literary work apparently produced in the very last years of Bavarian rule at The Hague, namely "Master Jan Froissart's chronicle, translated from the French into our German tongue by Gerard Potter van der Loo."[68] Or perhaps we ought to consider this book the first (and at the same time the last) product of *Burgundian* court culture in Holland. Whatever the answer, this Froissart translation by Dirk Potter's son marks in an almost symbolic way both the continuity *and* the expiration of literature at the court of Holland-Bavaria. Inasmuch as the author is a Potter van der Loo, he embodies (like his father, incidentally, who also took service with the Burgundians) the continuity of a tradition, not only within a family but also at the court in The Hague. That Froissart's work should have been chosen for translation is no less significant: it is a monument to chivalry erected almost half a century earlier, and even then as a bulwark of a waning culture, by the Hainaut master historiographer for distant relatives of John of Bavaria. Anyone who today picks up the impressive codex of Gerard Potter's Middle Dutch translation in the Royal Library at The Hague (see figs. 19 and 34) will have come as close as possible to the waning of Holland's courtly age. No less symbolic in this connection seems the fact that Potter's translation is incomplete; one wonders whether parts of the book have been lost or whether the translator abandoned the enterprise in full flow.

34.   Gerard Potter's translation of Froissart: opening miniature. (Koninklijke
Bibliotheek, The Hague, MS. 130 B 21, fol. 1r)

In any case, Gerard Potter's use of language is characteristic of the
changes occurring at court: for much as Potter Senior's work had a German flavor, so his son's has a French touch. The translation teems with
French hybrids: *aariergaerde, apparencie, balengier, desesperacie, exami-
neren, frontiere, injurie, cabaret, conquesteren, murmuracie, oistayge, pa-
vays, sustineren, travalye, vitalie*, and the like. These neologisms should
not be blamed on Gerard's lack of translation experience, nor should it
be thought that he used Frenchified terms simply because he could not
think of the Dutch equivalent—there are too many passages in which
he uses French-sounding words quite unlike those found in the original
version: *dissimulacie* for *sans fraude, exceptie* for *reservacion, kyvaedse* for
noise, presentacie for *offre, solaisse* for *reviel, getransfereert* for *envoié, visi-
teren* for *véoir*. The explanation must be something other than incom-
petence, namely that French was once again *bon ton* at The Hague. The
language difference between Potter van der Loo Senior and Junior, in-

deed, symbolizes the difference between Bavarian and Burgundian court culture in Holland.

For Middle Dutch court literature, this change was a serious setback, to say the least. What had been a great stimulus, namely the linguistic bonds between rulers and the people, was nullified, and the divide typical of the Hainaut period restored. In another respect, too, the Hainaut situation returned: with the Burgundians, the county again had rulers that set foot on the soil of Holland as little as possible. Not for a moment would they have considered copying Albert's example of taking up residence in The Hague. To men with their traditions and politics, Holland, though a(nother) pearl in their crown, was but a remote backyard. It was a backyard in cultural respects, too, particularly for men used to a courtly life-style that made even that of kings look inferior.

Both considerations had repercussions on the court at The Hague.[69] To be sure, a skeleton staff was retained under a Hainaut stadtholder, and the court, to use a then-current expression, remained a *hotel* for incidental visits by Burgundians; but now that The Hague had ceased to be a residence, the court lost its meaning, its very soul. A court without a prince was a court without real life—and without literature. History bears this last point out: Gerard Potter's translation of Froissart (circa 1430) was apparently the last literary creation to be produced at the court of Holland for a long time. Two generations of flourishing literary activity had preceded it—a period that, anything but accidentally, had coincided with the Bavarian presence in The Hague. Both before and after that period, (Middle Dutch) literature was silent, a silence presided over by a remote, foreign, and French-speaking administration—first under the Hainaut rulers and then under the Burgundians.

The subsequent fate of Holland-Bavarian court literature makes tragic reading for anyone sympathetic to the preceding chapters. It had no real future at the court in The Hague. True, a manuscript of Dirk of Delft's *Tafel* was retained in the Burgundian library, no doubt for its beautiful miniatures—that is, for its external, not its intrinsic, merits.[70] Middle Dutch texts, in short, survived thanks to their appeal to a public outside the Hague court. Sometimes works continued to be published in tandem, as in the case of a manuscript dating back to about 1480 which included both *Der minnen loep* and writings by Hildegaersberch.[71] Moreover, these texts traveled far, sometimes along paths that cannot be retraced. A late-fifteenth-century, simply illustrated manuscript of *Der minnen loep* was sufficiently small and its cover soft enough to fit neatly into any traveler's hand luggage. Much more checkered was the career of Potter's only other extant manuscript: anyone intending to recite passages from the *Blome der doechden*, especially those devoted to the clergy and to unchastity, will find that the Franciscan monks in Maastricht felt compelled to add a host of marginal "omit" instructions.[72] Much of the material in the small book with compositions by Fabri and Boy was excised; and of the large repertoire of courtly love poetry, only the *Haags liederenhandschrift* found a safe haven in the library of the Nassaus of Breda (and later of the princes of Orange, and later still in the Royal Library).

In both quantitative and qualitative terms, Dirk's *Tafel* fared best of all—as we saw in Chapter V, section 4, its second life among nuns and Beguines was almost more appropriate to its contents than its original perusal at court had been; in any case, that second life was the more intense.[73] Actually, the *Tafel* had a third life as well: it was the only text produced at the Holland-Bavarian court to reach the new printing presses, though only after the (Utrecht?) incunabulum of this so-called *Tafelboec* had been stripped of all scholastic discussions. As a result, nothing remained of Dirk of Delft's original text save the bare narrative bones on which the work had been fleshed out. Precisely what had made the original *Tafel vanden kersten ghelove* so unique in its day was spirited away in the *Tafelboec*, so much so that it hardly matters that the names of Dirk of Delft and of Albert of Bavaria were missing from the prologue.

This case was typical: if the literature produced at the court of Holland-Bavaria was to reach a wider public in the fifteenth-century Dutch-speaking world, then its quality had to be changed, even debased, for the sake of numbers. Most of these texts, moreover, were not thought to merit even that effort; only the work of Dirk of Delft was considered worth mutilating for the sake of publication in print. Certainly, other texts originating from the court of Holland-Bavaria were reproduced during the incunabula period, but (as if printing had not been invented in the meantime) only in manuscript form: their public was and remained small enough to be satisfied with a goose quill.

Let us take one final example. Even when the Holland-Bavarian line had long since disappeared, the Herald's chronicles continued to be read, but their bias had been totally changed. Thus, in 1476, one copyist of the *Wereldkroniek*, revising the work with painstaking precision, neutered or even reversed the Herald's many outbursts against the foul and heathenish Frisians. In the new version, Pippin of Herstal merely drew up against "heathenish people": he no longer waged "fierce war on that heathenish Frisian scum and on Rabout, their duke." Willibrord's work of conversion in Friesland, similarly, was made to appear more successful than it had been in the original; and the title to Frisian independence—whose seals, the Herald had claimed, would melt like butter in the sun—had now become quite solid.[74] Now, as the (possibly) Frisian-derived patronymic of this reviser, Scheen Wissenzoon van Kerckwerf, may suggest, he probably had personal reasons for protecting the Frisians—but that is another story. What matters here is that he was driven by impulses different from the Herald's: the *Wereldkroniek* had long since lost its appeal as a call for a crusade in the north, with the goals of revenge and chivalric honor. What had inspired the original author and his patron at the court of Holland-Bavaria in the early fifteenth century had ceased to interest readers who lived in quite different circumstances in the latter part of that same century. The Bavarian chronicles were no longer anything but jaded history books. The word of honor had made way for the word of yore.

Notes

Some of the original notes have been updated and now include works published since the appearance of the Dutch edition.

I. COURT AND LITERATURE

1. See, for instance, Volmuller 1981, II, 628.

2. Willems 1843, book 6, lines 3949–52. Another Brabantine historian, Hennen of Merchtenen, explained that William V of Holland "fell into a rage, his mouth stretching from ear to ear" (Merchtenen 1896, lines 3475–76); does this phrase mean that the count was screaming mad? Filled with compassion for a compatriot, William of Hildegaersberch (see Chapter II) described the count in about 1358 as a prince "used to great honors while his life was good; may God preserve his noble blood" (LXIII/50–53).

3. The most recent account (with the appropriate primary and secondary literature) can be found in Brokken 1982, 105–8.

4. Van Foreest 1964, 165. Not all historians have a favorable opinion of Albert's statesmanship; a biography of this important ruler is currently being prepared by Dr. D.E.H. de Boer.

5. See Brokken [1979]; Van Foreest 1964, 155–64; and Blok 1885, 258–60.

6. Quoted in Jansma 1974, 64; detailed descriptions of this hall can be found in C. H. Peters 1905 and Kuyper 1984.

7. See Brokken 1984, 14–15; and Rozema 1985. Less recent but packed with important information on all aspects of court life is "'s Gravenhage onder de regering der graven uit de huizen van Holland, Henegouwen en Beijeren" 1863, 261–81. Rather romanticized, sparsely documented, but far from unrewarding is C. H. Peters 1909, 135–206. See also Calkoen 1902; Pabon 1924.

8. See Niermeyer 1951, 111–12; and particularly van Riemsdijk 1908.

9. Bumke 1979, 58–65; see also Van Oostrom 1983a, 123–24.

10. See Jappe Alberts 1984; Nijsten 1986.

11. For the Persoenresone entries in the county accounts, see Jansen 1967b, 323n.31; and Jansen 1966, 36, where the first line of the poem is given a rather odd interpretation, corrected in Pleij 1984a, 6–8. For Peter Potter's drinking song, see Chapter VII, sec. 1, below; see also the short love poem in the margin of an official document (quoted in Chapter III, sec. 1).

12. These flourishes included particularly long downstrokes twisting to the right and small dots in the capital letters. I am indebted for this observation (and also for the next one) to J. P. Gumbert.

13. The marriage ties to the Burgundian house made sure that French would remain an important medium for external contacts; consider, for instance, the French book presented to the wife of William of Oostervant (see sec. 4 below), and the fact that her generosity was praised by Christine de Pisan in the *Cité des dames*. Fabri's French poems in the *Haags liederenhandschrift* (see Chapter III, secs. 1 and 2) are further indications of this trend. In addition, French literature may well have influenced Holland-Bavarian writers (particularly through Hainaut); for the possible influence of the Condés on William of Hildegaersberch, see Chapter II, sec. 2; and on Dirk Potter, see Van Buuren 1988, n. 11.

14. For contacts between Froissart and Albert and William VI, see Verwijs 1869, vi–x. Froissart also appears in John of Blois's accounts, as "Frosset the speaker"; see Jonckbloet 1854, 644. Further evidence of the counts' ties with French is to be found in a French Bible manuscript that bore the arms of Bavaria-Hainaut; see *De librije van Filips de Goede* 1967, no. 2 (also no. 5).

15. This phenomenon is known elsewhere as well: Prevenier (1972, 57), for example, mentions that secretaries of Westphalian origin working in the Hanse office in Bruges adapted their Lower German to the West Flemish tongue and larded the result with French words in order to be understood and accepted more readily.

16. The most recent publication on the subject is Gerritsen and Schludermann 1976, which also refers to older literature relevant to our discussion. Still, the *barbarolexis* hypothesis seems to have less bearing on Holland-Bavarian literature than do dynastic and political factors; all the more intriguing are the problems posed by the Gruuthuse manuscript.

17. See H. J. Smit 1924–39, 3:220.

18. Hainaut literature still awaits systematic study; Ribard 1969 provides valuable starting points; and Janet van der Meulen, Leiden, is currently preparing a thesis on the subject.

19. See Dehaisnes 1886, 1:156–57.

20. See Sillem 1900, 224.

21. See Ribard 1969, 74–75.

22. The document is quoted in Te Winkel 1922, 99. (On dress and status, see Chapter V, sec. 2; and for a wider context, Chapter VII, sec. 2.) It is far from certain whether Te Winkel is right to claim that the person concerned can be identified with the one who had received a grant of eight pounds from William III six years earlier. That William IV patronized Dutch- as well as French-speaking authors is borne out by text no. 42 in the *Haagse liederenhandschrift* ("A piteous plaint"), where "Lady Bountiful" is made to praise the late William IV in lines 470–89 for his generosity to "good people," including "many a poor companion"—a term often used to refer to (itinerant) professional poets.

23. The most striking result of the Middle Dutch poets' turning to patrons outside the central court in this period was the close link between Louis of Velthem and the court at Voorne; see Van Oostrom 1982, 35–38.

24. The literary and cultural life at the Blois court merits a separate study, especially now that the Blois archives have been analyzed more closely (see Schmidt-Ernsthausen 1982). A mass of literary and historical material on the Blois court was first presented in Jonckbloet 1854, app. B; see also Sillem 1900;

and Lingbeek-Schalekamp 1984, 132–34, 197–99. For an early sketch of life at the Blois court, see De Lange van Wijngaerden 1813.

25. See especially Lods 1951; the episode discussed below is referred to at greater length on page 138 of that book. My attention to the Holland-Hainaut antecedents of *Perceforest* was drawn by J. D. Janssens.

26. For an inventory based on published account entries, see Te Winkel 1922, 98; I am indebted for complementary data to T. Meder, who published the relevant entries in an appendix to his doctoral thesis in 1991.

27. See *ML* II, 706 (the commentary by the editor, Leendertz, is wide of the mark); I, 2505; and II, 4202–5; and *BD* 12/3; cf. Te Winkel 1922, 130–31; and Brinkman 1987. The German influence, incidentally, is considerably more marked in *ML* than in Potter's two other works. Was that because the *ML* is a more courtly work, or was it rather because of the difference in date, the two later works having been written during the Burgundian period? (See further Chapter VI, sec. 3; and Chapter VII, sec. 4.)

28. For a recent discussion of the count's library, see Korteweg 1984.

29. Could there also have been an influence in the opposite direction? Cases in point might have been not only Dirk of Delft's *Tafel vanden kersten ghelove*, but also Maerlant's Lower-German–tinged manuscripts *Alexanders geesten*, *Historie van Troyen*, and *Merlijn*, all dating back to about 1400. For the warm welcome given to Maerlant's work at the court of Holland-Bavaria, see Chapter VII, sec. 1.

30. See the beginning of the translated version of *De nugis curialium* in Map 1983, 2–3. Map's aphorism, incidentally, was a playful variation of Saint Augustine's famous dictum about time: "I exist in it and speak of it but what it is I know not."

31. See especially Van Riemsdijk 1908; and C. H. Peters 1909, sec. 2, of which what follows is a (slightly simplified) summary; see also H. J. Smit 1924–39, vol. 3, chap. 1.

32. Important studies on life at the Dutch-Bavarian court are Kroon 1852; Jonckbloet 1854, app. A; "'s Gravenhage onder regering der graven" 1863; Calkoen 1902; and C. H. Peters 1909. Unless stated otherwise, the following passages are based on these authors' conclusions. More recent studies of specific forms of art at court include: Tóth-Ubbens 1963 (arts and crafts and the fine arts); Lingbeek-Schalekamp 1984; and A. Janse 1986 (music). For information on newer findings, particularly with reference to literature, I am indebted to the researches of W. van Anrooij and T. Meder.

33. See Eberle 1985; and, of course, Huizinga 1919. Holland-Bavarian court authors repeatedly averred that great gentlemen had to live in great estate: for instance Hildegaersberch VII/27–31; and Dirk Potter, *ML* IV, 540–41. For Dirk of Delft, see various quotations in Chapter V, sec. 2. In a much broader context, see also Chapter VII, secs. 2 and 3.

34. See the entry in *De rekeningen van de Grafelijkheid van Holland* 1980–83, ser. 3, 80.

35. See Nijsten 1985, 138–39.

36. See Devillers 1887, 189; and Van Foreest 1965–66, 130.

37. See Blok 1885, 266.

38. I am indebted for this item to W. van Anrooij.

39. The most important study of the accounts in this sector is Tóth-Ubbens 1963, from which the following information is taken (unless otherwise specified).

40. See Devillers 1886, 480.

41. For this robe, see Guyot 1858.

42. See the entry in Devillers 1887, 196–97. For New Year presents, see Holtorf 1973; the (second version of) the *Hollandse kroniek* is linked to the custom of giving precious items as New Year presents as well: see Chapter IV, sec. 3.

43. For the golden crown of thorns, see J. Smit 1923, 20, 21–22, 37. It is a particular pity that all that is left of the magnificent tomb of Margaret, Albert's first wife, is a detailed reconstruction: see Tóth-Ubbens 1957; and Van der Klooster 1984.

44. In addition to Tóth-Ubbens 1963; and "'s Gravenhage onder de regering der graven" 1863, 298–299; see extracts from the accounts in the Netherlands State Archives, e.g., AGH 1257, fols. 47v (Albert's wife purchased "all manner of paintings and pictures") and 54r (she bought "three little paintings"); AGH 1261, fol. 107v ("three little paintings" for my lady); and AGH 1262, fols. 59v (contacts between the countess and "Dirk the painter") and 94r (the lady of Holland receiving "pictores"). I am indebted to W. van Anrooij for this information.

45. In discussing the visual arts, caution is in order, for secular art seems to have suffered heavy losses over the intervening centuries. The court also played a paramount role in commissioning magnificently illustrated manuscripts (in Haarlem and particularly in Utrecht), including the dedication copy of Dirk of Delft's *Tafel vanden kersten ghelove* (see Chapter V) and Margaret of Cleves's breviary (see sec. 4 below). For the fine arts at the court of Holland-Bavaria, see also Kurz 1956; and the discussion in Chapter III, sec. 4, and Chapter VII, secs. 1 and 4. On the enjoyment that the rulers of Holland found in music, see above all Pietzsch 1969; Lingbeek-Schalekamp 1984; and Janse 1986, on which the following discussion is chiefly based.

46. With acknowledgments to T. Meder.

47. AGH 1254, fol. 107; with grateful acknowledgments to J. G. Smit, who discovered this important entry in the accounts and made it available for publication.

48. In addition to the extracts from the accounts published in Jonckbloet 1854; "'s Gravenhage onder de regering der graven" 1863; and Tóth-Ubbens 1963, I was able to make grateful use for this section of the account entries brought to light by W. van Anrooij and T. Meder.

49. I am indebted to T. Meder for this account entry.

50. For more on this manuscript, see Gorissen 1973, 253, 441; Meiss 1974, 1:97; Marrow 1987, 298–301; and Hindman 1987, 439. In view of the considerable value of this breviary, it is almost inconceivable that it was not mentioned in the accounts, and yet no one entry can be assigned to it incontrovertibly. The book that Margaret commissioned shortly after her arrival in Holland (see the quotation in Chapter VII, sec. 3) was made too early (in 1395) to be identified

with this breviary; nor can the book by William the Confessor (see Chapter VII, secs. 1 and 3) be so identified. A more likely candidate is the book that Margaret had illuminated in 1398 by a "man from Utrecht" (again see Chapter VII, sec. 3); or could there be a connection with Dirk of Delft's first book? (Cf. Chapter V, sec. 1.)

51. See Tóth-Ubbens 1963, no. 135. Does the explicit mention of the "German" character of the book suggest that such writing was unusual during the early years of Bavarian rule? (Cf. sec. 2, above.)

52. See Bumke 1979, chap. 5; and, for Middle Dutch literature, Hogenelst and De Vries 1982.

53. See Van Foreest 1965–66, 123n.1.

54. Women's political influence was not inevitably low, however; see Crawford 1981. For good reasons, scholars also attribute a considerable influence to Margaret of Brieg, Duke Albert's first wife; see Van Foreest 1965–66, 121–22.

55. The accounts reference is at AGH 1258, fol. 50r; with acknowledgments to W. van Anrooij.

56. See Devillers 1886.

57. See Jacqueline's testament in *Codex diplomaticus neerlandicus* 1852, 176 (also 186) and 182; see also Löher 1862–69, 2:505–6; Jansen 1976, 117; and Chapter VII, sec. 4.

58. See Leupen 1981, 1975. A general analysis suggests that the Latin text (and the same is true of the following two works) is too distant from the Middle Dutch literature associated with the court of Holland-Bavaria to be treated fruitfully in this book; nevertheless, the subject merits closer investigation.

59. See the edition by the marquis de Fortia d'Urban (Guyse 1826–38). The chronicle has not yet received adequate attention; but see Wilmans 1847.

60. See Gaspar and Lyna 1937, 1:300–304.

61. For William VI, see, e.g., AGH 71, fol. 6r ("this account which my dear lord himself read over from beginning to end"); and AGH 1261, fol. 155v ("the secret letter my lord wrote himself"); with grateful acknowledgments to W. van Anrooij.

62. See further Chapter VII, sec. 4; this event is also mentioned in Jansen 1966, 69. Jansen, who calls the murder attempt "clumsy" (?), suggests that Count John probably had the habit of wetting his fingers to turn the pages. He may also have customarily kissed his prayerbook at the beginning and end of his devotions.

63. This order was placed on 1 November 1383, according to AGH 1238, fol. 137; with acknowledgments to J. G. Smit. For Utrecht as a center of North Netherlandish book illumination for ecclesiastical and temporal patrons, see Finke 1963. It is practically certain that the dedication copy of Dirk of Delft's *Tafel vanden kersten ghelove* was made in Utrecht as well; see Rickert 1949. Literary historians would do well to make a thorough study of these art-historical publications; see further Chapter VII, sec. 1.

64. The date and dedication of this incinerated book are under dispute; the most recent art-historical publications on the subject are Brand Philip 1971, excursus 1; Delaissé 1972; and Dhanens 1980, 162.

65. For Duke Albert, see the reference in Verwijs 1869, 60, to the "small chest" Albert took with him on the first Frisian campaign and in which "all manner of my lord's books were conveyed" (see also Chapter IV, sec. 4); for William VI, see the account entry concerning a payment in 1405 for "a chest for locking up my lord's books"; AGH 1259, fol. 33v (with acknowledgments to W. van Anrooij).

66. See "De bibliotheek van de kapel op het hof" 1876; and J. Smit 1923; fourteenth-century records of (liturgical) books in the court chapel are included in Lingbeek-Schalekamp 1984, 29–30. The inventory includes a manuscript of Philip of Leiden's treatise and hence introduces a factor that impedes determination of the books kept at the Hague court: namely, the possible inclusion of "old" copies handed down by earlier counts. See, for a wider context, Chapter VII, sec. 1.

67. See Nijsten 1986 (the Egmond inventory is currently being prepared for publication); Chapter III; and Matzel 1979. All three of these noble libraries, incidentally, reflect their owners' interest not only in chivalric but also in devotional literature, didactic poems, and technical manuals; much as medieval burghers did not confine their reading to edifying literature, so noblemen did not confine theirs to tales of chivalric exploits.

68. See Boehm 1982, 175.

69. See Buddingh 1843, 71–72; and Buddingh 1842, 44.

70. AGH 1262, fol. 104v (with acknowledgments to W. van Anrooij); see also "'s Gravenhage onder de regering der graven" 1863, 315.

71. This development had started as early as the thirteenth century (with Maerlant) and culminated in the ideal of a prince versed in the humanities—an ideal prevalent during the reign of the Emperor Maximilian I. For this trend, see Müller 1982; for an introduction to the earlier developments, see Van Oostrom 1985a. Orme 1983 arrives at much the same conclusions for the English court in about 1400.

72. See *BD* 124–25; and *ML* I, 2792, 3282; II, 162, 200, 2665; III, 473, 1020; and IV, 1458. Is it an accident that most of the writing was done by women and that the only man of whom Potter said "Rhyming and writing he could do" (I, 2792) seems to have been a *rara avis*? The *Hollandse kroniek* calls Zweder uter Loo, the dean of Utrecht, "a man of the world, for he could neither sing nor read" (fol. 113v).

73. On the Latin background to the writings of Dirk Potter, see particularly Van Buuren 1979.

74. For more on this subject, see Chapter VI, secs. 1 and 3. On his travels to England, Potter probably spoke French; when traveling eastward, he was able to hold his own in the Hollandish-German "intermediate language" that left its imprint on his literary work as well.

75. See, for example, *BD* 67/6–8. Some knowledge of Latin, however, could not have been uncommon among worldly courtiers, even outside private prayer and the liturgy: see, e.g., the Latin song L2 in the Leiden *chansonnier* (see under Martinus Fabri and Hugo Boy in the Note on Editions in the frontmatter).

76. For Tristan, see *ML* II, 3616–19, 4206–8; for Troy, I, 3107; II, 1967, 2169,

3869–70; for Perceval, I, 1296; II, 1204 (remarkably, Potter attributes the discovery of the Grail to Perceval; was he familiar with a Chrétien continuation rather than with the *Prose Lancelot?*); for Reynard, I, 1841; for *Titurel* and Neidhard, see sec. 2 above. Potter's references to epic writing ought, incidentally, to keep us from thinking that interest in romantic literature had dried up at the court of Holland; see further Chapter VII, sec. 1.

77. See particularly *ML* I, 2469–2508 (note the variant in L—was the editor of this manuscript unable to place his literary heroines properly?), I, 3239–53; II, 1675–90; and, more modestly, II, 3869–76 and 4202–13. Even if Potter included these lists partly to exhibit his own book learning, they nevertheless presuppose that his readers were reasonably familiar with the books in question. The matter-of-course way in which the extant remains of songs by the court composers Fabri and Boy (see Chapter III, sec. 1) refer to Orpheus and Pygmalion, and in which the related Utrecht fragments refer to Jason, Helen, and Troy, points in the same direction.

78. The same is true of the archives of other courts: see J. Vale 1982, 51.

79. Lingbeek-Schalekamp 1984, 197. The same accounts also mention two ducal minstrels in 1361; see Jonckbloet 1854, 618, 619, 632. The meaning of the term *minstrel*, incidentally, is not clear-cut: the concept changed during the Bavarian period from singer-musician to pure instrumentalist.

80. See Jonckbloet 1854, 620, 652; Lingbeek-Schalekamp 1984, 177.

81. Jonckbloet 1854, 605–6.

82. See ibid., 605, 617, 619, 620, 621, 622, 623. Most likely, the *catridder*, in full harness (see ibid., 623), was dressed up as a cat (and made hilarious leaps?), while his colleagues, dressed as "wild knights," tried to frighten the assembled table company by their outrageous behavior. Did the "wild wench Hillekijn" (ibid., 607) perform a similar act, or was hers a more naughty turn?

83. The most important primary sources are listed in Jonckbloet 1854, app. A; and Lingbeek-Schalekamp 1984; the principal studies on the subject are Te Winkel 1922, 49–102; Pleij 1977; and U. Peters 1983, chap. 3, sec. 1. For the most recent discussion and extensive original material, see Meder 1991.

84. See "'s Gravenhage onder de regering der graven" 1863, 316. Or was more than singing involved here? Van Foreest 1965–66, 125n.1 mentions an "Adelaide of Houthuizen who as early as March 1393, less than six months after the murder [of Adelaide of Poelgeest], had an affair with Albert"; see further Chapter III, sec. 4.

85. See the account entries in Jonckbloet 1854, 509; and the commentary in *Middelnederlandsch Woordenboek* 2:271 (with acknowledgments to H. Pleij).

86. For these quotations, see Lingbeek-Schalekamp 1984, 172, 169.

87. See Jonckbloet 1854, 616. The carnival entertainments provided at the court, incidentally, are a story in themselves; see "'s Gravenhage onder de regering der graven" 1863, 319, 330–31; and Chapter VII, sec. 1.

88. See "'s Gravenhage onder de regering der graven" 1863, 317; q.v. also for our next quotation, which is discussed in U. Peters 1983, 199n.83.

89. See Hummelen 1977, 239–41; an important discussion can also be found in U. Peters 1983, 198–206. The only unequivocal reference to the performance

of plays at the court of Holland-Bavaria occurs in Dirk of Delft: on Mid-Lent Sunday "the clerks in many monasteries were wont to perform plays . . . in winter and in summer. And the winter is bleak and terribly raw and the summer green and merrily fresh . . . but the winter with all its banes must make way and bow out. Then doth summer appear and quicken all our spirits" ("S" I/35–41).

90. See Lievens 1964. Because Augustijnken, a very small number of whose writings has come down to us, is mentioned not only in the Blois accounts but also in those of the county of Holland, he deserves more attention in this book than I have been able to pay him; his work is the subject of a separate study currently being undertaken by A. M. J. van Buuren.

91. See Mundschau 1972, 88; and the entry mentioned at the end of Chapter IV, sec. 4.

II. WILLIAM OF HILDEGAERSBERCH

1. For the Adelaide of Poelgeest affair, see Jansen 1982, 314, which includes references to the most important older texts.

2. See Van Heeringen 1983, 113.

3. For the relevant details, see *Rekeningen van de Grafelijkheid van Holland* 1980–83, ser. 3, 80–83, 100–102.

4. The following quote is from Meder 1991, 553; cf. Lingbeek-Schalekamp 1984, 180–81. The entry seems more detailed than the quotation in Jonckbloet 1855, 608, on which Van Oostrom 1986a, 64–65, is based.

5. In that case, the final lines of the poem (169–74) might indicate that such changes had already been made. In general, it must be borne in mind that the textual form in which William's poems appear in the (later) manuscripts can differ markedly from the form in which they were originally recited, the latter being subject to variation as well. Flexibility was one of the tricks of the trade of the didactic poet/reciter.

6. For more detailed documentation, see Meder 1991, which contains, in particular, a much fuller account of Hildegaersberch and his work than could be fit into the framework of the present book.

7. See Wailes 1975.

8. For statements in the first person singular, see poems CXIX, LXVI, XLVI, LXXXVII, CXIII, XII, CXV, XLII, and XXIII. The problem of the autobiographical features in such poetry is examined in Wenzel 1983.

9. See Ribard 1969, 1981; and U. Peters 1983, 189–90; cf. Chapter I, sec. 2, above. Hainaut literature was, however, more courtly in tone than William's poetry.

10. See the introduction to *Gedichten* (cited in full in the Note on Editions); Jonckbloet's view can be found there, p. xix; cf. De Vooys 1939, 266.

11. See, e.g., XXXII, LXVIII/15–23, LXXIV/12–26.

12. See, e.g., XIII/73, XX/17, XXII/67, XXXIX/28, XXXVIII/36, and prologue to LXXXI.

13. See, e.g., the prologues to XXI, XXXIII, and LXI; see also LXXXVI/16–17. Was William perhaps thinking of Dirk of Delft? Cf. Chapter V and, more generally, the beginning of Chapter VII, sec. 3.

14. See Ragotzky 1980a; and Franz 1974, para. 4.2.

15. See especially poem LXXXIII.

16. See poem LVI, discussed in the previous section; for a more detailed treatment of these problems, see Meder 1991.

17. There may, however, be a different explanation, namely that William was making a distinction between the small presents he could expect of the lords and the great favors for which he depended on his sovereign lord.

18. After having been disdained for years, this type of author seems to have become the chosen subject of many medievalists. Recent books in this field (and ones also relevant to studies of Hildegaersberch and his Middle Dutch fellow writers) include Lämmert 1970; Wachinger 1973; and Franz 1974.

19. See LXXXIII/55, where William is referred to as a "free master."

20. See Wachinger 1973, 116–20, 303–7; and Ribard 1981, 279.

21. See the prologues to VII and LXIV, and also XXI/12–17; see further sec. 3 below.

22. See, e.g., IV/533–35, XIX/196, XXI/18–20, XXXIII/88, LVIII/68, LXXXI/269, and XCIII/21–24.

23. See Franz 1974, 68–77; and Lämmert 1970, 142–44.

24. See Thum 1981, esp. 159–61.

25. Ibid., 164. It may be that a legal aspect came into play here as well: the chance that William would have to answer legally for his blunt criticisms of named persons. G. M. de Meyer (Schalkhaar) has drawn my attention to the repeated mention in medieval lawbooks of convictions for unduly severe attacks on the magistrature. The court of Holland-Bavaria, too, is known to have passed sentences for "discourteous words"; see "'s Gravenhage onder de regering der graven" 1863, 259.

26. See the prologues to VII, XXXI, XLI, LXIV, CXII, and CXVIII.

27. See also XXXIII/4–5; and Van Oostrom 1984b, on which the following remarks, too, are based, although that publication dwells more on the tactical than on the aesthetic dimension of the method.

28. The link between poetry and history has been stressed earlier by Jonckbloet and, later, by Verwijs and Te Winkel; the most recent of these discussions can be found in te Winkel 1922, 106–7. I am indebted for complementary information to R. van Oosten (Utrecht). There are several other indications of the special links between William and Leiden. For example, two of his appearances before the Guelders court took place in Leiden; see the discussion of poem LXXXIII in the introduction to *Gedichten*, xv–xvi; and Meder 1991.

29. Remarkably, even Philip of Leiden used this method to introduce a delicate political discussion; see Leupen 1981, 97.

30. For the "revelation of the truth" as William's self-appointed task, see XXIV/19 and CXII/11; for public "plaints," see, e.g., LXX/III. More generally, see Thum 1980, 1981; and Ragotzky 1981, para. 7.2.

31. For "censure" as a poetic duty, see XXIV/18 and LXXXII/5; for "counsel," see LXIII/168 (quoted here), LIX/157, LXXXVI/123–26, and XCVI/278.

32. See, e.g., LXXXI/488 and CVI/6.

33. For his own opinion, see XXXII/74, the prologue to XXXIII, and LIV/40. The word *dichten* (writing poetry) often occurs in association with *leren*

(teaching): see the prologue to LXXVIII, CXI/12, LXVIII/30–33, and also the epilogue of "Van feeste van hylic" (On the wedding feast), quoted in sec. 1 above.

34. See XXXIX/30; LXXIII/242, 4–5, 33; LXII/30–32; XCVI/91; XI/58–59; and generally, see Chapter VII, sec. 2.

35. See particularly his outburst against "the peasant" in "Vander drierehande staet der werelt" (On the three estates of the world; XCVII/344–77, but cf. line 321). William's ambivalent view of the third estate warrants a special study: on the one hand he condemns the social ferment that manifests itself within the upwardly mobile bourgeoisie, but on the other hand, in some of his poems (II, X, XXVII, LI/17) he sympathizes with town and trade. In this context, William's (alleged) contacts with Leiden are interesting (see sec. 2 above), as are his (rare?) appearances before municipal leaders (see sec. 1).

36. See Van Oostrom 1984b.

37. The interpretation of this fable, incidentally, is far from straightforward: to what extent is the dog an ambiguous, or even negative, figure? For related fables about dogs, see poems XLIV and XLII. In Dirk Potter's work, too, dogs have more than one symbolic meaning: see, on the one hand, *ML* III/103 and, on the other, *BD* 67–68. According to Köhn 1979, 230–31n.10, the court-dog symbol has a rich tradition.

38. See Van Oostrom 1983b, 20–21; Franz 1974, 72; Ribard 1981, 283.

39. See, particularly, Wackers 1986, 73–90.

40. See poems XXXIX, XLII, LV, LXX, LXXIII, and XCVI.

41. See poems X, LXXII, and CXVII.

42. See XXI/154–75 and XLVII/101.

43. See also LXVIII/116–24. The "invisibility" of injustice was probably ensured by bribes (see below).

44. See also XI, 61–64; and XLIX/198–205.

45. See LXVI/37–43, LXIII/137–38, LXXIII, XVII/16–17, and CII/10–11.

46. See XIX/97–112, XLVII, CII, LXII, CXVIII/191–93, and XXXVI.

47. See LXIII/139–40, LXIX/64–65, XI, and CXII/109–12.

48. See, e.g., LI, VII/82, and X; and, more generally, U. Peters 1983, 261–63. See also Chapter VI, note 76.

49. See LII, LXIII, XCIII, XLI/93–112, XL/78–83, CVII/58–60, and CX. Hildegaersberch—once again—was not the only didactic poet to place himself above the parties; see Lämmert 1970, 87, 167–71. He expected impartiality from the sovereign (CXVII/55–62, LVI/103–5), and we know that Duke Albert did aim to act accordingly; see Van Oostrom 1984b, 56.

50. The fact that William never mentions party names may also serve as a refutation of Brokken 1982, 200, who concludes from William's failure to mention the parties by name in his famous "Hoe deerste partyen in Hollant quamen" (LXIII) that such names were not in vogue before 1389 (the *terminus ante quem* of this poem).

51. Cf. Brokken 1982, 216–17.

52. See Cuvelier 1921; and Bos-Rops 1982; see further the discussion in Chapter VI, sec. 4.

53. The problems of a money economy as a destabilizing factor for the court's supremacy are more complex than can be shown in this work; see Ragotzky 1980b and, more generally, Chapter VII, sec. 2.

54. See Hermesdorf 1980, 139; and Berents 1985, 169.

55. The decision-making processes at the court of Holland became increasingly complex as the balance of social forces shifted: see H. J. Smit 1924–39, 3:220–31.

56. See, e.g., VIII/2–24, the prologue to XI, XXXI/120–25, XXXIX/39–53, XLVII/22–25, LXII/26, and the prologue to LXIII; also, more generally, Chapter VII, sec. 2.

57. In his well-known "Hoe deerste partyen in Hollant quamen" (LXIII/1–3), he points out that only one generation earlier, that is under William III, the county lived in peace and amity: "Great wonders may they tell you now who whilom were young bloods." Elsewhere, however, William seems to be singing the praises of a less settled past.

58. For William's disparagement of artistic malaise, see, e.g., XXIV/8–20, XLI/1–5, the prologue to LXIV, and LXXXIII; also Chapter VII, sec. 2.

59. William dwelled at far greater length on the internal dissensions than he did on the schism, however; see Van Buuren 1987a.

60. See also lines 108–13 and XXXI/83–86, quoted below.

61. According to Duinhoven 1977, 109–14, this passage contains several nonoriginal verses; the basic tenor, however, remained unchanged.

62. See, e.g., poems XXI, XL, and LXIV.

63. See De Boer 1978. The gap between literature and reality may be gathered from the fact that Hildegaersberch made very few references to even so important a historical disaster as the plague.

64. See, e.g., poems CVIII and CXIII.

65. See, e.g., poems CXV, CIX, XX, LIX, CIV.

66. See, e.g., poems XIII and LIX.

67. See Chapter V, sec. 4, and Chapter VI, secs. 3–4, and the secondary literature mentioned there.

68. Cf. poem CXVII. William of Hildegaersberch's idea of the good prince was influenced by what could be called "bourgeois" ideas; see Hugenholtz 1959, 164. See also William's conception of the "common good" and the relevant literature mentioned in sec. 3, above.

69. See LXXIV/445–48 and LXXXI/472–73.

70. See, e.g., XXV, LXIV, LXIX, LXX, LXXXIX, XCII, and XCVIII.

71. See also the conclusion of poem XXXVII; was the prayer for pardon and reform meant for the clergy in particular?

72. For other complaints about the failing priesthood, see, e.g., XLVII/42–46 and XCVII/253–58.

73. See particularly the last chapter of Stackmann 1958; Lämmert 1970, 126–32, 177–82; and Heinzle 1984, 29–30, 128–31. Asselbergs 1957 provides a starting point for Middle Dutch. A closer study of the relationship between this type of poetry and the more popular devotional forms is needed. It is characteristic of Axters (1953) that, in his history of piety in the Netherlands, he discussed Hil-

degaersberch under the heading of "Lay piety on the fringes of the church." The influence of this type of sermon on lay circles (even among the elite) may well have equaled that of Dirk of Delft; see Chapter V, sec. 4.

74. Even in the original recitation setting, William's poems must have made fairly high demands on the courtiers' powers of comprehension; see Lievens 1964, 224, on Augustijnken.

75. See, e.g., LVI/166, quoted in Chapter II, sec. 1; see also XII/45, XXXII/ 76–80, and IV/626.

76. Cf. LXVIII/23 and LXXIII/3.

III. THE HAGUE SONG MANUSCRIPT

1. Needless to say, the fact that much of the lyrical poetry is lost forever is equally true of other courts; it is no accident that nowhere is the Middle Dutch literary tradition more defective than in the lyrical sphere. See Boffey 1983; and Wilkins 1983.

2. See the splendid edition by Van Biezen and Gumbert (listed in the Note on Editions) from which many passages and data below have been taken; see A. Janse 1986 for the location of Fabri at Albert's court.

3. This profession seems to have changed during the late fourteenth century from poet/singer/musician to instrumentalist; see Te Winkel 1922, chap. 26; and U. Peters 1976, 242–43 (which makes finer distinctions than U. Peters 1983, 177n.17).

4. See Koppmann 1877 (here quoted with emendations); I am indebted to W. van Anrooij for drawing my attention to this obscure publication.

5. See the entries in Jonckbloet 1854, 600 (2×), 602. Research by T. Meder has revealed six other mentions of Jonkheer (alias Master Peter) van der Minne in the Holland accounts.

6. See the entry in Jonckbloet 1854, 620; his appendix contains several other mentions of singers in the service of noble ladies, for instance the ladies of Guelders and Voorne.

7. For a summary, see the introduction to the Hague Song Manuscript (*HLH*; referenced in full in the Note on Editions). The Rhenish background stressed by Glier 1981 may apply to some of the texts (see Ramondt 1944; and Rheinheimer 1975), but I consider it less likely to relate to the manuscript as a whole.

8. See Deschamps 1972, no. 42; and *De verluchte handschriften en incunabelen van de Koninklijke Bibliotheek* 1985, no. 117.

9. For the Breda Nassaus, see Jansen 1979; for their library, see Korteweg 1984 (the most recent contribution), as well as Chapter I, sec. 4; Chapter V, sec. 4; and Chapter VII, sec. 4. The links between the Nassaus and the court of Holland-Bavaria were very close in about 1400. According to one entry in the accounts (for which I am indebted to W. van Anrooij), for example, Count William IV and the *joncheer* of Nassau agreed on a joint plan of campaign; messages between both were conveyed by no one less than Bavaria Herald (see Chapter IV).

10. See Nijland 1896, 138; Introduction to *HLH*, 1; Rheinheimer 1975, 22. If

we trace the family tree of the Polanen-Duvenvoordes back to ca. 1340, we come across the fascinating figure of Herman de Bonghere, minstrel to William of Duvenvoorde and born in the county of Loon—that is, in the Rhine/Meuse area (see Lieftinck 1965, 64). Clearly the links between the aristocracy of Holland and that of the eastern regions had grown closer even before the arrival of the Bavarian dynasty; see Ramondt 1944.

11. See Van Buuren 1985a; for further examples see nos. 78–79 in *HLH*. Often the "independent unit" of this sort of poetry was not a whole poem but a separate verse; see Willaert 1986; Petzsch 1971; and nos. 29 and 41 in the manuscript under discussion.

12. For a telling example, see Willaert 1986. Winkelman 1990 differs on some of the conclusions presented here; several detailed interpretations of the German-tinged texts in the song manuscript have been adjusted accordingly.

13. Van Mierlo [1949], 16.

14. Verdam (1890, 275) coined the phrase "dog Middle High German"; see also Kloeke 1943, 77. More recently, Gerritsen and Schludermann (1976) have opened up new perspectives on this linguistic phenomenon by approaching it from a stylistic-rhetorical standpoint; this approach complements the functional-historical one used in this book. See Chapter I, sec. 2.

15. Feudal love metaphor, though not very dominant in the *Haags liederenhandschrift*, is nevertheless present: e.g., 40A/14, 50/23–25, 59/III, 102/43–54, and 113/6. More generally, see Warning 1979, 141.

16. Poems in which the idea of homage to women is central include nos. 18, 50, 65, 80, and 89.

17. See, e.g., poem no. 26, discussed above, and also I/128–31, II/52–53, 52/6–8, 54/90–92, 89, and 95/6–7.

18. Cf. 50/34 and 84/v. 9.

19. For the portrayal of women, see, e.g., poems 9, 50, and 86.

20. Characteristic poems portraying men include nos. 28, 33, 38, 49, 89, and 108.

21. On this issue, see the important book by Schnell 1985.

22. See, e.g., 60/55–56 and poem 51, discussed in sec. 3 below.

23. Cf. 4B, 43A, and II/61.

24. See II/37 and 10/21–28, from which it also appears that the similarity in character is determined by the planets and by the partners' constitution. Dirk Potter, too, was familiar with this view, which he proffered in the name of Plato (*BD* 14/14–16; cf. 125/11–12) and, elsewhere, of Aristotle (*BD* 80/9–10). For medieval views on "natural" love and its causes, see Schnell 1985, which contains a wealth of references to older sources.

25. See, e.g., the idyllic poem no. 59 and the meetings dreamed of in nos. 56 and 65.

26. See, e.g., nos. 9 and 80.

27. See, e.g., poems 33, 45 (quoted in the next section), 48, 57C, 70, 72, and 108.

28. See, e.g., 24*, the conclusion to 59, 64, 74/15–17, and 100; and, more generally, Chapter VII, sec. 2.

29. See, e.g., the conclusion to 60, 63/78–85, the conclusion to 86, and 100.

30. See, e.g., poem 26 (discussed above) and 59/105–8, the conclusion to 60, 87, and 98/197–206. Interesting, in this context, is also 20/vv. 39–41, in which the lady advises her lover to pretend that he is sadder than he really is so as to mislead outsiders (cf. 1/v. 38 and, by contrast, 98/134–35).

31. See, e.g., 2, the conclusion to 47, 49, and 69.

32. See, e.g., 25, 48/13–16, 105/1–8. Still, the urge to bold action inspired by love creates a fresh problem for the lovers: they must part and miss each other (or be unfaithful) while the hero is away fighting in foreign lands (see nos. 25, 27, and 92). According to Brunner 1978, 123, 136, the lovers' physical separation only became a stock theme in the later minnesongs; in the *Haags liederenhandschrift* it is associated (e.g., 27/62 and 92/21) with the Prussian (and Frisian?) campaigns (see Chapter IV, sec. 4).

33. In addition to the conclusion of the poem quoted above, see 34, 67/136–41, and 4B (repeated as 43B).

34. See Warning 1979, 159. On the development of the honor concept (which, as we saw in Chapter II, sec. 3, was also important to Hildegaersberch) in the *HLH*, see also the discussion of poem 19 in the next section; on honor as a dominant theme in Holland-Bavarian court literature as a whole, see particularly Chapter VII, sec. 2.

35. See, e.g., poems 33, 47, 57C, 72, 102, and 108.

36. See section 2 above. Other poems with a feminine viewpoint are nos. 25, 64, 88, and 104. The manner in which such poems were "executed" is an interesting question: were they presented by women reciters/singers? Women artists are known from the Holland-Bavarian accounts (though they constitute a small minority): for examples, see Chapter I, sec. 4.

37. Cases in point are a number of acrostics (see Willaert 1986), the poem (no. 62) complaining about Clara discussed in the previous section, and some allegorical verse riddles that apparently referred to specific situations, for instance nos. 51 (to be discussed below) and 102*.

38. A telling example is poem 52, discussed in the previous section. Further examples include nos. 50, 86, 96, and 113.

39. For another example, see no. 87; cf. Pfeffer 1985. Elsewhere in Holland-Bavarian court literature, too, interest in sayings, proverbs, and the like was rife: Hildegaersberch and Potter used them frequently, while the Herald included several in his *Kladboek* (Jotter). A closer investigation is needed, however—for instance of possible links with the reception of the (pseudo-)Cato or with chivalric devices.

40. For further examples, see the conclusions to nos. 60 and 102 and, in a sense, also 111 (discussed in section 4 below).

41. See, e.g., poems 39, 54, 83, 88, 114, and 115.

42. The following remarks require an apology to specialists: the frame of this book does not allow us to enter into the problems of allegory in the *Haags liederenhandschrift* in nearly as great detail as a true professional study demands. J. Flach is currently writing a thesis on the subject.

43. This extensive use of allegory seems to be one of the most striking "modern" features of the manuscript: during the Middle Ages, courtly love po-

etry changed not so much in conception as in execution (see Schnell 1985), thanks particularly to the increasing use of allegory. See also Brunner 1978, 128.

44. See Blank 1970, 54–104.

45. See the important study by Jauss [1968] 1977, para. 8.

46. See, e.g., nos. 7, 17, 21, 22, 34, 42, 67, 87, and 98.

47. See Glier 1971, 278. The systematic approach is not necessarily linked to personification; see, e.g., nos. 39 and 54. According to Glier, the didactic tendency in the *minnereden* (amorous address) genre is particularly marked in the *Haags liederenhandschrift*. See further Chapter VII, sec. 2.

48. See, e.g., nos. 22, 87, and 114 (combinations of symbolic and personification allegories) and 17, 90, 101, 102, 102*, 103, and 111, in addition to the examples about to be discussed. (It appears that this allegorical type was used more and more frequently toward the end of the manuscript.)

49. The requisite source, a poem, does, in fact, seem to exist in Middle Dutch literature: the Van Hulthem manuscript, for instance, includes "Den hoet van minnen," a poem in which the allegorical wreath of virtue worn by the ideal woman is made from six flowers; see the version in *Vaderlandsch Museum* 1 (1855): 384–86.

50. This fact is stressed in Jauss [1968] 1977, para 5.

51. See Ohly [1970] 1977.

52. What we have here is a form of satire designed for the delight and appreciation of "insiders": the very playful character of courtly literature demands that the strict reins of courtly adoration be relaxed from time to time. See section 4 below; and, more generally, Neumeister 1969. Veldeke already made use of such courtly self-ridicule.

53. See particularly Willaert 1984 and Rierink 1989. The remarkable feature of the *Haags liederenhandschrift* in this connection is that it was obviously a collection of poems contributed by *many* writers. Their number before Gruuthuse is under dispute, but the evidence suggests that it was small; Hadewijch's was, of course, a lone voice.

54. See the important article by Peters [1980].

55. For rhyming and metrical schemes, see the notes in the Kossmann edition; for acrostics, Willaert 1986; for wordplay, for instance, 53*[A], the concluding verse to 62, 109, and 110.

56. Stutterheim (1967) was the first to appreciate the ambiguous character of the poem; earlier scholars simply read it as a straightforward piece (e.g. Heeroma as late as 1968; cf. Stutterheim 1969). The method, incidentally, was widespread in courtly poetry: see not only Van Buuren 1985a for other Middle Dutch examples; but also Stengel and Vogt 1956, 205–6; and Stevens 1961, 162.

57. Nijland 1896, 142.

58. See Jansen 1979; for Joanna as the possible recipient of the manuscript, see Nijland 1896, 138.

59. For a full account, see Tóth-Ubbens 1964–65.

60. For an early account, see "'s Gravenhage onder de regering der graven" 1863, 276; cf. Van Foreest 1965–66, 124; and *Rekeningen van de Grafelijkheid van Holland* 1983, 81.

61. For more details about this lady and about the others discussed below, see Van Foreest 1965–66, 124–25.

62. See ibid., 124. For bathing facilities at the Holland-Bavarian court, see C. H. Peters 1909, 165–66; and H. Janse 1980, 16.

63. As so often, William's words were carefully chosen: adultery was the result not only of personal desire (*wille*), but also of the thirst for honor—that is, for a reputation as a great lover (see Chapter VII, sec. 2 for a more detailed discussion).

64. See also Chapter V, sec. 2. This antipathy is borne out by the fact that Dirk of Delft, for instance, was anything but sympathetic to the children of adulterous unions: "God scourges these children so that they become twisted and bad, shed their good qualities, turn into thieves and murderers, die a terrible death, become a shame and a disgrace unto this world, their family and standing suffering great humiliation" (*W* XXXII/489–93).

65. See Mathew 1968, chap. 14.

66. The following remarks are based on Green 1980, 115–34; Green 1983; Stevens 1961, chaps. 8–10; U. Peters 1972, [1980]; Neumeister 1969; Liebertz-Grün 1977, 113–21; Kleinschmidt 1976. Huizinga 1919 (chap. 4)—not surprisingly—treated the courtly lover as a *homo ludens*.

67. See Green 1980, 120–22; Poirion 1965, para. 1.3; basic data in Straub 1961; and Potvin 1886. See also Bozzolo et al. 1982.

68. For this drawing, see Kurz 1956; Van Luttervelt 1957; and Ferbeek 1985.

69. See Chapter VI, sec. 2; and "'s Gravenhage onder de regering der graven" 1863, 280–81.

70. For this print, see Van Luttervelt 1957 (highly speculative); and Vignau Wilberg-Schuurman 1983, 7–8. *The Small Love Garden* by the same master must also be mentioned in this context—again, see Vignau Wilberg-Schuurman 1983.

71. See "'s Gravenhage onder de regering der graven" 1863, 317, from which the next example is taken as well.

72. See ibid., 330, from which the next example is taken as well; see also Chapter VII, sec. 1.

73. Nos. L3 and L5, respectively, in the Gumbert/Van Biezen edition. For the literary genre of medieval New Year's greetings and their folkloristic background, see Holtorf 1973.

74. See Sarfatij 1984; and Winkelman 1986. The sayings carved into the leather slippers, too, seem to have been taken straight from courtly literature: "Love makes me wander; ever glad yet ever sad" (see sec. 2 above). We also know of an entry in the Holland-Bavarian court accounts that fits in well with the above remarks: it appears that Albert of Bavaria and Adelaide of Poelgeest presented *scaloedsen* (slippers) to each other (see Van Foreest 1965–66, 130n.6).

75. See U. Peters 1972, which contains further bibliographical material. In the same context, mention must also be made of the courtly parlor game "Le roi qui ne ment" (the Middle Dutch *koningsspel*, or king's game), most recently discussed in Green 1990. This type of text is not represented in the *HLH* but can be found in a manuscript linked to the court of Holland-Bavaria, namely *Van vrouwen ende van minnen* (Of ladies and of love) (see Chapter VII, sec. 1).

76. In addition to the poem about to be discussed, see also 92, 93, and the prologue of 110. Dirk Potter's *ML* III, 418–42, is part of the same tradition, as well: the narrator introduces a love problem with "Now shall a question I you ask" and "answers" it with "This question shall I never solve." Was that perhaps the opening of a lively group discussion in Potter's intimate circles (see Chapter VI)?

77. For examples of joy-giving women in *HLH*, see sec. 2 above, to which the following can be added (among many others): 20/v. 43, 42/514–21, 48/21–24, 63/95–98, 88/28–32, and 96/12–13. See also the important contribution in Willaert 1984, para 2.3.

78. See Schnell 1985, 124.

79. For outbursts against the villagers in *HLH*, see also 18*; for "good society," see, e.g., 87/297, 99/119, 100/62, and 102/40. It is remarkable that the last-named formula should also be Hildegaersberch's favorite epithet for his public; see Van Oostrom 1984a, 71n.29. The term also occurs in official sources and merits further investigation.

80. For the prominent role of women in courtly culture, see Liebertz-Grün 1977, 118–19; Chapter I, secs. 3–4; and Chapter VII, sec. 3.

81. See, e.g., 52/16 (and other poems quoted in sec. 2) and 109/v. 13; it is also characteristic of the *HLH* (and the genre as a whole) that women are so often presented as morally superior to men (for instance in poem no. 66, discussed in section 2) and that the personifications of the feminine sex always have a positive connotation (with the ambivalent Venus as a special case).

82. See Steinhausen 1899, 5; cf. Nijsten 1986.

83. See Leupen 1975, 196.

IV. BAVARIA HERALD

1. This anecdote is discussed in Jansen 1982, 314–16; Verwijs 1869, xiii–xxv; Brill 1876, 48–49.

2. For further information on heralds in the Middle Ages see Wagner 1956; Keen 1981, 1984; U. Peters 1976; and Van Anrooij 1986a,b, on which the following remarks are based.

3. For these entries in the accounts, see, respectively, Jonckbloet 1854, 599, 602; Pietsch 1966, 169; Jonckbloet 1854, 603 (2×), 598, 604; and Beelaerts van Blokland 1933, 3.

4. For recent studies of Bavaria Herald see Van Anrooij 1986a,b (where references to the older literature can also be found); Nijsten 1986; and especially Van Anrooij 1990.

5. This event was entered in the accounts on 5 December 1405 (AGH 1260, fol. 103v) and was discovered by W. van Anrooij. See also Chapter VII, sec. 3.

6. See particularly Coenen van 's Gravesloot 1875; cf. sec. 4 below.

7. See Van Anrooij 1988.

8. Muller Fz. 1885; the following quotations are taken from pages 109 and 3, respectively.

9. Ibid., 31.

10. See Guenée 1980, 212.

11. The variant of the manuscript of the *Wereldkroniek* (*WK*) kept in the Museum Meermanno, and its prologue, published in Van Vloten 1851, 122–23, merit special mention: "this Jacob van Maerlant hath joined into German rhymes from fair Latin histories, but here it is offered in prose." Pending further analysis, this variant must be considered a secondary source.

12. For the Hercules passage, see below; for Moses, compare *WK* 8v with *Alexanders geesten* III, 690–702.

13. See Verbij-Schillings 1987, on which much of the preceding and following comments are based.

14. Muller Fz. 1885, 3, 28. Beelaerts van Blokland (1933, 7) went one step further still: he called the *Wereldkroniek* a "compilation of the worst kind."

15. This view has recently gained ground in assessments of Old French and Middle High German compilation-chronicles as well; see Kusternig 1982, 33–34; Guenée 1980, 214; and Ott 1985.

16. He was, however, interested in martyrs (see, e.g., *WK* 44v–46r): was that because they shed their blood and could therefore be considered predecessors of the crusaders? A similar interest in martyrology was rife in the Teutonic Order, whose crusading spirit the Herald shared; see Richert 1978; and sec. 4 below.

17. Modern research lays considerable emphasis on medieval historiography as *Gegenwartsdeutung* (interpretation of current affairs); see Wenzel 1980. (It is open to question whether *modern* historiography takes a fundamentally different approach . . . with acknowledgments to T. Anbeek.)

18. See, e.g., the addition of this adjective to the sources given in *WK* 14v and 19r, and the many other qualifications in the passages dealing with "this old and fair state, its noble king and noble race." No less automatically, the Herald ascribes to the Frisians (on whom more below) such pejorative descriptions as "evil" and "foul."

19. See, e.g., the telling passage in *WK* 15v–16r, taken partly from the *Spiegel historiael* I, bk. 2, chap. 19.

20. The destruction of noble Troy puzzled many medieval writers: why did God permit it? Dirk Potter, too, seems to have wrestled with this problem, and came up with a secondary rationalization that I have been unable to discover in any other text: "for the populace there [i.e., in Troy] was too crowded and the rest of the world sparsely populated, so that it was necessary for them to be scattered over the wide world" (*BD* 97/14–16).

21. See Verbij-Schillings 1987, 46; fresh data on the sources of the Herald's Hercules story were presented by J. van der Hulst at a recent seminar.

22. The Herald's sources were the *Spiegel historiael* (III, bk. 8, chap. 89, lines 39–68) and the *Rijmkroniek van Vlaanderen* (Rhymed chronicle of Flanders; Kausler 1840, lines 19–26); cf. the short Flemish rhymed chronicle in his own hand, MS. 131 G 37. The coat of arms described (the Herald's own addition) is that of "Old Flanders." (With grateful acknowledgments to W. van Anrooij and J. Verbij-Schillings.)

23. In addition to the case of Charles Martel discussed below, see also 24r, 32r, 43r, and 61v; cf. Verbij-Schillings 1987. Characteristically, pay is the only form in which "bourgeois" money is mentioned in this chivalric chronicle.

24. See Verbij-Schillings 1987, 53; Martinus Polonus himself had nothing to say about the boastful "knights' Latin" used in the veterans' home.

25. See, e.g., 35r and 44v. The attention the *WK* pays to burial is remarkable: see, e.g., 15v, 33r, 37v, 41v, 43v, 48v, 51r, 52r, and 55r. This undoubtedly has to do with the belief that a close link exists between an honorable life and an honorable burial; the same link is also stressed in the *Hollandse kroniek* (*HK*; see sec. 3) and played a role in the Frisian wars.

26. See, e.g., 20r, 50v, 67v, 78r, and 78v. Was this fascination perhaps connected with the liturgical ritual of Duke Albert's Order of Saint Anthony (see sec. 4), on which Keen (1984, 196) has cast a most interesting, though still tentative, light?

27. Cf. *WK* 15v and the *Spiegel historiael* I, bk. 2, chap. 18, line 113; *WK* 72v and the *Spiegel* III, bk. 8, chap. 74, lines 71–80; *WK* 70v; and Beke 1982, 13. The same tendency to define and explain titles and genealogy can be found in *HK*; see sec. 3 below.

28. See Van Anrooij 1988.

29. Compare *Rijmbijbel* 7061–67 with *WK* 9r; see also Verbij-Schillings 1987, 54, which quotes a comparable historical example: while the Herald's source had Cadmus move on after a while, the Herald had him chased off by force of arms.

30. Cf. the *Historie van Troyen* 915–70 and *WK* 10v; see also Verbij-Schillings 1987, 54.

31. *WK* 72v; similar views are expressed in *HK* 11r. Dirk Potter, too, speaks of the "great haughtiness of France which has been sorely vexed and humiliated" (*BD* 86/44–45).

32. See *WK* 31r; also Verbij-Schillings 1987, 56.

33. Basic information on the *Kladboek* can be found in Beelaerts van Blokland 1933; and Van Anrooij 1986a, 158; the rhyming maxims are included in Suringar 1891, app. B; and Beets 1885, app. 1. Muller Fz. 1885, 108–9, was the first to identify the *Kladboek* as the Herald's autograph.

34. On this subject, see, in addition to the tentative conclusions in Muller Fz. 1885, Verbij-Schillings (1991). This section is based on the second version of the *Hollandse kroniek* in the authorized form of the Brussels (dedication?) autograph. For the first version, see Bruch 1954–55; the conclusion to this section; and Verbij-Schillings (1991).

35. For this scene, see *HK* 66v–68v; Beke 1982, chap. 66; and De Geer van Jutphaas 1867, 89–96. "King of the Romans" was virtually an honorary title, empty of actual power and having little or nothing to do with Rome. The Holy Roman (German) Emperor sometimes gave it to his possible heir. Richard of Cornwall, the brother of Henry III of England, for example, was "king of the Romans."

36. I am indebted for this information to the keen eye of J. Verbij-Schillings, who is preparing a publication on the subject.

37. For heraldry, see the examples given below. For titles, see *HK* 97r; for genealogy, 25r, 36v–37r, and various minor additions connected with family relationships; for (liturgical) ceremonial, 14r, 23v, 74v, 82v. The same tendencies are found in *WK*; see sec. 2 above; and Verbij-Schillings 1987.

38. See Beke 1982, chap. 68, line 305; and *HK* 75r; the Clerk (in De Geer van Jutphaas 1867, 113) simply mentions "the king's arms." A similar example is the Herald's version (61r) of the case of the two knights, which he saw fit to associate with the arms of the Persijn family; cf. Beke 1982, 106; and the Clerk, in De Geer van Jutphaas 1867, 80.

39. For the Herald and his panegyrics, see Van Anrooij 1990; and Nolte 1983.

40. See, e.g., *HK* 92r, 115v–116r, 117r, and 118v–119r.

41. See *HK* 81v (based on Beke 1982, 147) and *HK* 124v. Such precision is no mere pedantry; to maintain a family's honor (see Chapter VII, sec. 2), it was of vital importance to establish that its forebears had been present at a certain battle, and in this area the historical accounts of a herald had authoritative status. It may be assumed that the Herald was particularly scrupulous in this regard: one name more or less could make or break a family.

42. See *HK* 94v and 90r; in both places the Herald followed Beka faithfully. It might be added that the Herald's idea of God was a projection of his chivalric outlook: not only does God grant victory on the battlefield (35v), but above all he is the Supreme Avenger (4v, 7r, 50v, 51r, 52v). Conversely, Christ's crucifixion cries out for vengeance in this chivalric scheme; see 67v.

43. See *HK* 78r–79v. Characteristically, the Herald complements Stoke's version by adding that Floris "preferred tournaments above all."

44. The tombs of the counts of Holland-Bavaria lie hidden beneath the present-day Ministry of Government (Ministerie van Algemene Zaken). The tomb of Margaret of Brieg, in particular, must have been a showpiece; see Van der Klooster 1984.

45. The Herald's fury is reflected in his wording of this old story (*HK* 75r).

46. Cf. *HK* 85v, 91v, and 121v (quoted below).

47. This account was not added to Beka's version until the second edition (Beke 1982, 116–17). Was heresy added for the express purpose of winning the bishop of Utrecht over for the anti-Frisian cause?

48. See, e.g., *HK* 85v–86r and 91v. Beka himself may well have had the union of Holland and Utrecht against Friesland in mind (consider his double formulation of the mandate); see Bruch 1984, 243. Was the Herald's own pair of chronicles perhaps intended to be the county of Holland's "answer" to Beka's presentation of the bishopric of Utrecht's case?

49. The most important studies in this continuing stream of publications are Keen 1983 and (especially) 1984; M. Vale 1981; and J. Vale 1982. The 1959 study by Hugenholtz, too, added important nuances to the picture of declining chivalry.

50. See Jonckbloet 1854, 610.

51. See (also for the following discussion) Van Anrooij 1985; and *WK* 38r: Boendale's *Lekenspiegel* (II, 15/133–38) was the possible source of this legend.

52. See Coenen van 's Gravesloot 1875, 32.

53. See *HK* 61r and 65r–v. In the second case, the Herald, echoing Beka, even speaks of "idle praise"; it is, however, inconceivable that he should have considered this type of praise "idle" in the sense that the clerics Beka and Dirk of Delft did (cf. Chapter V, sec. 2).

54. For a sound introduction, see Keen 1984, chaps. 5 and 11; Fleckenstein 1985; and Bumke 1986, chap. 4.3.

55. With regard to the following discussion, see De Boer 1986.

56. See (following Huizinga 1919) Keen 1984, chap. 10; M. Vale 1981, chap. 2; and Boulton 1987.

57. See Noordeloos 1949, 486–97; Kurz 1956, 119–24; Keen 1984, 196; and *De heraldiek in the handschriften voor 1600* 1985, 55. Is there also a link between this order and the chapel dedicated to Saint Anthony, and apparently built during the last years of Bavarian rule, in the forest at The Hague? See Kroon 1852, 205–6; "'s Gravenhage onder de regering der graven" 1863, 304–6; and Pabon 1936, 50.

58. See Keen 1984, 196; and sec. 3 above.

59. For an introduction, see Beelaerts van Blokland 1929.

60. For the Prussian crusades, see especially Keen 1984, 171–74; Christiansen 1980, chap. 6; and Paravicini 1981, 1986.

61. See Smit 1924–39, 3:396; cf. Van Gelder 1975; and Devillers 1878.

62. On the negative view of the Frisians in the older historiography, see Gerritsen 1979, 80; and 1981, 382; for Froissart's view, see Froissart 1852, bk. 4, chap. 50, p. 249. In some texts the Frisians are painted to resemble the other archenemies of the court (of Holland), namely the "villagers"; see, e.g., *HLH* no. 93; and the anecdote told by Huizinga (1919, 488) about a dispute at the court at The Hague between Burgundian nobles and a Frisian delegation who disturbed the Burgundians' night rest by playing tag in the attic wearing clogs.

63. Cf. Niermeyer 1951, 117, who argues that, in this respect, the Frisian wars were not unlike the crusades against the Moors, Turks, and Lithuanians, "although fellow-Christians were involved."

64. See De Boer 1986, 11.

65. See Beelaerts van Blokland 1929, cols. 356–66. It is a striking fact that William VI seems subsequently to have admitted vanquished Frisian nobles to the Order of the Garden and to have invested them with extremely valuable badges (see Verwijs 1869, xcii)—was he perhaps trying to ensure their future loyalty?

66. For the accounts entry of the acquisition of the chest, see Verwijs 1869, 60; and see ibid., xxxi, xliii–xliv, for Albert's attempt to legitimize his claims to Friesland by displaying charters brought out from "a chest, in which were kept the covenants of the East Frisians."

67. See Beelaerts van Blokland 1933, 4.

68. For the entry in the accounts (not by chance in 1398–99!), see Jonckbloet 1854, 611; and the commentary in U. Peters 1983, 186–88. The first of these two sources is interesting for other reasons as well: in the first place, it seems to indicate that Monnikendam boasted a village speaker (see Chapter VII, sec. 1, more generally); and in the second place, it would appear (see Chapter I, sec. 4) that occasional poems were also being handed out on loose pages—which needless to say, are no longer extant.

69. See the relevant accounts entry in Verwijs 1869, 388.

70. Froissart 1852, 246.

71. See Verwijs 1869, xxxix. Frisians also took part in the "genuine" crusades; see, e.g., Hugenholtz 1950, 5–7.

72. See Jansen and Hoppenbrouwers 1979, 14, on which the preceding remarks are based. The poor quality of these recruits explains why Bavaria Herald kept harping (see sec. 2) on adequate pay for "hired knights." Clearly, he did not feel that appreciation of mercenaries and love of chivalry were mutually exclusive, a view not shared by others; see Maso 1982, 312–13.

73. See C. H. Peters 1909, pp. 126–127.

74. Partly for that reason, Albert and his first wife were buried in tombs considered among the most splendid erected in the North at the time. Bavaria Herald paid particular attention to the manner in which rulers were buried; see Chapter I, sec. 3, as well and the preceding sections of the present chapter.

75. Thus Hildegaersberch declared before the assembled court at The Hague (at the request of the abbess of Rijnsburg!) that "Should your father have been slain, / brother, uncle, cousin, fain / vengeance you must leave to God" (IV/288–90); see also his "Vander wrake Gods" (On God's vengeance; XXXV). The Herald would have been better pleased with the declaration by "Lady (!) Manliness" (*HLH* 34/579–80) that "worthy knights hold fast e'en unto death." Nevertheless, *HLH*, too, contains passages more in the line of Hildegaersberch and Potter: "Little honor can be found, where spite and vengeance do abound; 'tis far nobler to forgive and in harmony to live" (39/30–34).

76. See *BD* 49/28; and Chapter VI, sec. 3.

77. *HK* 123v. (Stone)busses were primitive cannons capable of firing stone balls. In the early fifteenth century, they were relatively modern weapons, and the Herald may well have considered it unchivalrous to use them against foot soldiers. It is well known that the advent of firearms gave rise to fierce discussions about (im)moral methods of warfare, and ultimately led to the decline of chivalry; see M. Vale 1981. (William VI, too, used busses during the siege of Hagestein; see Heniger 1982.)

78. See Bos-Rops 1982, 46–47.

V. DIRK OF DELFT

1. Unless stated otherwise, the following biographical details are taken from Daniëls 1932, chap. 1; and the introduction to the 1937–39 edition of *Tafel vanden kersten ghelove* (*TKG*).

2. See Posthumus Meyjes 1979.

3. The letter is reproduced in De Vooys 1903, 1–2; Daniëls 1932, 27; and in the introduction to *TKG*, 25. It is still unclear what Albert meant when he mentioned the "initial services" Dirk had rendered his lord even before December 1399; the most plausible surmise is that he had come to The Hague to preach or that he had undertaken missions for the count while traveling on his own behalf.

4. According to Verwijs 1869, cxx–cxxi, Albert sent a messenger to the towns on 19 December 1399, that is, two days later, asking them to "prepare for the Frisian campaign."

5. See "'s Gravenhage onder de regering der graven" 1863, 306; see also Chapter VII, sec. 3. In particular, she had a good understanding with such clerics as William the Confessor and later with Dirk himself (see below), and played an important part in the foundation of the Dominican convent (see sec. 4 below). An entry in the accounts in December 1403 (discovered by W. van Anrooij) mentions a "missal from which masses are said daily for my ladies." (Did Albert and William of Oostervant hear mass less frequently?) In general, the women at medieval courts make a more pious impression than their menfolk.

6. For this type of cleric at the court of Holland, see Van Riemsdijk 1908; however, the distinction between such priests and court chaplains was not strict, and sometimes the functions of the two were combined; see ibid., 138–40. An interesting representative is mentioned in Henderikx 1977, 123.

7. See Bumke 1986, 446–51; and Köhn 1979, 234; for the early Middle Ages, see particularly the monumental study by Fleckenstein 1959–66.

8. For William the Confessor, see Chapter VII, secs. 1 and 3; see also sec. 4 below for a "successor" to Dirk.

9. See Meier 1934, 235; and the introduction to *TKG*, 21.

10. For the relevant search of the accounts I am, as so often, indebted to W. van Anrooij and T. Meder.

11. I am indebted for this item to Meder 1991, 558.

12. Cf. the spectacular case of William the Confessor's book; see Chapter VII, sec. 1.

13. It must be stressed that Dirk, too, railed against avarice (see, e.g., "W" XXV/147–79 and XXVI/67–83); the difference was one of degree. Does the explanation lie in the difference between the groups at which the respective criticisms of the two men was leveled—with Hildegaersberch the circle round the sovereign, with Dirk of Delft the sovereign himself? (Incidentally, Dirk of Delft did not believe that the abuses discussed in this section were confined to the court; in the framework of this study, however, we cannot explore this further dimension.)

14. The quotes are from "S" XLV/354 and 361. See the interesting discussion of the tasks and importance of peasants, taken by Dirk from an as yet unidentified source and included in "S" XLV/347–401; in a wider context, see Van Buuren 1987b.

15. The quotes are from "S" XXXVII/89–91 ("source unknown" according to Daniëls's note); XL/316–17; and XLV/252–60 (Daniëls: "Perhaps inserted by D. of D. himself").

16. See, in addition to the quotations below, "W" XVI/26–35, XXXII 454–553, XLIX/67–79; "S" XXXVII/105–10, XLIX/30–42; and Van Moolenbroek 1986.

17. "S" XLVI/184–99; characteristically, being a pragmatic man of the world, Dirk Potter (see Chapter VI) used quite different terms in this context: he advised women to seek out husbands with fresh breath (*ML* I, 991).

18. Other important chapters on confession and penance are "W" XXVIII–XXX, "S" XXXIX, and "S" XLVIII. For more detailed background information, see Tentler 1977.

19. Other important chapters and passages on the importance of priests and the respect that the faithful owe them are "W" XXXII/311–37, "S" XIX, "S" XX/270–83, and "S" XXXIV.

20. For further details on how Dirk regarded the count of Holland, see sec. 4; and Van Oostrom 1987a.

21. See also "S" XLVI, esp. 19–24, to which Dirk refers explicitly in his chapter on rhyming sermons (mentioned earlier), as an example of indirect criticism of rulers by means of parables. More generally, see Van Oostrom 1984b.

22. See, e.g., "W" XIX/194–201, XXXII/65–71, and XXXIV/93–96; and also the (perhaps secondary—see the following note) chapter on the religious disputation between Pope Sylvester and the Jews. Even when it came to the sin of sexual relations between Christians and Jews, Dirk of Delft left the way open for absolution ("W" XXIX/31–33), whereas the otherwise liberal Dirk Potter (see Chapter VI, sec. 2) thought such lapses called for the stake and not for mercy (*ML* III, 1163).

23. See, e.g., "W" XLI/51–54 and "S" VI. Dirk's "moderate anti-Semitism" still awaits more detailed comparison with other texts and events at the court of Holland-Bavaria. With his relative tolerance toward Jews, Dirk fits into the tradition of those learned Schoolmen who stressed the importance of a rational approach to other religions; as far as that is concerned, the appendix to the chapter on the "Disputation Between Pope Silvester and the Jews" in Daniëls 1932, pt. IIIb, might well have been written by Dirk himself. True, Dirk saw fit to mention books that expanded on the cruelty of the Jews to the Son of God, but he added that he preferred to adhere to the biblical account ("S" VI). For Dirk's own account of the cruel treatment of Jesus, see "W" LIII/93–101 and various passages in "S" IV–VII.

24. On the giving of a sword to Judas Maccabaeus, see "W" XIX/173–76.

25. For this distinction, see Russell 1975; and for Dirk's sporadic references to just wars, see "S" XIV/173 (quoted below) and XXVII/26. Closer investigation is still needed to establish whether Dirk of Delft's relative coolness to the idea of holy wars was as typical of the attitude of clerics in his circle and age as it seems to have been—and Keen (1984) is correct in stating that the crusade ideal was inspired more by chivalric than by religious motives. This latter situation seems, in any case, to have been true of the later Middle Ages; see Chapter IV, sec. 4.

26. Cf. "W" XLIX/80–93; "S" XXVI/71–119 and XXVII/86–135. True, Albert is also called "lord of Friesland" in the prologue ("S," p. 7), and Dirk cited the quest for "mountains of gold" in Friesland as a rare delusion ("W" XI/95)—was that perhaps his way of hinting that love of booty, and not honor alone, inspired the Frisian campaigns (see Chapter IV, sec. 4, and Chapter VII, sec. 2)?

27. See (in addition to the examples about to be discussed), e.g., "W" XVIII/186–252, XIX/140–76; "S" IV, VII/541–691, XVI/426–41 (Daniëls: "source unknown"), XL/70–88, XLI/148–215, and XLII/85–117. For an incisive image of God's knight, see e.g., "S" III/244, XXXI/95–97, and XXXVIII/27–28. For Dirk's equally martial version of the Gospel of Nicodemus ("S" IX), see Daniëls 1932, 124–26; and De Vooys 1903, 15, 22–28.

28. This passage was added to his main source, Dirk claims, from the writ-

ings of "master Alanus." Though it has not yet been possible to trace the addition back to Alanus ab Insulis, the imagery used has a rich tradition; see Wang 1975.

29. See, e.g., "S" XL/318, XLVI/65, and LII/97–108. See also Chapter VII, sec. 2. (I am indebted to E. Kooreman for a careful analysis of the honor concept in *TKG*.)

30. See "W" XVIII/201–3 and XIX/152–53; "S" XLI/172–74 and 212–15.

31. Note Dirk's hierarchical view of how that court is run (undoubtedly delighting his earliest readers): table companions of rank are served by humble attendants. More generally, see Dinzelbacher 1979a,b; and also sec. 4 below. (Hildegaersberch, too, used the parallel between court and Heaven, if less majestically: see poem XCV.)

32. On the structure of the *Tafel*, see Daniëls 1932, 93–100; and the introduction to *TKG*, 48–50. The carefully planned basic structure of the *Tafel* does not preclude (some parts of) various chapters from constituting digressions; see Daniëls 1932 and the introduction to *TKG* for a discussion of this matter.

33. That Dirk of Delft should have used this division inspired by the *Legenda aurea* for his *Tafel*—which, after all, is based more closely on the *summa* tradition (see below)—is rather puzzling. Was it his intention to render his encyclopedic work more suitable for selected readings adapted to the church calendar?

34. See "W" XXXI/10 and XLVII.

35. It should be noted that, when it came to these whorls, Dirk failed (or is this a case of text corruption?) to provide cross-references to other parts of the *Tafel*, though both themes are treated at greater length in other parts of the book: see "S" XVI and "W" XVII.

36. See, e.g., "W" XXXIII and "S" XLI. (Dirk believed that their lack of the right religious perspective rendered them less reliable guides on the deeper issues.)

37. See Daniëls 1932, chap. 2 and passim; and the introduction to *TKG*, secs. 2 and 3.

38. See, e.g., "W" XVIII/337–38 and XXXVII/176–95; "S" VII/716–832 and VIII/264–335 (in both cases, verse fragments not remarked upon by Daniëls indicate a Middle Dutch rhymed source) as well as XII/204–34 and XLI/139–43 (do the above remarks apply to these passages too?).

39. An exception to this rule is the reference to the *Dietse Catoen* (the Middle Dutch version of the widely read *Disticha Catonis*) in "S" XLII/70–74, and perhaps also that to the *Spieghel menscheliker behoudinghe* in "S" XI/221–25.

40. Dirk does, however, seem to have been familiar with Maerlant's work, at least with the *Strofische gedichten* (Strophic poems), which is further evidence of the enormous influence that the "father of all Dutch poets" exerted through this work particularly (which was also translated into Latin). For possible traces of Maerlant's work in the *Tafel* , see "W" XIX/128–29 and "S" VII/296–333; see also, more generally, Chapter VII, sec. 1.

41. See Rosenplenter 1982, 26. There is, however, an odd exception even in this case: in "S" XV, Dirk of Delft distances himself from the views of "Rabbi [!] Moses," who, according to him, tried to determine how far the soul had to

travel from the earth to the furthermost heaven; "But methinks it is not worth the trouble to read about it, since our souls can, in one moment, fly beyond all the heavens" (236–38).

42. This difference is reflected in their respective views of the Trinity: while the layman William of Hildegaersberch confined himself to stating, "Hard though to grasp the truth may be, that three be one and one be three; yet have I known it well since yore, and shall believe it evermore" (XIV/5–8), the theologian Dirk of Delft devoted a more profound discussion to the subject ("W" I; cf. p. 48 of the introduction to *TKG*). Another important difference between the two was that Dirk of Delft's treatment of Christian doctrine was systematic, whereas Hildegaersberch's was eclectic.

43. See Grabmann 1909, 34, also quoted in Daniëls's introduction to *TKG*, 53. For further details on (the role of authorities in) scholastic thought, see de Rijk 1977, chap. 4. A more penetrating analysis of Dirk of Delft as a Schoolman-theologian, unfortunately, is beyond the scope of this work.

44. Considering the readership of the *Tafel*, what mattered here, unlike in academic instruction, was not so much the discussion as such as the answers. Even so, Dirk's arguments remained academic enough; see sec. 4 below for more on this topic.

45. See "S" XIII/199–235 (also quoted as an example in Daniëls 1932, 103–4).

46. According to Daniëls's notes, Dirk used a much greater number of forties than his sources.

47. For this tradition, see Dempf 1925.

48. *Urede = Vrede*. Medieval Dutch writers made no functional distinction between *v* and *u*.

49. See, e.g., the quotation in sec. 2 above. Cf. Huizinga 1919, chap. 7, where this way of thinking is called a "sickness" and a "purely mechanical" search for "trivial arithmetical sums."

50. See "S" XX, 306–11, appropriately presented as a game of questions and answers played by a "master" and a young nobleman, thus clearly reflecting the distribution of roles between Dirk and his public.

51. See, e.g., "W" XLII/60–80, together with Daniëls's note. Cf. Jacobs 1915, 129, 143. Dirk's version of the "rules that knights ought to make their own" was revealing as well—he added a characteristic twelfth rule for knights to Beka's eleven: "that, in respect of fasting, observation, prayer, and knowledge of the Gospels, they will gladly obey the commands of the holy church" ("S" XLV/323–25).

52. See Pleij 1979, chap. 4.

53. This becomes particularly clear in Dirk's treatment of the *Ludus scaccorum*, where the social order is exemplified by the various chessmen ("S" XLVI). That chapter merits a more detailed discussion than we can give it here, and particularly a closer comparison with the Latin sources and with the contemporary Middle Dutch version of Franconis, and possibly also with Philip of Leyden's vision of society.

54. Or rather, to "laicization"; for this term, see Steer 1981, 1983. Steer prefers that term to "secularization" for good reasons: church dogma was not so much being rendered more worldly as being made more accessible to laymen.

55. See Daniëls 1932, 189; and the introduction to *TKG*, 59. Anyone reading between Dirk's lines can see that he was thoroughly familiar with mystical thought and the appropriate terms: apart from Daniëls's work, see also Axters 1937, 47. If the Bruges sermons to be discussed below can be traced back to Dirk of Delft with certainty, then the least doubts about his familiarity with mysticism will have been dispelled. That the aristocratic life was not wholly incompatible with mysticism is borne out by the fact that the library of John IV of Nassau and his wife (see Chapter I, sec. 4, and Chapter III, sec. 1) contained a translation of Suso.

56. See "S" XVI/301–7; "W" XVIII/120–23; "S" XXIV/43–46; "S" XVI/435–41; "W" XII/117–21; "W" XI/55–58; "W" XI/88–91; "S" XVI/551–55; and "S" XXII/126–29. "S" XVI/426–41 probably wins out in this connection: according to Dirk, the Holy Ghost descended on the apostles at Whitsun because kings were wont to hold court at that time.

57. See "S" XIV/328–31, XIX/190–91, XXVIII/144–46, XII/196; "W" XXXVII/39–40 and 159–60; and "S" XIX/74–75.

58. See Rickert 1949; Finke 1963; and Van Oostrom 1987a. A closer study of this miniature tradition as a possible *Bildprogramm* ("picture program") may be called for, to which purpose the miniatures in the New York manuscript of the *Tafel* (which possibly belonged to the same dedication set as the one in Baltimore) might prove useful.

59. The completion of the book may have suffered a serious setback by Albert's death on 16 December 1404; in any case, the history of the *Tafel* was more complicated than can be shown here. See Van Oostrom 1987a.

60. Does this formulation suggest that the *Tafel* was intended primarily for meditative reading in private rather than for being read out loud? Perhaps this view is an oversimplification; other indications, such as the strongly rhetorical style of the chapter endings (sometimes concluded with an Amen), suggest the opposite. The problem applies to most Middle Dutch texts (see Pleij 1987a); those subsumed under the *Tafel* genre might well have been used for various practical purposes (see Frühwald 1963, chap. 5).

61. For this and related events (culled from the accounts), see C. H. Peters 1909, 221; and Bartelink 1985, 50–56. If we may take it that such visits were not unwelcome to the noble sisters, they tell us as much about their piety as about that of Albert and company; see Schotel 1851, chap. 19. For the (not very close) relations between the Bavarian counts of Holland and Egmont Abbey, see (in addition to Bartelink 1985) Hof 1973, 384–87.

62. Huizinga 1919, 294–95.

63. See the accounts entry in Jonckbloet 1854, 604; and the commentary in U. Peters 1983, 188. Hildegaersberch, too, penned a (strophic) poem to Our Lady (XLV).

64. See Chapter I, sec. 4, and Chapter III, sec. 1; also Korteweg 1984.

65. Other passages of the *Tafel* also presuppose familiarity with the Bible: see, e.g., "W" XXVII/30–31 on Melchizedek and "S" XIX/227–29 on the Levites. Dirk Potter and William of Hildegaersberch also took it for granted that their readers were familiar with the Scriptures.

66. On the court church and chapels, see Lingbeek-Schalekamp 1984, 6–7,

29; C. H. Peters 1909, 161–63, 219–28; "'s Gravenhage onder de regering der graven" 1863, 292–306.

67. See Keen 1984, 196 (including n. 72); and Chapter IV, sec. 4.

68. See Jonckbloet 1854, 606; and Verwijs 1869, ci–cii.

69. See the quotation in C. H. Peters 1909, 123; and cf. 226–27. For further details, see, "'s Gravenhage onder de regering der graven" 1863, 293; and *Hollandse kroniek* 112v.

70. See Huizinga 1919; and, for the court of Holland in particular, C. H. Peters 1909, 219–28, from which the following examples are taken; cf. Kroon 1852, 78–80.

71. See C. H. Peters 1909, 223; and Tóth-Ubbens 1963, 92.

72. For the seven works of charity and the seven sacraments, see, e.g., "S" XXII–XXXVIII. The court itself seemed to have realized, however, that such outer displays of religious fervor might degenerate into empty routine. William of Hildegaersberch, too, had seen fit to remind them that confession was more than dressing up to make a good impression on one's priest (CXV/61–72).

73. See Cuvelier 1921, 97–105, for an impressive list of such generosity to the church on the part of William of Duvenvoorde, who, being an upstart millionaire, felt compelled to make an extra show of altruism.

74. See Chapter VI, sec. 3, for further details. Or must we consider the great attention the *Tafel* paid to the Lord Jesus and its relatively small interest in the saints a vague token of the new trend? In any case, Dirk's text was also read in circles associated with the *devotio moderna*; see Van Oostrom 1987a.

75. See esp. "S" XXVIII–XXIX.

76. See, e.g., Daniëls 1932, 31; "'s Gravenhage onder de regering der graven" 1863, 306–7; and Wolfs 1973, 51–52n.18.

77. See the introduction to *TKG*, 46.

78. Cf., e.g., such Middle Dutch texts as *Der leken spiegel* (The layman's mirror), with which the *Tafel* has often been compared; and *Des coninx summe* (The king's *summa*), which is much less a *summa* in the classical sense than Dirk's *Tafel*; and Troelstra 1901. For a non-Dutch interpretation, see Weidenhiller 1965. Crucial for this comparison is the use of popular language: in contrast to learned Latin catechisms, the *Tafel* was intended to serve more practical ends; see Post 1957, 225.

79. See "W" XLI/1–105; "W" XXXV/170–98; "W" XXXVIII/142–70; "S" XV/464–511; "W" XLVII/165–82; "W" XLII/119–33.

80. See Axters 1937, 45–49. In general, Dirk felt free to "bastardize" a great many Latin words; examples include *approbieren, commendacie, concupiscencien, confortatief, consentieren, meliocatief, prepucio, signakel, substanciael,* and *tribuleren* (with acknowledgments to P. van Geest and A. Wilhelm, two of my students).

81. See sec. 1 above. One might even argue that with his writings Dirk was trying to make up for what verbal instructions he had failed to convey to the courtiers. It is probably significant that the *Tafel*, in referring to the giving of "good counsel" ("W" XIX/113–14), states that it teaches the faithful what to do and what not to do "as if from the master's mouth."

82. See Van Riemsdijk 1908, 138; and Verwijs 1869, cxlvi. It is, of course, possible that Dirk continued to serve Albert's widow, for whom he had, after

all, been writing books as well (see sec. 1 above); but there is no evidence that he did. By all accounts, he seems to have had no successors at the court, much as he had had no predecessors (though consider the interesting figure of the Dominican confessor, Jan van Neck, discussed in Jongkees 1942, 56, 67; and sec. 1 above).

83. See Axters 1956, 316–17; the manuscript is kept in the Bruges Municipal Library (MS. 408). I am indebted to A.M.J. van Buuren for drawing my attention to the sermons, and to my former assistants J. van Rooden and G. Warnar for copying and examining the texts. The Bruges manuscript, incidentally, contains yet a third sermon (fol. 282v–285r) of which Dirk of Delft is most likely to have been the author (referred to as *doctuer vanden predicaren*: doctor of the order of preaching friars); I am indebted for this suggestion to A.M.C.B. de Jong.

84. See Van Oostrom 1987a. Whether these circles also stood in need of Dirk's secularized imagery and some of his lessons is open to question.

VI. DIRK POTTER

1. See Overmaat 1952.

2. For the (Hague) bailiff's office, see, in addition to Overmaat 1952, "'s Gravenhage onder de regering der graven" 1863, 253–61; and *Rekeningen van de Grafelijkheid van Holland* 1980, xii–xiii. Cf. sec. 4 below.

3. When referring to this mission in *Der minnen loep*, he described it as "a secret ploy beyond the plowman's ken."

4. See Bos-Rops 1982, 47; cf. Chapter IV, sec. 4. His work, too, shows Potter as an advocate of amicable settlements; see secs. 3 and 4 below.

5. On his reaction to homophile deportment in Italy, see *ML* II, 731–40; III, 98–150. For the rest, he deplored (*BD* 89/23 and 9/27–28) the untrustworthiness of his Italian contacts.

6. See *ML* I, 69–76; *BD* 81/8, 18/47, and 213–14 ("you, young man"); for "my friends," see, e.g., *ML* I, 1236, 3025; II, 3477; III, 416, 1104; and several passages in the prologue and in short verses in *BD*. His calling his audience "my friends" (in *ML*, men as well as women) may, however, have been a purely rhetorical device; see Ragotzky 1981, 137.

7. A passage in *Der minnen loep* supports this interpretation: the narrator begs leave "dat ic arbeyde op minen kost, die wile ic hebbe sin ende lost" (II, 635–36). The interpretation of Van Buuren 1979, 133 ("He must be allowed to earn his living for as long as he wants to") seems less plausible than the more literal translation: that he works (i.e., writes?) for himself as long as he wants to; was the author trying to present his poetry as a work of love? The fact that Potter wrote as a hobby does not, of course, mean that he had nothing serious to say, as this chapter will show. It does, however, provide some explanation of why Potter as a writer was less strict and consistent than his colleagues. In particular, the fourth book of *ML* looks rather thin in comparison with the second, and the later chapters of *BD* seem rather hurried. See also the vague forward reference in *BD* 114/115.

8. See the introduction to the *Mellibeus* (listed in the Note on Editions).

9. For the problems posed by the sources of these two works, see Van Buuren 1979, 1984b, and 1985 (with references to the older literature); and, more recently, Van Oostrom 1987b on *BD*.

10. See Scattergood 1983, 32, 38; Stevens 1961, 156–57; and Pearsall 1977, 73–74. For the (attractive but risky) parallel between Chaucer and Potter, see also sec. 4 (with notes 78 and 80) below.

11. Van Buuren 1979, however admirable in other respects, goes too far when he calls the book "a paean of praise to marriage," thus ignoring Potter's libertine side (see below). Perhaps it is characteristic that Potter referred to married love as "permitted" love while contending that "good" love could occur even outside marriage; that the concept of "good love" was apparently Potter's very own; and that the second book was almost twice the size of the fourth.

12. Cf. *ML* II, 1761–66 and 1778–83, and the story of Sabina and Floridamas that follows.

13. Various comparative studies of medieval writings on love and morals refer to *Der minnen loep* as an exceptional work; see, e.g., Schnell 1985, index; and Glier 1971, 286–88. Kooper 1985, 237–39, makes an interesting comparison between Potter and Chaucer.

14. For background information, see, in addition to the literature cited in Chapter II, sec. 1, and Chapter III, sec. 4, Dallapiazza 1981. One detail in Potter's *Blome der doechden* (for which see sec. 3 below) is striking in this respect: Potter states with some emphasis that although Dido was deserted by Aeneas and the latter had meanwhile founded Rome, "she would not change her mind, nor alter her love for him, even though she loved her country" (fol. 57r, omitted in the Schoutens edition). Did even Potter expect a princess to abandon her lover for the sake of her country? Cf. *ML* II, 1372–1404. (Does this passage indicate that the *Blome* was written during the reign of Jacqueline of Bavaria? See the beginning of sec. 3 and Chapter VII, sec. 4.)

15. It must again be stressed that this interpretation is an oversimplification. Some authorities emphasize that, even among medieval nobles, marriage for love was less exceptional than is generally believed: see, e.g., Kelly 1975; and Mathew 1968. It is difficult to tell to what extent the issue is colored by the fact that these writers drew a large part of their material from such court authors as Chaucer and Gower, who, like Potter, came from the ranks of the lower nobility.

16. See *ML* I, 1179–1219; II, 2628–32 and 1345–1560.

17. In this respect, too, Potter was more modern (and more bourgeois: see below) than other authors at the court of Holland, most of whom were extremely critical of people crossing the class border; see, e.g., Hildegaersberch XCVII/344–77; and Chapter II, sec. 3.

18. See *ML* I, 2712–42; in the opposite case Potter seems less optimistic: the man might easily conclude that he was free to do as he pleased.

19. See *ML* III, 309–1227; cf. Pleij 1979, 224; and Van Buuren 1984a, 62. Does this lengthy discussion suggest that incest was fairly common in Potter's circles, or at least a serious problem? In view of the relatively self-contained

character of court life, it does not seem inconceivable; yet, so far, little concrete corroborative evidence has been found. It does, however, strike one when, in the *Blome*, Potter calls the camel the symbol of moderation inasmuch as it is, on the one hand, so *luxurioes* that it will run a good hundred miles to find a wife, yet, on the other hand, "so temperate and unyielding to his lust that he will not pursue his sister nor have his pleasure with her, albeit she daily stands by his side and they browse together in one and the same herd" (4520–27). The Herald, for his part, when describing the sinfulness of the people of Walcheren under Bishop Frederic, declared that "not only did brother sleep there with his sister, but also the son with his mother" (*HK* 16r).

20. Cf. II, 1969–1978, where Potter states that he prefers premature fourth-degree sex to "real crimes," although he adds that those who have "chosen to wait" are wise to do so. Does that mean that he considered full sexual intercourse permissible whenever marriage was out of the question? That is certainly true of some of the examples of fourth-degree love he described in positive terms in book two, for instance between Tristan and Iseult, Neptanabus and Olympia (see below), and the Parisian couple, but not between Sabina and Floridamas, who marry in the end but nevertheless go to the fourth degree beforehand. But cf. *ML* II, 1561–1810, where Potter gives the impression of holding stricter views.

21. Cf. *ML* IV, 405–10. Note that Potter here (and also in subsequent passages) assumes that the man was committing adultery with an unmarried woman. He had had experience of this type of adultery in his own family: his half-brother was Dirc Potter *bastaird* (see Overmaat 1952); and according to Van Foreest 1965–66, 125n.4, Duke Albert lodged his mistress Catherine of Domburg temporarily in Potter's parental home.

22. See, e.g., *ML* IV, 365–404 and 857–72.

23. See *ML* IV, 968–84 and 2233–45. That Christian women might do likewise is to Potter inconceivable: 2246–50. Probably he was thinking more in terms of "informal concubinage" than of real bigamy; for the latter, many stiff punishments were meted out during his bailiffship; see Berents 1985, 43–44; and Hermesdorf 1980, 301–2.

24. Cf. *ML* II, 731–40; and III, 98–150.

25. For "good love," see, e.g., II, 1798–1810; for "forbidden love," III, 1257–62 (quoted above); for adultery, IV, 613–22; see also the index in Van Buuren 1979 under *heimelycheit* (secrecy) and *heelghesel* (secret accomplice). Cf. Van Oostrom 1986b; and, more generally, Chapter VII, sec. 2.

26. See, e.g., II, 3147–49 and 3287–98, and some of the exemplary tales in book two, including the one mentioned below; see also the index in Van Buuren 1979 under *list* (ruses or stratagems). A fascinating body of scholarly writing on ruses and stratagems exists that would be well worth exploring in connection with Potter's work and medieval Dutch literature in general: e.g., Könneker 1970; Cramer 1974; Van Kampen and Pleij 1981; Ragotzky 1977, 1981; and Hahn 1985. Potter's attitude to stratagems seemed to reflect his pragmatic and rational attitude (on which more in the next two sections). Remarkably, the more aristocratic-idealistic (and less male chauvinistic? cf. Chapter III, sec. 4)

conception of love in the *HLH* went hand in hand with a more reserved approach: men often become unfaithful once they have "succeeded in conquering women with their ruses" (6327–73). Dirk of Delft, for his part, spoke out strongly against men who used ruses to rob "good women and maidens" of their honor ("W" XXXII/632; cf. XX/34).

27. The question of whether *Der minnen loep*—and Potter's other (prose) writings—were meant from the outset to be read out loud poses a special problem. On the one hand, the text emphatically acknowledges the narrator's role, which seems to support the view that it was intended for recitation; on the other hand, one of the (later) manuscripts "is a small book eminently suited to be taken on one's travels by those wishing to read about love whenever time allows" (Obbema 1979, 23). See also Pleij 1987a.

28. Cf. Van Buuren 1979, 305, on Potter's humor; the author pleads eloquently for a closer study.

29. For a good example see *ML* I, 736–824.

30. See, e.g., I, 159–76; II, 86–109 and 2392–2476.

31. Compare such passages as II, 3497–3526, 4125–34; IV, 876–92 and conclusion; with I, 928–46, 2642–2758; IV, 931–98 and 1839–1918. See also Schnell 1985, 176–77, 483, 508, setting Potter's apparently inconsistent views in a wider context. Potter, incidentally, was by no means the only writer to combine pro- and antifeminism in what for modern readers is a most peculiar manner; see Rocher 1979; and Williamson 1985. Roessingh 1914 takes a relatively favorable view of Potter's attitude toward women (cf. Van Buuren 1979, 43); but then, Roessingh was comparing *Der minnen loep* with Middle Dutch texts written from a clerical viewpoint.

32. See particularly the lengthy apology with which he begins and ends book two; also II, 1703–4, 4237–39; and IV, 915–16.

33. For a detailed account, see Van Buuren 1979, chaps. 1 and 3; and Van Buuren 1985b; for an interpretation of the lines from the prologue to *BD* quoted above, see particularly Van Buuren 1979, 29.

34. For this acrostic, see Overmaat 1950, 11–15; in reproducing it here, I have altered some spelling, word divisions, and punctuation in accord with Overmaat's interpretation. *Der minnen loep*, too, was signed by its author with an acrostic: the first letters of the final lines form the name *Dirc Potter*.

35. For further details on the dating of Potter's writings, see Van Buuren 1979, 28–30.

36. The framework of this book prevents me from discussing the complex problem of the sources of Potter's work at greater length. For a general overview, see sec. 1 above; for more detailed comments, see Overmaat 1950; Van Buuren 1985b; and Van Oostrom 1987b. Further study is, however, required.

37. See, e.g., *BD* 12/40, 34/30, 35/35, and 68/19.

38. See, e.g., the chapter on unchastity (80–83) and 109/7 ("the great sin of adultery").

39. See Glier 1971, 287–88.

40. Compare the prologue to *ML* with *BD* 9/16–20.

41. This blurring applies particularly to the pairs that have no (known) par-

allels in the *Fiore* tradition, and may therefore have been Potter's own contribution: for instance, the noble-ignoble pair (discussed in sec. 4 below).

42. The last group includes the chapters on moderation, nobility, modesty, righteousness, disobedience, meekness, and wisdom. It was not by chance that these were more deeply rooted in Potter's ethics and personal life than any others.

43. See *ML* I, 1298–1311; and the prologues to books two and four.

44. See Van Buuren 1985b; and Chapter V, sec. 2; also Chapter VII, sec. 3.

45. In the introduction to that edition, p. x.

46. See manuscript, fols. 73v–74r (omitted from p. 70 of the printed edition); 63r (omitted from p. 61); 45v (omitted from p. 46); 75r (omitted from p. 71). Numerous other passages might be added to this list of omissions, for instance the many passages in *BD* in which pope, priests, and monks are referred to negatively, and Potter's repeated references (also in *ML*) to the old men spying on the chaste Susanna as "hypocritical priests." See *BD* 33, 55, 78, 110; and *ML* II, 2494–2584; cf. Van Buuren 1979, 271–79.

47. The literature on the subject is as large as the problems involved; for three important general studies, see Trinkaus and Oberman 1974; Trinkaus 1976; and Oberman 1978. For the Netherlands, see Van Herwaarden and De Keyser 1980; and Van Herwaarden 1983. Evidence of the influence of the *devotio moderna* at the court of Holland-Bavaria is (as far as we can tell at present) too scant to be convincing; thus, the fact that Henrik Mande was a clerk to William of Oostervant in his youth seems accidental rather than significant. Needless to say, this does not mean that certain parallels cannot be drawn; see Van Buuren 1985b.

48. Both factors left traces even on the *Blome*: the first in Potter's attacks on clerical hypocrisy (see above), the second in the prologue quoted earlier. (In respect of the first, I learned at a meeting of the Leiden Working Group "Holland 1300–1500" that Potter's dislike of the clergy may well have involved social factors: during the very years that Potter was active at the court, laymen had to compete for court appointments with clerics. Does that help to explain the bloody fight [see sec. 1 above] between the Potters and the court clergy in 1400?)

49. It goes without saying that we must proceed cautiously here—who would swear that the future will not show that he was the slavish follower of thus far undiscovered sources?

50. See also the immediately following (rather puzzling) lines. Cf. *BD* 31/27–28. Other passages in which the author stands up for his own opinions include 14/33 and III/13; cf. *ML* II, 413.

51. There is no incontrovertible proof that this work was Potter's (sole) source of information on Troy, particularly since he takes so many liberties with it; the most important differences can, however, be convincingly attributed to Potter himself. The detail in *BD* 97/19–20 concerning the slaying of Achilles by Paris was added by Maerlant to his own sources; see Jongen 1988. According to Franck in Maerlant n.d., xvii, Potter may also have been familiar with Maerlant's *Alexanders geesten*; the story in that work of the *vipera* may have been the source (through word corruption) of the comments in *BD* 82/35–42 on the *nepa*.

Compare, too, the description of the nature of the fox in *BD* 103/14–25 with *Der naturen bloeme* II, 3889–3952. There seems little doubt that, in about 1400, court circles in Holland were familiar with these writings by Maerlant; see Chapter IV; and Chapter VII, sec. 1.

52. *BD* 97/1–27; no parallel in the *Fiore* tradition has so far been discovered for the benevolence-anger pair.

53. *Historie van Troyen* 25316–18; cf. Jongen 1988.

54. For Maerlant's very negative portrayal of Ulixes, see Jongen 1988; for Potter's portrayal, see Van Buuren 1979, index.

55. See *ML* II, 2885–2958. Van Buuren (1979, 244) states that Bartsch attributes this passage to some French source; but until that source is discovered, Maerlant must be considered Potter's authority even here.

56. See particularly the chapters on wisdom and competence and their opposites (discussed in sec. 4 below). In general, the "rational" dimension is more marked in *BD* than it is in the *Fiore*; see van Oostrom 1987b; and Van Gorp 1912.

57. See *HLH* 10/29, 99/123 62*MDSU/5; cf. *TKG* "S" XLV/107–17. The fact that this concept also appears in other writings does not mean that Potter did not attach special importance to it; this is particularly true of the stress he laid on "reason," a concept also emphasized by Hadewijch. Careful semantic research is needed to clarify the fine differences between Potter's concepts of moderation, honor, wisdom, and reason and those found e.g. in (Maerlant's?) *Torec*; the analysis by Vanderheyden 1933 seems too superficial.

58. See, in addition to the passages discussed below, *BD* 93/24–25; the chapters on strength (49–52) and benevolence (92–96); 106/43–44; and 109/45–46; see also sec. 4 below. *Der minnen loep* takes a similar view: see, e.g., III, 541, 684–88, 1103, and 1136–60; IV, 1276–1306 and 2209–10; cf. Verdam 1898, 12–13.

59. As far as we can tell from the published versions, *prudenza* plays a much less dominant role in the *Fiore* tradition than "wisdom" does in Potter's work.

60. *ML* II, 694–95 (quoted in sec. 2 above); cf. I, 2857.

61. See, e.g., *ML* I, 2288; II, 1234–36 and 2070–71; III, 982; IV, 589.

62. In addition to Middle Dutch writings on ruses, stratagems, and deceits (mentioned in sec. 2 above), see especially the work of Herman Pleij (with an abundance of references to the primary and secondary literature), especially 1979, 156–63; 1982, 34–38; and, most particularly, 1984b. It is a great pity that Pleij has not (yet) analyzed the relations between Potter and "bourgeois morality"; can Potter help to preserve us from arriving at an overly simplistic polarization of (ethics and literature in) court and town? Cf. Ragotzky 1981 on the idea of wisdom in Der Stricker, an author who had much in common with Potter.

63. For fuller quotations (also in respect of what follows), see Van Oostrom 1987b.

64. See, e.g., "W" XIX/222–77; when Dirk of Delft discusses "wisdom" in the context of the four cardinal virtues, he endows it with characteristics that were to set their stamp on the "bourgeois" view: see "W" XVIII/31–113 and "S" XLII/109–40. Among other authors at the court of Holland, William of Hildegaersberch's use of "wisdom" was closest to Potter's; see, e.g., II/18–19 (a very

"townish" poem) and XXXV/12. "Reason" was prized by Hildegaersberch as well: see, e.g., XXXVIII/90–102 (quoted in Chapter II, sec. 4) and XC/241–58. It is not surprising that the nonaristocratic, self-made Hildegaersberch should have been closest to Potter in this respect (see below).

65. The bastard William Snickerieme (Duvenvoorde) had acted similarly; see Cuvelier 1921. For William Eggert, see the interesting study by Bos-Rops (1982); cf. Van Oostrom 1987b.

66. See *BD* 59/40–47 and 62/15–19 (the pair humility-pride is a typical illustration of Potter's writing and thinking). Can (many of) the newcomers at court reviled here be identified with the "rogues" whose baneful influence Hildegaersberch so deplored (see Chapter II, sec. 3)? Or would Hildegaersberch have counted someone like Potter among the "rogues"? It is, incidentally, odd that Potter, consummate courtier though he was, should have used the term *rogues* so sparingly.

67. See *BD* 105/47–48, 112/11–12, 59/6, and 124/14–16 (all quoted in Van Oostrom 1987b, where other relevant references can also be found). Even in his first book, Potter argued that (in matters of love) humility was often more helpful than swagger; see the story of Orphaen and Lympiose (*ML* IV, 1095–1326).

68. *BD* 42/6–40 (quoted in Van Oostrom 1987b with other relevant examples). Despite research into the *Gesta romanorum* tradition, the source of Potter's example (which is not found in any known *Fiore* version) has not yet been discovered; it is therefore impossible to determine whether our author gave the story a significant twist of his own.

69. For Potter's life, see especially Overmaat 1952; also Van Buuren 1979, chap. 1, sec. 4; and Van Oostrom 1987b. To the bibliography listed in the last work must be added Plomp 1985 and (for the later Potters) Meesters 1985.

70. Bailiffs wielded considerable power, and inasmuch as they received a share of the fines, they were susceptible to corruption and apparently succumbed on many occasions; see Berents 1985, 163–68. In Middle Dutch writings, the bailiff traditionally plays a negative role. In Jacob van Maerlant's *Alexanders geesten*, for example, Antipater, the murderer of Alexander the Great, is said to have been a *baliu*, a story that Bavaria Herald repeated in *WK* 30v.

71. See Overmaat 1952, 131–32. If that marriage did indeed take place, it places Potter's ideas on marriages between different classes (see sec. 2 above) in particularly sharp relief.

72. For further details, see Van Oostrom 1987b, from which much of what follows has been taken.

73. On this widely discussed subject, see, e.g., Borck 1978; and for the late-medieval (bourgeois) approach to the *Tugendadel* (nobility from virtue) concept, see Honemann 1984.

74. Note that Potter concludes with a sarcastic allusion to the credo of (courtly) love propounded, e.g., in the *Haags liederenhandschrift* (see Chapter III, sec. 2).

75. See Van Riemsdijk 1908, 304.

76. Overmaat 1952, 137. In this connection, it should also be noted that Pot-

ter's (once again like Hildegaersberch's) concept of *gemeyn oerbore* (common interest) seemed to be informed by more modern political thought reflecting the rise of the towns; cf. *gemeyner nutz* (common benefit) in U. Peters 1983. For relevant passages in Potter, see, e.g., *BD* 72/46 and 37/10–13. For Hildegaersberch, see Chapter II, sec. 3.

77. According to J. Vale 1982, 2, the circle of officials around the medieval ruler was "perhaps the area of greatest social mobility outside the Church." See also Paravicini 1977; and Prevenier 1972. Potter seems to have embodied all the symptoms of the complex described by Prevenier: the crossing of class barriers, the quest for material advantage and social prestige, being the son of an official, being a professional technocrat, being obsequious yet critical of his noble employer, and, to some extent, having a double moral standard.

78. See Godding and De Smidt 1980, 174; see also the life of the (noble) Baldwin of Zwieten as drawn by Van Kan 1981. Potter was fully aware of this trend: see the above-quoted passage in *BD* 124/15–16 on the career of educated clerks. The portrait of Chaucer in Coleman 1983 makes it clear that the several portraits of Potter as (a) an author well versed in the classics (Van Buuren 1979) and (b) a (modern) well-traveled official (as described in this section), far from being mutually exclusive, are complementary: his education helped Potter to get on in the world.

79. It should be added that in my reconstruction I have exaggerated Potter's "modern" side at the expense of the more conventional facets of his thought. Potter's close links with tradition are emphasized in Van Buuren 1979. It is, moreover, striking that all early publications on Potter see him as a writer in whom modernity and traditionalism go hand in hand; Busken Huet (1882, 664), for example, considered him a guarantor of the continuity between the old and the new. See also the comments on Potter in Kalff 1906, 553–72 (contradicted by Vanderheyden 1933); and Glier 1971, 287–88.

80. See sec. 1 above and Chapter VII, sec. 3. Once again the parallel with Chaucer comes to mind: he, too, was a clerk writing for his own pleasure, well traveled (he had been as far as Italy), a translator of the *Mellibeus*, and a man opposed to chivalric fanaticism. One sees particularly striking similarities between Potter and the portrait of Chaucer drawn in Coleman 1983. True, Chaucer was a great deal more indebted to modern Italy than Potter; but the latter, too, owed much to Italy: all three of his books had Italian antecedents. According to Potter himself, the idea for his *ML* first came to him in Rome; the *Mellibeus* goes back to the work of Albertanus of Brescia (via the French); and *BD* may well have been the first Dutch translation of an Italian text.

81. The last, that is, if we exclude his son Gerard; see Chapter VII, sec. 4.

VII. COURT LITERATURE

1. I am indebted to R. L. Falkenburg for the following remarks. For a fuller discussion, see Van Oostrom 1985b; I hope to return to the subject at a later time.

2. For possible traces of Maerlant's work in the *Tafel*, see Chapter V, sec. 3; for Maerlant's influence on Hildegaersberch, see Chapter II, sec. 2; for the links

between Maerlant and Potter, see Chapter VI, sec. 3; and for Maerlant's links with the Herald see, above all, Chapter IV, sec. 2.

3. See particularly Rickert 1949; and Finke 1963; and, more recently, Hindman 1987. It is remarkable (and satisfying) to note how often these studies use art-historical criteria for bracketing together manuscripts that can also be correlated on (literary) historical grounds. See the discussion of William the Confessor below. Significant contributions can also be found in *The Golden Age of Dutch Manuscript Painting* 1989; and Van Oostrom 1991.

4. This entry, as well as the preceding one, was discovered by T. Meder. (This example alone shows that interest in court literature was not confined to the ruling dynasty. See sec. 3 below and, for instance, the double dedication of *HK* [see Chapter IV, secs. 3–4] to William VI and the bishop of Utrecht.)

5. See Warnar 1988–89.

6. See Overmaat 1952, 118–20; (especially) Overmaat 1977; and (for the musical notation) Stam 1977. Below is the first verse of the (again, strongly German-tinged) song, quoted from Overmaat 1977, 37, but with modernized spelling and added punctuation. In addition to the drinking song, the index lists two Latin proverbs and a German-Dutch epigram. The (unacknowledged) witticism (*ML* IV, 77–79) that the married state, unlike the monastic, cannot, alas, be dissolved after one year may be found in much the same words in the writings of Peter's brother Dirk.

7. Even the elegant *HLH*, which (like Hildegaersberch in his sphere) was undoubtedly the most polished of its kind, adopts a more popular tone from time to time; see, e.g., song no. 62, quoted in Chapter III, sec. 2. The accounts, too, repeatedly mention singers with what must have been a fairly popular repertoire; see Jonckbloet 1854. The reference there (p. 646, Mainz 1371) to "3 servants who sang the song of Vermof Merdas at my lord's tavern" is rather enigmatic. Jonckbloet suspects that "Vermof Merdas" must have been the name of the songwriter or of some other person, but it could equally well have been a (misread, Germanized, or bastardized) *incipit*. Cf. the (equally cryptic) reference in *ML* IV, 1975, "*Soemen van Roseboom* was wont to sing," in connection with the spicy Schiedam affair discussed in Chapter VI, sec. 2.

8. See L9 in Van Biezen–Gumbert 1985 (cited in the Note on Editions). Nos. 7, 10, and 11 have erotic overtones as well. Is it an accident that all of them are French songs? The most risqué song in *HLH*, too, is in French, namely no. 73 (discussed in Chapter III, sec. 2).

9. See poems XXVI and LXXXV, discussed in Chapter II, sec. 4. Some of Potter's stories, too, sail close to the wind; see Chapter VI, sec. 2. *Of women and of love*, for example, a manuscript discussed below, contains several bits of low farce.

10. I am indebted to D.E.H. de Boer for this item. In a sense, the combination of illustrations and pious sayings was also an important reflection of the court's attitude toward the sacral sphere; see Chapter V, sec. 4, more generally.

11. Van Foreest 1965–66, 128. The Leiden song manuscript, too, contains a carnival song in addition to compositions by Fabri and Boy; see L17 in that edition. See also (in passing) Chapter III, sec. 4, and Chapter IV, sec. 4.

12. For this entry, see Jonckbloet 1854, 616; cf. Chapter I, sec. 4.

13. See Verwijs 1871; and, among later writers, esp. Pleij 1979. Nijland 1896, 140–41 (and 147) also associates the manuscript with Holland-Bavarian cultural influences. Cf. Brinkman 1987.

14. For an assessment of musical life, see Wagenaar-Nolthenius 1969 (on Fabri and Boy), 308; for the fine arts, see Van Luttervelt 1957; and Kurz 1956.

15. We need only recall the double marriage of Albert's children to members of the House of Burgundy (see Chapter II, sec. 1); the marriage of his second daughter, Joanna, to King Wenceslas; and the arranged marriages of Jacqueline of Bavaria to the French crown prince and the duke of Brabant. As Boehm (1981, 116) rightly observes, this was a two-sided coin: these marriages increasingly drove Holland into the arms of the great powers, until it ultimately lost its very identity (to the Burgundians; see sec. 4 below).

16. On politics and music in a Holland caught between these two worlds, see De Boer 1986; and A. Janse 1986.

17. See U. Peters 1983 for an important and balanced account; Holland is treated in chap. 3, sec. 1, of that work.

18. See the entries in Jonckbloet 1854, 602, 613; and the discussion in Mundschau 1972, 85. U. Peters (1983, 194) mentions a payment recorded in the Blois accounts to "Master Peter, the speaker from Breda." Speakers from towns in Flanders and Brabant are mentioned earlier and more often; see Pleij 1987b.

19. See, for the English court, Mathew 1968; Green 1980; and Alexander 1983; for the French court during the same period, Poirion 1965; and for Burgundian literature, Vaughan 1970, 155–60; Vaughan 1979, 191–95.

20. For Guelders, see Nijsten 1985, 1986. In general, the court of Brabant was as prominent a center of Middle Dutch literature as the court of Holland, but after the mid–fourteenth century French became the language of cultured circles in Brabant under Wenzel (Wenceslaus) of Luxembourg; see Van Oostrom 1982; and Chapter I, sec. 2, and Chapter VII, sec. 4.

21. For a bird's-eye view of literature at the court of Holland, see Van Oostrom 1985b, 1986a.

22. The "opening up" of literary potential, incidentally, was not confined to late-fourteenth-century Holland but was a characteristic of literature generally during that period; see the masterly survey in Kuhn 1980, 57–75.

23. For Potter, see Chapter VI, secs. 1, 2, and 4 (and for Tristan, also *HLH* I/st. 6/47); for Christian names in the accounts, see Jonckbloet 1854, 611; and Nijsten 1984, 187n.45. (I am obliged to the author for permission to consult his doctoral thesis, about to be presented to Nijmegen University.)

24. See Schnell 1978, 79; Haug 1982, 56–57; and esp. Cramer 1983.

25. See Van Oostrom 1984a, on which the following discussion is based. For "thematic fatigue," see esp. Haug 1980.

26. Another pointer is the Herald's insistence in the prologue of *HK* that he had compiled his history "as short as I knew how to" (for the relevant quotation in a wider context, see sec. 3 below). He followed this declaration by quoting William VI's personal commission to him; cf. *TKG* "W" XXXVIII/170.

27. For Holland, see the life of, say, Baldwin of Zwieten, as outlined in Van Kan 1981.

28. The poem in *HLH* about the maid, the old knight, and the young fop (no. 66, quoted in Chapter III, sec. 2 above) is characteristic of this trend.

29. Tuchman 1978. Other studies treating the fourteenth century as one of decay include Wood 1983; and Van Caenegem 1982. Schnell 1978; and Liebertz-Grün 1984, 63–64, take a different view.

30. See *TKG* "W" XXXIV/240–41; *HLH* 98/385–92; *BD* 114/47–115/3; *HK* 78v (with significant minor differences from Beke and Stoke). Other laments about the age can be found in, e.g., *BD* 17/47–48, 69/12, 70/18–21, 73/30–32, 77/32–35; *TKG* "S" XLI/135–37 (quoted in Chapter V, sec. 2); and *HLH* 15A, 90, 107.

31. See Hildegaersberch's prologues to XXIV, XLI, LXIV, and LXXXIII; *TKG* "W" XIX/128–29; and *BD* 69/10–13. *HLH* and the Herald are not quite so explicit. Other references to the good old times can be found in *TKG* "S" XLI/20–80, and abundantly in William of Hildegaersberch: see Chapter II, sec. 3.

32. Of course, Holland was prospering economically in the second half of the fourteenth century; see Jansen 1976. But however advantageous that might have been for the count's treasury, urban expansion went hand in hand with urban power politics, a trend that, from the court's (and hence our authors') point of view, was not unreservedly welcome. It is also against this background that we must view the tension between the accumulation of worldly goods and the quest for honor, as reflected in much of the literature of the times: a hankering after possessions tends to disturb the established order. See the pertinent discussion in Ragotzky 1980b; also Chapter II, sec. 3.

33. *HLH* 98. The fact that the work of Augustijnken—which was at least partly associated with the (early) court of Holland-Bavaria—has not been treated more systematically in this book must be considered a serious shortcoming. A.M.J. van Buuren is currently engaged on a special Augustijnken study. (Did "Vanden scepe" have a much more concrete and timely significance in its own day than the general and abstract one suggested here? Cf. Hildegaersberch's "Vanden sloetel" [On the key], discussed in Chapter II, sec. 2.)

34. Given the confines of this work, it is impossible to enter into the complicated question of how the then-prevailing conception of literature differed from our own. Important studies of the literary conception(s) of late-medieval (court) circles can be found in Allen 1982; Coleman 1981; Stevens 1961, chap. 10; Kuhn 1980; and Janota 1983. Needless to say, the arguments presented here in no way detract from the remarks on comic court literature in the last section, nor should the entertainment value of medieval literature be underestimated: even a moralist like (the later) Potter spoke up for the "many poets who . . . put all manner of agreeable inventions into verse, the better to please those who like to hear that sort of thing" (*BD* 36/32–35).

35. Most stated their didactive purpose explicitly: for Hildegaersberch, see the relevant quotations in Chapter II, sec. 4; for *HLH*, see 78/2, quoted in Chapter III, sec. 3 (and also 114/78); for Dirk of Delft, see Chapter V, sec. 4; and for Dirk Potter, see the prologues to *ML* and to *BD*. Only the Herald did not say in so many words that he was out to instruct his readers, but his prologues betray that very intention; nor is it without significance that he said of Charlemagne

that "when he sat at table, he loved to hear stories of lords, of arms, of wisdom, and of wars so as to learn and remember" (*WK* 79r).

36. See Huizinga 1919; and Van Oostrom 1986b. The relative conservatism of Holland-Bavarian culture is also reflected in music and prosody; see Wagenaar-Nolthenius 1969, 308; and Van den Berg 1983, 224.

37. The literature in this field is vast; masterly studies impinging on anthropology, sociology, and intellectual and literary history include Peristiany 1966; Maurer 1971a,b; Elias 1977, 144–56; Robreau 1981; Maso 1982; Ward 1982–83; Künzel 1983; and Fischer 1983. For research into Middle Dutch material, see Van Buuren 1984b; Van Oostrom 1986b; and esp. Van Buuren 1988. Chapter 11 of Huizinga 1919 ("The Forms of Thought and Practical Life," English chapter 18) contains a trenchant discussion of "honor culture" at medieval courts.

38. See, e.g., *TKG* "W" XII/156–66 and XXIII/190–93 (however, the honor concept occurs much more often in the writings of Dirk of Delft, as I learned from my student E. Kooreman); cf. *HK* 37v–38r; William of Hildegaersberch LXXVI/273–79 (quoted in Chapter II, sec. 4) and CXV/69; *BD* 106/21 and 110/13.

39. See Van Oostrom 1986b; the following conclusion is offered pending a more "conscientious" investigation, and introduces no more than fresh nuances: cf. Van Buuren (1988) and what follows below. Relevant passages in Potter's writing include particularly *ML* I, 917–27; II, 3285–98, 3598–3612; III, 646–68; IV, 591–652 and 774–78.

40. It is generally believed that the honor concept evolved from a purely external notion (respect) toward a more internalized one (virtue). Students of Professor F. Willaert have drawn my attention to the parallel with the development of conscience attributed to "modern man" by the sociologist L. Kohlberg—from externally imposed norms (those of one's parents and social environment) to an independent attitude. Cf. Reiner 1956.

41. See Chapter II, sec. 3, Chapter III, sec. 2, and Chapter VI, sec. 2; cf. such passages as *ML* III, 345; IV, 1638–86 and 1821–28; *BD* 26/2–3 and the chapter on *scalckheit* (roguery); *TKG* "W" XXVIII/25–36 and XXXII/394–424. Here, too, striking parallels can be drawn with other shame cultures; see Versnel 1984, 39.

42. This short poem was fittingly marked by the copyist with a marginal *nota bene* and repeated as maxim no. 112*. Sir Honorful and Lady Honor (interchangeable; see the variant in 112*) are personifications of absolute honor.

43. This anecdote taken from Froissart is found in Verwijs 1869, xlv.

44. See the incisive study by Thum (1980).

45. See Schneider 1913, app. V; and Götze 1878. A comparable example is the satirical song about King Louis the Bavarian quoted in Bach 1964, 508. For obvious reasons, many of these satirical songs have been lost. Another good example is what *Dat boec exemplaer* (The book of exemplars) had to say about Julius Caesar (see Heeroma 1958–59, 194), namely that he took it in good spirit when "they wrote poems about him and improper songs that belittled him."

46. Poem XXIX, lines 146–49, in Primisser 1827; I have slightly modernized the spelling of the passage. My attention to it was drawn by W. van Anrooij; see

Van Anrooij 1990 for further details on Suchenwirt and his connections with the court of Holland-Bavaria and with the Herald.

47. Cf. the skepticism of various contributors to *English Court Culture in the Later Middle Ages* (e.g., Scattergood 1983), though the introduction by J. A. Burrow should not be ignored.

48. The Muider Circle, which flourished during the first half of the seventeenth century, included such luminaries as Grotius, Vondel, and Huygens. The circle gathered around P. C. Hooft, *drost* (or sheriff) of Muiden, whence its name.

49. See Spies 1984.

50. See Van Buuren 1984b, 58–59.

51. AGH 1262, fol. 61v. This entry in the accounts was discovered by W. van Anrooij.

52. Compare *ML* III, 833–908, and I, 2515–2686, with *WK* 5v–6r and 35v–36r; and *BD* 93/21–25 with *WK* 31v, respectively. See Warnar 1986; exploratory research by Warnar has also uncovered other Potter passages that may go back to the Herald, although Potter has rephrased them freely.

53. In general, the princes of (medieval) courts, that of Holland-Bavaria included, were on much closer terms with members of their household staff than we tend to think; in that sense, the term *huysgesinde* (familiars) is revealing. See, e.g., Lingbeek-Schalekamp 1984, 117–18.

54. Unless the phrase "tot sonderlinghe bevelinghe" (for the special consideration of) in the commissioning brief of the *TKG* is taken to mean "on the orders of" Albert of Bavaria. But that seems an unlikely interpretation.

55. Was that a reference to the (extant) breviary of Margaret of Cleves? See Chapter I, sec. 4; and Hindman 1987, 439. (The accounts entry [and the following one as well] were discovered by T. Meder; see Meder 1991 for a survey of entries in the county accounts bearing on literary life at court.)

56. See Chapter I, sec. 4, and sec. 1 above. The later copy of the book was also intended for a lady, namely the lady of Kruiningen; see Warnar 1988–89.

57. Albert's death quashed these pious hopes. For philological and historical reasons, moreover, it is far from certain that Dirk addressed these words directly to Albert; see Chapter V, sec. 4; and Van Oostrom 1987a.

58. See Chapter V, sec. 4; and Van Oostrom 1987a.

59. Brill 1876, 38.

60. For Jacqueline's turbulent life and reign, see Jansen 1976; and Löher 1862–69.

61. See Chapter I, sec. 4; and Jansen 1967, 58–60; for the (by no means generally accepted) link between his poisoning and his death, see Jansen 1980, which includes references to the earlier literature.

62. See the inventory of Jacqueline's estate, published in *Codex diplomaticus neerlandicus* 1852, esp. 176, 186, 182; cf. Chapter I, sec. 4.

63. See Schneider 1913, 142–49.

64. For his links with the court of Holland-Bavaria, see ibid., 143; Kurz 1956, 129; and Weale 1908, xxvii–xxviii, xxx–xxxi. Dhanens (1980, 162) considers it possible that both the *Fishing Party* and the *Cavalcade* are copies of original work by Van Eyck.

65. See Schneider 1913, 143, from which the following information is taken as well.

66. See Crowe and Cavalcaselle 1875, 40n.1; and Jonckbloet 1854, 612–17, where several speakers by the same name are mentioned.

67. Schneider 1913, 143–44.

68. See Muller 1888; the presumed date of the (incomplete) Hague manuscript text has since been advanced from ca. 1430 to ca. 1460; see *Verluchte handschriften* 1985, no. 249. Under the aegis of W. P. Gerritsen, M. Desage is currently writing a thesis on the translation, one more reason for confining the present discussion to preliminary impressions based on the incomplete De Pauw (1898–1909) edition.

69. See Calkoen 1902, 68–84; Ebels-Hoving 1985, 32; and Lingbeek-Schalekamp 1984, 7, 143. It appears that the cultural history of the Hainaut period was repeated in another respect as well: much as artists from Holland had formerly sought employment with the lower nobility at the court in Voorne (see Van Oostrom 1982, 35–36), so they now turned increasingly to Frank of Borselen (and later to the Brederodes?). For the rest, the Hague court shared in the Burgundian luster on many special occasions; see, e.g., Smit 1923; and Kuyper 1984, 26–27.

70. See Rickert 1949, 101n.37; and Van Oostrom 1987a. Possibly it was also along this route that the (since lost) manuscript of Maerlant's *Historie van Troyen* came into Burgundian hands, as reported in *Vlaamse kunst of perkament* 1981, 210 sub a (with acknowledgments to L. Jongen). Another case is the manuscript of *HK* that came into the possession of Edmond de Dynter, secretary to Philip the Good, who, as a historian, was obviously interested in the contents; see Muller 1885, 33.

71. Royal Library, The Hague, MS. 128 E 6. Other examples of texts originating in the court of Holland-Bavaria and later existing jointly are manuscripts of *TKG* and *WK* that once belonged to the library of the Magdalene Convent in Haarlem (Leiden University Library, Lit. 338 [lost in 1914] and BPL 76C), and *HLH* and a manuscript of *WK* (Royal Library, The Hague, MS. 128 E 10) belonging to the library of John IV of Nassau (see Chapter III, sec. 1).

72. See Chapter VI, sec. 3; the illustration in the manuscript (fig. 27 above) might well indicate that it was originally intended for secular circles.

73. See Van Oostrom 1987a (also for the following discussion).

74. See the manuscript in Leiden University Library (BPL 76C), fols. 42r and 48v, respectively; I am indebted for this information to P. Rodenburg, who compared the different versions at a doctoral seminar.

Bibliography

Alexander, J.J.G. 1983. "Painting and Manuscript Illumination for Royal Patrons in the Later Middle Ages." In *English Court Culture in the Later Middle Ages*, ed. V. J. Scattergood, 141–62. London.

Allen, J. B. 1982. *The Ethical Poetic of the Later Middle Ages: A Decorum of Convenient Distinction*. Toronto.

Anrooij, W. van. 1985. "Dichter, kroniekschrijver en wapenkundige: heraut Gelre en zijn werk." *Literatuur* 5:244–51.

———. 1986a. "Heraut Beieren en heraut Gelre: oude theorieën in nieuw perspectief." *Bijdragen en mededelingen betreffende de geschiedenis der Nederlanden* 101:153–76.

———. 1986b. "Herauten in de middeleeuwen." *Spiegel historiael* 21:270–79.

———. 1988. "Het Haagse handschrift van heraut Beyeren: de wordingsgeschiedenis van een autograaf." *Tijdschrift voor Nederlandse taal- en letterkunde* 104:1–20.

———. 1990. *Spiegel van ridderschap. Heraut Gelre en zijn ereredes*. Amsterdam.

Asselbergs, W. 1957. "De bijbel in de late middeleeuwen." In *De bijbel in de literatuur*, 30–43. The Hague.

Axters, S. 1937. *Scholastiek lexicon*. Antwerp.

———. 1939. "Meester Dirc van Delf en zijn Dietsche Summa." *Kultuurleven* 10:350–54.

———. 1940. "De geestelijke physionomie van meester Dirc van Delf." *Roeping*, 583–96.

———. 1953. *Geschiedenis van de vroomheid in de Nederlanden*. Vol. 2. Antwerp.

———. 1956. *Geschiedenis van de vroomheid in de Nederlanden*. Vol. 3. Antwerp.

Bach, A. 1964. *Germanistisch-historische Studien*. Bonn.

Bartelink, J.T.N. 1985. "Vroom of wereldwijs: eigenkloosters van de graven van Holland." *Groniek*, no. 93: 45–59.

Beelaerts van Blokland, W. A. 1929. "De Hollandsche Tuin en de Orde van St. Anthonis." *Maandblad van het genealogisch-heraldisch genootschap "De Nederlandsche leeuw"* 47, cols. 363–66.

———. 1933. *Beyeren quondam Gelre armorum rex de Ruyris. Een historisch-heraldische studie*. The Hague.

Beets, A. 1885. *De "Disticha Catonis" in het Middelnederlandsch*. Groningen.

Beke, Johannes de. 1982. *Croniken van den Stichte van Utrecht ende van Hollant*. Edited by H. Bruch. The Hague.

Berents, D. A. 1985. *Het werk van de vos. Samenleving en criminaliteit in de late middeleeuwen*. Zutphen.

Berg, E. van den. 1983. *Middelnederlandse versbouw en syntaxis. Ontwikkelingen in de versifikatie van verhalende poëzie ca. 1200–ca. 1400.* Utrecht.

"De bibliotheek van de kapel op het hof in Den Haag." 1876. *Mededeelingen van de Vereeniging ter beoefening der geschiedenis van 's Gravenhage* 2:16–19.

Bibliothèque Jhr. J.F.L. Coenen van 's Gravesloot (auction catalogue). 1918. Amsterdam.

Blank, W. 1970. *Die deutsche Minneallegorie. Gestaltung und Funktion einer spätmittelalterlichen Dichtungsform.* Stuttgart.

Blok, P. J. 1885. "De eerste regeeringsjaren van Hertog Albrecht van Beieren 1358–1374." *Bijdragen voor vaderlandsche geschiedenis en oudheidkunde,* 3d ser., 2: 244–84.

Boehm, L. 1981. "Das Haus Wittelsbach in den Niederlanden." *Zeitschrift für bayerische Landesgeschichte* 44:93–130.

———. 1982. "Das mittelalterliche Erziehungs- und Bildungswesen." In *Propyläen Geschichte der Literatur II: Die mittelalterliche Welt, 600–1400,* 143–81. Berlin.

Boer, D.E.H. de. 1978. *Graaf en grafiek. Sociale en economische ontwikkelingen in het middeleeuwse "Noordholland" tussen ca. 1345 en ca. 1415.* Leiden.

———. 1986. "Vorst tussen twee werelden: het hof van Albrecht van Beieren (1336–1404)." *Fibula* 27, no. 2: 4–11.

———. 1987. "Ein Dreieck wird gespannt: der Weggang Albrechts von Bayern-Straubing in die Niederlande im Licht der Territorien bildung." *Jahresbericht des Historischen Vereins für Straubing und Umgebung* 89:33–56.

Boffey, J. 1983. "The Manuscripts of English Courtly Love Lyrics in the Fifteenth Century." In *Manuscripts and Readers in Fifteenth-Century England,* edited by D. Pearsall, 3–14. London.

Borck, K. H. 1978. "Adel, Tugend und Geblüt: Thesen und Beobachtungen zur Vorstellung des Tugendadels in der deutschen Literatur des 12. und 13. Jahrhunderts." *Beiträge zur Geschichte der deutschen Sprache und Literatur* 100: 423–457.

Bos-Rops, J.A.M.Y. 1982. "Willem Eggert (ca. 1360–1417): een Amsterdams koopman in grafelijke dienst." *Hollandse studiën* 12:37–72.

Boulton, D'A.J.D. 1987. *The Knights of the Crown: The Monarchical Orders of Knighthood in Later Medieval Europe, 1325–1520.* Woodbridge, Eng.

Bozzolo, C., and H. Loyau. 1982. *La cour amoureuse dite de Charles VI.* Vol. 1. Paris.

Brand Philip, L. 1971. *The Ghent Altarpiece and the Art of Jan van Eyck.* Princeton.

Brill, W. G. 1876. "Holland onder het huis van Beieren." *Voorlezingen over de geschiedenis der Nederlanden* 2, pt. 3: 1–84.

Brinkman, H. 1987. "Neidhart in de Nederlanden: *Vanden Kaerlen* en de literaire traditie." *Literatuur* 4:205–11.

Brokken, H. M. [1979]. "Het beleg van Delft in 1359." In *De stad Delft. Cultuur en maatschappij tot 1572,* 19–22. Delft.

———. 1982. *Het ontstaan van de Hoekse en Kabeljauwse twisten.* Zutphen.

———. 1984. "Het Hof in Den Haag: grafelijke residentie en centrum van bestuur." In *Het Binnenhof. Van grafelijke residentie tot regeringscentrum,* edited by R. J. van Pelt et al., 13–20. Dieren.

Bruch, H. 1954–55. "De Clerc uten laghen landen." *Bijdragen tot de geschiedenis der Nederlanden* 9:38–48.

———. 1984. "Johannes de Beke en Friesland." *It Beaken* 46:238–50.

Brunner, H. 1978. "Das deutsche Liebeslied um 1400." In *Gesammelte Vorträge der 66-Jahrfeier Oswalds von Wolkenstein,* edited by H.-D. Mück et al., 105–46. Göppingen.

Buddingh, D. 1842. *Geschiedenis van opvoeding en onderwijs, met betrekking tot het Bijbellezen en godsdienstig onderrigt op de scholen in de Nederlanden.* Pt. 1. The Hague.

———. 1843. *Bijdragen of geschied- en letterkundig mengelwerk, betrekkelijk de geschiedenis van opvoeding en onderwijs in de Nederlanden.* Pt. 1. The Hague.

Bumke, J. 1979. *Mäzene im Mittelalter. Die Gönner und Auftraggeber der höfischen Literatur in Deutschland, 1150–1300.* Munich.

———. 1986. *Höfische Kultur. Literatur und Gesellschaft im hohen Mittelalter.* 2 vols. Munich.

Busken Huet, C. 1882. *Het land van Rembrand.* Vol. 1. Haarlem.

Buuren, A.M.J. van. 1979. *Der minnen loep van Dirc Potter. Studie over een Middelnederlandse ars amandi.* Utrecht.

———. 1984a. "Dat scamelheit thoechste poent es van minnen." In *Ic ga daer ic hebbe te doene. Opstellen aangeboden aan Prof. Dr. F. Lulofs,* edited by J.J.T.M. Tersteeg et al., 127–48. Groningen.

———. 1984b. "*Die Minne staet op aventuer.*" *Jaarboek Fonteine* 34:49–63.

———. 1985a. "Ernst of boert." *Vooys* 4 (special issue: *Liber amicorum Jules van Oostrom*): 17–21.

———. 1985b. "Een seer notabel boeck: *Blome der doechden* van Dirc Potter." In *Tussentijds. Bundel studies aangeboden aan W. P. Gerritsen,* edited by A.M.J. van Buuren et al., 41–55. Utrecht.

———. 1987a. "*Nu woent die paus tot Avenyoen?*" In *Leidschrift special. Gescheurd geloven,* 29–56. Leiden.

———. 1987b. "*Ay hoor van desen abuze:* enkele dorpers uit de Middelnederlandse literatuur." In *Gewone mensen in de middeleeuwen. Bundel studies aangeboden aan F.W.N. Hugenholtz,* edited by R.E.V. Stuip et al., 137–59. Utrecht.

———. 1988. "Eer en schande in enkele laat-Middelnederlandse literaire teksten." In *Soete minne en helsche boosheit. Seksuele voorstellingen in Nederland, 1300–1850,* edited by G. Hekma et al., 23–41. Nijmegen.

Caenegem, R. C. van. 1982. "Slotreferaat." In *Hoofsheid en devotie in de middeleeuwse maatschappij,* edited by J. D. Janssens, 240–59. Brussels.

Calkoen, G. C. 1902. "Het Binnenhof van 1247–1747 (volgens de Rentmeestersrekeningen van Noord-Holland)." *Die Haghe,* 35–182.

Carasso-Kok, M. 1981. *Repertorium van verhalende historische bronnen uit de middeleeuwen.* The Hague.

Christiansen, E. 1980. *The Northern Crusades: The Baltic and the Catholic Frontier, 1100–1525.* London.

348   Bibliography

Codex diplomaticus neerlandicus. Verzameling van oorkonden, betrekkelijk de vader-landsche geschiedenis. 1852. 2d ser., vol. 1. Utrecht.

Coenen van 's Gravesloot, J.F.L. 1875. "Wapenboek door den wapenkoning Beyeren uit het begin der XVde eeuw." *Heraldische Bibliotheek* [4]:30–34.

Coleman, J. 1981. *English Literature in History: 1350–1400—Medieval Readers and Writers.* London.

———. 1983. "English Culture in the Fourteenth Century." In *Chaucer and the Italian Trecento,* edited by P. Boitani, 33–63. Cambridge.

Cramer, T. 1974. "Normenkonflikte im *Pfaffen Amis* und im *Willehalm von Wenden." Zeitschrift für deutsche Philologie* 93 (special issue): 124–40.

———. 1983. "Aspekte des höfischen Romans im 14. Jahrhundert." In *Zur deutschen Literatur und Sprache des 14. Jahrhunderts,* edited by W. Haug et al., 208–20. Heidelberg.

Crawford, A. 1981. "The King's Burden? The Consequences of Royal Marriage in Fifteenth-Century England." In *Patronage, the Crown, and the Provinces in Later Medieval England,* edited by R. A. Griffiths, 33–56. Gloucester.

Crowe, J. A., and G. B. Cavalcaselle. 1875. *Geschichte der altniederländischen Malerei.* Leipzig.

Cuvelier, J. 1921. *Les origines de la fortune de la maison d'Orange-Nassau.* Brussels.

Dallapiazza, M. 1981. *Minne, husere und das ehlich leben. Zur Konstitution bürgerlicher Lebensmuster in spätmittelalterlichen und frühhumanistischen Didaktiken.* Frankfurt.

Daniëls, F. L. M. 1932. *Meester Dirc van Delf. Zijn persoon en zijn werk.* Nijmegen.

Dehaisnes, [C]. 1886. *Documents et extraits divers concernant l'histoire de l'art dans la Flandre, l'Artois et le Hainaut avant le XVe siècle.* 2 vols. Lille.

Delaissé, L.M.J. 1972. "The Miniatures Added in the Low Countries to the Turin-Milan Hours and Their Political Significance." In *Kunst-historische Forschungen Otto Pächt zu seinem 70. Geburtstag,* 135–149. Salzburg.

Dempf, A. 1925. *Die Hauptform mittelalterlicher Weltanschauung. Eine geisteswissenschaftliche Studie über die Summa.* Munich.

Deschamps, J. 1972. *Middelnederlandse handschriften uit europese en amerikaanse bibliotheken.* 2d rev. ed. Leiden.

Devillers, L. 1878. "Sur les expéditions des comtes de Hainaut et de Hollande en Prusse." *Compte rendu des séances de la Commission royale d'histoire,* 4th ser., 5: 127–44.

———. 1886/1887. "La naissance et les premières années de Jacqueline de Bavière." *Messager des sciences historiques* 1886:273–305, 456–89; 1887:185–210.

Dhanens, E. 1980. *Hubert en Jan van Eyck.* Antwerp.

Dinzelbacher, P. 1979a. "Klassen und Hierarchien im Jenseits." In *Soziale Ordnungen im Selbstverständnis des Mittelalters,* edited by A. Zimmermann, 1:20–40.

———. 1979b. "Reflexionen irdischer Sozialstrukturen in mittelalterlichen Jenseitsschilderungen." *Archiv für Kulturgeschichte* 61:16–34.

Duinhoven, A. M. 1977. "Corruptie is overal." *De nieuwe taalgids* 70:97–120.

Ebels-Hoving, B. 1985. "Johannes a Leydis en de eerste humanistische geschiedschrijving van Holland." *Bijdragen en mededelingen betreffende de geschiedenis der Nederlanden* 100:26–51.

Eberle, P. J. 1985. "The Politics of Courtly Style at the Court of Richard II." In *The Spirit of the Court: Selected Proceedings of the Fourth Congress of the International Courtly Literature Society (Toronto 1983)*, edited by G. S. Burgess et al., 168–78. Cambridge.

Elias, N. 1977. *Die höfische Gesellschaft.* 3d ed. Darmstadt.

Ferbeek, E. 1985. "Ende zij waren hoofs . . . Ridderschap en hoofsheid in Holland." *Groniek*, no. 93: 79–91.

Finke, U. 1963. "Utrecht: Zentrum nordniederländischer Buchmalerei." *Oud Holland* 78:27–66.

Fischer, H. 1983. *Ehre, Hof und Abenteuer in Hartmanns "Iwein." Vorarbeiten zu einer historischen Poetik des höfischen Epos.* Munich.

Fleckenstein, J. 1959–66. *Die Hofkapelle der deutschen Könige.* 2 vols. Stuttgart.

———, ed. 1985. *Das ritterliche Turnier im Mittelalter.* Göttingen.

Foreest, H. A. van. 1964/1965–66/1968–69. "Traditie en werkelijkheid." *Bijdragen voor de geschiedenis der Nederlanden* 18 (1964): 143–66; 20 (1965–66): 110–46; 22 (1968–69): 171–208.

Franz, K. 1974. *Studien zur Soziologie des Spruchdichters in Deutschland im späten 13. Jahrhundert.* Göppingen.

Froissart, Jean. 1852. *Les chroniques.* Vol. 3. Edited by J.A.C. Buchon. Paris.

Frühwald, W. 1963. *Der St. Georgener Prediger. Studien zur Wandlung des geistlichen Gehaltes.* Berlin.

Gaspar, C., and F. Lyna. 1937. *Les principaux manuscrits à peintures de la Bibliothèque Royale de Belgique.* 2 vols. Paris.

[Geer van Jutphaas, B.J.L. de, ed.] 1867. *Kronijk van Holland van een ongenoemden geestelijke.* Utrecht.

Gelder, H. E. van. 1975. "De reiskas van graaf Willem IV." In *Driekwart eeuw historisch leven in Den Haag*, 51–65. The Hague.

Gerritsen, W. P. 1979. "Wat voor boeken zou Floris V gelezen hebben?" In *Floris V. Leven, wonen en werken aan het einde van de dertiende eeuw*, 71–86. The Hague.

———. 1981. "Jacob van Maerlant and Geoffrey of Monmouth." In *An Arthurian Tapestry: Essays in Memory of Lewis Thorpe*, edited by K. Varty, 368–88. Glasgow.

Gerritsen, W. P., and B. Schludermann. 1976. "Deutsch-niederländische Literaturbeziehungen im Mittelalter: Sprachmischung als Kommunikationsweise und als poetisches Mittel." In *Akten des V. Internationalen Germanisten-Kongresses Cambridge 1975*, edited by L. Forster et al., 2:329–39. Bern.

Glier, I. 1971. *Artes amandi. Untersuchung zu Geschichte, Überlieferung und Typologie der deutschen Minnereden.* Munich.

———. 1981. "Haager Liederhandschrift." In *Die deutsche Literatur des Mittelalters. Verfasserlexikon*, 2d ed., 3: cols. 358–60. Berlin.

Godding, P., and J.T.H. de Smidt. 1980. "Evolutie van het recht in samenhang met de instellingen." *Algemene geschiedenis der Nederlanden* (Haarlem) 4: 172–181.

The Golden Age of Dutch Manuscript Painting. 1989. Intro. by J. H. Marrow; catalogue by H.L.M. Defoer et al. Stuttgart.

Gorissen, F. 1973. *Das Stundenbuch der Katharina von Kleve. Analyse und Kommentar.* Berlin.

Gorp, K. van. 1912. "Hans Vintlers *Pluemen der Tugent* en Dirc Potters *Blome der doechden.*" *Verslagen en mededeelingen Koninklijke Vlaamse Academie,* 525–41.

Götze, L. 1878. "Ein Scheltbrief des Grafen Johann III von Nassau-Dillenburg gegen den Herzog Johann von Bayern und Holland." *Monatschrift für die Geschichte Westdeutschlands* 4:63–73.

Grabmann, M. 1909. *Die Geschichte der scholastischen Methode.* Vol. 1. Frieburg.

"'s Gravenhage onder de regering der graven uit de huizen van Holland, Henegouwen en Beijeren." 1863. *Mededeelingen van de Vereeniging ter beoefening der geschiedenis van 's Gravenhage* 1:207–342.

Green, R. F. 1980. *Poets and Princepleasers: Literature and the English Court in the Late Middle Ages.* Toronto.

———. 1983. "The *Familia regis* and the *Familia cupidinis.*" In *English Court Culture in the Later Middle Ages,* edited by V. J. Scattergood et al., 88–108. London.

———. 1990. "*Le roi qui ne ment* and Aristocratic Courtship." In *Courtly Literature: Culture and Context,* edited by K. Busby and E. Kooper, 211–25. Amsterdam.

Guenée, B. 1980. *Histoire et culture historique dans l'occident médiéval.* Paris.

Guyot, P.C.G. 1858. "Rood, wit en blaauw, de landsheerlijke kleuren van Holland onder de graven uit het huis van Beijeren; en graauw, namelijk bleekblauw, de kleur van de hofkleding dier graven." *Bijdragen voor vaderlandsche geschiedenis en oudheidkunde* 10:344–54.

Guyse, Jacques de. 1826–38. *Histoire de Hainaut.* 21 vols. Edited by the marquis de Fortia d'Urban. Paris.

Hahn, I. 1985. "Das Ethos der *Kraft:* zur Bedeutung der Massenschlachten in Strickers *Daniel von dem Blühenden Tal.*" *Deutsche Vierteljahrsschrift* 59:173–94.

Haug, W. 1980. "Paradigmatische Poesie: der spätere deutsche Artusroman auf dem Weg zu einer 'nachklassischen' Ästhetik." *Deutsche Vierteljahrsschrift* 54:204–31.

———. 1982. "Das Bildprogramm im Sommerhaus von Runkelstein." In *Runkelstein. Die Wandmalereien des Sommerhauses,* 15–62. Wiesbaden.

Heeringen, R. M. van. 1983. "'s Gravenhage in archeologisch perspectief." In *De bodem van 's Gravenhage,* edited by E.F.J. de Mulder, 96–126. The Hague.

Heeroma, K. 1958–59. "Nieuwe Middelnederlandse fragmenten: *Dat Boec Exemplaer.*" *Tijdschrift voor Nederlandse taal- en letterkunde* 76:178–98.

———. 1968. "Augustijnkens meilied." *Tijdschrift voor Nederlandse taal- en letterkunde* 84:38–52.

Heinzle, J. 1984. *Geschichte der deutschen Literatur von den Anfängen bis zum Beginn der Neuzeit.* Vol. 2/2: *Wandlungen und Neuansätze im 13. Jahrhundert.* Königstein.

Henderikx, P. A. 1977. *De oudste bedelordekloosters in het graafschap Holland en Zeeland*. Dordrecht.

Heniger, J. 1982. "Beleg van Hagestein in 1405." *In 't land van Brederode* 7, no. 2/ 3: 32–44.

De heraldiek in de handschriften voor 1600. 1985. Catalogue compiled by C. van den Bergen-Pantens. Brussels.

Hermesdorf, B.H.D. 1980. *Rechtsspiegel. Een rechtshistorische terugblik in de Lage Landen van het herfsttij*. Nijmegen.

Herwaarden, J. van. 1983. "Geloof en geloofsuitingen in de late middeleeuwen in de Nederlanden: Jerusalembedevaarten, lijdensdevotie en kruiswegverering." *Bijdragen en mededelingen betreffende de geschiedenis der Nederlanden* 98:400–429.

Herwaarden, J. van, and R. de Keyser. 1980. "Het gelovige volk in de late middeleeuwen." In *Algemene geschiedenis der Nederlanden* 4:405–20. Haarlem.

Heures de Milan. 1911. With an introduction by G. H. de Loo. Brussels.

Heures de Turin. 1902. Paris.

Hindman, S. 1987. "Dutch Manuscript Illumination Around 1400: Some Cuttings in Darmstadt (MS. 2296)." In *Miscellanea neerlandica. Opstellen voor dr. Jan Deschamps*, edited by E. Cockx-Indestege et al., 419–440. Louvain.

Hof, J. 1973. *De abdij van Egmond van de aanvang tot 1573*. The Hague.

Hogenelst, D., and S. de Vries. 1982. "*Die scone die mi peisen doet*... De vrouw als opdrachtgeefster van middeleeuwse literatuur." *Tijdschrift voor vrouwenstudies* 3:325–46.

Holtorf, A. 1973. *Neujarhswünsche im Liebesliede des ausgehenden Mittelalters*. Göppingen.

Honemann, V. 1984. "Aspekte des 'Tugendadels' im europäischen Spätmittelalter." In *Literatur und Laienbildung im Spätmittelalter und in der Reformationszeit*, edited by L. Grenzmann et al., 274–88. Stuttgart.

Hugenholtz, F.W.N. 1950. *De kruistocht in de Noordnederlandse historiografie der Middeleeuwen*. Haarlem.

———. 1959. *Ridderkrijg en burgervrede. West-Europa aan de vooravond van de Honderdjarige Oorlog*. Haarlem.

Huizinga, J. 1919. *Herfsttij der Middeleeuwen. Studie over levens- en gedachtenvormen der veertiende en vijftiende eeuw in Frankrijk en de Nederlanden*. Haarlem.

Hummelen, W.M.H. 1977. "Tekst en toneelinrichting in de abele spelen." *De nieuwe taalgids* 70:229–42.

Jacobs, J. H. 1915. *Jan de Weert's Nieuwe doctrinael of Spieghel van sonden*. The Hague.

Janota, J. 1983. "Das vierzehnte Jahrhundert: ein eigener literarhistorischer Zeitabschnitt?" In *Zur deutschen Literatur und Sprache des 14. Jahrhunderts*, edited by W. Haug et al., 9–24. Heidelberg.

Janse, A. 1986. "Muziekleven aan het hof van Albrecht van Beieren (1358–1404) in Den Haag." *Tijdschrift voor Nederlandse muziekgeschiedenis* 26:136–57.

Janse, H. 1980. *Zeven eeuwen bouwen. De bouwwereld in 's Gravenhage van 1280– 1980*. The Hague.

Jansen, H.P.H. 1966. *Hoekse en Kabeljauwse twisten*. Fibula Series 17. Bussum.

————. 1967a. *Jacoba van Beieren*. The Hague.

————. 1967b. "Het eerste Kabeljauwse jaar in Holland en de rekening van Philips Persoenressone (1351)." In *Miscellanea Mediaevalia in memoriam Jan Frederik Niermeyer*, 317–23. Groningen.

————. 1971. "Willem V." *Spiegel historiael* 6: 424–30.

————. 1976. *Hollands voorsprong*. Leiden.

————. 1979. "De Bredase Nassaus." In *Nassau en Oranje in de Nederlandse geschiedenis*, edited by C. A. Tamse, 11–44. Alphen.

————. 1980. "Modernization of the Government: The Advent of Philip the Good in Holland." *Bijdragen en mededelingen betreffende de geschiedenis der Nederlanden* 95:254–64.

————. 1982. "Holland, Zeeland en het Sticht 1100–1433." In *Algemene geschiedenis der Nederlanden* 2:281–323. Haarlem.

Jansen, H.P.H., and P.C.M. Hoppenbrouwers. 1979. "Heervaart in Holland." *Bijdragen en mededelingen betreffende de geschiedenis der Nederlanden* 94:1–26.

Jansma, T. S. 1974. "Les Pays-Bas du Nord et la Bourgogne du XVe siècle." In *Tekst en uitleg*, 54–71. The Hague.

Janssen, W. 1970. "Ein niederrheinischer Fürstenhof um die Mitte des 14. Jahrhunderts." *Rheinische Vierteljahrsblätter* 34:219–51.

Jappe Alberts, W. 1984. *De graven en hertogen van Gelre op reis (13de–15de eeuw)*. Utrecht.

Jauss, H. R. [1968] 1977. "Entstehung und Strukturwandel der allegorischen Dichtung." Reprinted in *Alterität und Modernität der mittelalterlichen Literatur. Gesammelte Aufsätze, 1956–1976*, [154]–[218]. Munich.

Jonckbloet, W.J.A. 1854. *Geschiedenis der middennederlandsche dichtkunst*. Vol. 3. Amsterdam.

Jongen, L.E.I.M. 1988. *Van Achilles tellen langhe. Onderzoekingen over Maerlants bewerking van Statius' "Achilleis" in de "Historie van Troyen."* Deventer.

Jongkees, A. G. 1942. *Staat en kerk in Holland en Zeeland onder de Bourgondische hertogen, 1425–1477*. Groningen.

Kalff, G. 1906. *Geschiedenis der Nederlandsche letterkunde*. Vol. 1. Groningen.

Kampen, H. van, and H. Pleij, eds. 1981. *De pastoor van Kalenberg*. Muiderberg.

Kan, F.J.W. van. 1981. "Boudijn van Zwieten, tresorier van Holland." *Holland* 13:288–305.

Kausler, E., ed. 1840. *Reimchronik von Flandern*. Tübingen.

Keen, M. 1981. "Chivalry, Heralds, and History." In *The Writing of History in the Middle Ages: Essays Presented to R. W. Southern*, 393–414. Oxford.

————. 1983. "Chaucer's Knight, the English Aristocracy, and the Crusade." In *English Court Culture in the Later Middle Ages*, edited by V. J. Scattergood et al., 45–62. London.

————. 1984. *Chivalry*. New Haven.

Kelly, H. A. 1975. *Love and Marriage in the Age of Chaucer*. Ithaca.

Kleinschmidt, E. 1976. "Minnesang als höfisches Zeremonialhandeln." *Archiv für Kulturgeschichte* 58:35–76.

Kloeke, G. 1943. Review of the *Haags liederenhandschrift*. *Tijdschrift voor Nederlandse taal- en letterkunde* 62:73–80.

Klooster, L. J. van der. 1984. "De hofkapel." In *Het binnenhof. Van grafelijke residentie tot regeringscentrum,* edited by R. J. van Pelt et al., 29–40. Dieren.

Köhn, R. 1979. *"Militia curialis:* die Kritik am geistlichen Hofdienst bei Peter von Blois und in der lateinischen Literatur des 9.–12. Jahrhunderts." In *Soziale Ordnungen im Selbstverständnis des Mittelalters* 1:227–57. Berlin.

Könnecker, B. 1970. "Strickers *Pfaffe Amis* und das Volksbuch von *Ulenspiegel.*" *Euphorion* 64:242–80.

Kooper, E. S. 1985. *Love, Marriage, and Salvation in Chaucer's Book of the Duchess and Parlement of Foules.* Utrecht.

Koppmann, K. 1877. "Liebesgruss." *Jahrbuch des Vereins für niederdeutsche Sprachforschung,* 8.

Korteweg, A. S. 1984. "De bibliotheek van Willem van Oranje: de handschriften." In *Boeken van en rond Willem van Oranje,* 9–28. The Hague.

Kroon, A. W. 1852. *Beschrijving van 's Gravenhage, uit echte bronnen geput.* The Hague.

Kuhn, H. 1980. *Entwürfe zu einer Literatursystematik des Spätmittelalters.* Tübingen.

Künzel, R. E. 1983. "Over schuld en schaamte in enige verhalende bronnen uit de tiende en elfde eeuw." *Bijdragen en mededelingen betreffende de geschiedenis der Nederlanden* 98:358–72.

Kurz, O. 1956. "A Fishing Party at the Court of William VI, Count of Holland, Zeeland, and Hainault: Notes on a Drawing in the Louvre." *Oud-Holland* 71:117–31.

Kusternig, A. 1982. *Erzählende Quellen des Mittelalters. Die Problematik mittelalterlicher Historiographie am Beispiel der Schlacht bei Dürnkrut und Jedenspeigen 1278.* Vienna.

Kuyper, W. 1984. "De Koninklijke Zaal." In *Het Binnenhof. Van grafelijke residentie tot regeringscentrum,* edited by R. J. van Pelt et al., 21–28. Dieren.

Lämmert, E. 1970. *Reimsprecherkunst im Spätmittelalter. Eine Untersuchung der Teichnerreden.* Stuttgart.

Lange van Wijngaerden, C. J. de. 1813. *Geschiedenis der heeren en beschrijving der stad van der Goude.* Vol. 1. Amsterdam.

Leupen, P.H.D. 1975. "Filips van Leiden: een onderzoek naar ontstaan, vorm en inhoud van zijn traktaat 'De cura reipublicae et sorte principantis.'" Ph.D. diss., University of Amsterdam.

———. 1981. *Philip of Leyden: A Fourteenth-Century Jurist.* The Hague.

De librije van Filips de Goede. Tentoonstelling, georganiseerd bij de 500e verjaardag van de dood van de hertog. 1967. Brussels.

Liebertz-Grün, U. 1977. *Zur Soziologie des "amour courtois." Umrisse der Forschung.* Heidelberg.

———. 1984. *Das andere Mittelalter. Erzählte Geschichte und Geschichtserkenntnis um 1300.* Munich.

Lieftinck, G. I. 1965. "Pleidooi voor de philologie in de oude en eerbiedwaardige ruime betekenis van het woord." *Tijdschrift voor Nederlandse taal- en letterkunde* 81:58–84.

Lievens, R. 1964. "Een pocketboek van Augustijnken." *Verslagen en Mededelingen Vlaamse Academie,* 223–27.

Lingbeek-Schalekamp, C. 1984. *Overheid en muziek in Holland tot 1672. Een onderzoek naar de rechten en plichten van zangers, organisten, beiaardiers en speellieden, in overheidsdienst in de Nederlanden, in het bijzonder in Holland, tot 1672.* [Rotterdam.]

Lods, J. 1951. *Le roman de Perceforest.* Geneva.

Löher, F. 1862–69. *Jakobäa von Bayern und ihre Zeit.* 2 vols. Nördlingen.

Luttervelt, R. van. 1957. "Bijdragen tot de iconographie van de graven van Holland, naar aanleiding van de beelden uit de Amsterdamse vierschaar." *Oud-Holland* 72:73–91, 139–50, 218–34.

Maerlant, Jacob van. N.d. *Alexanders Geesten.* Edited by J. Franck. Leiden.

Map, Walter. 1983. *De nugis curialium.* Edited by M. R. James; revised by C.N.L. Brooke and R.A.B. Mynors. Oxford.

Marrow, J. H. 1987. "Prolegomena to a New Descriptive Catalogue of Dutch Illuminated Manuscripts." In *Miscellanea neerlandica. Opstellen aangeboden aan dr. Jan Deschamps,* edited by E. Cockx-Indestege et al., 295–309. Louvain.

Maso, B. 1982. "Riddereer en riddermoed: ontwikkelingen van de aanvalslust in de late middeleeuwen." *Sociologische gids* 29:296–325.

Mathew, G. 1968. *The Court of Richard II.* London.

Matzel, K. 1979. "Ein Bücherverzeichnis eines bayerischen Ritters aus dem 14. Jahrhundert." In *Medium aevum deutsch. Beiträge zur deutschen Literatur des hohen und späten Mittelalters. Festschrift für Kurt Ruh zum 65. Geburtstag,* edited by D. Huschenbett et al., 237–45. Tübingen.

Maurer, F. 1971a. "'Tugend' und 'Ehre.'" In *Dichtung und Sprache des Mittelalters,* 335–45. Bern.

———. 1971b. "Die Ehre im Menschenbild der deutschen Dichtung um 1200." In *Dichtung und Sprache des Mittelalters,* 406–20. Bern.

Meder, T. 1991. *Sprookspreker in Holland. Leven en werk van Willem van Hildegaersberch (omstreeks 1400).* Amsterdam.

Meesters, G. L. 1985. "Waarom de één in Brussel wel Potter van der Loo genoemd wilde worden en de ander in Dordrecht niet." In *Liber amicorum Jhr. Mr. C. C. van Valkenburg,* 207–18. The Hague.

Meier, L. 1934. "Der Studiengang des Ex-Dominikaners Narcissus Pfister O.S.B. an der Universität Köln." *Archivum fratrum praedicatorum* 4: 228–57.

Meiss, M. 1974. *French Painting in the Time of Jean de Berry: The Limbourgs and Their Contemporaries.* 2 vols. New York.

Merchtenen, Hennen van. 1896. *Cornicke van Brabant.* Edited by G. Gezelle. Ghent.

Mierlo, J. van. [1949]. *De letterkunde van de Middeleeuwen.* 2d ed., rev. and enl. Vol. 2. 's Hertogenbosch.

Moolenbroek, J. J. van. 1986. "Seksuele onthouding als norm en waarde in laat-middeleeuws Nederland: verkenningen in officiële en niet-officiële cultuur." In *In de schaduw van de eeuwigheid,* edited by N. Lettinck et al., 109–33. Utrecht.

Müller, J. D. 1982. *Gedechtnus. Literatur und Hofgesellschaft um Maximilian I.* Munich.

Muller, J. W. 1888. "Gerijt Potter van der Loo en zijne vertaling van Froissart." *Tijdschrift voor Nederlandsche taal- en letterkunde* 8:264–95.

Muller Fz., S. 1885. "Die Hollantsche Cronike van den Heraut: eene studie over de Hollandsche geschiedbronnen uit het Beijersche tijdperk." *Bijdragen voor geschiedenis en oudheidkunde,* 3d ser., 2:1–124.

Mundschau, H. 1972. *Sprecher als Träger der "tradition vivante" in der Gattung Märe.* Göppingen.

Neumeister, S. 1969. *Das Spiel mit der höfischen Liebe. Das altprovenzalische Partimen.* Munich.

Niermeyer, J. F. 1951. "Henegouwen, Holland en Zeeland onder Willem III en Willem IV van Avesnes" and "Henegouwen, Holland en Zeeland onder het huis Wittelsbach." In *Algemene geschiedenis der Nederlanden* 3:63–91 and 92–124. Utrecht.

Nijland, J. A. 1896. *Gedichten uit het Haagsche liederhandschrift, uitgegeven en toegelicht uit de Middelhoogduitsche lyriek.* Leiden.

Nijsten, G. 1985. "Hertog en hof in Gelre: bronnen en perspectieven." *Groniek,* no. 93: 124–41.

———. 1986. "Van dichters en sprekers: het literaire leven aan het hof van de hertogen van Gelre (±1370–±1470)." *Literatuur* 3:289–96.

Nolte, T. 1983. *Lauda post mortem. Die deutschen und niederländischen Ehrenreden des Mittelalters.* Frankfurt.

Noordeloos, P. 1949. "Enige gegevens over broederschappen van S. Antonius." *Publications de la Société historique et archéologique dans le Limbourg, Miscellanea P.J.M. van Gils* 85:477–99.

Obbema, P.F.J. 1979. "Van schrijven naar drukken." In P.F.J. Obbema et al., *Boeken in Nederland. Vijfhonderd jaar schrijven, drukken en uitgeven,* 5–27. N.p.

Oberman, H. 1978. "Fourteenth-Century Religious Thought: A Premature Profile." *Speculum* 53:80–93.

Ohly, F. [1970] 1977. "Cor amantis non angustum: vom Wohnen im Herzen." In *Schriften zur mittelalterlichen Bedeutungs-forschung,* 128–55. Darmstadt.

Oostrom, F. P. van. 1982. "Maecenaat en Middelnederlandse letterkunde." In *Hoofsheid en devotie in de middeleeuwse maatschappij. De Nederlanden van de 12e tot de 15e eeuw,* edited by J. D. Janssens, 21–40. Brussels.

———. 1983a. "Hoofse cultuur en literatuur." In *Hoofse cultuur. Studies over een aspect van de middeleeuwse cultuur,* edited by R.E.V. Stuip et al., 119–38. Utrecht.

———. 1983b. *Reinaert primair. Over het geïntendeerde publiek en de oorspronkelijke functie van Van den vos Reinaerde.* Utrecht.

———. 1984a. "Achtergronden van een nieuwe vorm: de kleinschalige epiek van Willem van Hildegaersberch." In *Vorm en functie in tekst en taal. Bundel opstellen verschenen ter gelegenheid van de voltooiing van het honderdste deel van het "Tijdschrift voor Nederlandse taal- en letterkunde,"* 48–72. Leiden.

———. 1984b. "De vrijheid van de Middelnederlandse dichter." In *Ic ga daer ic hebbe te doene. Opstellen aangeboden aan Prof. Dr. F. Lulofs,* edited by J.J.T.M. Tersteeg et al., 45–62. Groningen.

———. 1985a. "Jacob van Maerlant: een herwaardering." *Literatuur* 2:190–97.

———. 1985b. "Schetskaart of geschiedverhaal? Over methode en praktijk van (een) geschiedschrijving van de Middelnederlandse letterkunde." In *Tussen-tijds. Bundel studies aangeboden aan W. P. Gerritsen,* edited by A.M.J. van Buuren et al., 198–216. Utrecht.

———. 1986a. "Van hoofs tot herfsttij: literatuur aan het Hollandse hof, ca. 1200–ca. 1400." In *Dichter en hof. Verkenningen in veertien culturen,* edited by J.T.P. de Bruijn et al., 57–74. Utrecht.

———. 1986b. "De oude orde in verval? Hollandse hofliteratuur en Huizingas *Herfsttij.*" *Literatuur* 4:202–10.

———. 1987a. "Dirc van Delft en zijn lezers." In *Het woord aan de lezer,* edited by W. van den Berg et al., 49–71. Groningen.

———. 1987b. "Literatuur en levensloop: de succesmoraal van Dirc Potter, ambtenaar-auteur aan het Hollandse hof (ca. 1400)." In *De Nederlanden in de late middeleeuwen,* edited by D.E.H. de Boer et al., 98–112. Utrecht.

Orme, N. 1983. "The Education of the Courtier." In *English Court Culture in the Later Middle Ages,* edited by V. J. Scattergood et al., 63–86. London.

Ott, N. H. 1985. "Kompilation und Zitat in Weltchronik und Kathedralikono-graphie: zum Wahrheitsanspruch (pseudo-)historischer Gattungen." In *Ge-schichtsbewusstsein in der deutschen Literatur des Mittelalters. Tübinger Collo-quium 1983,* edited by C. Gerhardt et al., 119–35. Tübingen.

Overmaat, B. 1952. "Dirc Potter: nieuwe gegevens voor 's dichters biografie." *Tijdschrift voor Nederlandse taal- en letterkunde* 69:110–37.

———. 1977. "Een drinklied in het Rijksarchief." *De nieuwe taalgids* 70:34–41.

Pabon, N. J. 1924. "Die Haghe als ambacht, parochie en waterschap tot het einde der 16e eeuw." *Die Haghe,* 70–244.

———. 1936. "Bijdragen over het godsdienstig, zedelijk en maatschappelijk leven in Den Haag tot het einde der 16de eeuw." *Die Haghe,* 36–258.

Paravicini, W. 1977. "Soziale Schichtung und soziale Mobilität am Hof der Her-zöge von Burgund." *Francia* 5:127–82.

———. 1981. "Die Preussenreisen des europäischen Adels." *Historische Zeit-schrift* 232:25–38.

———. 1986. "Edelleute, Hansen, Brügger Bürger: die Finanzierung der west-europäischen Preussenreisen im 14. Jahrhundert." *Hansische Geschichtsblätter* 104:5–20.

Pauw, N. de, ed. 1898–1909. *Jehan Froissart's Cronyke van Vlaenderen.* 3 vols. Ghent.

Pearsall, D. 1977. "The *Troilus* Frontispiece and Chaucer's Audience." *Yearbook of English Studies* 7:68–74.

Peristiany, J. G., ed. 1966. *Honour and Shame: The Values of Mediterranean Soci-ety.* Chicago.

Peters, C. H. 1905. "Enkle bladzijden uit de geschiedenis der Groote of Hof-zaal." *Die Haghe,* 297–448.

———. 1909. "Het grafelijk leven in die Haghe, in de tweede helft der XIVe eeuw." *Die Haghe,* 113–268.

Peters, U. 1972. "*Cour d'amour*—Minnehof: ein Beitrag zum Verhältnis der französischen und deutschen Minnedichtung zu den Unterhaltungsformen ihres Publikums." *Zeitschrift für deutsches Altertum* 101:117–33.

————. 1976. "Herolde und Sprecher in mittelalterlichen Rechnungsbüchern." *Zeitschrift für deutsches Altertum* 105:233–50.

————. [1980]. "Le Minnesang en tant que 'poésie formelle': sur l'adaptation d'un paradigme de la critique littéraire." In *Musique, littérature et société au Moyen Age. Actes du colloque 24–29 Mars 1980*, edited by D. Buschinger et al., 323–42. Paris.

————. 1983. *Literatur in der Stadt. Studien zu den sozialen Voraussetzungen und kulturellen Organisationsformen städtischer Literatur im 13. und 14. Jahrhundert.* Tübingen.

Petzsch, C. 1971. "Das mittelalterliche Lied: res non confecta." *Zeitschrift für deutsche Philologie* 90 (special issue): 1–17.

Pfeffer, W. 1985. "The Riddle of the Proverb." In *The Spirit of the Court*, edited by G. Burgess et al., 254–63. Cambridge.

Pietzsch, G. 1966. *Fürsten und fürstliche Musiker im mittelalterlichen Köln.* Cologne.

————. 1969. "Archivalische Forschungen zur Musikgeschichte um 1400." In *Annales de la Fédération archéologique et historique de Belgique, annales du Congrès de Liège 1968*, 1:240–48. Liège.

Piponnier, F. 1970. *Costume et vie sociale. La cour d'Anjou XIVe–XVe siècle.* Civilisations et Sociétés 21. Paris.

Pleij, H. 1977. "Volksfeest en toneel in de middeleeuwen II: entertainers en akteurs." *De Revisor* 4:34–41.

————. 1979. *Het gilde van de Blauwe Schuit. Literatuur, volksfeest en burgermoraal in de late middeleeuwen.* Amsterdam.

————. 1982. *De wereld volgens Thomas van der Noot.* Muiderberg.

————. 1984a. *Het literaire leven in de middeleeuwen.* Leiden.

————. 1984b. "De laatmiddeleeuwse rederijkersliteratuur als vroeg-humanistische overtuigingskunst." *Jaarboek Fonteine* 34:65–95.

————. 1987a. "Met een boekje in een hoekje? Over literatuur en lezen in de middeleeuwen." In *Het woord aan de lezer*, edited by W. van den Berg et al., 16–48. Groningen.

————. 1987b. "Literatuur en stad in de middeleeuwen." *Literatuur* 4:116–23.

Plomp, N. 1985. "Adelsgunsten van de Rooms-koning Sigismund." In *Liber amicorum Jhr. Mr. C. C. van Valkenburg*, 235–250. The Hague.

Poirion, D. 1965. *Le poète et le prince. L'évolution du lyrisme courtois de Guillaume de Machaut à Charles d'Orléans.* Grenoble.

Post, R. R. 1957. *Kerkgeschiedenis van Nederland in de middeleeuwen.* Vol. 2. Utrecht.

Posthumus Meyjes, G.H.M. 1979. *Quasi stellae fulgebunt. Plaats en functie van de theologische doctor in de middeleeuwse maatschappij en kerk.* Leiden.

Potvin, C. 1886. "La charte de la cour d'amour de l'année 1401." *Bulletins de l'Académie royale des sciences, des lettres et des beaux-arts de Belgique*, 3d ser., 12: 191–220.

Prevenier, W. 1972. "Ambtenaren in stad en land in de Nederlanden. Socioprofessionele evoluties (veertiende tot zestiende eeuw)." *Bijdragen en mededelingen voor de geschiedenis der Nederlanden* 87:44–59.

Primisser, A., ed. 1827. *Peter Suchenwirts Werke aus dem vierzehnten Jahrhunderte.* Vienna.

Ragotzky, H. 1977. "Das Handlungsmodell der List und die Thematisierung der Bedeutung von guot." In *Literatur-Publikum-historischer Kontext,* 183–204. Bern.

———. 1980a. "Die *kunst der milte.* Anspruch und Funktion der *milte*-Diskussion in den Texten des Strickers." In *Gesellschaftliche Sinnangebote mittelalterlicher Literatur,* edited by G. Kaiser, 77–112. Munich.

———. 1980b. "Die Thematisierung der materiellen Bedeutung von *guot* in Texten des Strickers." In *Soziale Ordnungen im Selbstverständnis des Mittelalters,* edited by A. Zimmermann, 2:498–516. Berlin.

———. 1981. *Gattungserneuerung und Laienunterweisung in Texten des Strickers.* Tübingen.

Ramondt, M. 1944. "Problemen in en om het Haagse liederenhandschrift." *Tijdschrift voor Nederlandse taal- en letterkunde* 63:63–81.

Reiner, H. 1956. *Die Ehre. Kritische Sichtung einer abendländischen Lebens- und Sittlichkeitsform.* N.p.

De rekeningen van de Grafelijkheid van Holland uit de Beierse periode. 1980–83. Published by the Werkgroep "Holland 1300–1500." Ser. 3 (law officers)/ser. 2 (bailiffs), 1393–96. The Hague.

Rheinheimer, M. 1975. *Rheinische Minnereden. Untersuchungen und Edition.* Göppingen.

Ribard, J. 1969. *Un ménestrel du XIVe siècle: Jean de Condé.* Geneva.

———. 1981. "Littérature et société au XIVe siècle: le ménestrel Watriquet de Couvin." In *Court and Poet,* edited by G. S. Burgess, 277–86. Liverpool.

Richert, H.-G. 1978. "Die Literatur des deutschen Ritterordens." In *Neues Handbuch der Literaturwissenschaft* 8, edited by W. Erzgräber, 275–86. Wiesbaden.

Rickert, M. 1949. "The Illuminated Manuscripts of Meester Dirc van Delf's *Tafel vanden kersten ghelove." Journal of the Walters Art Gallery* 12:78–108.

Riemsdijk, T. van. 1908. *De tresorie en kanselarij van de graven van Holland en Zeeland uit het Henegouwsche en Beyersche huis.* The Hague.

Rierink, M. 1989. "Variaties en experimenten: de Gruuthusedichter als vormkunstenaar." *Spiegel der letteren* 31:161–77.

Rijk, L. M. de. 1977. *Middeleeuwse wijsbegeerte. Traditie en vernieuwing.* Assen.

Robreau, Y. 1981. *L'honneur et la honte. Leur expression dans les romans en prose du Lancelot-Graal (XIIe–XIIIe siècles).* Geneva.

Rocher, D. 1979. "Le *De amore* du Stricker et le sens de ses contradictions." In *Le récit bref au Moyen Age,* edited by D. Buschinger, 227–48. Paris.

Roessingh, A.L.A. 1914. *De vrouw bij de Dietsche moralisten.* Groningen.

Rosenplenter, L. 1982. *Zitat und Autoritätenberufung im Renner Hugos von Trimberg. Ein Beitrag zur Bildung des Laien im Spätmittelalter.* Frankfurt.

Rozema, B. 1985. "Burchten en kastelen in Holland." *Groniek,* no. 93:22–43.

Russell, F. H. 1975. *The Just War in the Middle Ages.* Cambridge.

Sarfatij, H. 1984. "Tristan op vrijersvoeten? Een bijzonder versieringsmotief op laat-middeleeuws schoeisel uit de Lage Landen." In *Ad fontes. Opstellen aangeboden aan C. van de Kieft,* 371–400. Amsterdam.

Scattergood, V. J. 1983. "Literary Culture at the Court of Richard II." In *English Court Culture in the Later Middle Ages,* edited by V. J. Scattergood et al., 29–44. London.

Schmidt-Ernsthausen, A.A.M. 1982. *Archief van de graven van Blois, 1304–1397.* The Hague.

Schneider, F. 1913. *Herzog Johann von Baiern. Erwählter Bischof von Lüttich und Graf von Holland (1373–1425).* Berlin.

Schnell, R. 1978. *Zum Verhältnis von hoch- und spätmittelalterlicher Literatur.* Berlin.

——. 1985. *Causa amoris. Liebeskonzeption und Liebesdarstellung in den mittelalterlichen Literatur.* Bern.

Schotel, G.D.I. 1851. *De abdij van Rijnsburg.* 's Hertogenbosch.

Sillem, J. A. 1900. "Aanteekeningen omtrent muzikanten en muziek, uit XIVe eeuwsche Noordnederlandsche bronnen." *Tijdschrift der Vereeniging voor Noord-Nederlandse muziekgeschiedenis* 6:218–32.

Smit, H. J., ed. 1924–39. *De rekeningen der graven en gravinnen uit het Henegouwsche huis.* 3 vols. Amsterdam.

Smit, J. 1923. "De kerkinventaris van de voormalige hofkapel in Den Haag." *Bijdragen voor de geschiedenis van het bisdom van Haarlem* 41:1–57.

Spies, M. 1984. "Van mythes en meningen: over de geschiedenis van de literatuurgeschiedenis." In *Historische letterkunde. Facetten van vakbeoefening,* edited by M. Spies, 171–93. Groningen.

Sproemberg, H. 1936. "Residenz und Territorium im niederländischen Raum." *Rheinische Vierteljahrsblätter* 6:113–39.

Stackmann, K. 1958. *Der Spruchdichter Heinrich von Mügeln. Vorstudien zur Erkenntnis seiner Individualität.* Heidelberg.

Stam, E. 1977. "De muzikale notities op het handschrift van Pieter Potter." *De nieuwe taalgids* 70:42–47.

Steer, G. 1981. *Hugo Ripelin von Strassburg. Zur Rezeptions- und Wirkungsgeschichte des "Compendium theologicae veritatis" im deutschen Spätmittelalter.* Tübingen.

——. 1983. "Der Laie als Auftraggeber und Adressat deutscher Prosaliteratur im 14. Jahrhundert." In *Zur deutschen Literatur und Sprache des 14. Jahrhunderts,* edited by W. Haug et al., 354–67. Heidelberg.

Steinhausen, G., ed. 1899. *Deutsche Privatbriefe des Mittelalters.* Vol. 1. Berlin.

Stengel, E. E., and F. Vogt. 1956. "Zwölf mittelhochdeutsche Minnelieder und Reimreden." *Archiv für Kulturgeschichte* 38:174–217.

Stevens, J. 1961. *Music and Poetry in the Early Tudor Court.* London.

Straub, T. 1961. "Die Gründung des Pariser Minnehofs von 1400." *Zeitschrift für romanische Philologie* 77:1–14.

Stutterheim, C.F.P. 1967. "Mens of duivel? Augustijnken's *Ridder die waldoen haet." Tijdschrift voor Nederlandse taal- en letterkunde* 83:81–107.

——. 1969. "Raadsel of grap? Nogmaals Augustijnken's 'Klacht'." *Tijdschrift voor Nederlandse taal- en letterkunde* 85:194–211.

Suringar, W.H.D., ed. 1891. *Die bouc van seden.* Leiden.

Tentler, T. N. 1977. *Sin and Confession on the Eve of the Reformation.* Princeton.

Thum, B. 1980. "Öffentlich-Machen, Öffentlichkeit, Recht: zu den Grundlagen und Verfahren der politischen Publizistik im Spätmittelalter mit Überlegungen zur sog. 'Rechtssprache.'" *Zeitschrift für Literaturwissenschaft und Linguistik* 10:12–69.

———. 1981. "Die Wahrheit des Publizisten und die Wahrheit im Recht: zum Aufbau gesellschaftlicher Wirklichkeit im späteren Mittelalter." In *De poeticis medii aevi quaestiones. Käte Hamburger zum 85. Geburtstag,* edited by J. Kühnel et al., 147–207. Göppingen.

Tóth-Ubbens, M. 1957. "De graftombe van Margaretha van Brieg, gemalin van Albrecht van Beieren." *Oud Holland* 72:59–72.

———. 1963. *"Van goude, zelver, juellen ende anderen saken.* Twintig jaren Haagse tresorie-rekeningen betreffende beeldende kunst en kunstnijverheid ten tijde van Albrecht van Beieren 1358–1378." *Oud Holland* 78:87–134.

———. 1964–65. "Een dubbel vorstenhuwelijk in het jaar 1385." *Bijdragen geschiedenis der Nederlanden* 19:101–32.

Trinkaus, C. 1976. "Humanism, Religion, Society: Concepts and Motivations of Some Recent Studies." *Renaissance Quarterly* 29:676–713.

Trinkaus, C., and H. Oberman, eds. 1974. *The Pursuit of Holiness in Late Medieval and Renaissance Religion.* Leiden.

Troelstra, A. 1901. *De toestand der catechese in Nederland gedurende de voorreformatorische eeuw.* Groningen.

Tuchman, B. W. 1978. *A Distant Mirror: The Calamitous 14th Century.* New York.

Vale, J. 1982. *Edward III and Chivalry: Chivalric Society and Its Context, 1270–1350.* Woodbridge, Eng.

Vale, M. 1981. *War and Chivalry: Warfare and Aristocratic Culture in England, France, and Burgundy at the End of the Middle Ages.* London.

Vanderheijden, J. 1933. *"Mate bij Dirk Potter." Leuvense bijdragen* 25:178–85.

Vaughan, R. 1970. *Philip the Good: The Apogee of Burgundy.* London.

———. 1979. *Philip the Bold: The Formation of the Burgundian State.* 2d ed. London.

Verbij-Schillings, J. 1987. "Die ieesten der princen. De *Wereldkroniek* van de heraut Beyeren (ca. 1405–1409)." In *Genoechlicke ende lustige historiën. Laatmiddeleeuwse geschiedschrijving in Nederland,* edited by B. Ebels-Hoving et al., 35–59. Hilversum.

———. 1991. "Heraut Beyeren en de Clerc uten laghen landen." *Tijdschrift voor Nederlandse taal- en letterkunde* 107:20–42.

Verdam, J. 1890. "Over de Oudvlaemsche liederen en andere gedichten der 14de en 15de eeuw." *Tijdschrift voor Nederlandsche taal- en letterkunde* 9:273–301.

———. 1898. "De Griseldis-novelle in het Nederlandsch." *Tijdschrift voor Nederlandsche taal- en letterkunde* 17:1–30.

De verluchte handschriften en incunabelen van de Koninklijke Bibliotheek. 1985. Compiled by J.P.J. Brandhorst and K. H. Broekhuijsen-Kruijer. The Hague.

Versnel, H. S. 1984. "Vrouw en vriend: vrouwen van het oude Athene in anthropologisch perspectief." *Lampas* 17:28–45.

Verwijs, E. 1869. *De oorlogen van hertog Albrecht van Beieren met de Friezen in de laatste jaren der XIV de eeuw.* Utrecht.

————, ed. 1871. *Van vrouwen ende van minne. Middelnederlandse gedichten uit de XIVde en XVde eeuw.* Groningen.

Vignau Wilberg-Schuurman, T. 1983. *Hoofse minne en burgerlijke liefde in de prentkunst rond 1500.* Leiden.

Vlaamse kunst op perkament. Handschriften te Brugge van de 12de tot de 16de eeuw. 1981. Brugge.

[Vloten, J. van.] 1851. *Verzameling van nederlandsche prozastukken van 1229–1476, naar tijdsorde gerangschikt.* Leiden.

Volmuller, H.W.J., ed. 1981. *Nijhoffs Geschiedenislexicon Nederland en België.* The Hague.

Vooys, C.G.N. de. 1903. "Iets over Dirc van Delf en zijn *Tafel vanden kersten ghelove.*" *Tijdschrift voor Nederlandsche taal- en letterkunde* 22:1–36.

————. 1939. "Bijdragen tot de Middelnederlandse woordgeografie en woordchronologie VII. Noord-Nederlandse bestanddelen in de woordvoorraad van Willem van Hildegaersberch." *Tijdschrift voor Nederlandsche taal- en letterkunde* 58:266–76.

Wachinger, B. 1973. *Sängerkrieg. Untersuchungen zur Spruchdichtung des 13. Jahrhunderts.* Munich.

Wackers, P.W.M. 1986. *De waarheid als leugen. Een interpretatie van Reynaerts historie.* Utrecht.

Wagenaar-Nolthenius, H. 1969. "De Leidse fragmenten. Nederlandse polifonie uit het einde der 14de eeuw." In *Renaissance-muziek 1400–1600. Donum natalicum R. B. Lenaerts,* 303–15. Louvain.

Wagner, A. R. 1956. *Heralds and Heraldry in the Middle Ages.* 2d ed. Oxford.

Wailes, S. I. 1975. "Oswald von Wolkenstein and the *Alterslied.*" *Germanic Review* 50:5–18.

Wang, A. 1975. *Der "miles christianus" im 16. und 17. Jahrhundert und seine mittelalterliche Tradition.* Bern.

Ward, D. 1982–83. "Honor and Shame in the Middle Ages: An Open Letter to Lutz Röhrich." *Jahrbuch für Volksliedforschung* 27–28:1–16.

Warnar, G. 1986. "Potters kuisheidsgordel." *Meta* 21:78–80.

————. 1988–89. "Het *Nuttelijc boec* en het Hollandse hof." *Spektator* 18:290–304.

Warning, R. 1979. "Lyrisches Ich und Öffentlichkeit bei den Trobadors." In *Deutsche Literatur im Mittelalter. Kontakte und Perspektiven,* edited by C. Cormeau, 120–59. Stuttgart.

Weale, W.H.J. 1908. *Hubert and John van Eyck: Their Life and Work.* London.

Weidenhiller, E. 1965. *Untersuchungen zur deutschsprachigen katechetischen Literatur des späten Mittelalters.* Munich.

Wenzel, H. 1980. *Höfische Geschichte. Literarische Tradition und Gegenwartsdeutung in den volkssprachigen Chroniken des hohen und späten Mittelalters.* Bern.

————. 1983. "Typus und Individualität: zur literarischen Selbstdeutung Walthers von der Vogelweide." *Internationales Archiv für Sozialgeschichte der deutschen Literatur* 8:1–34.

Wilkins, N. 1983. "Music and Poetry at Court: England and France in the Late

Middle Ages." In *English Court Culture in the Later Middle Ages,* edited by V. J. Scattergood et al., 183–204. London.

Willaert, F. 1984. *De poëtica van Hadewijch in de Strofische Gedichten.* Utrecht.

———. 1986. "Vier acrostichons in het Haagse liederhandschrift." In *'t Ondersoeck leert. Studies over middeleeuwse en 17de-eeuwse literatuur ter nagedachtenis van Prof. Dr. L. Rens,* edited by G. van Eemeren et al., 93–104. Louvain.

Willems, J. F., ed. 1843. *De Brabantsche Yeesten, of Rymkronyk van Braband.* Vol. 2. Brussels.

Williamson, J. B. 1985. "Philippe de Mézière's Book for Married Ladies: A Book from the Entourage of the Court of Charles VI." In *The Spirit of the Court,* edited by G. S. Burgess et al., 393–408. Cambridge.

Wilmans, R. 1847. "Iacobi de Guisia Annales Hannoniae." *Archiv der Gesellschaft für ältere deutsche Geschichtskunde* 9:292–382.

Winkel, J. te. 1922. *De ontwikkelingsgang der Nederlandsche letterkunde.* Vol. 2. 2d ed. Haarlem.

Winkelman, J. H. 1986. "Tristan en Isolde in de minnetuin: over een versieringsmotief op laatmiddeleeuws schoeisel." *Amsterdamer Beiträge zur älteren Germanistik* 24:163–88.

———. 1990. "Potjesmiddelhoogduits in het Haagse liederenhandschrift? Een bijdrage tot de interpretatie van de Middelnederlandse minnezang." *Spiegel der letteren* 32:167–79.

Wolfs, S. P. 1973. *Studies over Noordnederlandse dominicanen in de middeleeuwen.* Assen.

Wood, C. T. 1983. *The Quest for Eternity: Manners and Morals in the Age of Chivalry.* Hanover.

Index

Abraham, the patriarch, 142
Achilles, in Dirk Potter, 245
Acrostics, 238, 317n55; in *Haags liederen-handschrift*, 316n37; in *Der minnen loep*, 334n34
Adalbert of Laon, 204–5
Adelaide of Houthuizen (mistress of Duke Albert), 309n84; gift-giving of, 309n74
Adelaide of Poelgeest (mistress of Duke Albert), 20, 113, 120; murder of, 37, 167
Adultery: in Dirk of Delft, 181–82, 211, 318n64; in Dirk Potter, 230–31, 333n21; in *Haags liederenhandschrift*, 114–15; at Holland-Bavaria court, 112–13; in William of Hildegaersberch, 113, 318n63
Aeneas, 140
Agincourt, battle of, 159
Albert (duke of Bavaria, count of Holland), 1; assistance to Dirk of Delft, 173, 289, 324n3; banquets given by, 19; conflict with Leiden, 54; death of, 153, 169, 217, 329n59, 343n57; dedication of *Tafel* to, 208–11, 266, 291, 292, 306n45, 307n63; and Dirk Potter, 219, 254, 255, 289; Frisian expeditions of, 283–84, 323n66; gift-giving of, 318n74; in *Hollandse kroniek*, 152; and Hook-Cod feud, 3–5; illegitimate children of, 112; interest in music, 22–23; and Jean Froissart, 304n14; library of, 28, 308n65; literary patronage of, 288–89; marriages of, 111; marriage to Margaret of Cleves, 37–39; membership in orders of knighthood, 162; military campaigns of, 152–53, 166; mistresses of, 42, 112–13, 333n21; musical compositions by, 119; patronage of education, 29; poetry by, 81–82; prayer books of, 28; quarrel with Delft, 3–5; quarrel with William of Oostervant, 167; recreations of, 20; regency of, 2–6; religious observances of, 214, 325n5; reorganization of government, 8; statesmanship of, 303n3; titles of, 5; tomb of, 324n74; tournaments of, 161, 167

Albertanus of Brescia, 249, 250
Alexanders geesten (Maerlant), 137, 142, 265, 305n29, 337n70
Alexander the Great, in *Der minnen loep*, 235
Allegory: aesthetic appeal of, 104; in *Haags liederenhandschrift*, 102–7, 316n42
Alterslied (old age song), 46
Animals, exotic: at Holland-Bavaria court, 20–21
Annales Hannoniae (Jacques de Guise), 26
Anrooij, W. van, 305n32, 306n44, 342n46
Antichrist, in Dirk of Delft, 192
Anti-Semitism, 186, 326n23
Aphorisms, in courtly love poetry, 100
Aportyf (lambskin vellum), 25
Aquinas, Thomas, 203
Aristocracy. *See* Courtiers; Nobility
Aristotle, 199
Arkel campaigns (of William VI), 158
Armorials (books of heraldry), 128, 132–33, 146
Ars nova (polyphonic song style), 78
Arthur, King, 273, 274
Arts, at Holland-Bavarian court, 20–21
Augustijnken (Middle Dutch poet), 12, 85, 278, 310n90, 341n33; ambiguity in, 109–10; in *Haags liederenhandschrift*, 83
Avarice: in Dirk of Delft, 178, 325n13; in William of Hildegaersberch, 60–62, 325n13
Axters, S., 217, 218, 313n73

Bailiffs, 337n70
Baldwin of Zwieten, 338n78, 340n27
Baptism, in Dirk of Delft, 189
Bathhouses, 113, 318n62
Baudouin de Sebourc (epic), 11
Bavaria, House of. *See* Holland-Bavaria, House of
Bavaria Herald, 23, 264; access of to books, 28; armorials by, 132–33, 149, 160; campaigns in Prussia, 165, 166; chivalry in, 275; dialect of, 10; and Dirk Potter, 343n52; early life of, 129–32; eulogy of the duke of Gulik, 160; friend-

Compositor: Graphic Composition, Inc.
Text: 10/13 Galliard
Display: Galliard
Printer: Malloy Lithographing, Inc.
Binder: John H. Dekker & Sons